URBAN LIFE AND URBAN LANDSCAPE

Zane L. Miller, Series Editor

A LITTLE MORE FREEDOM

African Americans Enter the
Urban Midwest, 1860—1930

JACK S. BLOCKER

THE OHIO STATE UNIVERSITY PRESS / COLUMBUS

Library of Congress Cataloging-in-Publication Data
 A little more freedom : African Americans enter the urban Midwest, 1860–1930 /
Jack S. Blocker.
        p. cm. — (Urban life and urban landscape)
Includes bibliographical references and index.
ISBN-13: 978-0-8142-1067-3 (cloth : alk. paper)
ISBN-10: 0-8142-1067-8 (cloth : alk. paper)
1. African Americans—Middle West—History. 2. Human geography—Middle West.
3. African Americans—Migrations—History. 4. Migration, Internal—United States—
History. 5. Urbanization—Middle West—History. 6. Racism—Middle West—History.
7. Middle West—History. I. Title.

 E185.915.B55 2008
 977'.0496073—dc22
                            2007022590

This book is available in the following editions:
Cloth (ISBN 978-08142-1067-3)
CD-ROM (ISBN 978-08142-9152-8)
Paper (ISBN: 978-0-8142-5616-9)
Cover design by Laurence Nozik
Type set in Adobe Caslon by Jennifer Forsythe

TO SUSAN AND DAVID, FOR ALL THE REASONS;
AND TO THE MEMORY OF

Katherine Irene (Blocker) Anderson (1952-2004)

CONTENTS

LIST OF ILLUSTRATIONS

LIST OF TABLES

LIST OF ABBREVIATIONS

AH	*Agricultural History*
AnRS	*Annual Review of Sociology*
AS	*The American Slave: A Composite Autobiography,* ed. George P. Rawick, 41 vols. (Westport, CT: Greenwood Press, 1972–79)
ASR	*American Sociological Review*
BMOHP	Black Muncie Oral History Project, Archives and Special Collections, Bracken Library, Ball State University, Muncie, Indiana
BMP	Black Middletown Project, Archives and Special Collections, Bracken Library, Ball State University, Muncie, Indiana
BOHCO	Black Oral History of Canton, Ohio, Stark County District Library, Canton
C&C	*City and Community*
CC	*Charities and the Commons*
CDP	*Contemporary Drug Problems*
CHS	Chicago Historical Society, Chicago, Illinois
CHSB	*Cincinnati Historical Society Bulletin*
CO	*Camera Obscura*
CWH	*Civil War History*
EEBH	*Essays in Economic and Business History*
EEH	*Explorations in Economic History*
EG	*Economic Geography*
Eh	*Ethnohistory*
GHQ	*Georgia Historical Quarterly*
GR	*Geographical Review*
HM	*Historical Methods*
HS/SH	*Histoire sociale/Social History*
IHJ	*Illinois Historical Journal*
IHS	Indiana Historical Society
IJSF	*International Journal of Sociology of the Family*
IMH	*Indiana Magazine of History*
IMR	*International Migration Review*
IWP	Illinois Writers Project Collection, Vivian G. Harsh Research Collection, Chicago Public Library, Chicago

JAEH	*Journal of American Ethnic History*
JAH	*Journal of American History*
JEH	*Journal of Economic History*
JES	*Journal of Ethnic Studies*
JIH	*Journal of Interdisciplinary History*
JIlH	*Journal of Illinois History*
JISHS	*Journal of the Illinois State Historical Society*
JMF	*Journal of Marriage and the Family*
JNH	*Journal of Negro History*
JSoH	*Journal of Social History*
JSH	*Journal of Southern History*
JUH	*Journal of Urban History*
LH	*Labor History*
MHR	*Missouri Historical Review*
MVHR	*Mississippi Valley Historical Review*
NCHR	*North Carolina Historical Review*
NHB	*Negro History Bulletin*
NP	*New Politics*
OH	*Ohio History*
OHS	Ohio Historical Society, Columbus
OH-TPL	Oral History Collection, Toledo-Lucas County Public Library, Toledo, Ohio
OHUIS	Oral History Office Collection, University of Illinois–Springfield Archives, Brookens Library, University of Illinois–Springfield (formerly Sangamon State University), Springfield
OVH	*Ohio Valley History*
PCS	*Politics, Culture, and Society*
PMHB	*Pennsylvania Magazine of History and Biography*
SF	*Social Forces*
SJOHP	St. James AME Church (Cleveland) Oral History Project, Western Reserve Historical Society, Cleveland, Ohio
SP	*Social Problems*
SSH	*Social Science History*
SW	*Southern Workman*
WHQ	*Western Historical Quarterly*
WUL	Wilberforce University Library, Wilberforce, Ohio

ACKNOWLEDGMENTS

A s is perhaps appropriate for a study of migration, this book has traveled the longest road of any of my projects, and the debts incurred
along the way are correspondingly numerous. I might not have tried to
retool from a historian of alcohol and temperance into a student of African
American migration had it not been for the example of my departmental
colleague Gary Owens, who negotiated the transition from Tudor-Stuart
history to modern Ireland with blazing success. For the methods and
approaches used I credit most of the inspiration to the late Dick Alcorn.
Dick not only helped to initiate me into quantitative analysis, but also
accustomed me to thinking about towns and cities as parts of urban systems and taught me the importance of human mobility across the historical
landscape. At about the same time as I was learning from Dick Alcorn, I
read Lawrence Levine's *Black Culture and Black Consciousness*. This pioneering work both revealed new possibilities in studying African American life
at the grassroots and boldly proclaimed the centrality of agency in African
American migration.

The route from inspiration to interesting and useful findings lay through
numerous archives, and I would certainly have lost my way without the
assistance of their custodians. I wish particularly to thank three guides who
went out of their way to help: Nancy Turner, former curator of the Archives
and Special Collections, Ball State University; Wilma Gibbs, archivist at
the Indiana Historical Society and editor of *Black History News and Notes;*
and Lena Calhoun at the Stark County District Library in Canton, Ohio,
whose job description did not include enthusiastically providing crucial
help to visiting researchers, but who did anyway. Mrs. Carrie Pope Banks
in Champaign, Illinois, and Dr. Norma Snipes Marcere in Canton, Ohio,
graciously consented to be interviewed.

Equally necessary to the success of this project was the diligent, efficient,
and thoughtful work of my research assistants. The principal contributors,

who now know more than they ever wanted to learn about the vagaries of the U.S. federal manuscript census, were Rebecca Surtees, Stacey Demay, Shannon Stettner, and Jennifer Carson. Colin Fitzsimons drew the maps, and Laura Wackman and Kirk Hammond also made significant contributions.

Long as it was, the road from initial questions to final manuscript would have been even longer without the funding generously provided by the Canadian people through the Social Sciences and Humanities Research Council of Canada and the Faculty of Arts and Social Science of Huron University College, and by the people of Indiana through an Indiana Historical Society Director's Grant. In addition, the Conference on Race, Ethnicity, and Migration at the University of Minnesota furnished support for travel to read a paper at that conference.

At the Minnesota conference and others where I presented work in progress, discerning scholars did their best to keep me on the right track. I would especially like to thank S. Charles Bolton, Marvin McInnis, Kimberley Phillips, Spencer Crew, Felix Armfield, Joe Trotter, and Walter Kamphoefner. Nelson Ouellet also gave me helpful feedback. Shirley Portwood and Sundiata Cha-Jua invited me to their stimulating second conference on African Americans in Illinois history, and I benefited both from the opportunity to present preliminary findings and from the chance to discuss my work with these pioneers in midwestern African American community history. My always dependable critics in the American historians' seminar at the University of Western Ontario read several papers and chapters in draft; suggestions by Monda Halpern, George Emery, and Margaret Kellow were particularly helpful. As I neared the end of the trip, David Gerber and David Macleod read a very long manuscript in its entirety and made many useful suggestions, as did Zane Miller and an anonymous reader for The Ohio State University Press. At Huron University College, Julie Bennett cheerfully provided crucial late-stage assistance with file conversion. My wife, Susan, and my son, David, were tolerant of, and supportive despite, long absences from home during research trips. If, despite the guidance and assistance given by all these companions on the journey, this traveler has lost his way, the responsibility is mine alone.

A portion of chapter 5 appeared in *Ohio Valley History* 6, no. 1 (Spring 2006), and is reproduced here by permission of the publishers, Cincinnati Museum Center and the Filson Historical Society. Permission to quote from oral history transcripts in their collections has been granted by the Indiana Historical Society for the Martha Lattimore Papers; Professor Rutledge M. Dennis for the Black Middletown Project; Archives/Special

Collections, Brookens Library, University of Illinois at Springfield, for the Oral History Collection; the Chicago History Museum; the Stark County (Ohio) District Library; the Western Reserve Historical Society for the St. James AME Church Oral History Project; and the Local History and Genealogy Department, Toledo-Lucas County Public Library.

INTRODUCTION

This project began with the bullet holes in the courthouse door. Nearly thirty years ago, research on another topic brought me to Washington Court House, a small town in southwestern Ohio. Most of my work was conducted in the Fayette County courthouse, an impressive sandstone building of 1880s vintage. While passing back and forth to the various county offices where the records were stored, I noticed about a dozen small holes irregularly spaced across the pair of tall, heavy oak doors in one of the main entrances. Inquiring, I was told that the holes were caused by the National Guard firing through the doors during "the race riot in 1894." Race riot? My research focused on the 1870s, and I knew that during the Civil War and postwar years Washington Court House had attracted a substantial African American cohort, who by 1880 made up more than 13 percent of the town's population. At the time, African Americans represented less than 3 percent of Ohioans. Looking around me in the Washington Court House of a hundred years later, I could see that the African American presence was now only a fraction of what it had been.[1] Could there be some connection, I wondered, between the "race riot" and the decline of this small-town African American community? In the Midwest, and across the United States as well, African Americans were now an overwhelmingly metropolitan people. Their movement from country to big city had been rapid in historical terms. Certainly it had been swifter than that of European Americans, whose metropolitan shift had occurred through stages encompassing a protracted period in small towns, an "age of the village." Could the African American experience in Washington Court House be in any way typical of the African American experience in other midwestern small towns? Was there an age of the village for African Americans, a forgotten stage between ruralism and the big city? And, most intriguing, could

1

African Americans' village experience offer any clue to the historical rapidity of their movement to the metropolis?

Curiosity about the bullet holes in the courthouse thus had led me to questions about one of the most significant chapters in African American history. The migrations from the rural South to the metropolitan North arguably represent, along with the civil rights movement, one of the principal changes that African Americans wrought in their lives since emancipation. Furthermore, metropolitan migration and the civil rights movement were indissolubly linked as complementary strategies. Urbanization in both the South and the North created new kinds of African American communities, not only more densely populated but also wealthier, better organized, and more diverse than southern rural communities.[2] Movement to the North regained political rights stolen in the South, which could then be exercised to good effect by the new metropolitan communities. In the absence of the African American vote concentrated in key states, the national administrations since 1940 would have been far more reluctant to listen to demands for civil rights. To explain how and why African Americans moved so rapidly up the urban hierarchy is therefore to open a new window on a critical phase of African American history. Some inkling of the possibilities behind the bullet holes registered in my mind at the time, but meanwhile I had another book to write.[3]

Returning to the question years later, I discovered that Washington Court House was indeed representative, not in the size of its postbellum African American population, which was proportionately larger than most, but in its pattern of rise and decline. The same pattern occurred in many small towns and midsize cities in Ohio and Indiana before 1910. As fine studies by historians David Gerber and Emma Lou Thornbrough demonstrated, during the 1880s African Americans began to move from the rural areas and smaller communities where they had previously settled to the metropolitan centers of Cincinnati, Columbus, Cleveland, and Indianapolis. Gerber and Thornbrough believed that the African American metropolitan shift was part of a general cityward movement involving whites as well as blacks, but their focus on African Americans prevented them from making the detailed comparisons necessary to document this.[4] Early indicators I found suggested that this movement was distinctively African American. In order to understand why African Americans left nonmetropolitan communities for large cities, it would be necessary for me to examine closely both black and white mobility between 1860 and 1910 across these two states.

As if this were not a sufficiently daunting task, I quickly added Illinois to the study area. In terms of their African American migration experience, the three states seemed to form a natural unit, since they stood apart from the other midwestern states by virtue of the larger size of their migration flows.[5] Together, Ohio, Indiana, and Illinois received an estimated total of more than 750,000 African American migrants between the outbreak of the Civil War and the eve of the Great Depression, more than one-third of all those who left the South.[6] In 1860 African Americans represented a tiny minority in each of the three states, but seventy years later migration had made them a significant factor within the region, a mixture of a few old and many new midwesterners whose presence had begun to reshape culture, politics, and urban geography. Another reason to include Illinois was Chicago, the metropolis not only for its state but for the region as a whole, as well as a powerful magnet for African American migration. The unity of the three states in terms of their African American migration history was reinforced by a rough similarity among their economies, all diversified but fairly balanced, with strong agricultural, commercial, and industrial components. Their urban systems, however, were quite different. Ohio contained a multiplicity of dynamic cities, the Big Three before 1900 joined by fast-growing upstarts Akron, Dayton, Toledo, and Youngstown afterward. In Indiana, the most rural of the three states, the urban hierarchy was dominated by a single center, Indianapolis, but rapid growth occurred in the Calumet region in the state's northwestern corner near Chicago after 1900. Chicago overshadowed all other urban places in Illinois, but downstate towns also felt the influence of St. Louis across the Mississippi River. Both the similarities and the differences among the three states of what I was now calling the Lower Midwest encouraged comparison.

During the late nineteenth and early twentieth centuries, Ohio, Indiana, and Illinois reached the apex of their collective importance and influence in American society and politics. A region already populated by the "old" immigration from northwestern Europe attracted "new" immigrants from southern and eastern Europe to fill the industrial jobs that multiplied in its cities. Meanwhile, native-born sons and daughters of the Lower Midwest moved on to the fertile agricultural territory further west. In 1900 Illinois was the nation's third most populous state, Ohio fourth, and Indiana eighth. The region formed a key sector on the battleground of national politics, and both major parties recognized this fact by regularly calling its sons to head their ticket. Between 1860 and 1928, the Lower Midwest had produced eight of the thirteen victorious presidential candidates. Because of the region's political importance, its role as conveyor of American values to new immigrants, and its fecundity in producing migrants to other regions, the pattern of race relations hammered out within its borders could well have influenced the nation's.

3

To explain why the African American metropolitan shift occurred, then, a regional framework would be appropriate. Only a regional study could both analyze the shifting channels of migration within a state and compare these changes to patterns in other states. Regional studies have not been common in American urban history, and in research on African American urbanization they represent a new and as yet rarely used approach.[7] Historians have preferred instead to examine single communities, but such a focus, while allowing considerable descriptive depth, forecloses the possibility of explaining why migrants chose one destination over another.[8] For such a task, comparison is essential. When combined with well-chosen local case studies, a regional focus might provide the graphic detail available in a single-community monograph together with the broad comparative reach necessary for analysis.

With the issue of the proper spatial context in which to place Washington Court House's bullet holes settled, the question of time required consideration. The Civil War clearly formed a watershed in the history of African American migration by endowing African Americans with a degree of choice unprecedented in their history. Indeed, the war itself stimulated the largest black influx to that point in the history of the Lower Midwest. The contrast between the numbers who came to the Midwest after 1860 and the few who resided in the region when the war began clearly indicated the opening of a new chapter in Afro-Midwesterners' story. Within the region, the metropolitan shift that began in the 1880s was measurably well under way by 1910 (at least in Ohio and Indiana), so the study period could have ended there. A good reason to go on lay in the fact that the relation of the volume of African American migration to the Midwest before 1915 to that of the ensuing fifteen years—the First Great Migration period—was as a trickle to a flood. Why African Americans began to abandon smaller urban places for larger ones before the Great Migration, while a fascinating question in itself, would become even more fruitful if that current could be placed in relation to the larger tide that followed. The most prominent scholars who had studied African American migration on a large scale hypothesized that the earlier migration streams "developed pathways and linkages that served as mechanisms for facilitating and even encouraging later movements."[9] Neither they nor anyone else, however, had found a way to test this proposition empirically on anything more than the local level. Once my research had delineated patterns of African American mobility before the First Great Migration of 1916–1930, I would be in a good position to do so. The Great Depression temporarily diminished the appeal of the North in African American eyes, so 1930 seemed a good place to stop.[10]

Within my chosen space and time, research began to focus on three questions. What was life like for African Americans in small towns and other nonmetropolitan urban communities? What relation did African American movement within the North bear to migration into the region? What role did antiblack violence play in relation to other factors in stimulating African American mobility? At the time this project began, all these questions were drastically underresearched.

Since 1990, however, we have learned much about the African American small-town experience in the North through studies that have ranged from America's premier resort towns through gritty industrial communities, from places in which blacks represented a tiny minority to all-black communities.[11] The rich and complex picture that has begun to emerge shows that the quality of African American life in small towns depended upon the interaction of many factors. Following historian Kenneth Kusmer, these can be grouped into three categories. First, structural factors such as the nature of the local economy or the town's location in relation to networks of transportation and communication placed limits on the options available to blacks as well as whites. Second, the attitudes and actions of the European American majority, whether on the local, state, or national level, represented forces to which African Americans often had to respond. Third, the past and present condition of the African American community framed choices. Relations between transient and stable community members; divisions of class, gender, color, and religion; the sex ratio and family structure; the density of the institutional network; and the character of leadership, together with other factors internal to the black community, all could play a role in shaping its history.[12]

My goal is to add to this picture by constructing a comprehensive portrait of small-town life in the Lower Midwest, particularly for the crucial years between 1860 and 1910. Since in 1910 the region held 364 communities containing a population between 2,500 and 100,000, this is no small task. I have collected information bearing on dozens of these towns and have relied on historical studies of the few that have been closely examined.[13] In addition, I will present in-depth studies of four towns distinguished by various combinations of local economy, race relations, and migration history. Washington Court House must be included, if only because of the bullet holes. The Fayette County seat was a market center for a rich agricultural hinterland. Its "race riot" in 1894—actually a foiled lynching—coincided with an African American exodus that followed a period of strong inflow. Springfield, Ohio, a larger industrial city, experienced a pair of true race riots in 1904 and 1906, which similarly capped a period of powerful black inflow and tarnished Springfield's luster in the eyes of would-be migrants. The third town is another Springfield, Illinois's state capital, whose local economy was based on government and coal mining. Its vicious race riot in 1908 set off a national shock wave that culminated in the founding of the National Association for the Advancement of Colored People (NAACP). Before the riot, the African American community in Springfield grew, but more slowly than the state's black urban population as a whole. This pattern continued after the riot. The fourth case study, Muncie, Indiana, was a small industrial city with a steadily growing African American community. No antiblack collective violence is known to have marred race relations in Muncie, although during the 1920s, when it became famous as the site and subject of Robert and Helen Lynd's sociological classic *Middletown*, the town was divided between fervent support for and outspoken opposition to the Ku Klux Klan.[14] Through a close examination of the status and behavior of the African American community in each of the four towns I hope to provide contexts for both white violence and African American decisions to stay or to move on. More generally, I wish to bridge the gap between migration researchers who focus on movement and those who study processes of integration and assimilation within settlement communities.[15]

The question I posed as I pondered the shrunken African American community of Washington Court House centered upon intrastate and intraregional migration. Why did African Americans abandon the small towns of the Lower Midwest for the region's large cities? But I soon realized that this issue was inseparable both conceptually and empirically from the question of interstate and interregional migration flows. A metropolitan shift could have occurred only if both residents of small towns and new southern emigrants chose big-city destinations. Otherwise the places in small towns of veteran black Midwesterners who moved to the city would have been filled by new migrants from the South. Both types of mobility therefore had to be considered in relation to each other.

The question of the contributions made to the metropolitan shift by interstate and interregional migration opened a Pandora's box of collateral issues. We know that the sources of northern migration steadily shifted southward. Before 1915, the border states were the prime generators; afterward, the Deep South. What implications did the changing backgrounds of interregional migrants hold for the metropolitan shift? Another possibly significant facet of the migration stream was its sex composition. Were men or women more likely to migrate into the Lower Midwest early or late in the period, and how could any such change have affected destination choices? Transportation and communication also figured in the rapidly expanding equation. Did changes in the transportation system predispose travelers toward certain destinations? If conditions in small towns became increasingly inhospitable to African Americans, could potential migrants in the South have known this? Finally, there was the question of migration sequences. Did interregional migrants habitually travel to the Midwest in a single jump, or did they carry out step migration, moving up, down, or across the urban hierarchy? Answers to these and other questions were necessary before I could identify which migrants were making what decisions, and for what reasons.

Reflection on these questions led me to define a central goal of the project as delineation of the migration field of African American migrants to and within the Lower Midwest. The concept of a migration field was inspired by the notion of a "mental map" employed by geographers, psychologists, and other social scientists. Each resident of a community, it is said, carries about inside his or her head a map of that community defined by his or her work, history, interests, and connections. Each mental map is therefore personal and may bear little resemblance either to the mental maps of other community residents or to published maps—which of course are themselves arbitrary in selecting which features of a community to include. Nevertheless, comparison of individuals' mental maps generally reveals some degree of correspondence, both with those of other local residents and with real features of the landscape or cityscape.[16]

This concept can be extended to migrants. Potential migrants must have a mental image of the area to which they consider migrating. This image may be scant and totally inaccurate for those with little or no background information, or it may be rich in detail and chronologically deep for those with long residence in the general area and access to the best intelligence. For much human travel, "route knowledge," which consists of awareness of landmarks and turning directions at each landmark, is sufficient. When information about distances and different routes is added, we have acquired "survey knowledge."[17] Whatever its amplitude or quality, the image of the area to be traversed guides decisions about whether, when, and where to move. For all migrants during a period of time, the aggregate of their images of the region of interest is the migration field of that cohort.

When due allowance is made for transportation corridors that channel human mobility, a cohort's migration field should be definable by inference from its locational choices. That is, among the array of potential destinations enjoying equality of access, the places chosen should be the locations preferred. For historical actors, inference will probably be the only guide, since extant records rarely contain anything more than tantalizing clues to the size, shape, or configuration of anyone's mental map. Even when asked directly, "Why did you choose this destination?" respondents to oral history interviews usually offer answers that are no more than implicitly comparative and therefore reveal only a glimpse of a small portion of her or his personal map of accessible terrain.[18] Whatever method is used, defining the migration fields of one's subjects must be a central task of migration research.[19] As a recent review of the scholarly literature on African American migration concludes, "There is much more that we need to learn about the processes that led migrants to select particular destinations in the North and about the wide-ranging consequences of their choices."[20]

The potential motive for migration that initially caught my attention was, of course, white violence. A substantial scholarly literature on racial violence appeared during the twentieth century, focused first on lynching and later on race riots. Most of this literature sought to explain the actions of lynchers or rioters, whether white or black. The most recent historical scholarship on lynching portrays antiblack violence as arising from interaction between black aspirations and behavior and white repression. As George Wright states, "Afro-Americans were lynched for getting out of the place assigned them by white society."[21] Definition and enforcement of that place could vary across both space and time. After tracing a "geography of lynching" in Georgia and Virginia, Fitzhugh Brundage concludes:

> Lynch mobs seem to have flourished within the boundaries of the plantation South, where sharecropping, monoculture agriculture, and a stark line separating white landowners and black tenants existed. In such areas, mob violence became part of the very rhythm of life.[22]

Based on a sophisticated statistical analysis of lynchings across ten southern states, sociologists Stewart Tolnay and E. M. Beck agree. "Mob violence," they write, played a "fundamental role . . . in the maintenance of southern society and economy. . . . [L]ynching was an integral element of an agricultural economy that required a large, cheap, and docile labor force."[23] Existing tallies indicate that lynchings in the North followed a similar chronological pattern to those in the South, with the peak of violence occurring in the two decades around the turn of the century. My own count for Ohio, Indiana, and Illinois shows more than thirty lynchings, attempted lynchings, mobbings, and race riots between 1885 and 1910. No one has yet conducted an analytical study of antiblack violence in the North, where none of the specific conditions cited to explain southern lynching existed. A long step toward such an analysis has been taken, however, in a book published after my research was nearly completed, sociologist James Loewen's *Sundown Towns*. According to Loewen, the heightened white racism across the United States at the turn of the twentieth century led many European Americans in towns and suburbs outside the Deep South to regard the mere presence of African Americans in their communities as unacceptable. As a result, through discrimination, harassment, and violence, African Americans were driven from such places.[24] Loewen's argument, which is both complementary and competitive to mine, will be addressed in chapters to follow. Here I will simply note my belief that, without excusing the racist attitudes that motivated white actions, a full explanation should take into account the dynamics of racial interaction, including the struggles of African Americans for the freedoms they had left the South to find. If northern whites did assign African American a "place" in their communities and society and African Americans in search of full citizenship, not merely a subordinate place, transgressed their prescribed boundaries, then the fundamental trigger of southern lynching may well have produced racial explosions in the North as well. Assessing this hypothesis will require both a comparative examination of violent and peaceful communities and in-depth analysis of specific events.

In contrast to the issue of lynching motivation, fewer historians have attempted to explore how African Americans responded to racially motivated violence. Brundage describes how African Americans in Virginia and Georgia organized politically against lynching, and Wright portrays a range of responses in Kentucky, from lobbying and petition campaigns to armed self-defense.[25] Tolnay and Beck add outmigration to the list of responses, concluding that "blacks were more likely to leave areas in which lynching was more common." Furthermore, across the South a justified fear of lynching acted independently of other variables such as urban or rural residence, illiteracy, and factors influencing both black and white migration.[26] The first post–Civil War mass migration to the North, the Kansas Exodus of 1879, has been portrayed as in part a response to European American violence and intimidation.[27] How much of this repertoire of responses was relevant to northern communities, where antiblack violence is generally considered to have been less common and African American communities were usually smaller, but where the vote offered a political channel to reply? As in the case of lynching motivation, an answer should be based both on comparative analysis across communities and close examination of specific events.

Answering the questions outlined above is the goal of this book. As I suggested above, my purpose in constructing answers is to shed light on some of the most powerful forces shaping American society in the twentieth century. For example, the story of African Americans' movement to large cities forms a significant part of the larger history of the transformation of the United States from a rural to an urban, and then a metropolitan and suburban society. As African Americans changed the setting in which they lived, from the rural South to the metropolitan North, they altered the patterns of their lives through both personal and institutional transmutation. Their movement into northern cities in turn triggered responses from their European American coresidents ranging across a wide spectrum from neglect through cooperation to violent resistance and suburban mobility. Metropolitan migration spread cultural forms born or nurtured in the South—music, dance, and language, for example—not only across the nation, but also into the society's most dynamic cultural centers. As northern migration regained the suffrage for African Americans, metropolitan concentration amplified the power of their vote, a development eventually to carry important consequences for the prospects of the civil rights movement. The full flowering of African American metropolitan migration took place after the end of my story, but its seedtime and germination before 1930 set the pattern for its later growth.

The methods used to answer my questions will become clear as the book proceeds, but here I want to make clear my stance on two basic issues of historical research: quantitative versus qualitative approaches and the truth value of what we as historians produce. This study seeks to explain the attitudes and behavior of ordinary people by defining the conditions under which they lived and the choices they made about their lives. Of the 750,000 African Americans who migrated to the Lower Midwest between 1860 and 1930, the voices of only a small fraction can be heard in surviving sources. To elucidate the locational choices of the multitude and the experiences of those whom history has rendered silent, quantitative evidence is unavoidable, despite its deficiencies, and quantitative analysis is useful, in spite of its tendency to obscure through aggregation. I have consciously tried to counter the homogenizing effect of a quantitative approach by searching in memoirs, newspapers, and, above all, oral history sources for individual voices, and paying attention to what they have to say. As one student of African American migration has observed, "the pattern of movement and the experiences of the individuals involved are both essential to an adequate understanding of the dynamics of human migration."[28] My approach, therefore, is eclectic and inclusive, rather than methodologically focused.

I have tried to tell the story of the African Americans who came to the Lower Midwest, but in the end I do not pretend that it is their story. Instead, it is my story about them. The facts of this story are as true as any set of facts can be. Their selection and arrangement, however, represent only one of an infinitude of possible interpretations.[29]

A word about terminology. "African American" and its parallel term,

"European American," will be used to designate Americans of African and European descent, respectively, but since I cannot establish a full and accurate genealogy for any of the actors in this story, the application of these terms must necessarily depend upon how they were perceived during their lifetimes. Those who were seen and treated as "Negroes" or "colored people" or "Afro-Americans" will be considered to be African Americans. Those who were considered to be "white" will be described here as European Americans. The terms "black" and "white" will be used as interchangeable, respectively, with "African American" and "European American." The noun "race" and its adjectival forms are unavoidable in describing relations between African Americans and European Americans, but I shall try to avoid using them in any way that asserts the reality of discrete racial groups. It should be understood that in this study the terms "race," "racial," "interracial," and the like refer to contemporary perceptions and behaviors, not biological entities. As anthropologist Malcolm Chapman notes, "[T]he notion of a finite, biologically defined and biologically self-reproducing population as the basis of an ethnic group is largely fictional."[30] A burgeoning volume of historical scholarship now treats "whiteness" and "blackness" as social constructions, linguistic and conceptual weapons deployed to create and maintain a relationship of domination by one set of Americans over another.[31] Demonstrating the historical contingency of that relationship is precisely a goal of this study.

Through the bullet holes in the court house doors in Washington Court House I perceived an ever-widening historiographic space. I have tried to furnish as much of that space as possible, but I do not pretend that I have filled it all. This is the first analytical study to employ both qualitative and quantitative methods to study African American migration over such a large area and such a long time. I hope it will not be the last.

Chapter 1 identifies and charts the first two waves of migration into the Lower Midwest: the rush of the Civil War years and the more deliberate movement during the quarter century that followed. Migrant characteristics and patterns of mobility are delineated, a sketch of the Lower Midwest and its race relations is drawn, and migrant choices of destination are traced. Chapters 2 through 5 focus on the conditions migrants found in nonmetropolitan communities and how they dealt with those conditions, emphasizing family life, jobs, wealth, housing, and politics. Within this section, the story proceeds from matters of everyday life to the sporadic outbreaks of violence directed against African Americans and how they responded. In the final three chapters, the focus widens to encompass not only the case study communities, but also the choices made by migrants before leaving the South as well as those that brought them to some destinations rather than others in the Lower Midwest. Locational choices within Ohio, Indiana, and Illinois are examined both during the period of accelerated inmigration around the turn of the twentieth century and during the even more stepped-up surge of the Great Migration period, after 1910. A brief conclusion reflects on the meanings and implications of the story the book tells.

PART ONE

Getting There, 1860–1890

1

RECONNAISSANCE
PARTIES

Man is emphatically a migratory animal.
—Frederick Douglass, 1862[1]

I don' b'lieve in movin' ev'ry year, lak a lot o' people. But if I tek a mine teh move,
I tell you one thing—ain't nobody kin *stop* me!
—An Afro-Mississippian, 1930s[2]

[W]e've always wanted equality. We didn't always know the technique to go about
obtaining [it,] but we have always wanted to be equal.
—Austin Andrews, Canton, Ohio, 1970s[3]

A frican American migration to the Lower Midwest between 1860 and 1890 responded to changes forced by the Civil War on both sides of the Ohio River. A deluge poured into Ohio, Indiana, and Illinois during the terrifying yet liberating turbulence of the war, but the stream slowed to a dribble afterward, as most African Americans chose to test the limits of their new freedom in the South. The war and its attendant changes altered much in the Midwest, stimulating its farms and industries and stretching the narrow limits within which Euro-Midwesterners had historically confined their African American neighbors. With mixed hope and prudence, African American newcomers seized the new opportunities they and their fellows North and South had helped to create.

TWO MIGRATIONS

The wartime migration to the Lower Midwest probably began as soon as troop movements, pitched battles, and internecine conflict in the disputed states of Kentucky and Missouri disrupted slaveholders' patterns of control. As Union troops moved farther south in the war's western theater, more slaves grasped the opportunity for freedom. Some walked or rode to free states on their own. One such pair were Missouri slave Henry Clay Bruce and his betrothed, who took his master's horse, rode to a railway line, and caught a train to the Missouri River, where they crossed to free territory in Kansas.[4] Other ex-slaves were gathered by the Union army and, beginning in 1862, were held at a huge contraband camp in Cairo, at the southernmost tip of Illinois.[5] As historian Michael Johnson points out, "[T]hese refugees from Dixie comprised the largest voluntary interstate migration of African Americans in the first century of the nation's history, over 80,000 in all."[6] About 21,000 came to Ohio, more than 11,000 to Indiana, and 20,000 to Illinois.[7] The wartime migrants may have planned their departure or even made more than one attempt before succeeding, but in the end it was the war's convulsive impact that provided the catalyst for their movement.

Three other characteristics marked the wartime migrants. First, having seized war-generated opportunities to escape from slavery, they were dirt poor. Second, evidence from Kansas and Iowa indicates that they tended to move as families.[8] Oral histories from the Ohio Valley states, too, reflect family migration. For Adah Isabelle Suggs, the actions of her mother, Harriott McClain, were crucial. Born in slavery in Henderson County, Kentucky, in the early 1850s, Adah was taken from her mother at the age of four and put under her mistress's care. Adah's mother attempted several times to escape with Adah to save her daughter from the threat of sexual assault by her master when the girl reached puberty, but her initial efforts were unsuccessful. Although the enlistments of Harriott's husband and son in an African American Union regiment should have brought emancipation for Adah and Harriott, Adah's owner refused to comply with the federal law. When Adah was about twelve, Harriott McClain finally succeeded in escaping with her daughter. They were transported across the Ohio River by federal troops and taken in by the African American community in Evansville, Indiana.[9] Much of that community consisted of newly arrived fellow Kentuckians, and most lived in black-headed households.[10] Fleeing guerilla-war-torn Missouri, the Blue, Barnett, and Mallory families migrated together from Paris to Jacksonville, Illinois; so did the Kirk family from Carrollton.[11] Migrants to rural Pulaski County, Illinois, tended to arrive in family groups and to settle near relatives.[12] As in slavery, the family served as a buffer against a threatening world.

Finally, the wartime migrants were distinguished from all succeeding waves by the role played by whites in aiding their flight. White help was especially useful because established midwestern African American communities were relatively small and the likelihood of slaves' contact with them correspondingly slight. Most slaves had probably never visited free territory.[13] With little or no knowledge of the terrain, no money, and few or no family or friends to assist upon arrival, help from European Americans was no doubt welcome. Migrants, especially those on their own, therefore sometimes sought out white assistance, but the circumstances under which it was sought and rendered suggest exchange and mutuality as much as charity and dependence. After running away from his Missouri plantation, William Nelson hunted for turtle eggs until he filled a bucket. Taking the bucket to the river, he found Yankee soldiers who bought his eggs and took him on board a boat. A Union officer, whom Nelson referred to as "Mars Ben," "tol 'em he take cair me and he did. Den Marse Ben got sick and cum home and brung me along [to Ohio] and I staid with 'em 'til I was about fo'ty, when I gets married and moved to Wyllis Hill."[14] David A. Hall was "brought north" to Ohio by a Union soldier named Kuhns, whom he had met in North Carolina during the war. Hall found work in a flour mill in Tiffin. When he moved to Canton in 1866, Kuhns offered him a job in a mill of which he was part owner. Hall worked in the mill for the next seventy years. In this exchange, Hall received the help he needed to find his way north (but perhaps not to find a job); Kuhns obtained an experienced and loyal employee.[15] In Ohio Union officers and abolitionist and humanitarian organizations were active in recruiting and transporting African Americans to work as domestic servants. At the war's end, the Union commander in northern Kentucky issued free travel passes—via rail or steamboat if necessary—to both free blacks and slaves, and many used the passes to travel north.[16]

In a few cases, family support and white assistance were the same. Orville Artis's grandmother, a slave on a Kentucky plantation, was brought with her four children to Logan County, Illinois, by her master, the father of Orville's mother. The children called him Dr. George, and Artis's mother, Georgiana, was named after him. Dr. George moved on to Chicago, but he provided Georgiana's mother with a house and regular financial support, returning periodically for visits. When Georgiana married Tom Artis, Dr. George bought first a sixty-acre, then a two-hundred-acre farm for his daughter and her husband. "He's one white man," Orville Artis recalled of his grandfather, who "tried to set a record straight as he could."[17]

The sheer volume of wartime migration represented an unprecedented turn in midwestern history. Ohio's prewar African American population of 36,673, by far the largest of the three states, leaped by 72 percent during the decade. Indiana's more than doubled, from 11,428 to 24,560. The tiny African American population of Illinois, only 7,628 at the war's outset, nearly quadrupled to 28,762. In significant ways, however, the wartime flood, by compressing them in time, only underscored prewar patterns. European

Americans had historically played a significant role in facilitating African American migration and settlement in the region. Repentant slaveholders such as Dr. George had settled their slave mistresses, natural children, and other manumitted bondspeople on midwestern lands. Abolitionists had assisted in creating Underground Railroad routes that whisked some fugitives through to Canada and encouraged others to settle nearby. Quaker settlements became well known for their sympathy, and many black communities grew up in their vicinity.[18] As the war to preserve the Union became a war of liberation, northern white opinion toward blacks polarized, largely along partisan lines. Many of those who took the side of the freedpeople accepted the duty of manifesting their principles in deeds.[19]

For every slave who escaped before the war, flight was more than fulfillment of a personal need: it was a form of active resistance to a system grounded upon denial of African American volition. Once the seceded states mobilized for war, escape took on an even more portentous political dimension. Every fugitive deprived the Confederacy of a badly needed worker. When the Union armies began to enlist African Americans on a large scale in the aftermath of the Emancipation Proclamation, flight from slavery became for many only the first phase of a campaign to destroy the slave system. In the border slave states, the message sent by the fugitives was slightly different but no less political: The end of slavery was at hand. When nearly 24,000 Afro-Kentuckians gained legal freedom for themselves and their dependents—totaling 71 percent of Kentucky's slaves—by leaving their farms and plantations to enlist in the Union army, they all but guaranteed its realization.[20] A step toward African American freedom during the antebellum years, flight in the wartime crisis quickened the pace toward that elusive goal.

The wartime migration probably extended into 1867, when the rapid turn toward Radical Reconstruction began to open new opportunities in the South. It was succeeded during the following quarter century by a different kind of movement, more tentative and gradual than the sometimes premeditated but often precipitate departures of the apocalyptic wartime years. The Lower Midwest experienced nothing like the sudden surge of migrants who left the Deep South for Kansas in the spring of 1879. Because it was incremental, the new migration usually attracted far less notice and much less support or opposition from whites. African American migration could generate intense reactions during these years, as became clear during the Kansas Exodus, when newspapers across the country dissected the motives and probed the political implications of the movement.[21] Some of the fallout splashed across the Midwest, as Democratic charges that Republicans were importing voters into closely divided Indiana sparked a congressional

Sex Ratio of Net Black Migration to Ohio, Indiana and Illinois, 1870-1930

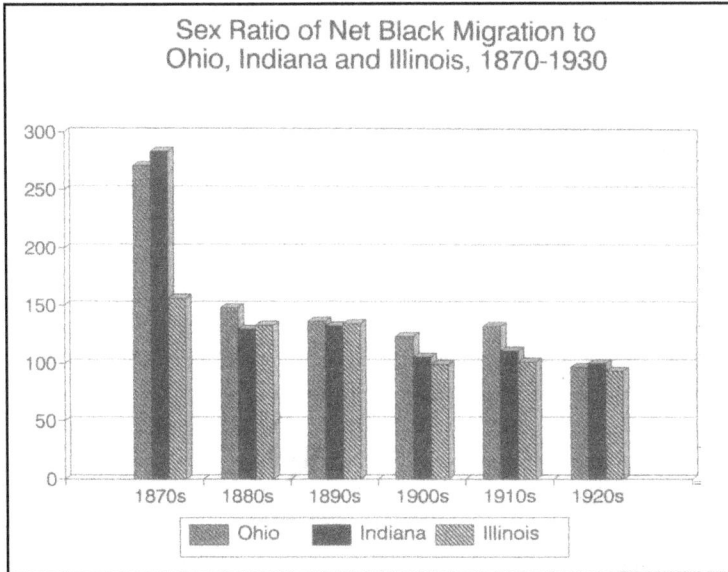

Figure 1.1 Sex Ratio of Net Black Migration to Ohio, Indiana, and Illinois, 1870–1930. Source: Everett S. Lee et al., *Methodological Considerations and Reference Tables,* vol. 1 of *Population Redistribution and Economic Growth, United States, 1870–1950,* ed. S. Kuznets and D. S. Thomas, 3 vols. (Philadelphia: American Philosophical Society, 1957–64), 136, 138–39, 191

investigation.[22] But this was the exception to the rule. The Gilded Age migration was far more under African American control than any previous African American migration. Its political implications for the migrants and their new communities were left unexplored by Congress or anyone else, and other consequences it might bring in its train were probably equally unanticipated by blacks and whites alike as the migration proceeded.

African American migration to the Lower Midwest during the Gilded Age brought about the same number of migrants to the region as the wartime movement, but the flow extended over a period nearly four times as long (1867–1890). The Civil War flood dwindled to a trickle.[23] Nevertheless, by the time the current began to flow more strongly in the 1890s, the trickle had made significant additions to the region's African American population. Population growth, most of which was provided by migration, added 38 percent in Ohio between the censuses of 1870 and 1890, 84 percent in Indiana, and 98 percent in Illinois. In Ohio black population growth kept pace with white. In Indiana and Illinois the African American growth rate substantially exceeded the European American.

Most of the Gilded Age migrants were former slaves, young, and male. Evidence on individual migrant histories comes from the ex-slave

19

interviews conducted by the Federal Writers' Project (FWP) during the 1930s (see appendix C). Of thirty-three oral history respondents for whom an age at the time of their migration to the North can be calculated, all but three were under thirty years. Their median age was eighteen years. Of forty-three whose sex is known, 70 percent were male. The male majority among the FWP migrants is also apparent in the census, which shows extremely high sex ratios in the migrant streams for all three states during the 1870s, in excess of three males for every two females. More women and girls came during the 1880s, but not enough to produce parity (figure 1.1). In moving north, the FWP migrants also moved townward. More than 90 percent of oral history subjects were born in rural areas (thirty-four of thirty-seven), but only one-third made their first northern stop a rural one (six of seventeen). Fewer than one-fifth were still living in a rural community when they were interviewed (six of thirty-five).

For some migrants, migration was initiated or accelerated by the sort of dramatic incident that plays a central role in the literary and artistic representations of African American migration. African American migration narratives are marked by a "pivotal moment" in which "an event . . . propels the action northward."[24] For some Gilded Age migrants, literature reflected life. Mrs. Preston, a migrant from Kentucky to Indiana, reported that Klansmen gave her family ten days to leave their land, and then burned their home when her father dared to return.[25] Another Kentuckian told how white farmers organized in an attempt to deny their black sharecroppers a share of the crops, and how his family left for Indiana as a result.[26]

Other migrants recalled conflicts with individual whites that figured in their decisions to move on. Ex-slave Kisey McKimm and her mother left the farm in Bourbon County, Kentucky, that they had been given by their former master after the master died and his son threatened to burn them out.[27] After emancipation another Kentuckian, young Watt Jordan, was bound out by his mother to Matt Clay. After about ten years working for Clay, Jordan left.

> I left Clay's atter he flew en er rage one day en wuz goin' ter whip me. I wuz eighteen den, en I knowed I wuz jes' as good er man as Clay wuz; so, when he started en ter whip me, I jes' whipped him en left. He tried ter git me back, en come to town en raised er racket, but folks all tole him I wuz free ter do what I wanted, en so he left me erlone.[28]

John William Matheus stayed after emancipation on the West Virginia farm of his former owners, until a verbal conflict with his former master brought him to the decision to leave.

I stayed with Michael and Mary Blue till I was nineteen. They were supposed to give me a saddle and bridle, clothes and a hundred dollars. The
massa made me mad one day. I was rendering hog fat. When the crackling
would fizzle, he hollo [*sic*] and say "don't put so much fire." He came out
again and said, "I told you not to [p]ut too much fire" and he threatened to
give me a thrashing. I said, "If you do I will throw rocks at you."

After that I decided to leave and I told Anna Blue I was going. She
say, "Don't do it, you are too young to go out into the world." I say, I don't
care. . . . [29]

Clearly the migrants felt such incidents to be important turning points in
their personal lives, as they recalled them many years later for interviewers
who were often strangers.

Although such dramatic incidents were connected in the migrants' minds
with a decision to move, they were not always, or even often, related to a
decision to move north. After receiving the Klan's warning, Mrs. Preston's
family did take what the Klan paid them for their farm and came north. But
after a period in the North, her father returned to Kentucky. When the Klan
burned his house, he and part of his family remained in their old neighborhood under the protection of their former owner.[30] Under threat of being
burned out, Kisey McKimm and her mother abandoned their Kentucky
farm, but they went only as far as Paris, Kentucky. Kisey McKimm did not
move north until after she had married and borne two children.[31] After
beating Matt Clay, Watt Jordan did not go north right away; instead he
moved to Carlisle, Kentucky, only later migrating to Ohio.[32] John William
Matheus left the Blues' farm in about 1879 after arguing with his former
master, but he went only as far as his uncle's farm nearby. He worked in a
tannery and presumably husbanded his resources, then Matheus crossed the
Ohio River to Steubenville. After eighteen months working in Steubenville,
Matheus returned to West Virginia, moving permanently to Steubenville
only in 1884, five years after the conflict he remembered so clearly more
than half a century later. For Jordan and Matheus, the successful dispute
with a white man probably symbolized coming to manhood, a transition
that, for Matheus at least, also embraced migration north. Like Jordan's stay
in Carlisle, the time that elapsed between the clearly remembered incident
and the final relocation, the testing of northern waters in Steubenville followed by Matheus's return to home ground, suggest a deliberate process of
decision making. John Matheus himself noted a possible reason for his hesi-
tation: "The old folks told me they were stoned when they came across the
river to Ohio after the surrender and that the colored people were treated
like cats and dogs."[33]

21

Table 1.1 Step Migration in Three Periods

	Period		
	1859–1889	1890–1915	1916–1930
Percentage who:			
Made no recorded stops	8.1	36.7	39.6
Made stops in the South	29.7	10.0	26.4
Made stops in the North	43.2	26.7	13.2
Made stops in both North and South	18.9	26.7	20.8
Total	99.9*	100.1*	100.0
N	37	30	53

* Does not equal 100.0 because of rounding

Note: A migrant was considered to have made a stop if he or she indicated living in a place rather than merely stopping over, but no precise quantitative distinction was possible.

Source: Oral history respondents (see appendix C).

Step migration—movement by stages, usually from smaller to larger places—does seem to have been characteristic of Gilded Age migrants to the Lower Midwest.[34] Pre-1890 migrants were less likely than later ones to make the move north in a single jump (table 1.1).[35] Lloyd Phillips escaped from slavery in Kentucky in 1864. Eight years and two Ohio stops later, he arrived in rural Paulding County in northwestern Ohio.[36] Elizabeth Russell took three years to work her way north from Georgia to Kentucky. After staying "awhile" in Covington, she finally crossed into Indiana.[37] William Williams's journey from rural North Carolina to Canton, Ohio, included stops in both the South and the North:

> I did not stay with my father and mother long as I was only about 14 when I started north. I worked for farmers every place I could find work and sometimes would work a month or maybe two. The last farmer I worked for I stayed a year and I got my board and room and five dollars a month which was paid at the end of every six months. I stayed in Pennsylvania for some years and came to Canton in 1884.[38]

Step migration is a common pattern in rural-urban migration.[39] But it was especially useful, indeed necessary, when potential migrants had to rely upon word-of-mouth communication to gain knowledge of potential destinations. During these years few northern African American newspapers circulated in the South, and widespread illiteracy restricted the impact of those that did.[40] Southern newspapers sometimes received correspondence from the North, but this was rare and less authoritative than a northern newspaper.[41] Communication by letters and personal contact was less common than it would become when northern black communities grew and north–south railway links multiplied.[42] The prevalence of step migration among the early migrants suggests how much they needed and valued foreknowledge of potential northern destinations.

Long-distance transportation was also problematic, although one must be careful not to judge nineteenth-century facilities by twenty-first-century standards.[43] The southern railway network, much less extensive than in the North at the war's outset, was systematically destroyed by both Union and Confederate forces seeking to deny each other use of the railways. Rebuilding was delayed during the 1870s by the South's credit shortage and the severe national depression of 1873–1879. Only during the 1880s did significant expansion and harmonization with the northern system take place. The southern system was realigned from east–west to north–south, and in 1886 most of the South's trackage was changed to the northern standard gauge. The first railway bridge across the Ohio River was built at Louisville in 1870, the second seven years later at Cincinnati, and in 1889 the Illinois Central bridge at Cairo connected Illinois with the South.[44] By 1890, then, all three states of the Lower Midwest enjoyed southern rail connections. Whether southern blacks in large numbers could afford to ride them—or wished to endure long-distance travel in Jim Crow cars—was another question.

Railway travel for African Americans from the Deep South to the North during the 1870s and 1880s generally meant discomfort at best and conflict at worst. Humiliation was likely in either case. As the southern rail system was extended, the railroads became a focus of struggle between whites demanding separation and blacks insisting on equal rights. The upshot was state laws requiring the railroads to provide separate and equal accommodations for African Americans, which began to spread across the South during the late 1880s.[45] The accommodations, however, were not equal. In the North by the 1880s, Pullman Palace Cars were transforming long-distance travel into an adventure that was not only fast but comfortable, but southern black emigrants traveling by train experienced an entirely different sort of adventure. To travel from, say, Selma, Alabama, to Toledo, Ohio, in 1893 meant a thirty-one-hour, twenty-minute journey sitting up on wooden benches and eating and drinking only what the traveler could manage to bring along. Along the way were two changes from one railway line to another—fortunately, in the same stations—in Chattanooga and Cincinnati. A traveler from Clarksdale, Mississippi, to Chicago needed to make only one change, but had to endure the same conditions for about the same length of time.[46]

Railroads, however, were not the only way to leave the South. Despite increasing competition from railroads, steamboats cruised the Ohio, Mississippi, Missouri, and other midwestern rivers throughout the nineteenth century, and carried passengers more cheaply than the railways. Steamboats played an indispensable role in the most widely publicized African American migration of the Gilded Age, the "Exodus" to Kansas in 1879. When the Exodus began in the early spring, Exodusters flocked to the Mississippi River ports and riverbanks, hoping to catch steamboats that would take them to St. Louis. From St. Louis they could embark by rail or Missouri River steamer to Kansas. The steamboat fare was four dollars from Vicksburg to St. Louis, and another $2.50 from St. Louis to Wyandotte, Kansas. Threatened by the loss of their labor force, planters and merchants sought to stop the movement. For about a month beginning in late April 1879, the principal Mississippi River steamboat companies refused to carry would-be migrants, and the steamboat boycott effectively interdicted African American mobility from the Deep South to Kansas. Historians agree that more African Americans tried to leave the Deep South in 1879 than were able to do so, and one argues that the impetus of the movement was broken by the migrants' stranding on the river banks.[47] What the flood and ebb of the Kansas Exodus demonstrate is that in normal times the steamboat offered a relatively inexpensive means of long-distance travel out of the South. More than 7,500 migrants from the Deep South states managed to reach Kansas during the 1870s, and most of these traveled by water. Its value decreased, however, with a would-be migrant's distance from a navigable river. On the other hand, a penniless but able-bodied man who was able to reach a steamboat landing might be able to pay for his passage by helping to load fuel or cargo.

During the Kansas Exodus, public discussion focused primarily on migrants from the Deep South. In fact, many more migrants to Kansas during the 1870s hailed from the Upper South states of Kentucky and Tennessee than from the Deep South states of Alabama, Mississippi, Louisiana, Texas, and Arkansas.[48] Kentucky was also the leading source of Gilded Age migrants to the Lower Midwest, and Tennessee was not far behind.[49] Compared to later migratory streams, the Lower Midwest's Gilded Age migrants traveled shorter distances, but, despite their proximity to their destinations, they were more likely to travel in stages.

When all the evidence is weighed, the migration of the 1867–1890 period looks more like a deliberate movement in search of opportunity than a headlong flight from oppression. The fact that greater numbers came to the Lower Midwest during the wartime years than during the postwar period tends to discount the deterrent effects of absent railroad links and few sources of information. More could have moved than did. Those who did migrate were predominantly young men, typically the group that responds most readily to the lure of new opportunities. They left the South during a time when most African Americans still retained the right to vote, before the wave of disfranchisement legislation stimulated by the Mississippi Plan of 1890.[50] The migrants effectively counteracted the scarcity of information through step migration. The relatively short range of their migration, from the border states to the Lower Midwest, facilitated communication with families and kept open the possibility of return. If conditions in their new homes proved welcoming, they could serve as a reconnaissance party for larger detachments to follow. Whether any individual migrant stayed or returned south, the migration widened the scope of informed choice for African Americans collectively by exploring new territory.

THE LOWER MIDWEST

During the postwar years the prospects of that new territory—the Lower Midwest—certainly generated abundant optimism among its residents. The Midwest in general, and the states of the Lower Midwest in particular, were entering their peak years of wealth and national influence, emerging economically and politically from the shadow of the older states to the east. In Lincoln the Lower Midwest had elected its first president, and five more followed him to the White House before the century ended. A maturing agricultural economy and a lusty, youthful industrial one shaped the region's population dynamics. Yet Midwesterners were forced to temper their optimism when boom regularly turned to bust. Native-born women and an increasingly foreign-born industrial working class challenged the order ruled by native-born white men. Deep and persistent partisan divisions both reflected other conflicts and generated their own. As the Midwest gained power to shape the nation's course, no one could easily foretell what heading the region would choose.

The Midwest's historic strength stemmed from its bountiful land. During the Gilded Age, its regional metropolis, Chicago, acquired dominance because of the city's ability to control markets for the massive quantities of grain, livestock, and timber produced on that land.[51] Supplies of coal and natural gas and ready access to iron ore fueled the growth of manufacturing. The Midwest was distinguished by "the sustained, simultaneous growth of agriculture and industry."[52] All three states consistently ranked among the nation's leaders in agriculture, and Ohio and Illinois repeated the achievement in manufacturing. Agriculture and industry, however, produced different effects upon population movements. Even as midwestern agriculture came to lead the nation, rising land prices and high machinery costs drove the sons and daughters of farm families to seek opportunity in states farther west. During the decades from the Civil War to the eve of the Great Depression, each state typically lost more native-born white males and females than it gained. Industry, in contrast, attracted to the region large numbers of immigrants, mostly to Ohio and Illinois, an influx that sustained the white population's growth rate.[53] Urban growth, another notable feature of the region's history during this period, resulted from the convergence in the cities of immigrants and the stay-behind surplus agricultural population.[54]

Urbanization provides as good a gauge as any of the explosive growth of the Lower Midwest. Between 1860 and 1890, the number of urban places (those of 2,500+ population) more than doubled in Illinois, tripled in Ohio, and quadrupled in Indiana. Urban populations grew at a similar pace. In 1860 Indiana contained no city larger than 25,000, but by 1890 Indianapolis had passed the 100,000 mark. Cleveland joined Cincinnati at the apex of Ohio's urban hierarchy, and Chicago swelled from a population smaller than Cincinnati's in 1860 to more than one million residents by 1890, a size that dwarfed all other midwestern cities. Hamlets blossomed into villages, villages grew into towns, and towns became cities. Washington Court House and Muncie, beneath the urban threshold in 1860, expanded respectively from 1,035 and 1,782 to 5,742 and 11,345. Springfield, Illinois, grew from 9,320 to 24,963, but even so found itself surpassed by the Ohio Springfield, which multiplied its 7,002 into 31,895. Within each state, population, agriculture, industry, and wealth were beginning to shift north from the Ohio River valley as the draining of northern swamplands, the growth of Chicago, and the building of new rail lines along the southern shores of Lakes Erie and Michigan created mutually reinforcing incentives for development.[55]

Midwestern politics shared the dynamism of the midwestern economy. No other subject received such consistent and dramatic coverage from the region's flourishing and omnipresent newspaper press. Frequent elections mobilized virtually all of the able-bodied adult males, as well as some who were not so able. Fixed during the Civil War, partisan loyalty formed a major component of male identity.[56] Political partisanship became the lens through which events were commonly viewed. The cause of the Kansas Exodus, for example, to Republicans was southern white oppression of the freedpeople; to Democrats, it was Yankee meddling. During the Exodus, several hundred African Americans migrated from North Carolina to Indiana, which had narrowly voted Democratic in the previous presidential election. Democrats perceived the migration as a nefarious attempt by Republicans to tilt the state's electoral balance, and some Republicans fed their suspicions. The resulting investigation by a U.S. Senate committee predictably produced diametrically opposed conclusions by its Democratic majority and Republican minority.[57]

Given the white South's growing attachment to the Democratic party and New England's and the West's solid Republican loyalties, the Midwest and the Middle Atlantic states became the main battleground of national politics. Within the Midwest, the three states of the Lower Midwest formed the front lines. Early southern migration to the lower reaches of Ohio, Indiana, and Illinois created fertile soil for Democratic doctrines. The peopling of their northern sectors by New Yorkers and New Englanders did the same for Republican principles. Still, within most communities could be found thriving detachments of both major parties, with the minority biding its time until the right combination of local, state, and national conditions allowed it to turn out the current governing party. Factions thrived in both Democratic and Republican ranks.[58] Complicating the picture still further, the Prohibition Party, formed in Chicago in 1869, gained strength throughout the 1870s and 1880s by attracting dissident Republicans, especially in the Prohibitionists' Lower-Midwestern heartland.[59]

The partisan political spectacles worn by nearly all native-born male Midwesterners equipped them poorly to comprehend challenges that arose during the Gilded Age from sources beyond party and governmental machinery. The first of these appeared in the winter of 1873–74, when tens of thousands of women—mostly white, native-born, and middle-class—suddenly began to march on saloons and other liquor retailers in hundreds of towns across the region and beyond.[60] Simultaneously, what was to become a severe economic depression commenced with the unexpected failure of one of the country's largest banking houses. The Women's Crusade ended by the summer of 1874, but it left behind a new national women's temperance organization, the Woman's Christian Temperance Union (WCTU), organized in Cleveland in the fall of that year and later headquartered in Chicago. The Lower Midwest formed the seedbed for both the Crusade and the WCTU, as temperance women energized the antiliquor cause in communities across the region for years after the marches ended.[61] The depression lingered nearly through the end of the decade, annually generating thousands of unemployed workers who traveled the countryside seeking work. In 1877 hard times helped to bring on the nation's first national railway strike.

The railway strike was only the most visible early conflict between capital and labor during the Gilded Age. African Americans had already been brought to Ohio's Hocking Valley and other places in the Lower Midwest in 1873–74 to supplant European American coal miners.[62] Strife in the coal-mining regions of all three states continued through the century's end, and it often pitted black miners against whites.[63] In 1886, Chicago police attacked eight-hour-day protestors, and the subsequent bombing of police in Haymarket Square brought midwestern newspapers' routine antianarchist hatred to fever pitch.[64] Eight years later, another national railway strike spread outward from Chicago after the American Railway Union chose to support striking workers at George Pullman's suburban plant and model town.[65] If the Midwest represented America's future, as many Midwesterners liked to believe, then from the perspective of the Gilded Age that future appeared to be conflict ridden.

On the question of African Americans in the Midwest's—and, by extension, America's—future, white Midwesterners were not only divided, as responses to the small black migration of 1879–80 showed, they were changeable. Ohio's relatively large African American population in 1860 could be traced in large part to the fact that the Buckeye State was the only one of the three that had not prohibited African Americans by constitution or statute from entering the state. Ohio also allowed African Americans to enter the state without having to post a bond for good behavior, to testify in court, and to attend publicly supported separate schools. The schools, however, were generally inadequate, and state law prohibited African Americans from serving on juries or in the militia or receiving public relief.[66] In 1851 Indiana's new state constitution had ratcheted up its antiblack legal proscriptions by adopting, with enthusiastic popular support, an article that read, "No negro or mulatto shall come into, or settle in the State, after the adoption of this Constitution."[67] As a result, as Indiana's governor pointed out in 1865, "No negro who has come into Indiana since 1850 can make a valid contract; he can not acquire title to a piece of land, because the law makes the deed void, and every man who gives him employment is subject to prosecution and fine."[68] Black Hoosiers were banned by state law from voting, serving in the militia, attending public schools, and testifying in cases involving whites. Intermarriage between whites and persons having one-eighth or more "Negro" blood was prohibited.[69] Illinois's Black Laws generally echoed those of Indiana.[70]

These structures of legal discrimination, built up piece by piece during the half century since Ohio, Indiana, and Illinois achieved statehood, eroded rapidly in the tumult of change brought by the Civil War. Most white Midwesterners at the war's outset did not expect the conflict to expand black freedom. In fact, they steadfastly resisted such an outcome. During the war's first year, Illinois led in the ratification of a proposed but abortive U.S. constitutional amendment that would have prevented the Emancipation Proclamation or any other federal action toward abolition. Illinois voters followed the path charted by their legislature by approving incorporation of the state's Black Laws into the constitution.[71] Ohio's legislators responded to the possibility of former slaves migrating into the state by passing a new law forbidding all sexual contact, including marriage, between blacks and whites. White dock workers in Toledo and Cincinnati attacked African American workers and property during the summer of 1862, as did a mob in New Albany, Indiana.[72] The secretary of war's order in September 1862 to disperse African Americans from the massive contraband camp in Cairo evoked racist fears that swept Democrats into office across the Lower Midwest in the subsequent elections.[73] The 1862 elections, however, proved to be the high-water mark for midwestern racism.

Union victories at Vicksburg and Gettysburg in July 1863 turned the tide, not only of the war itself, but also of European American opinion in the Lower Midwest. "Carried along by the religious and patriotic currents that swept in the wake of Gettysburg and Vicksburg," Jacque Voegeli writes,

> more and more people viewed the war as a fight for liberty and embraced the idea that the antislavery policy had endowed the Union with moral superiority that would help to conquer the South and also ultimately elevate the national character by purging the country of its sole remaining defect.[74]

In January 1865 the Illinois legislature repealed the exclusion law and gave African Americans access to the courts. Five years later, Illinois voters adopted a new state constitution incorporating the principles of universal public schooling and a desegregated militia.[75] Indiana took no steps toward legal equality during the war, but in 1866 the Indiana Supreme Court ruled that the constitutional exclusion clause was void in light of the recently passed federal civil rights act granting African American citizenship.[76] Three years later, the Indiana legislature required local authorities to provide schooling for African American children.[77] Ohio removed the ban on relief and improved facilities for separate black schools.[78]

African Americans played an active role in changing white public opinion and dismantling the structures of midwestern discrimination. During the war, African Americans moved into the Lower Midwest in numbers large enough to disprove racist claims that slavery was their natural condition and to provide badly needed laborers for manpower-depleted midwestern farms. But the migration was insufficiently voluminous, and the migrants' behavior insufficiently threatening, to fulfill Democratic predictions of job competition, declining wage levels, rising criminality, and proliferating immorality. African Americans did act, however, so as to realize one Democratic nightmare, the entry of a new political force into the volatile midwestern polity. They organized conventions and petition campaigns and lobbied for equal rights. The crucial decision by the Indiana Supreme Court was delivered in a suit brought by an African American, Jacob Smith of Marion County, and appealed by him to the court. Most important, African Americans contributed to the war effort. Only six weeks after Cincinnati's antiblack riot, almost a thousand African American men, dubbed the "Black Brigade," worked for three weeks to build fortifications to protect the city against an approaching Confederate army. Once the Emancipation Proclamation cleared their way, a substantial proportion of the African American population of military age enlisted in the region's black regiments. When African American enlistments reduced the need for European Americans to fight and die, whites were forced to recognize the African American contribution to the struggle to save the Union.[79]

Given the degree of antiblack prejudice in the antebellum Lower Midwest, the changes of the Civil War and Reconstruction were indeed dramatic. Yet their cumulative effect was only to grant to African Americans a "cramped, meager degree of equal rights."[80] Through the Civil Rights Act of 1866 and the Fourteenth and Fifteenth Amendments, the federal government had forced African American citizenship and suffrage on the region. Ohio voters, in fact, explicitly rejected African American male suffrage in 1867, only to have the Fifteenth Amendment impose it three years later.[81] Much remained to be done. The meaning of the wartime and postwar changes and the European American will to support the new order were unclear. The new order itself left African Americans with significant disabilities. White racism had been "tempered," but not "purged."[82]

DESTINATIONS SOUGHT AND SHUNNED

Although white racism lingered in both midwestern law and custom during the late nineteenth century, the legal and institutional changes that had occurred as a result of the Civil War gave grounds for hope that racist structures and practices could be further eroded in the years to come. The postwar period was "a time of unparalleled hope, laden with possibility, when black men and women acted to shape their own destiny."[83] To those who lived through the titanic struggle that brought about the death of slavery and the winning of citizenship and suffrage by those who only a few years before had been declared by the nation's highest court to have "no rights that the white man was bound to respect," the changes were breathtaking, even if incomplete. Nor did that sense of expanding possibilities die with those who experienced personally the transition from slavery to freedom. They inculcated in their children born in freedom an expectation of exercising full civil rights.[84]

In this atmosphere of cautious hope, the wartime and postwar migrants entered the Lower Midwest and chose destinations. The patterns of their locational choices are clear and consistent across all three states.[85] In each state at least two-thirds of the African American population had lived in rural areas on the eve of the Civil War, but African Americans were still a more urban people than European Americans. Although the wartime and Gilded Age migrations bolstered African American rural populations, in no state did rural populations grow as rapidly as the number of urban dwellers. African American rural population growth did, however, nearly match the increase in the largest cities of Ohio and Indiana, and in Illinois substantially exceeded Chicago's gain.[86] Although the largest cities attracted African American migrants, the migration stream did not concentrate there either. Instead, African Americans distributed themselves across the urban hierarchy, settling in small towns and midsized cities as well as in Chicago, Indianapolis, Cleveland and Cincinnati, and the rural areas.[87] As a result, in 1890 blacks were a significantly more metropolitan population than whites only in Indiana, where Indianapolis held one-fifth of blacks compared to one-twentieth of whites.[88] Yet even in Indiana, twice as many African Americans lived in other urban places as in Indianapolis. In Ohio African Americans were only slightly more concentrated in Cincinnati and Cleveland than European Americans. In Illinois, despite the fifteenfold multiplication of Chicago's African American population, a larger proportion of the state's European American population (29 percent) than its African American population (25 percent) lived in the regional metropolis in 1890 (tables A.1–A.3).

As they scattered across the landscape of the Lower Midwest, African American migrants generally bypassed prewar centers of African American population. In 1860 New Albany held 23 percent of Indiana's African American urban population, the largest share of any community. By 1890, despite tripling the number of its African American citizens, New Albany's share dropped to less than 7 percent. The story was the same upriver in Cincinnati, which in 1860 contained one-third of Ohio's African American urbanites, the region's largest concentration. Despite tripling their numbers over the next thirty years, Afro-Cincinnatians in 1890 represented 10 percent less of their state's African American urban dwellers than they had in 1860. Chicago varied from the pattern, however, increasing its share of Illinois's African American urban population from 39 to 42 percent. In Ohio and Indiana, African American urban growth was most rapid in the towns that

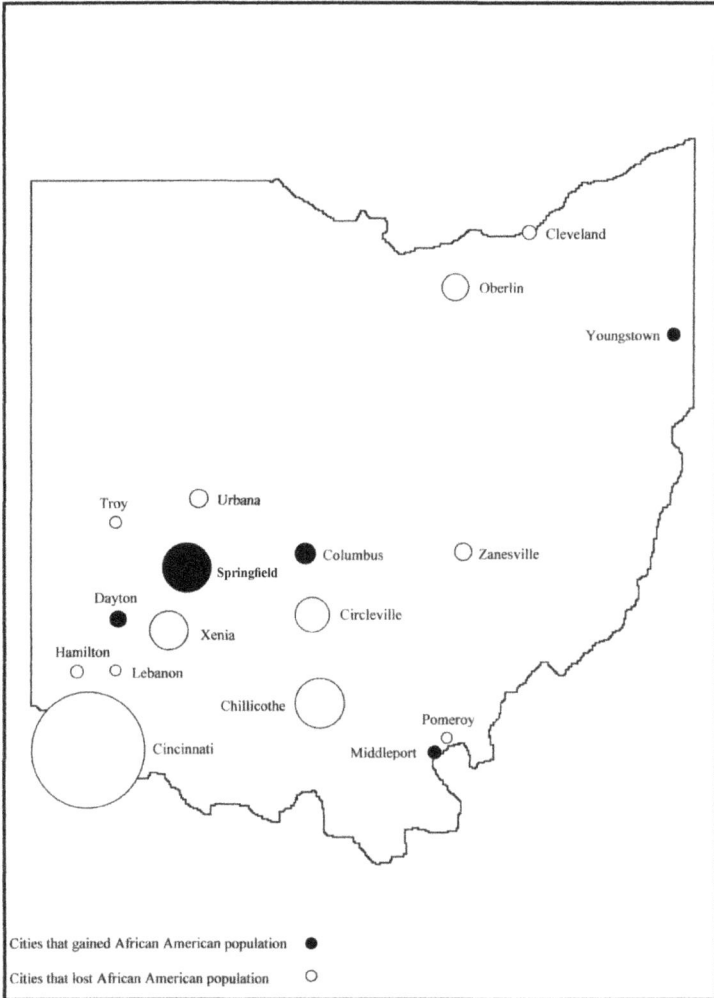

Figure 1.2 Gainers and Losers in African American Urban Population Share in Ohio, 1860–1890.

contained fewest African Americans on the eve of the Civil War. In Illinois the same trend appears outside of Chicago. Beyond Chicago, Gilded Age migrants to the Lower Midwest dispersed themselves across a rapidly growing urban system. They avoided existing black clusters and instead selected communities where few or no African Americans had lived before.[89]

Some historians believe that African American migrants were deterred from locating in communities containing large numbers of European immigrants, and they explain this by the threat of job competition. To the extent

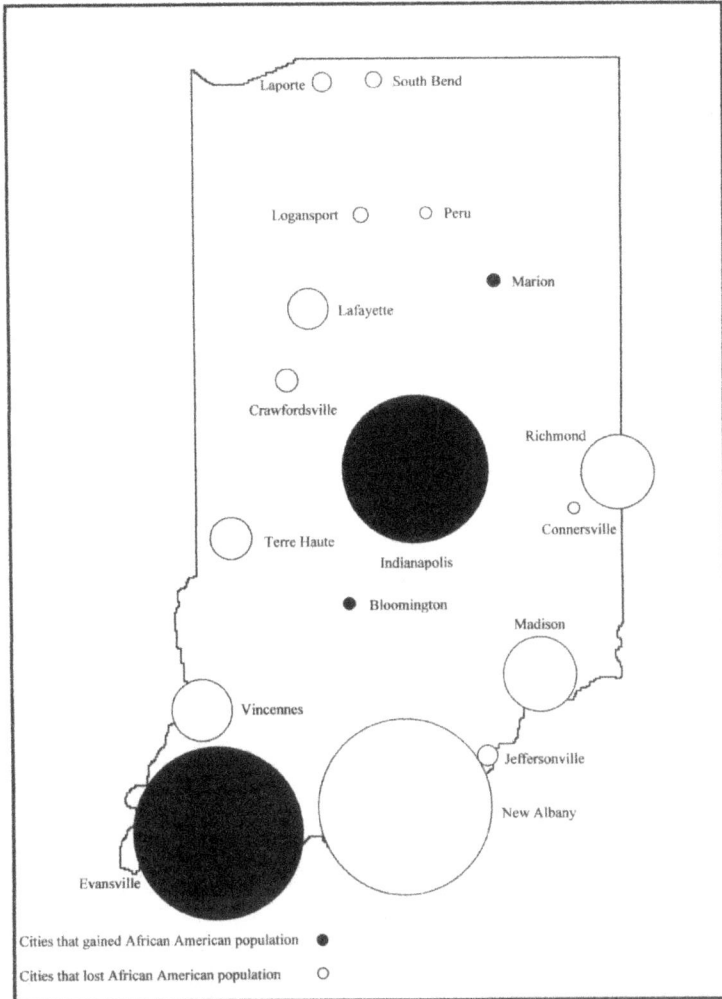

Figure 1.3 Gainers and Losers of African American Urban Population Share in Indiana, 1860–1890.

that both migration streams were composed of former agricultural workers, they might have been expected to compete with each other in the industrializing Lower Midwest for lower-skilled jobs.[90] If the Gilded Age African American migrants to the Lower Midwest anticipated such competition, however, they seem not to have expected to lose. Migrants chose destinations without reference to the size of their immigrant populations.[91]

Migrants also did not make their locational choices in accordance with gross spatial changes in the regional economy. In all three states, the locus

33

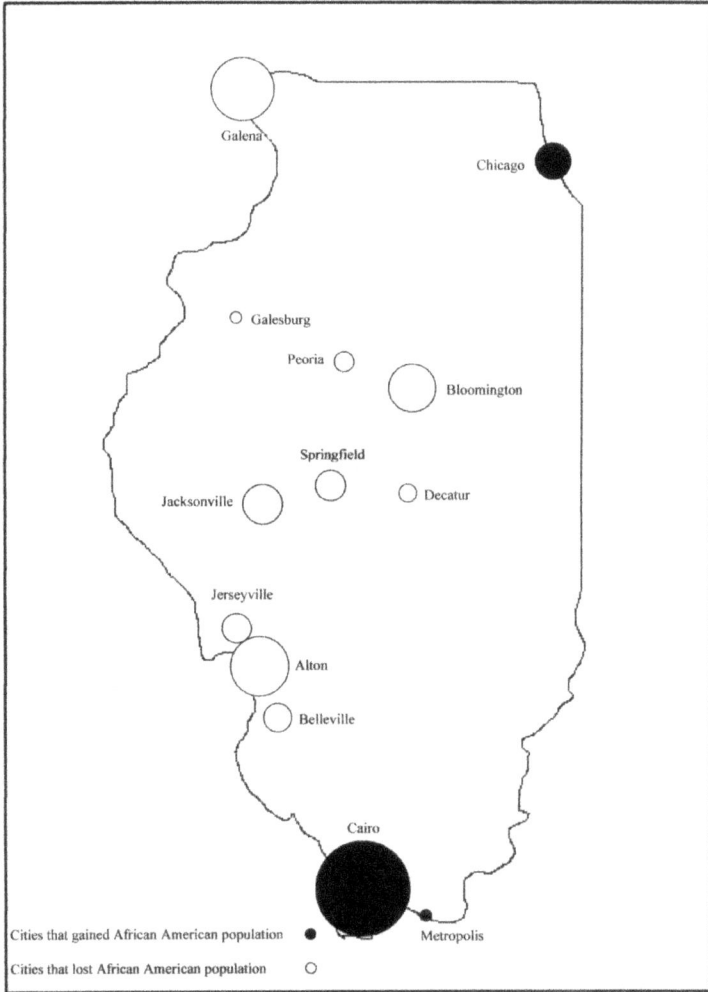

Figure 1.4 Gainers and Losers of African American Urban Population Share in Illinois, 1860–1890.

of state economies was shifting northward from the Ohio River valley. In Ohio, however, most of the significant gains and losses in African American population took place among towns and cities in the southwest quadrant of the state, where most African Americans lived (figure 1.2).[92]

Indiana's principal gainers and losers were more scattered, but the biggest gain appeared in Evansville on the Ohio River, and the losses were distributed across the entire state (figure 1.3).

In Illinois, too, the largest share gain took place in an Ohio River town, Cairo. The principal losers were dispersed across the central part of the state except for the biggest, Galena, which was located in the extreme northwest corner (figure 1.4).

Migrants made more precise choices than those dictated by large-scale economic shifts. In every state they chose rapidly growing villages, towns, and cities and rejected slowly growing ones. In other words, within Ohio, Indiana, and Illinois, African American migration streams flowed parallel to European American ones.[93] New Albany and Cincinnati were bypassed by many African American migrants at least partly because they were their respective states' biggest losers of total urban population share.[94] Chicago's gain in African American urban population share rested upon its huge jump in its proportion of Illinois's urban dwellers, from 46 to 65 percent. Whatever sources of information about the dynamics of midwestern economies migrants managed to unearth, the leads they obtained were usually accurate.

African American migrants to the Lower Midwest may well have been dislodged from their southern homes by Civil War fighting, by the wave of terrorism launched by white southerners to halt black progress after the war, or by the threat of such violence.[95] Their locational choices in the Lower Midwest, however, suggest that their primary concern in the North was jobs, not security in numbers. If so, they seem to have expected the North to be less threatening than the South. The migrants proceeded cautiously, to be sure, and chose the kinds of places and sought the type of work with which they were familiar. Favorite destinations Evansville and Cairo lay just across the Ohio River from families and friends in central and western Kentucky. Landscapes and climate north of the Ohio were similar to those to which they were accustomed. The small towns to which so many traveled, urban settings tightly enmeshed within an agricultural economy and culture, represented continuity with rural backgrounds.

The white worlds within those towns, however, were something new. In 1860, one out of five Kentuckians was African American, and the proportion was much higher in the parts of the state where African Americans were concentrated. In contrast, only 3 of the 236 urban places in the Lower Midwest held as large a proportion of African Americans in 1890 as the entire state of Kentucky thirty years before.[96] The old abolitionist strongholds, such as Oberlin in Ohio and Galesburg in Illinois, and the welcoming Quaker communities of the antebellum years, such as Richmond, Indiana, did not attract the new migrants.[97] Instead they pioneered settlements in places where African Americans before the war had been less welcome—but where expanding economies demanded workers. If the migrants manifested caution in remaining close to rural roots, they also showed daring in venturing into those hitherto white worlds.

PART TWO

Black Striving in White Worlds, 1860–1910

African American migrants from the South to the Lower Midwest immediately set to work to create institutions that would bind them together with other African Americans both within and beyond the places in which they settled. Through the private and semipublic instruments of family, church, and voluntary society they cultivated one side of their double identity. At the same time, they sought to realize another kind of hope in northern freedom by striving to become equal participants in a more public setting, the economy and politics of their adopted communities. Their goals, and the means they employed to pursue them, probably differed in no significant way from those of the majority of their European American fellow citizens. But their efforts to realize these aspirations in the context of the midwestern small town sometimes proved disruptive to precarious balances.

2

SMALL TOWN
Washington Court House, 1860–1900

[W]ith all the recognized ability of the race as artisans, laborers, and professional men and women, we find, with few exceptions, that on account of the most unreasonable and un-American race prejudice, the avenues of mercantile and industrial activities are closed against [Afro-Americans].
—Manifesto of the Afro-American League of Illinois, 1895[1]

I . . . know that it is in the heart of nearly every white, both North and South, to keep the Negro or colored man, woman or child down in a servant's place, and allow me to say they are in a fair way to do it.
—"Uncle Sam," Springfield, Illinois, 1894[2]

"Always have your own little patch of ground and your own house if it's nothing but a shack," I was taught.

It took Grandfather twenty years to achieve it. . . . He and Grandmother often went without food to pay for it and keep up the taxes. To his family it was more than a home; it was a monument to Grandfather's courage and tenacity.

There was something solid and indestructible about Grandfather's house. It wasn't very large—it had only six rooms—and it wasn't nearly so fine as his brother Richard's house, but it was free and clear of debt and Grandfather had supervised the laying of each board and brick and shingle although he could see the work only through his fingers. It was as if he had built himself into the structure, for it had his stubborn character.
—Pauli Murray, 1956[3]

I f we are to understand why African American migrants were first attracted to small towns and cities and later abandoned them, it is necessary to probe the place and progress of African Americans in such communities. State-level studies of Ohio and Indiana have demonstrated that African Americans generally were unable to gain entry to highly skilled or prestigious occupations or to accumulate significant wealth holdings.[4] But those studies were not designed to penetrate beneath aggregated statistics, and without such microanalysis African Americans cannot be located within the social structures of the communities in which they lived. This chapter and the one that follows attempt to accomplish that task.

One cannot spend long on a study of midwestern communities without realizing that finding a typical town is impossible. Each community represents a unique combination of traits that were generally shared. The best that can be done is to compare the situation of African American residents in communities of different sizes and varied economies, so as to distinguish those aspects of their situation that were common from those that were due to particular characteristics of the community. This chapter and the next examine three case study communities at the end of the nineteenth century, Ohio's Washington Court House and Springfield and Illinois's Springfield. These communities were selected for close analysis because they differed in size, economic base, and timing and volume of African American inmigration. Despite these differences, each town produced at least one violent attack upon African Americans individually or collectively, an attempted lynching in Washington Court House and major race riots in the Springfields. Those episodes will be discussed in chapter 5, for which these chapters serve as a prologue, in addition to their primary purpose.[5]

JOBS, WEALTH, AND HOMES

Washington Court House was a sleepy market town and county seat until the coming of a railroad connection to Cincinnati in the 1850s. This link to the Midwest's pork-packing center stimulated agriculture in Fayette County, oriented it to the market, and tilted it decisively toward production of corn and hogs. The town's population doubled in the 1850s and doubled again during the Civil War decade as its agricultural hinterland prospered. But the railroad carried more than hogs out of Washington Court House. What manufacturing had existed in the county seat mostly vanished as local residents found it cheaper to import processed goods from elsewhere than to produce them locally. Local editors began to chant the mantra of industrial development, but no one answered.[6] Washington Court House continued to prosper during the 1870s, but it was commerce, not industry, that provided its wealth. In 1900 Washington Court House ranked sixty-first in population among 101 Ohio towns and cities and eighty-first in value of manufactured products. After the 1860s, the county seat's growth came at the expense of its hinterland. Through the early twentieth century, Fayette County remained one of Ohio's top corn and hog producers. But when all the county's cultivable farmland was put into production, new opportunities on the farm dwindled. Population growth in Washington Court House continued robust during the 1880s. Outmigration no doubt exceeded inflow during the depressed decade of the 1890s, but after 1900 population growth resumed, although at a slower rate than during the post–Civil War years.[7]

Located in the Virginia Military District, where western land was granted to Virginia veterans of the Revolutionary War, Washington Court House initially attracted settlers from that state. Its railroad-induced prosperity during the 1850s brought German and Irish immigrants, and by 1870 they and their children made up about one-sixth of the town's population. African American migrants began to arrive in significant numbers during the Civil War, mainly from North Carolina and Virginia, and the inflow continued through the 1870s. At first, African Americans who arrived in Washington Court House tended to pass on through. During the 1860s only 15 percent remained across the decade, compared to 38 percent of whites.[8] After 1870, however, the African American population stabilized. Thirty-five percent remained from one census to another, a rate not far behind the European American persistence rate (41 percent). During the generally prosperous 1880s, the African American population continued to grow, although at a rate slightly slower than that of European Americans. In 1890 the 742 black Washingtonians made up 13 percent of the town's population, the eighth-largest African American proportion among Ohio towns.[9] Against the background of the overwhelmingly male migration stream to Ohio during the early postwar years, Washington Court House was unusual in its ability to attract a relatively symmetrical flow of African American females and males. In 1870 the sex ratio was almost perfectly even, 124 females and 126 males. The sexes remained fairly well balanced numerically over the next thirty years.

As the relatively even sex ratios suggest, Washington Court House was a town of families. In 1880, more than four-fifths of both males and females lived with other members of their nuclear or extended family, a proportion that fell only slightly behind the figure for European Americans.[10] These figures and this comparison are especially striking when one reflects that nearly all of the African Americans living in Washington Court House in 1880 were migrants to the community, and many no doubt were former slaves. An exact count of migrants is not possible, but a minimum figure can be established. Neither those born outside Ohio nor newcomers to the community since 1870 could have been native Washingtonians.[11] By this logic, no more than one out of fifteen adult African Americans resident in 1880 was a native Washingtonian, compared to one out of five adult European Americans.[12] Some of the families recorded in 1880 were formed after arrival in Washington Court House. But, taken together with the continuation of a robust inflow through the 1870s and the balanced sex ratio, the evidence of family coresidence strongly suggests a pattern of family migration. That suggestion is supported by coresidence patterns among those who

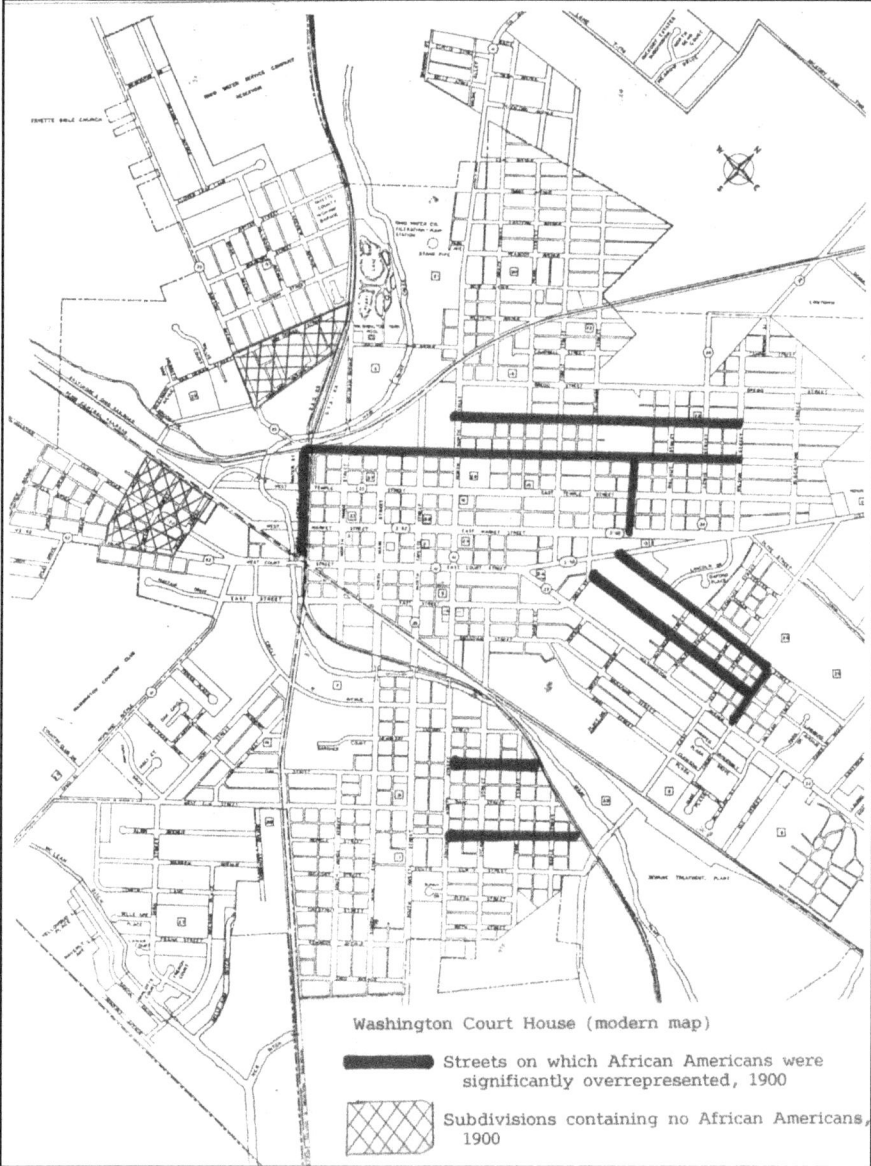

Washington Court House (modern map)

Streets on which African Americans were significantly overrepresented, 1900

Subdivisions containing no African Americans, 1900

Figure 2.1 Map of Washington Court House.

Table 2.1 Occupational Category of Workers, Washington Court House, Ohio, 1890 (in percentages)

| | *African Americans* | | *European Americans* | |
	Men	Women	Men	Women
High white collar	0.0	0.0	10.2	0.0
Low white collar	3.4	25.0	37.9	46.2
Blue collar skilled	22.5	50.0	31.1	35.9
Blue collar semiskilled & unskilled	74.2	25.0	20.8	17.9
Total	100.1*	100.0	100.0	100.0
N	89	4	586	39

* Does not equal 100 percent because of rounding

Sources: U.S. census manuscripts for Fayette County, OH, 1880, 1900; R. L. Polk's Directory for Washington C. H. 1889–90 (Washington Court House, OH: Sandy Fackler, 1995).

had arrived in Washington Court House since 1870. Although the family coresidence rate was somewhat lower among adult blacks than whites, the fact that about three-quarters of the adult newcomers lived with kin seems to confirm the family's importance in migration.[13]

By 1900, when the total population of Washington Court House approached 6,000, the town contained nothing resembling an urban ghetto. African Americans lived on thirty-three of the town's fifty-six streets. In the older, central part of town their homes were intermingled with those of European Americans. African Americans were overrepresented on streets ringing the downtown on the north, east, and west. None of these clusters, however, was entirely African American. On the west side, however, all-white suburbs had begun to appear, perhaps signaling a new configuration contrasting with the older pattern of integrated clustering (figure 2.1).

But if Washington Court House exhibited only a relatively small degree of residential segregation, the work world in 1890 told an entirely different story. Compared to large cities, Washington Court House did not possess an elaborate occupational structure. Nevertheless, more than a quarter of a century after they began to arrive in significant numbers, African American citizens had not scaled its low heights (table 2.1).[14]

Few African American women appeared to hold gainful occupations, but this is because the source used as a starting point to construct the town profile in 1890 was a city directory.[15] A crude labor force participation rate calculated using the last extant census before 1890 (1880) shows that African American women were almost twice as likely to hold gainful occupations as their European American counterparts.[16] The smaller proportion

Table 2.2 African American Wealth and Population Shares, Washington Court House, Ohio, 1860–1890 (in percentages)

	1860	1870	1880	1890
Census Wealth	0.04	2.0	N/A	N/A
Assessed Wealth	N/A	0.8	1.4	1.6
Population	6.2	11.8	13.5	12.9

Sources: U.S. census manuscripts for Fayette County, OH, 1860, 1870, 1880, 1900; *R. L. Polk's Directory for Washington C. H. 1889–90* (Washington Court House, OH: Sandy Fackler, 1995); Auditor's Tax Duplicate, Fayette County, OH, 1870, 1880, 1890.

of European American women who worked outside the home, however, monopolized the needle trades, teaching, sales, and nursing—all the non-domestic jobs available to women. African American women found work outside the home only in laundry and domestic service.[17]

In sharp contrast to European American men, African American men were concentrated in semiskilled and unskilled jobs. The job situation, however, was even worse than these broad categories suggest. A study of the occupational profiles of African Americans in North Carolina towns—probably the origin of some migrants to Washington Court House—identifies a set of occupations dominated by African American workers.[18] The occupations in this set that were found in Washington Court House in 1890 were barber, laborer, restaurant or saloonkeeper (or worker), servant, and brickmaker. Eighty-two percent of the African American men listed with occupations in Washington Court House held these positions. European American male workers also could be found in these occupations, but the categories of barber, laborer, waiter, servant, and brickmaker were numerically dominated by African Americans, even though together they made up only a little more than one-eighth of the male work force. "Negro jobs" in the South, it seems, were also "Negro jobs" in this part of the North.[19]

Occupational categories such as those used in table 2.1 are unavoidably prone to twentieth-century biases. Notions of "white collar" and "blue collar" work, as well as ideas of what constitutes skill, may reflect modern perceptions rather than nineteenth-century perspectives. For these reasons, wealth is a better gauge than occupation of an individual's or group's place and progress within a local economy.

Black Washingtonians expanded their wealth holdings between 1860 and 1890, both absolutely and relatively (table 2.2). Their share of local wealth reported by the federal census increased from virtually none in 1860 to two percent by 1870. Over the next twenty years, their share doubled. Their place in the local wealth structure was undoubtedly more favorable in

1880 and 1890 than table 2.2 indicates, since the figures for these years are derived from local tax assessment lists, which consistently underenumerated African American property holders and, when they were included, undervalued their holdings.[20] Nevertheless, progress was exceedingly slow. Even if underassessment reduced reported African American wealth share by as much as a factor of three in 1890, that share still falls far behind the African American proportion of population.

But were individual African Americans able to find and exploit economic opportunity in this small town during the late nineteenth century? Because it is static, the profile of the Washington Court House occupational structure in 1890 cannot answer this question. Nor can the charting of the African American wealth share over thirty years, because it reflects behavior in the aggregate. Individuals who remained in Washington Court House could have prospered while growth in aggregate holdings was retarded by destitute inmigrants. Alternatively, growth in African American property could have resulted from a prosperous inmigration rather than from local success stories. If a structure of opportunity existed, then it should be reflected in higher rates of accumulation among those who had the longest exposure to the community.[21] In his study of the African American community in Monroe, Michigan, James DeVries found that stability in Monroe did make a difference.

> In Monroe, black individuals belonging to lineages enjoyed an existence with a modicum of rewards; those who were not members of these kinship groups did not. The key ingredients in the creation of these groupings were the timing of arrival and duration of their stay. The Duncansons and Smiths came when the city was first emerging, and the Wickliffes, Bromleys, Millers, and Fosters planted roots in Monroe in the Civil War era, when communities throughout the nation were undergoing vast and rapid transitions. Furthermore, each of these families persisted for several decades in the area. They were well known within the community and occupied the special status of "town folk."[22]

DeVries, however, did not compare the persistence, status, and wealth of Monroe's African Americans and European Americans. As we have seen, African Americans during the 1860s and 1870s were more likely than European Americans to move on from Washington Court House, so the lower African American wealth share could have been a result of their higher turnover. To be useful, an analysis must distinguish between newcomers to the community and persisters. Age should also be taken into account, since differences between black and white wealth could have resulted from

45

Table 2.3 Possible Determinants of Wealth-Holding, Adult Males, Washington Court House, Ohio, 1890

A. Mean Assessed Wealth Holdings by Characteristic

| | *African Americans* | | *European Americans* | |
	Group Size	Mean Wealth	Group Size	Mean Wealth
Persistence				
Newcomer since 1880	44	$76	265	$773
Present in 1880	57	87	401	1,282
Age				
Age 21–39 years	44	45	295	602
40 years and over	59	114	376	1,454
Origin				
Southern-born	71	111	69	763
Northern-born	32	27	547	1,118
Foreign-born	0	—	54	1,110
All	103	85	671	1,079

B. Correlation Matrices

| | | *African Americans* | |
	Persistence	Age	Origin**
Assessed wealth	+.03	+.19*	−.21*
Persistence		+.15	+.00
Age			−.41*

| | | *European Americans* | |
	Persistence	Age	Origin**
Assessed wealth	+.08*	+.02	+.03
Persistence		+.07*	−.16*
Age			−.02

* Significant at the .05 level

** Excluding foreign-born

Source: U.S. census manuscripts for Fayette County, OH, 1880, 1900; *R. L. Polk's Directory for Washington C.H. 1889–90* (Washington Court House, OH: Sandy Fackler, 1995); Auditor's Tax Duplicate, Fayette County, OH, 1890.

Table 2.4 Possible Determinants of Wealth-Holding, Adult Females, Washington Court House, Ohio, 1890

A. Mean Assessed Wealth Holdings by Characteristic

| | *African Americans* | | *European Americans* | |
	Group Size	Mean Wealth	Group Size	Mean Wealth
Persistence				
Newcomer since 1880	12	$139	124	$747
Present in 1880	25	233	253	693
Age				
Age 21–39 years	16	151	156	320
40 years and over	21	242	223	978
Origin				
Southern-born	24	268	25	909
Northern-born	13	81	339	681
Foreign-born	0	—	15	972
All	37	203	379	707

B. Correlation Matrices

| | *African Americans* | | |
	Persistence	Age	Origin**
Assessed wealth	+.17	+.35*	−.35*
Persistence		+.05	−.09
Age			−.53*

| | *European Americans* | | |
	Persistence	Age	Origin**
Assessed wealth	−.02	+.00	−.04
Persistence		+.06	−.11*
Age			−.15*

* Significant at the .05 level

** Excluding foreign-born

Source: U.S. census manuscripts for Fayette County, OH, 1880, 1900; *R. L. Polk's Directory for Washington C.H. 1889–90* (Washington Court House, OH: Sandy Fackler, 1995); Auditor's Tax Duplicate, Fayette County, OH, 1890.

differing age structures in the two populations. So should regional origins, because migrants from the underdeveloped South could have been disadvantaged by their origins compared to Northerners.[23]

White men owned the bulk of assessed wealth in Washington Court House in 1890, and for them, whether immigrant or native-born, the town furnished lucrative opportunities (tables 2.3 and 2.4).

Town residence for at least ten years boosted wealth by 66 percent compared to newcomers. Furthermore, no other variable was associated with wealth at a statistically significant level. In contrast, no variable was correlated with wealth for white women, whose restricted wage-earning opportunities meant that gifts or inheritance most likely represented the principal means of property acquisition.

While time in the community paid off for European American men and male European immigrants, it did not for either African American men or women. Interestingly, African American women had higher average property holdings than men, and the women's proportion of African American property holdings was significantly larger (46 percent) than women's proportion of European American wealth (27 percent). Some of these women were widowed or separated, but others were married women living with their husbands. For both men and women, age and southern origin paid off in increased wealth. The two variables were intercorrelated, however, since the southern-born tended to be older than the northern-born. When the variables competed freely with each other in a stepwise multiple regression procedure, origin proved the stronger for men, and age for women.

In these facts lies an ominous message for men's aspirations in this small midwestern town. The downward pull of northern birth suggests poor conditions before 1890 for advancement in the region in which migrants had invested their hopes. And the insignificant effect of persistence in Washington Court House implies the same for this local setting. Assets won in the town boosted the African American community's aggregate holdings slightly, but it appears that the arrival of propertied older, southern-born migrants helped even more. If one's skin was "white," the more time spent in the North, the better were the chances of wealth accumulation. The important point is that for African Americans, factors independent of the local setting (southern origin and age) influenced wealth holding, while for immigrant and native-born white men, persistence in Washington Court House paid off in accumulated wealth. These extralocal factors that influenced African American wealth holding, however, were not powerful enough to offset the advantage of "white" skin. Whites usually came to Washington Court House with far more property than blacks, and whites, especially the men, then gained more from their residence in the community than blacks. In summary, this analysis allows a precise quantitative answer to the question, what were the "wages of whiteness" in Washington Court House?[24] About $500 for women and $1,000 for men.[25]

Washington Court House did reward its African American residents in one possibly significant way. They were able to gain ownership of the homes in which they lived at a rate that nearly equaled that of European Americans, and one that was almost certainly higher than what was possible in most other settings. In 1900, the first year for which such information is available, 48 percent of the blacks designated by the census as household heads lived in family-owned homes, compared to 49 percent of white "heads," virtually a dead heat. More of the African American families' homes were mortgaged (51 percent to 36 percent), but at least African Americans were able to obtain home mortgages. Across the state of Ohio, only 27 percent of African American nonfarm homes were owned by the family occupying them.[26] Perhaps the homes of black Washington Court House families were more humble than those of their European American counterparts, but at least they were theirs. Some of them may have been self-built, but ownership of homes built with "sweat equity" did not necessarily distinguish African American workers from European American ones.[27]

The advantages obtained from home ownership should not be underestimated. As other historians point out, "In the early twentieth century the purchase of a home was the most common form of wealth accumulation achieved by persisting unskilled workers and newcomers to the city." This was because

> homeowning had several distinct advantages over renting. In addition to providing a sense of status, it gave the owners greater control over their environment, provided a form of enforced savings with a resultant equity, and had the potential of providing a source of income.[28]

"Workers," adds a historical geographer, "viewed their homes as a source of security in times of unemployment, sickness, and old age. Among a group of people who had little say in how their work was done, the home could be a place of real, if limited autonomy."[29]

The home-owning record of African American families in Washington Court House suggests that some small towns, where good jobs for African Americans were few and wealth acquisition difficult, yet offered one tangible form of reward in improved chances to own one's home.[30] Possibly this was because of lower prices for land or housing. Or small-town lenders may have shown greater willingness than in larger centers to offer mortgages to known residents. In Washington Court House, land speculation was one of

the principal routes to wealth, and some of the town's most active specula-
tors also controlled local sources of credit.[31] In this limited yet significant
way, decisions to remain in Washington Court House paid off for African
Americans. Whether these or some other factors were at work, the result
meant that this small town could offer African Americans one meaningful
incentive to come and to remain.

MIGRANT FAMILIES

Historians agree on the importance of the African American family both
during slavery and after emancipation. In Monroe, Michigan, after the Civil
War, the family acted as a buffer between its members and the white world.
As James DeVries explains:

> Without question, the Afro-American family was the most important
> ameliorative agency in Monroe. The black kinship networks that evolved
> in the nineteenth century functioned as mediating structures between their
> members and the larger community. These support structures cushioned
> the blows of prejudice and discrimination and devised strategies for success
> and survival in a difficult milieu.[32]

Precisely because of its importance, the family carried a heavy burden. To
migrants who left behind some family members, friends, and community,
those kin who traveled alongside became the primary or only source of
economic and emotional support. On arrival, the male breadwinner role
that was central to nineteenth-century separate-spheres ideology created
expectations that were extremely difficult to meet within the discriminatory
employment structures of midwestern towns. Sometimes the burden became
too great to bear, and families broke under the strain. The collective and
individual lives of family groups in Washington Court House illustrate both
the rewards and the burdens of family ties.

The Andersons

The Andersons were a large clan, many light skinned, who came to Fayette
County during the 1860s and 1870s from Granville County, North
Carolina.[33] Indeed, use of the word "clan" to describe the Andersons may
exaggerate the extent of the blood ties among them, which are not discern-
able in census or most other records among those living in separate house-

holds. Nevertheless, there is evidence of both common experience and cooperation among the Anderson households, and their journeys to Washington Court House demonstrate the strength of a migration chain that operated across more than a decade, pulling Andersons from a rural neighborhood in North Carolina to a small town in southwestern Ohio.

On the eve of the Civil War, five Anderson couples who were later to travel to Fayette County lived in close rural proximity among other Anderson families in a free black settlement in Granville County, located in the Piedmont region of North Carolina. They were farmers and artisans, but the "thin, sandy soil" of Granville County provided a poor medium for any crop but tobacco.[34] All five couples had acquired modest holdings in both real and personal property, the realty ranging from $75 to $250 and the personalty from $50 to $300.[35] The families of two artisans were the first to appear in Fayette County, found there sometime during 1862 or 1863 by a special census commissioned by the Ohio state government in response to Democratic-inspired fears of an African American inundation.[36] "The Anderson family," the local auditor noted on the census report, evidently referring to the nineteen persons he listed with that name, "contemplate returning to their native home as soon as the war closes."[37] At least one artisan and his wife and two children remained long after Appomattox, as we shall see. Two farm families of Andersons arrived between 1863 and 1870, along with another Granville County family of Weavers, who were also free before the war. Another Anderson farm couple came to Washington Court House during the 1870s, bringing two of their six children (the rest were probably grown). The initial Anderson migrants' reasons for choosing Washington Court House are unknown. Tobacco culture could not have been the magnet that drew them, since Fayette County's soil was much richer than Granville's, and therefore suitable for growing far more lucrative crops than tobacco. But once some of them settled, the reports sent back to Granville County by what was now a reconnaissance party convinced others to follow over the next decade or more.

In 1870, Andersons were living in five main households in Washington Court House, three of which stood side by side. The oldest couple, possibly the patriarch and matriarch of the clan, were Peter Anderson, sixty-seven years old, an illiterate well digger, and his wife, Elizabeth, sixty-five. Also living in their household were a nineteen-year-old boy and eleven-year-old girl. Peter did not appear in the special census, so he, and probably Elizabeth as well, must have come since 1863. Despite their illiteracy and Peter's menial occupation, they reported real estate worth $1,500 and personal property valued at $2,000. These holdings represented a considerable improvement over the $100 in real estate and $50 in personal property recorded in Granville County ten years before. In 1880, however, the assessment list reported Peter holding only a single one-third acre parcel in town, valued at $170; Elizabeth held no listed property. Possibly the local assessor, normally neglectful of African American and female property holdings, missed property they had maintained since 1870. Alternatively, they could have lost most of their small wealth or passed it on to other family members. The two youths of 1870 disappeared from town records. Peter, and perhaps Elizabeth as well, died during the 1880s. The 1890 tax list reported his estate as an undeveloped land parcel about half the size of the plot he owned in 1870, valued at $130, less than the value of their North Carolina holdings. The economic story of their migration and life in Washington Court House was diminution of their property.

The next most senior couple among the Andersons were Bolding (sometimes "Bolen" or "Boldens") and Eliza Anderson. Bolding Anderson was in his fifties in 1870, and Eliza was about ten years younger. Like Peter and Elizabeth Anderson, they had arrived in Washington Court House after 1863. Bolding was a laborer, and was reported as being unable to write, which indicates that he could read. Eliza evidently was literate. They appear to have been renting, as no property was assessed. Ten years earlier in Granville County, the census had reported Bolding with $200 in real and $150 in personal property, which might have been sold to finance their move to Ohio. Bolding joined the Second Baptist Church, which had been founded before the Civil War by the handful of African Americans then living in Washington Court House. Sharing their household in 1870 were their daughters Maggie, twenty-one, her occupation listed as "house servant," but who also attended school, and Eliza, fourteen, also in school. A darker-skinned five-year-old boy, Whiteman Anderson, also lived with Bolding and Eliza.[38] In addition, James Anderson, a thirty-one-year-old farm laborer, lived in the household. James Anderson had served in the Civil War with several other Fayette Countians, including another Anderson.

Unlike Peter and Elizabeth Anderson, Bolding and Eliza acquired increasing property between 1870 and their deaths during the 1890s, although Bolding always worked as a laborer. By 1880 Bolding was assessed for two small undeveloped plots in Washington Court House worth $20 each, as well as $70 in chattel property. In 1890 Bolding owned a town lot of thirty-four-foot frontage valued at $600, which was probably their house lot on East Paint Street. In addition, Bolding and Eliza each held a small undeveloped lot valued at $150 and $160, respectively. Despite being consistently employed as an unskilled worker, Bolding and his wife had managed to make small gains, whether the benchmark is their premigration holdings or their property shortly after arrival in Washington Court House. They had acquired not only a home, but also additional land for their children or for speculative purposes. James Anderson, however, vanished from local records after 1870. So did Bolding and Eliza's daughter Eliza, although this could have been through marriage as well as death or departure from the community. Maggie in 1880 was single and living with her parents, as was their three-year-old granddaughter Ada, probably the child of either Maggie or her sister. Against the background of support for at least one of their daughters and a grandchild, Bolding and Eliza's economic progress appears even more hard-won. The expansion of the household of Bolding and Eliza Anderson—and of the household of Peter and Elizabeth—to take in grandchildren and other Anderson children exemplifies the importance of the extended family in African American life, a significance that could only have been magnified by migration.[39]

The other three principal Anderson households in 1870 were headed by members of a younger generation, possibly the children of Peter and Elizabeth. Betsey Anderson, thirty-five years old and illiterate, was the wife of William N. Anderson. William was almost certainly another Civil War veteran, as the African American Grand Army of the Republic (GAR) post in Washington Court House was later named in his honor. William and Betsey had arrived in Washington Court House from North Carolina early in the war years. William was not in Washington Court House at the time of the census, and he apparently died a few years later. Living with Betsey in 1870 were her four children: Alphina, twelve; William N., ten; Alonzo, seven; and Emma, three. She bore another daughter, Lula, in 1872. Betsey reported no occupation other than "keeping house," but she owned $800 worth of real estate and personal property valued at $100.

Betsey Anderson remained in Washington Court House until her death in 1913 at nearly eighty years of age, when she would have been one of the oldest living Washingtonians. A member of the community for more than fifty years, she was almost certainly one of its longest residents. By 1900 she had learned to read, and she retained her modest property holdings. Tragedy marked her family life, however. After her father's death in the 1870s, Alphina married Thomas Thornton, a barber and native Ohioan, and the young couple moved in next door to Betsey. They had at least three children, but by 1900 Alphina had died, Thomas had died or left Washington Court House, and one of their children, Irene, fifteen, was living with Betsey. Emma, too, had died, as had William, after working as a barber in partnership with his brother, Alonzo.

Betsey Anderson would have been able to take comfort, however, in Alonzo, who had made a life for himself in Fayette County. He continued to work as a barber, sometimes on his own and at other times with a partner, and by 1900 he had acquired a small plot of undeveloped land. In 1891 he married Hattie Stewart, the daughter of Hezekiah and Maggie Stewart, and they had two children. The older child was named William after Alonzo's father and brother, and the younger after Hattie's mother. Alonzo and Hattie were living in 1900 just outside Washington Court House in the home of Hezekiah, a Civil War veteran and laborer, who was paying off a mortgage on the property. Hattie Stewart Anderson and her mother were members of the African Methodist Episcopal (AME) Church in Washington Court House. By the time of Betsey's death in 1913, Alonzo and Hattie had moved back into town, into a house on Fourth Street, a predominantly black street. Betsey Anderson lived closer to downtown, on East Temple, a predominantly white street. Betsey had lived on East Temple, though not in the same house, since at least 1880. She is buried in the town cemetery. Alonzo joined her there in 1929.

Another Anderson who came to Washington Court House to stay was Alexander, who probably arrived after 1863. Alexander served with James Anderson in Company D, 45th Regiment, U.S. Colored Infantry Volunteers. In 1870 Alexander was in his early thirties, reported his occupation as "brick manufacturer," and listed $1,500 in real estate as well as $2,000 in personal property. He lived with his wife, Sarah, twenty-five, and their four daughters, ranging in age from six-year-old Melissa down to newborn Sarah Adeline. One daughter evidently died during the 1870s, but two more were born, and Sarah's childbearing stopped after the birth in 1879 of their first son, whom they named Bolding. Alexander Anderson did not remain a brick manufacturer for long. Unfortunately, he had arrived in the North at just the time when machines were rendering hand brickmakers obsolete.[40] Instead, he became a teamster, driving a one-horse express wagon through the town and countryside. Like Peter Anderson, his property holdings never again equaled the size reported in 1870, but in 1900 he owned outright the home he occupied with four of his daughters and his son. Their house stood on a majority-black street on the east side of town. By 1900 Sarah and Melissa had vanished from town records, and young Bolding, too, disappeared before 1906. None of the daughters is known to have worked in domestic service. During the early years of the twentieth century, Sarah Adeline and Faith gave their occupations as "book agent." Bolding's only listed occupation, when he was twenty, in 1900, was "farm day laborer."

Alexander Anderson played his principal community roles in the church and lodge hall. An early member of the Second Baptist Church, he soon became as well a mainstay of St. Luke's Lodge of the Prince Hall Masons. Alexander served as Worshipful Master of the lodge throughout much of the 1870s and 1880s and sporadically during the 1890s and the early years of

Photo credit: Jack Blocker

Figure 2.2 The headstone of Alexander Anderson, Civil War veteran and leading spirit in church and lodge.

the twentieth century. When he was not leading the lodge, he was ordering its affairs as senior warden or treasurer. He played a far larger part in community life than is indicated by his humble occupation or his simple headstone in the town cemetery, distinguished only by the five-pointed metal star of the GAR. Through his associational activity Alexander Anderson helped to knit together the sinews of the African American community within the white world of Washington Court House, a common and vital task in the small towns and cities across the Midwest where Civil War and postbellum migrants settled.[41] His headstone, however, memorializes only his contribution to making their migration possible: "A. Anderson Co. D. 45 U.S.C.Inf" (figure 2.2).

The male head of the fifth Anderson household in 1870 played an equally large though somewhat different role in the Washington Court House community. King David Anderson was as splendid as his name, and as flamboyant as Alexander was respectable. A man of many talents, he was variously identified as a butcher, a carpenter, and a saloonkeeper during the more than forty years he lived in Washington Court House between his arrival early in the Civil War and his death in 1904. A true jack-of-all-trades, in Granville County he had been a mat maker. In his late twenties King was one of the pioneering Andersons from Granville County, when he came to Washington Court House with his wife, Emily, a few years younger, and their two young daughters, Dora and Nancy. In September 1864, King enlisted in the 42nd Regiment, U.S. Colored Troops, and served until after the war's end. Army records describe him as five feet, seven inches tall, of light complexion, with blue eyes and dark hair.

The census enumerator in 1870 found King working as a butcher, and reported $2,300 in real estate and $1,200 in personal property. In the household, along with Emily, Dora, and Nancy, were Nelson Anderson, a forty-year-old journeyman carpenter (possibly King's brother), and seventeen-year-old Ellen Anderson, possibly Nelson's daughter. King was a member of the Second Baptist Church and a leading black Republican. By 1873 King had gone into business with a baker, John Keller, a German immigrant, thereby creating a rare biracial partnership. Along with bread and meat, the partners stocked something to wash down a meal, and this part of their business drew the attention of the town's women temperance crusaders when they began to march on liquor dealers in December 1873. After three days under siege by prayers and hymns, Anderson and Keller set a good example for the town's other dealers by surrendering and turning their stock over to the crusaders. Axes were given to the female relatives of some of the town's worst drinkers, and soon "Holland gin and old Bourbon" were flowing down the street and into Paint Creek. King Anderson and John Keller each made a "rousing speech" and were given three cheers by the crusaders, mostly women of the town's wealthiest families, and their male supporters, the men of those families. The partners spoke again at the movement's public meeting that evening, with "earnestness and the best of feeling." Their example was soon followed by the thirteen other liquor dealers of Washington Court House, which thereby became the first town in which the marching women won a complete victory.[42]

By 1880 King David Anderson was running a saloon again. In fact, his saloon, located in a small white-frame cottage at the corner of East Paint and Bereman streets, had a reputation as one of the town's "hot spots." Adjacent to King's place was a rare phenomenon in a midwestern small town: a saloon run by a woman.[43] Even more exotic, the saloonkeeper was an African American woman. Virginia-born Martha Lawson came to Washington Court House during the 1870s with her younger brother, ex-slave Henry Phillips. The neighborhood where King Anderson and Martha Lawson entertained was known as "Andersonville," certainly because of King's presence, probably because of the proximity of other Andersons, and possibly as a sarcastic analogy between the effects of the liquor sold there and the deadly fate of captured Union soldiers in a notorious Confederate prison. If it is possible to conceive of slumming in a small hog-trading town squatting on the flat landscape of southwestern Ohio—where the greatest excitement was normally generated by the monthly livestock sale—then that may be the best term to describe what drew thirsty Fayette Countians to Andersonville: Harlem on Paint Creek.

To understand King David Anderson's biography, however, a different question must be posed. What drew him back to saloonkeeping after his abrupt, impassioned, and evidently sincere exit from the liquor trade? Although, as we shall see, other African American men in Washington Court House gained reputations as hard drinkers, no such label is known to have attached itself to King. According to one account, he rarely even served drinks by his own hand to the patrons of his saloon, leaving that chore to a bartender. Although local law enforcement officials were not loath to lock up public drunks, neither King nor any other member of the numerous Anderson clan is known to have been jailed for this—or any other—reason.[44] The best answer is that he probably had little choice. Various avenues led into the retail liquor business during the late nineteenth century, and one well-traveled one carried artisans whose trades were threatened by the advance of mass production.[45] Local butchers across the North were being undercut by the competition of processed meats shipped from packinghouses in Chicago across the railway network in the new refrigerated boxcars.[46] The technique of balloon-frame construction using standardized wood sizes reduced the skills needed to build houses.[47] In the face of shrinking opportunities, European American craftsmen banded together to restrict competition, and their most vulnerable rivals were African American artisans. Saloonkeeping required little capital and less skill and offered a route to self-employment.[48] The only prerequisites were ease in human relations and a reputation for honesty, and King David Anderson seems to have possessed both.[49]

The man who was known to local topers as "the King of Andersonville" was experiencing difficulty, however, in his personal life. By the time he returned to the saloon trade in 1880, daughter Nancy had disappeared from local records, and he and Emily had just had another daughter, who was named after her mother. But the new baby was not enough to save King and Emily's marriage, which broke up during the ensuing decade. In 1890 they were living apart. Emily Anderson occupied a house on East Temple

Figure 2.3 The magnificent monument to the King of Andersonville.

Street near Betsey Anderson and was listed in the city directory as a widow, even though King was living around the corner. The family real estate, three undeveloped parcels and two town lots, was divided between Emily and Dora, while King occupied rented accommodations. King had returned to carpentry, which he pursued until his death. Emily died in 1899. Dora lived in Washington Court House for the rest of her long life, and never married. Before she died in 1927, she paid for a handsome monument for King's grave, carved of red granite, which overshadows the adjacent grave markers, Emily's headstone elsewhere in the town cemetery, and Dora's simple stone next to it (figure 2.3).[50]

Whether it was King David Anderson mobilizing black Republicans and enlivening the town's night life; or Alexander Anderson leading Masonic ritual; or Bolding, Alexander, and King bolstering the Second

Baptist Church through its early days; or Maggie and Hattie supporting the AME church, the Andersons made their presence felt in both the black and white worlds of Washington Court House. Some of these North Carolina migrants put down deep roots in the town and spent the remainder of their lives there. Their lives became intertwined with those of other residents, and they became an integral part of local memory. "Remember?" a white amateur local historian would later write: "When King Anderson run [*sic*] a saloon and was known as the King of Andersonville? There was a character for you, and one that knew all the insides of his business." "Alex Anderson, a well known colored citizen? He was a veteran of the Civil War, and drove a one horse express wagon for years."[51] Local memories of others, however, broke off when an Anderson left the town, as more and more of the younger ones tended to do. Young whites left, too, especially during the hard years of the 1890s. But after prosperity returned, the European American community in Washington Court House resumed its growth. The African American community did not.

The Chesters

When the Andersons began to arrive in Washington Court House, the Chesters were already there. Lewis Chester and Mary Good Chester arrived during the 1850s. Lewis was born in North Carolina in 1832, and Mary in South Carolina six years later.[52] Both were literate. In 1859, soon after their arrival in Washington Court House, their first child, Eugene, was born. A daughter, Madora, followed two years later, and a second daughter, Frances, two years after that. In 1860 Lewis reported his occupation as a plasterer and listed $300 in real estate and personal property valued at $55. Ten years later his real wealth had grown to $500 and his personal wealth to $350, and he now called himself a journeyman brickmason. All three children attended the "colored" school.

Lewis Chester became active in Republican politics as soon as the Fifteenth Amendment allowed African American men to vote in Ohio. Three years before, he and Mary had helped to organize an AME church in Washington Court House with the help of sympathetic whites. Mills Gardner, an attorney, former state senator and Lincoln presidential elector, and currently a representative in the lower house of the Ohio state legislature, became a charter member and one of three trustees, along with Lewis Chester. Another wealthy European American, David Rodgers, gave the fledging church a gift of $1,000 and a loan in the same amount to purchase the seven-year-old former Catholic church building, and the grateful members named their new church Rodgers Chapel. Lewis was also a leading figure in St. Luke's Lodge, holding several offices during the 1870s.

In May 1868, Lewis began to show the first public signs of an excessive fondness for the bottle, as he was arrested and briefly jailed for drunkenness, an episode that was repeated in June 1873, only three months after he oversaw the purchase of the new AME church building. Six months later, Mary Chester joined the temperance crusaders marching on the town's retail liquor dealers, the only African American woman to do so. She may have been one of the women given the honor of smashing the barrels and cask surrendered by Anderson and Keller. By 1880 Mary had taken the precaution of placing title to their house and lot in her name. She must have been concerned about Eugene, who in 1877 was working as a waiter; three years later, he left restaurant work to become a laundryman.

By 1890 Lewis and Mary separated. The city directory of 1889–90 listed Mary as a widow, but Lewis was still alive, although temporarily absent from Washington Court House. Mary now owned a second house and lot in addition to her home on East Temple Street, where she lived with Eugene. Eugene had returned to the food-and-drink business as a bartender, aided no doubt by what one memoirist referred to as his "famous smile." Madora had married, bore at least one child, and left Washington Court House. Frances, too, was married briefly, but in 1890 she lived with her six-year-old daughter in a rented house on Rawlings Street, two blocks north of Temple, and supported herself as a dressmaker.

Lewis Chester returned to Washington Court House politics in 1891 as the organizer of a flourishing black Republican club. His conduct as the decade wore on, however, brought no credit to his party. In 1896 he was jailed on a charge of drunk and disorderly conduct, and he was arrested twice more in 1899 for using obscene language. In 1900 he was boarding with another African American man. Fannie had disappeared from local records. Mary had lost her house and lived in rented quarters on Market Street with her granddaughter and her widowed mother. Nevertheless, she continued to make small donations to the AME church as long as she lived in Washington Court House. Eugene, still a bartender, had married Addie Anderson, the daughter of an Anderson couple who had arrived during the 1870s. Eugene and Addie were married in 1897, but their only child died. Living with them in their rented accommodations were Addie's mother and Madora's fifteen-year-old son.

Lewis Chester died on the first day of 1903. Eugene memorialized him with the word "Father" on a simple headstone. Sometime between 1906 and 1913, Eugene took his famous smile to Columbus. By 1913, for the first time in more than half a century, there were no Chesters in Washington

Figure 2.4 The obelisk of the Scott/Weaver family.

Court House, only memories. "Remember? When the Chester family of colored people were so well known?"[53]

Washington Court House had not been kind to the Chesters. Lewis and Mary began their lives in the town as a young couple active in both black and white worlds, in lodge, church, and political affairs. Lewis's inability to control his drinking contributed to the family's decline, but their slide could have been arrested or even reversed if Eugene had been able to find an occupation sufficiently remunerative to allow him to support his family, or if the husbands of Madora and Frances had been able to find jobs that would keep them in town. Eugene must have developed self-discipline, for despite the exposure to liquor entailed by his work as a waiter and his ultimate career as a bartender, he never followed his father into local jail cells. What he and other young African American men lacked was opportunity—that, and examples of older black men who were able to accumulate more than a modest competence. Eugene Chester was not driven from Washington

Figure 2.5 Headstones of the Scott/Weaver family.

Court House by the white mob that tried to lynch another young black man in 1894. Instead, he stayed, married, and tried to start a family. But in his late forties or early fifties, he gave up on the town where he had been born and lived his entire life, and moved to the nearest big city. His decision was typical of many others.

The Weavers

As one enters the Washington Court House cemetery, the first section ahead contains the graves and monuments of some of the town's most prominent European American families from the late nineteenth and early twentieth centuries. In the midst of this section stands a six-foot red granite obelisk. The obelisk marks no grave; the resting places of those it memorializes are arranged behind and beside the monument. Instead, the obelisk commemorates the Scott/Weaver family, and its siting announces the place they perceived themselves to occupy in the community (figures 2.4 and 2.5).[54]

The leading spirit of the family appears to have been Susan Scott, whose name is carved alone on the front of the obelisk: "Born in Granville Co. North Carolina in 1808 Moved to Fayette Co., O. in 1860, Died July 8, 1884, Aged 76 Y's. Blessed are the dead who die in the Lord."

In 1870 Susan Scott was living in Washington Court House with her thirty-three-year-old daughter, Emily, and an unrelated male boarder. She was listed as owning $700 in real estate and $200 in personal property. None of the house's three occupants were said to be able to read. Ten years later, Susan and Emily were still living together, but much else had changed. Susan's property holdings had diminished. Emily had been married to a man named Evans and widowed, but there were no surviving children living with her. Emily did, however, hold an undeveloped town lot. After Susan Scott's death, Emily Evans seems to have remained in Washington Court House until at least 1890, but whether she died or left town after that is unknown.

The other family household in Washington Court House in 1870 was that of Lytle (sometimes "Little") Weaver, a thirty-five-year-old laborer; his wife, Emily, a little younger; and their daughter, Ella, six. Lytle and Emily emigrated from Granville County in their native North Carolina during the Civil War, and Ella was born shortly after their arrival in Ohio. Neither Lytle nor Emily was described as illiterate in 1870 or 1880, but in 1900 Lytle was. Lytle was listed as propertyless in Granville County in 1860, but in Washington Court House ten years later he reported real estate worth $700 and personal property of $200.

Silas Weaver, a few years older than Lytle and probably his brother, was almost certainly in Fayette County in 1870, although he was not listed in the 1870 census, for his wife, Agnes, led in launching the AME church in 1867. Agnes and Silas never had children, or at least any who survived infancy. Sharing their house in Washington Court House in 1880 was their nephew, James F. Weaver, twenty, born in North Carolina; and their domestic servant, a young African American woman. It was unusual for an African American family in Washington Court House to hire a servant, and Silas and Agnes's ability to do so testifies to their solid material standing. Silas was a barber, and in 1880 he was assessed for a total of three town lots, valued in total at $1,360, as well as two plots of undeveloped land, valued at $440 and $130, respectively. James, who may have been the son of Lytle and Emily, was probably apprenticing with Silas. In 1890 Silas Weaver's assessed property value totaled about one-half its 1880 size, but he was still the wealthiest African American in Washington Court House. He was also a political activist, designated to serve as a marshal for the local Republican Party's torchlight parade and rally during the 1888 presidential campaign.

Silas Weaver's wealth in 1890, however, ranked him only 209th in the community, and he never managed to find a comfortable occupational niche. By 1890 he ran a saloon on the courthouse square, and Lytle was a bartender,

probably working for Silas. Such work must have created constant temptation for Lytle, who was known as "having a great fondness . . . for a drink."[55]
Agnes died, and in 1885 Silas married again. In 1900 Silas and his second
wife, Emma, were living on a farm that he owned outright. Six years later,
Silas had moved back into town but still listed himself as a farmer. He died
in 1907. Emma died in 1910, having invited her cousin Dora Anderson to
live with her during her last years after Silas's death.

Apart from his spell as a bartender, Lytle worked as a laborer or driver,
and never again reported as much property as he held in 1870. Widowed, he
was living in 1900 with his daughter, Ella, and her husband, Eddie Edwards,
also a teamster and laborer. Lytle died in 1912, almost certainly poorer than
during his first years in Washington Court House. Ella and Eddie had
married in 1888, and Ella gave birth to three children during the following
twelve years. They were renting in 1900. In 1913 Eddie was working in a
livery stable, and Ella and Eddie's oldest son was married, operated in partnership a barber shop near the courthouse square where Silas had once had
a saloon, and lived on Bereman Street, one block from the cottage where
King Anderson used to entertain.

James F. Weaver created an occupationally more stable, but not necessarily more remunerative, life in Washington Court House than Silas. He
always worked as a barber until his death just short of his fiftieth birthday.
He married in 1886, but neither of the two children born to him and his
wife, Anna, survived childhood. In 1900 they carried a mortgage on their
home. James followed Silas into Republican Party activism, helping King
Anderson to organize the large "colored" Republican club in 1891. Anna
survived him by fifteen years.

The Scott/Weavers appear to have been every bit the tightly knit family
their obelisk and the close grouping of their graves proclaim them to be.
Silas had probably assisted James into the barber trade and employed Lytle
in his saloon. Eddie and Ella Edwards lived in Lytle's home during the early
days of their marriage, and Lytle thereafter lived with them. They were also
respectable and law abiding; despite his reputed propensity for the bottle,
Lytle never spent time in the local jail, nor did any other Scott, Weaver, or
Edwards. Like the Andersons and Chesters, the Weavers became enshrined
in local memory, although more for Lytle's weakness than for Silas's
accomplishments. Their achievements were as solid as those of any African
American family in Washington Court House could be and justify the pride
their family monument displays. But their story also demonstrates the limits
in Washington Court House to African American aspirations.

The Oatneals

The fourth family came to Washington Court House late in the century. John T. Oatneal was born in 1865 in Franklin County, Virginia. Through the barber trade he made his way to the college department of Virginia Normal and Collegiate Institute in Petersburg, graduating with honors in 1890. He then enrolled in the law department of Shaw University in Raleigh, North Carolina, and graduated in 1892. He attempted to practice in Roanoke, Virginia, but then moved to Washington Court House, where he became the first and only African American attorney in the county. It was probably in Washington Court House that he met his wife, Victoria, a native Ohioan. They married in 1898. Both became active members of the AME church, and John served for many years as superintendent of the Sunday school. He was also a Republican Party activist.[56]

John Oatneal specialized in pursuing the pension claims of local Civil War veterans and their widows, both black and white, and by all reports he was good at it. What is striking about this pioneering African American attorney in Fayette County is how uncertain his legal practice must have been, and how reluctant some local whites were to recognize it. The 1900 census reported only that he was a barber. The 1906 city directory listed him as editor of a weekly newspaper, the *Ohio Leader,* and the cover of the directory carried a prominent advertisement for his barber shop. He and Victoria may have left Washington Court House for several years, as they did not appear in either the 1910 census or the 1913 city directory, although they donated to the AME church in 1907, 1911, and 1912. If they had not left town in 1913, then they were simply ignored by the compilers of the city directory. At some point, however, John was elected justice of the peace, which could only have been possible with the support of European American voters. John died in 1933 and is buried in the town cemetery. His grave is marked with a double headstone engraved with Victoria's name and birth year, but her year of death is blank.

What is known of the career of John T. Oatneal in Washington Court House suggests the ambiguous status of an African American professional in a small white world. He probably came to Washington Court House in the immediate aftermath of the foiled lynching of 1894, when the town was still seething with resentment toward the Ohio National Guard commander who had shot down their fellow townspeople to protect an African American alleged rapist. He must have expected that the supercharged racial atmosphere would not affect his prospects. To some extent, he was right. On

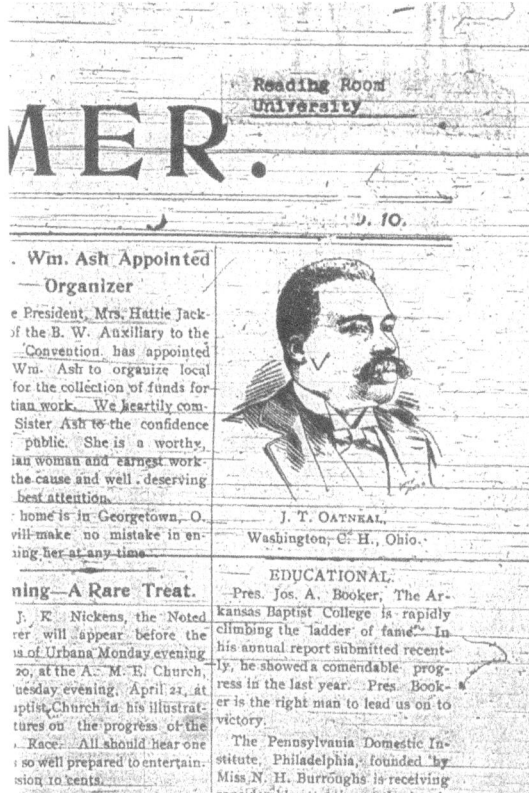

Figure 2.6 John T. Oatneal in 1903. *Urbana Informer,* April 1903.

one hand, he was "a very popular colored man," sufficiently well respected to be elected to a position previously held only by European Americans.[57] On the other, for at least a decade after his arrival, and probably longer, he struggled to establish a practice. If he ever did, he would have been in his fifties when it came about, nearly twenty years after he first came to Fayette County.[58] To the Oatneals, Washington Court House was not a totally hostile environment. But neither did it afford a field of opportunity commensurate with John's ambition and energies.

FAMILIES AND FATES

Clearly, African American families served their members in many different ways. Individuals of both sexes and all ages received shelter and support—and sometimes jobs—from other members of their extended families.

Such support no doubt helped to counteract the effect of the restricted job opportunities available in Washington Court House. As the case of Bolding and Eliza Anderson shows, a menial occupation was no bar to modest material progress. Immigrant and native-born white families performed the same functions, but the latter generally had greater resources to share, and neither group faced the same occupational restrictions as African Americans. Still, European and European American families were under pressure, too, and they too broke apart. But family breakups by separation or death were probably not as common among white families as they were among the Andersons, Chesters, and Weavers. Comparative evidence from other small towns at the turn of the century suggests as much.[59] While crude birth rates in Fayette County were comparable among blacks and whites during the last twenty years of the nineteenth century, black death rates consistently exceeded white.[60] Widowers were disproportionately common among African American men in Washington Court House, and some of them, like King Anderson and Lewis Chester, may actually have been separated.[61] Family support could mitigate the impact of occupational restrictions. But poverty placed limits on the nutrition and medical care that African American families could afford. Furthermore, restricted access to the remunerative jobs that would allow husbands and fathers to fulfill the breadwinner role demanded by the dominant gender ideology put distinct pressure upon African American families.

One specific pressure that may have affected African American families more than European American ones arose from the involvement of African Americans, and particularly African American men, in the retail liquor trade.[62] At least one male member of the Anderson, Chester, and Weaver families worked in the liquor business at some point in his life. It is extremely unlikely that any three randomly selected white families would have revealed such a history. The prime virtue of the liquor trade was its accessibility, but along with ease of access came some powerful disadvantages. First, it was dangerous.[63] During the late nineteenth century distilled spirits contributed most of the absolute alcohol consumed by American drinkers, so drunkenness was no doubt more common than in later years, when beer came to dominate American tastes. "Violence," a historian of the midwestern saloon writes, "frequently broke out where young men, liquor, and weapons mixed."[64] For saloonkeepers, bartenders, and waiters, exposure to violence constituted an occupational hazard. One white saloonkeeper in Washington Court House was attacked with an axe when he tried to cut off a group of drunks. Knives, glasses, chairs, and billiard balls regularly flew in Washington Court House saloons.[65] King Anderson had a reputation as a saloonkeeper who could anticipate barroom brawls, but even he was sometimes surprised. Second, the liquor trade was disreputable. Only one group of retail liquor sellers possessed wealth and prestige in small towns, and that was the physicians who supplied patients with "medicinal" alcohol through the drugstores they owned. Many saloonkeepers began as artisans, but none, in Washington Court House at least, rose to the pinnacle of the local structure of wealth or respectability—or even came close. Third, the liquor trade was uncertain. In addition to business cycle swings, which affected the liquor trade like other businesses, throughout the late nineteenth century, especially in the Midwest, the trade became the intense focus of continual political struggles. As time went on, more and more saloons were acquired by brewers, which may have reduced financial incertitude but also limited access and removed the trade's other attraction, self-employment. After the mid-1880s, the number of retail liquor outlets steadily contracted in per capita terms.[66] The existence of such potent disadvantages was, of course, precisely the reason why the retail liquor business was as open as it was to immigrants and African Americans. No one else wanted it.

Involvement in the liquor trade carried another threat specific to African Americans. When African Americans drank or dispensed liquor, or even entertained in song or dance that transgressed the extremely tight boundaries of Victorian respectability, they confirmed in European American eyes the charges of degeneracy and primitivism that southern racist demagogues were spewing forth at the turn of the century. The result was to introduce into the white side of the sort of black-white encounters that routinely took place in Andersonville powerful emotions of guilt and self-hatred, which could easily be projected toward the black drinker, bartender, saloonkeeper, or performer. When this happened, the normal danger, disreputability, and uncertainty of the liquor business gave way to an even more combustible mixture.

3

SMALL CITIES
The Springfields

[After emancipation,] I worked roun' on farms [in Kentucky], en finely in 1881, I came ter
Springfield [Ohio].
I built me er shanty on East Main St. jes' below de stan'pipe. All roun' wuz woods. East
Street shops was just startin' ter be built en I carried de hod fer it en de Arcade, en
Metallic Casket, en er Y.M.C.A.; en I mixed all er morter fer de Fairbanks Building.
—Charles Green, Springfield, Ohio, ca. 1937[1]

That's one thing too, that caused me to leave the school and go to work because the
teachment handed down from the older folks was, you just as well to work and earn a
living because if you get your education, there's nowhere for you to go here. . . .
—Rev. Harry Mann (born in Springfield, Illinois, 1903), 1974[2]

I was living in—as we call it in Springfield—the West End. There were only three Colored
families living in the neighborhood—it was a German neighborhood. I never felt I was
Black, we never used the word Black, but we were treated as people, as human beings.
I went along with the Whites and at no time would we ever feel that we were not
wanted. Our neighbors were wonderful.
—Mrs. Mary Blue Wynne (born in Springfield, Illinois, 1901), 1987[3]

Town size and the more complex economy that usually accompanies
greater size may be thought to mitigate racist prejudice and therefore make possible a less hostile welcome for African American migrants.
Springfield, Illinois, at 34,000 population in 1900, and Springfield, Ohio,
about 4,000 larger, stood several steps above Washington Court House on
the urban hierarchy. But as chapter 1 demonstrated, Civil War and postbellum migrants showed no preference for larger communities in the Lower
Midwest. If reputation made a difference, then the Illinois capital, well
known as home of the Great Emancipator, should have attracted many. But
in fact Lincoln's hometown, although seeing its African American population increase almost ninefold between 1860 and 1890, notably showed
a weaker attraction for migrants both black and white than most other
Illinois urban places (figure 1.4). Industry formed a crucial base for urban
growth during the Gilded Age, and here Ohio's Springfield held a crucial

advantage over its western counterpart as it edged ahead of most other Ohio urban places in growth of its European American population and leapt ahead in its African American population increase (figure 1.2). After 1900 the two Springfields' histories would converge in vicious mob attacks on their African American citizens. At the turn of the century, however, the two cities' disparate histories produced divergent conditions for African American work, family life, and housing.

METAL CITY

Founded in the early 1800s, Springfield, Ohio, sprang to life during the 1830s, when it became the western terminus of the National Road. The first railroad arrived in the mid-1840s. By the end of the Civil War decade, Springfield was already a center of manufacturing, notably of agricultural implements, farm and mill machinery, woolen goods, carriages, and flour. Rapid growth occurred during the 1860s, 1870s, and 1880s as the city's factories expanded and proliferated, a process capped during the early years of the 1880s with construction of the shops of the "Reaper King," William N. Whitely, the world's largest agricultural implement manufacturer. The Whitely company failed a few years later after a dramatic and mutually destructive open-shop battle with the Knights of Labor, who had organized two-thirds of the Reaper King's 1,500 workers. Springfield remained an agricultural implement manufacturing center after the Whitely collapse, its industrial economy now based upon many smaller plants, but city growth was slower for twenty years after the great confrontation. African American migration to Springfield tracked the pattern of urban growth, reaching its height during the heady years of industrial expansion lasting from the Civil War through the 1880s, as the city's African American population mush-roomed from 276 in 1860 to 3,549 in 1890.[4]

On the edge of the Virginia Military District, Springfield's Clark County was settled by Virginians, Marylanders, and Pennsylvanians. The railroads brought European immigrants, principally Irish and Germans. While Irish immigration seems to have peaked before the Civil War, the German inflow continued through the prosperous years of the Gilded Age. Springfield attracted little of the new immigration from central and southern Europe in the waning years of the century, but at century's end immigrants and their native-born children made up one-third of the city's population. Afro-Kentuckians moved up the Miami Valley to Springfield, and in 1900 they comprised nearly one-half of interstate migrants, with Virginians a distant second at about 20 percent. As an industrial city based

Table 3.1 Occupational Category of Workers, Springfield, Ohio, 1900 (in percentages)

| | *African Americans* | | *European Americans* | |
	Men	Women	Men	Women
High white collar	0.4	0.0	5.3	0.0
Low white collar	4.8	5.1	22.2	38.9
Blue collar skilled	18.5	12.8	52.6	36.1
Blue collar semiskilled & unskilled	76.3	82.1	19.9	25.0
Total	100.0	100.0	100.0	100.0
N	249	78	171	36

Source: Sampled manuscript U.S. census schedules for Clark County, OH, 1900.

on metalworking, Springfield was a magnet for African American men, whom employers stereotyped as able to tolerate work at high temperatures. The African American sex ratio was balanced in 1890, but tilted slightly toward the male side during the succeeding decade.[5]

A large majority of African American women lived with at least one other nuclear or extended family member, as did most European Americans of both sexes.[6] African American female coresidence patterns generally paralleled those in Washington Court House. Men's, however, were quite different. More men lived alone than in Washington Court House, and in Springfield African American men were far more likely to live on their own than European Americans. Whereas in Washington Court House more than three-quarters of male African Americans lived with their families, in Springfield less than seven out of ten did. The difference is accounted for by the much larger proportion of boarders or roomers in the industrial city (20.4 percent compared to 10.2). This reflected a higher rate of transiency among African American men in Springfield compared to European American men. The percentage of African American women in the 1900 sample who were identified in Springfield twenty years earlier was nearly the same as that for European American women (13.6 percent compared to 15.0 percent). Only 17.8 percent of African American men had persisted since 1880, however, while 29.9 percent of European American men had. Family migration appeared to figure as large in the African American female migration experience as in Washington Court House, but not as large in the male.[7] Instead, the industrial city drew a minority of males traveling alone or with non-kin.

Springfield's neighborhoods in 1900 appear to have been characterized by an even looser pattern of integrated clustering than in Washington Court

House. African Americans were fairly evenly distributed across the city's six wards; they were significantly underrepresented only in Ward Three, the city's smallest. Less than one-third of African American homes had African American neighbors on both sides; as many lived between two European American homes. Springfield, Ohio, was less segregated residentially than either Washington Court House or Springfield, Illinois.[8]

As a larger industrial city, Springfield's occupational profiles were quite different than those of Washington Court House (table 3.1). In the extent of labor force participation, women's experience mirrored the situation in Washington Court House. In Springfield, 32 percent of African American women were listed in the 1900 census with occupations, compared to only 18 percent of European American women. Springfield, however, offered African American women workers a wider and more varied range of work. In addition to the laundresses, washerwomen, and domestic servants who made up the largest groups of women workers in Washington Court House, African American women worked as seamstresses, dressmakers, milliners, and nurses. There was one African American bookkeeper and one clerk, but white women held all of the small number of jobs as cashiers, salesladies, and stenographers.

Springfield's industries in 1900 depended on a large corps of skilled male workers, a significant difference from industrially challenged Washington Court House. After the decline of the Knights of Labor, Springfield's white workers continued to organize, but in craft unions. In 1903 the city held 62 craft unions, which enlisted five-sevenths of the workers in the trades they represented.[9] But most craft unions probably did not admit African American workers. Furthermore, most employers would not hire African American men for anything but menial jobs.[10] A few did manage to surmount the barriers of discrimination. Among the sample, whites dominated the machinist trade, but there were nearly as many black iron molders as white.[11] The molders—probably the top rung of the industrial ladder for black men—represented only 3.5 percent of the African American male work force. Thus, while plenty of unskilled jobs were usually available for black men, little opportunity existed for advancement into skilled positions. Although the skilled sector of the work force was considerably larger in Springfield among European American men than in Washington Court House, among African American men it was smaller.

Home ownership was significantly less common in Springfield in 1900 than in Washington Court House. Only 38 percent of all homes in the industrial city were owned, compared to 49 percent in the smaller town.[12] Also unlike Washington Court House, the African American home ownership rate fell well behind the European American (23 to 38 percent), as well

Table 3.2 Possible Determinants of Home Ownership, Adult Males, Washington Court House, Ohio, 1900

A. Occupancy of Family-Owned Homes by Characteristic

| | African Americans | | European Americans | |
	Group Size	Percent Occupying Owned Homes	Group Size	Percent Occupying Owned Homes
Persistence				
Newcomer since 1880	210	14.3	129	31.8
Present in 1880	47	31.9	53	54.7
Age				
Age 21–39 years	144	14.6	99	31.3
40 years and over	113	21.2	83	47.0
Origin				
Southern-born	151	15.9	8	37.5
Northern-born	104	19.2	144	36.1
Foreign-born	0	—	28	50.0
All	257	17.5	182	38.5

B. Correlation Matrices

| | African Americans | | |
	Persistence	Age	Origin**
Family-owned home	+.18*	+.07	+.04
Persistence		+.16*	+.08
Age			−.41*

| | European Americans | | |
	Persistence	Age	Origin**
Family-owned home	+.21*	+.11	−.01
Persistence		+.21*	−.22*
Age			−.32*

* Significant at the .05 level

** Excluding foreign-born

Source: Sampled U.S. census manuscripts for Clark County, OH, 1900.

Table 3.3 Possible Determinants of Home Ownership, Adult Females, Springfield, Ohio, 1900

A. Occupancy of Family-Owned Homes by Characteristic

| | *African Americans* | | *European Americans* | |
	Group Size	Percent Occupying Owned Homes	Group Size	Percent Occupying Owned Homes
Persistence				
Newcomer since 1880	180	26.1	172	31.4
Present in 1880	27	51.9	31	71.0
Age				
Age 21–39 years	122	33.1	133	33.1
40 years and over	85	41.2	70	45.7
Origin				
Southern-born	102	34.3	9	44.0
Northern-born	103	25.2	167	35.3
Foreign-born	0	—	27	48.1
All	207	29.5	203	37.4

B. Correlation Matrices

| | *African Americans* | | |
	Persistence	Age	Origin**
Family-owned home	+.19*	+.23*	−.10
Persistence		+.20*	−.07
Age			−.44*

| | *European Americans* | | |
	Persistence	Age	Origin**
Family-owned home	+.29*	+.15*	−.04
Persistence		+.09	+.02
Age			−.02

* Significant at the .05 level

** Excluding foreign-born

Source: Sampled U.S. census manuscripts for Clark County, OH, 1900.

as behind the statewide black rate (27 percent). African American women's home ownership was close to that of European American women (29.5 to 37.4 percent), but African American men were less than half as likely as their European American counterparts to live in a family-owned home (17.5 to 38.5 percent; tables 3.2 and 3.3).

The presence of a sizable number of males living away from kin in Springfield explains part of the lag in male home ownership, but other factors operated as well to cause the deficit. African American men who had been present in the community for at least twenty years, men over forty, and the northern-born were all less likely than their European American counterparts to live in a family-owned home. These findings suggest that the bars blocking entry to higher-level jobs also hindered men's access to home ownership. Discrimination did not operate directly, through refusal of white vendors to sell properties to blacks. If this had been the case, African American women's home ownership rate would have fallen further behind that of European American women. Instead, white prejudice functioned indirectly, through occupational segregation affecting the principal breadwinners in African American families. Occupational segregation prevailed in Washington Court House, too, but perhaps in the smaller town lower housing costs worked to mitigate its effects.

Job discrimination and a low rate of male home ownership did not, however, preclude the presence of an opportunity structure. In fact, such a structure did influence home ownership patterns in Springfield. Those who remained in the community for twenty years or more nearly always enjoyed significantly higher rates of home ownership than newcomers after 1880.[13] Among African Americans of both sexes, persistence in the community doubled the likelihood of living in a family-owned dwelling. For both African American and European American men, no other factor—age or regional origin—was strongly correlated with home ownership. For women of both groups, aging brought improved chances for home ownership, but among African American women age is correlated with persistence. Further analysis using a stepwise multiple regression procedure that allows the variables to compete freely shows persistence to be the stronger variable, although when persistence is controlled, age still exerts an independent effect.[14] Finally, incorporating "color" into the analysis confirms the effect of job segregation on African American male home ownership. Among all men, "color" exerts an independent influence on home ownership after the effect of persistence is taken into account.[15]

In sum, Springfield presented a complex combination of advantages and disadvantages to African American migrants. In contrast to Washington Court House, the industrial center, especially during the dynamic years between 1860 and 1886, offered some jobs for men in factories and was prepared to yield some of these to African Americans. These jobs were probably seen as attractive by former Kentucky and Virginia farmers and farm workers. But after the decline of the Knights of Labor—racially integrated in policy, if not in practice—black artisans and skilled industrial workers found few opportunities to exercise their crafts, as they faced hostility from both white employers and white workers. Still, the larger and more complex economy in Springfield, together with the size of the African American population, created some opportunities in construction, transportation, and retail trade. African American women were also able to obtain access to a somewhat wider range of work than their counterparts in Washington Court House, which may have contributed to rates of home ownership that approached those of European American women. Job segregation in the male work world, in contrast, severely retarded African American men's access to home ownership. Those men and women who stuck it out in Springfield could improve their chances of buying a home. The value of persistence was demonstrated by the career of Robert J. Piles, who came to Ohio as a child in 1819. Later finding his way to Springfield, where he worked as a barber, Piles had accumulated by the time of his death in 1886 real estate, bank stock, and bonds reputedly worth between $85,000 and $125,000, and left his sons in white-collar jobs.[16] But few had Piles's patience. Although African Americans seem to have dominated the barber, waiter, and teamster trades in Springfield, these occupations offered few openings to the many who may have wished to move on from the dead-end, menial industrial jobs that were the best Springfield had to offer to most African American men.

LINCOLN'S TOWN

Illinois's capital differed in several ways from Washington Court House and its Ohio counterpart. Springfield, Illinois, contained more industry than Washington Court House, but its economy was more diversified than that of Springfield, Ohio. Government, the hospitality business the presence of the capital stimulated, and coal mining were all major employers. The Illinois Watch Company operated a large factory, and the city also contained several foundries. Similar in size to the Ohio Springfield, it grew at a different pace, surging during the 1860s, slowing through the 1870s and 1880s, then spurting again during the twenty years after 1890. Its African American population was larger than that of Washington Court House at every census from 1860 to 1930, but smaller than the other Springfield's. But as a proportion of the city's population, the capital's African American population generally lagged behind those in the other two case study communities.[17]

Initially settled by a varied American-born migration, Springfield's ethnic mixture became more variegated with the arrival before the Civil War of Irish and German immigrants. Toward the end of the century, the coal mines drew a trickle of new immigrants from southern and central Europe. By century's end, immigrants and their children made up nearly half of the city's white population. Among African Americans, Missourians formed the largest group of migrants, followed in order by Kentuckians, Tennesseeans, and Virginians. In 1890, African American males significantly outnumbered females, but more females entered the migration stream during the following decade, producing a nearly balanced sex ratio in 1900.[18]

Like migrants to the other two towns, African Americans tended to travel to Springfield, Illinois, in families.[19] Young Leota Harris came to Springfield in 1896 with her parents; "all my father's people were here," she recalled, plus her mother's uncle.[20] Even those who did not travel in a family group, such as twenty-two-year-old Clarence Liggins, arriving from Kentucky in 1900, may have migrated on the recommendation of a family member, in Liggins's case his cousin.[21] Approximately three-quarters of adult blacks resided in family groupings, not much less than adult whites. Most African Americans in 1900, like most European Americans, had arrived in the capital city during the previous two decades.[22] African Americans in 1900 resided in all of Springfield's seven wards, but they were clustered in seven distinct locations. The largest of these was an area of old, dilapidated housing known as the Badlands (in honor of its thriving vice business) in the northeastern quadrant of the downtown, which held about two-fifths of Springfield's African Americans. The second-largest cluster was in the southeast section, just inside the city limits and near coal mines, where another quarter of the black population lived. The level of residential segregation by ward was the highest among the three communities. As in Springfield, Ohio, and Washington Court House, these clusters were integrated.[23] Seventy-three percent of blacks had at least one white neighbor, and nearly 40 percent had two.

African American women's occupational profile resembled that in Springfield, Ohio, more than that of Washington Court House, in that they had access to something more than domestic-service jobs. As in the other two towns, more African American than European American women were listed with occupations (36 percent to 16), but little work was available for African American women beyond laundry, domestic service, and the needle trades (table 3.4). All of the clerks, stenographers, bookkeepers, and cashiers were whites. A few European American women worked for

Table 3.4 Occupational Category of Workers, Springfield, Illinois, 1900 (in percentages)

| | African Americans | | European Americans | |
	Men	Women	Men	Women
High white collar	0.0	0.0	7.3	0.0
Low white collar	5.9	0.0	25.5	27.5
Blue collar skilled	11.8	13.9	27.9	37.5
Blue collar semiskilled & unskilled	82.3	86.1	39.4	35.0
Total	100.0	100.0	100.1*	100.0
N	271	72	165	40

* Does not equal 100.0 percent because of rounding

Source: Sampled manuscript U.S. census schedules for Sangamon County, IL, 1900.

the Illinois Watch Company, the city's largest manufacturer, but the sole African American employee among its 900 workers was a janitor.[24] Among men in the sample, there was a smattering of white-collar occupations—a bookkeeper, a salesman, a state employee, a veterinarian, two preachers, a few clerks—but the most numerous occupations were laborer (28 percent of those known), coal miner (15 percent), porter (8 percent), janitor (5 percent), waiter, barber, and cook (each 4 percent).

Among Springfield whites in 1900, home ownership was slightly more common than in Washington Court House (52 percent to 49). Both, of course, contrasted with Springfield, Ohio, where only 38 percent of adult whites lived in family-owned homes. The African American home ownership rate in the Illinois capital (37 percent) stood midway between the rates in Springfield, Ohio (23 percent), and Washington Court House (48 percent). It was also significantly higher than the statewide rate in Illinois (24.5 percent).[25] Because the rate of white home ownership in Springfield, Illinois, was higher than in the Ohio Springfield, the gap between white and black home ownership rates in the two Springfields was almost exactly the same (15 percent). Home ownership was more readily available in the Illinois than in the Ohio Springfield, but blacks were just as far behind whites.

As in Springfield, Ohio, among whites the foreign-born had the highest rate of home ownership. In another pattern similar to the Ohio Springfield, among African Americans women were more likely than men to live in family-owned homes, and the gap between African Americans and European Americans was narrower among women than men. Like Springfield, Ohio, and unlike Washington Court House, a local structure of opportunity influenced the outcome for all groups, African Americans and

Table 3.5 Possible Determinants of Home Ownership, Adult Males, Springfield, Illinois, 1900

A. Occupancy of Family-Owned Homes by Characteristic

| | *African Americans* | | *European Americans* | |
	Group Size	Percent Occupying Owned Homes	Group Size	Percent Occupying Owned Homes
Persistence				
Newcomer since 1880	221	29.0	138	47.1
Present in 1880	41	58.5	39	74.4
Age				
Age 21–39 years	142	25.4	93	45.2
40 years and over	120	43.3	84	61.9
Origin				
Southern-born	174	31.6	11	36.4
Northern-born	84	36.9	108	50.0
Foreign-born	4	50.0	53	66.0
All	262	33.6	177	53.1

B. Correlation Matrices

| | *African Americans* | | |
	Persistence	Age	Origin**
Family-owned home	+.23*	+.20*	+.05
Persistence		+.12*	+.16*
Age			−.26*

| | *European Americans* | | |
	Persistence	Age	Origin**
Family-owned home	+.23*	+.16*	+.08
Persistence		+.16*	+.16*
Age			−.02*

* Significant at the .05 level

** Excluding foreign-born

Source: Sampled U.S. census manuscripts for Sangamon County, IL, 1900.

Table 3.6 Possible Determinants of Home Ownership, Adult Females, Springfield, Illinois, 1900

A. Occupancy of Family-Owned Homes by Characteristic

| | African Americans | | European Americans | |
	Group Size	Percent Occupying Owned Homes	Group Size	Percent Occupying Owned Homes
Persistence				
Newcomer since 1880	168	37.5	179	49.2
Present in 1880	24	70.8	35	65.7
Age				
Age 21–39 years	104	32.7	121	43.0
40 years and over	88	52.3	93	63.4
Origin				
Southern-born	116	38.8	21	57.1
Northern-born	74	45.9	144	44.4
Foreign-born	2	50.0	48	70.8
All	192	41.7	214	51.9

B. Correlation Matrices

| | *African Americans* | | |
	Persistence	Age	Origin**
Family-owned home	+.22*	+.20*	+.07
Persistence		+.21*	+.04
Age			−.42*

| | *European Americans* | | |
	Persistence	Age	Origin**
Family-owned home	+.12*	+.11	−.08
Persistence		+.30*	−.10
Age			−.38*

** Excluding foreign-born

Source: Sampled U.S. census manuscripts for Sangamon County, IL, 1900.

European Americans of both sexes. Persistence since 1880 reliably boosted one's chances of living in a family-owned home (tables 3.5 and 3.6).[26]

Leota Harris's parents are the apparent exception that proves the rule. In 1897 they bought a house only one year after their arrival, but they had the advantages of coming from Chicago (probably bringing some capital with them) and joining a large network of family in Springfield; they bought their house from Leota's maternal grandfather.[27] When "color" is incorporated into the analysis, the results, as might be expected, differ for men and women. Among men, persistence and age retain their impact upon home ownership patterns, and "color" exerts a lesser, yet still distinct, effect. As in Springfield, Ohio, the power of discrimination was probably exerted indirectly through occupational segregation more than through refusal to sell to blacks, since African American women's home ownership rate was higher than men's and closer to that of European American women than African American men's was to that of European American men. Among women, only persistence exerted a significant influence upon home ownership.

PATTERNS AND MIGRANT PERSPECTIVES

State-level and urban studies of African Americans in the Lower Midwest during the late nineteenth century have stressed the worsening prospects for black men in the job market.[28] The profiles of a small town, Washington Court House, and two small cities, the Springfields, confirm that opportunities to find remunerative skilled wage work or profitable self-employed work, although not completely absent, were severely limited. But while the types of work available to blacks in a community and the degree of occupational segregation certainly exerted a powerful influence on other aspects of African American life, jobs did not tell the whole story. Occupational segregation was extreme in all three of the case study communities, yet the towns varied considerably in the access to home ownership they provided for African Americans. Occupational segregation was also severe in larger cities, yet African American home ownership rates in 1900 were even lower there than the lowest rate in the case study communities. African American home ownership stood at 16 percent in Columbus and Indianapolis, 10.5 percent in Cleveland, and 5 percent in Cincinnati and Chicago, compared to 23 percent in Springfield, Ohio; 37 percent in Springfield, Illinois; and 48 percent in Washington Court House.[29] Rare in the metropolitan centers, African American access to home ownership tended to expand as urban size fell.[30] Community size itself reflects—no doubt imperfectly—the action of other factors such as lower housing costs or greater willingness of small-town lenders to grant mortgages to residents whom they knew personally. For whatever reason, nonmetropolitan urban communities offered greater opportunities for home ownership than larger cities, despite sharing metropolitan patterns of occupational segregation.

Separate analysis of women's and men's wealth and home ownership points to one way in which the effects of workplace segregation and discrimination may have been mitigated for African American families in nonmetropolitan settings. Although fewer women property holders could be identified in Washington Court House, average female wealth holdings exceeded men's. In both Springfields, African American women were considerably more likely than men to live in family-owned homes. This pattern is consistent with those found in antebellum Petersburg, Virginia, and postbellum Cincinnati by other locally based studies of sex differences in African American property holding.[31] Further investigation is required to explain the divergence between women and men. But it is already clear that African American women played a more significant economic role in contributing to or holding family property than has generally been recognized. The census, which typically underreported women's gainful work, usually found a larger proportion of African American than European American women holding paying occupations, as was the case in Washington Court House in 1880 and in both Springfields in 1900.[32] Furthermore, like their white counterparts, African American women contributed to family income through unreported industrial work at home, as well as often taking in laundry and caring for and feeding boarders. Their contributions to family income, whether as primary or secondary providers, may well have made the difference between renting and owning for their families.

Despite the lower rates of African American home ownership in the larger case study communities (the Springfields), at least persistence in these communities paid off in improved chances for home ownership. In Washington Court House, African Americans' share of town wealth doubled between 1870 and 1890. In 1890, however, persistence within the community showed no correlation with wealth holding. This implies that the increase between 1870 and 1890 resulted as much from black achievement elsewhere as from persistent effort within the Fayette County seat. Where was such achievement taking place, in the North or the South? Before 1890, southern-born migrants to Washington Court House enjoyed an economic advantage over the northern-born. In the two Springfields ten years later, however, no "southern" advantage could be found in African American home ownership. This evidence hints that, as the century progressed, so did African Americans' material circumstances in the North. The payoff to persistence in the Springfields suggests further that such gains were more likely to be achieved in larger than in smaller urban communities.

What do these town profiles tell us about the migration field of African American migrants to and within the Lower Midwest? If they were aware of the conditions prevailing in different towns (a question that will be addressed in later chapters), they faced complex and difficult choices. Where industrial work was available for men (Springfield, Ohio), chances for home ownership were more limited than in other small towns and small cities. Where home ownership was most accessible (Washington Court House), work for women beyond domestic service was scarce. Where residential segregation was least stringent (Springfield, Ohio), access to home ownership was more restricted than in other nonmetropolitan urban places. In cities containing the largest black communities (the metropolitan centers), owning a home was an evanescent dream for most. Choices among towns of disparate sizes and economies were difficult not because opportunities were equally bleak, but because urban communities offered such variant combinations of job type, residential segregation, and access to home ownership. The midwestern urban landscape presented African American migrants with a variety of choices: a shifting, tumbling kaleidoscope of opportunities and risks.[33]

But although choices were difficult, they were not impossible. African Americans in both South and North were accustomed to wide variation from place to place in treatment and condition.[34] Nor were African Americans a monolithic group: different migrants sought different goals, and people's goals changed at different stages of their lives. While thousands of African Americans were flocking to Chicago during the 1890s, Leota Harris's parents were leaving the Windy City for Springfield. Conditions facing African Americans were generally deteriorating across the Midwest during the late nineteenth century, but they were not universally grim or worsening. Although still far behind European Americans, the African American share of wealth in Washington Court House was growing, as Bolding and Eliza Anderson could have testified. African Americans who remained twenty years in both Springfields—as well as some new arrivals, such as the Harrises—did achieve home ownership. To cast down one's bucket where one was, or to pull it up and move on, could both be viable strategies.

4

IN WHITE WORLDS
Politics

Next to victory is the glory and happiness of manfully contending for it.
Therefore, contend! contend!
—Frederick Douglass, 1892[1]

It is evident that the prejudice to our people in many localities is growing worse each
year. This in my opinion is due to the rapid progress of the Negro rather than to his
former condition.
—Rev. Jordan Chavis, Illinois Afro-American Protective League, 1897[2]

Cairo was always "diabolically Democratic," at least until the "man and brother" from
the cotton-fields and jungles of the South parted company with the swamp alligators
and toothsome possoms [*sic*] of that region and came upon the town like the black ants
of his native Africa.
—H. C. Bradsby, Cairo, Illinois, 1883[3]

I would advise the colored voters, in view of the treatment they have received at the
hands of the Republican party in Ross county, to assert some political independence in
municipal elections. While we are Republicans in principle, yet I do not deem it necessary and right we should support men adverse to our civil and political rights.
—"Helmet," Chillicothe, Ohio, 1887[4]

African American migrants to midwestern towns entered fervently
partisan and deeply divided political environments. As easily identifiable newcomers who usually voted as a bloc, their political behavior was
closely scrutinized by both the white Republicans they normally helped
and the Democrats they hurt. But since existing state laws, federal and
state court decisions, and the action or inaction of local officials could have
a direct impact on their daily lives and the future of their children, African
Americans in pursuit of freedom had a strong incentive collectively to seek
political change. Such struggles were facilitated by a tradition of resistance to
oppression developed during slavery and nourished during the tumultuous
times since emancipation.[5] A recent historian of twentieth-century migrations finds "remarkable" how quickly African Americans in metropolitan
centers "developed political capacity," but that capacity had been cultivated
during the age of the village, which preceded the movement to midwestern

metropolises.[6] African Americans' quest for freedom, which had brought them to the Midwest, made them political actors in their new homes.

Historians have long recognized the years around the turn of the century as a period of worsening race relations in the United States. In the South disfranchisement and segregation were entrenched, having been brought to completion and then safeguarded by mob violence.[7] The white North not only acquiesced in the cancellation of southern blacks' constitutional rights, but also produced its own wave of mob violence, as well as a creeping tide of de facto segregation, job discrimination, and reduction of African American political influence.[8] Hardening of northern whites' racial attitudes has been attributed to the southern example and to factors such as a yearning for sectional reconciliation, the spread of racism in intellectual circles, growing sympathy for imperialism, and fear of class conflict, which white northern editorialists were increasingly associating with African Americans.[9] Such explanations implicitly portray black northerners as passive victims of forces originating from sources beyond their control. Yet in the face of discriminatory structures and practices, African Americans did have a choice whether to acquiesce or to resist. When they resisted, they added a new and turbulent cross-current to already troubled waters.

AT THE STATE LEVEL

Of the three levels of government, the local exerted the most direct and conspicuous impact on Americans during the late nineteenth century. Locally set and assessed property taxes were the only taxes paid directly by individuals.[10] Insofar as manufacturers' locational choices were affected by government action, only local inducements were offered.[11] Community liquor-licensing authorities, judges, police, and marshals held the keys to peace and order. Enforcement of state laws depended almost wholly upon local officials' willingness to cooperate. Nevertheless, local authorities operated within a legal context shaped by their state government and, much more distantly, by federal authority.

In the Lower Midwest, the drastic changes during the Civil War decade in state laws governing the status of African Americans still left significant disabilities. In every state, African Americans mobilized to dismantle the remaining framework of discrimination. Indispensable to these campaigns were the region's precariously balanced politics and adult African American males' status as voters following ratification of the Fifteenth Amendment in 1870. Between 1876 and 1892, the average gap between Republicans and Democrats in the east north central states was less than three percentage points, the second smallest among the nation's regions.[12] Major-party politi-cal battles in Ohio, Indiana, and Illinois during the 1870s, 1880s, and 1890s were fought in one of the most competitive environments in American political history. Joseph B. Foraker, Ohio governor, U.S. senator, and one of the central figures in Ohio politics during this period, later articulated a guiding belief of midwestern European American politicians: "The Negro vote was so large that it was not only an important but an essential factor in our considerations. It would not be possible for the Republican party to carry the state if that vote should be arrayed against us."[13] Although this belief depended upon several dubious assumptions, events seemed to con-firm it often enough that it took on "a life of its own."[14]

Although Afro-Midwesterners voted overwhelmingly Republican in most elections throughout the period, even before ratification of the Fifteenth Amendment the Democrats began to pursue their vote. This rep-resented a drastic about-face from the party's previous strategy toward black voting, which was to play the "race card" by scaremongering about the drastic political and social consequences that would allegedly follow black enfran-chisement. After African Americans began to vote, however, Democrats executed a "New Departure," in which they rubbed and scraped at the festering sore in the Republican–African American alliance, Republicans' unwillingness to reward African American voters with a proportionate share of political rewards.[15] By doing so, Democrats aimed to detach as much as possible of the African American vote from their Republican rivals. One Republican editor sarcastically portrayed the Democrats' change of attitude: "[B]efore the war the d——d nigger was a slave; after the war the ignorant negro was free; at the present time our intelligent fellow-citizen is a voter."[16] The New Departure accounts for an otherwise curious aspect of one of the principal political achievements of African Americans in the Lower Midwest during this era. In 1883 the U.S. Supreme Court struck down the federal Civil Rights Act. Shortly thereafter, state legislatures in Ohio (1884), Indiana (1885), and Illinois (1885) passed state civil rights acts outlawing racial discrimination in public accommodations. The responsible legislatures in Ohio and Indiana were under Democratic control. Democratic votes were also crucial to the passage of civil rights legislation through Illinois's divided legislature.[17]

In Ohio, where African American voters were most numerous both absolutely and proportionately, and where African American votes seemed to have contributed to election of a Democratic governor as well as the civil rights legislation, Democratic overtures set off a bidding war with Republicans that produced a series of statutory victories for blacks. In 1887 a Republican legislature repealed a law providing for separate schools for blacks, as well as one forbidding racial intermarriage. Ohio's African American legislators and their European American allies were able subsequently to head off retrogressive legislation and to introduce and shepherd to enactment bills prohibiting discrimination by life insurance companies (1889), strengthening the civil rights law (1894), and mandating sanctions for local officials who offered insufficient resistance to lynch mobs (1896).[18]

In Indiana, where African American voters remained more steadfast in their loyalty to the GOP, fewer legislative gains were won. Acts of 1869 and 1877 forbade local school authorities from excluding African American children, and in 1899 Indiana passed an antilynching law at the urging of a Republican governor. Two years later, another Republican governor, acting under the law's provisions, removed from office a sheriff whom he deemed to have been derelict in his duty of protecting an African American prisoner from a lynch mob. But at century's end, Indiana remained the only state in the Lower Midwest to exclude African Americans from militia service by statute, and one of only two northern states to forbid racial intermarriage.[19]

Whereas in Ohio enactment of a civil rights law initiated a series of African American legislative gains, in Illinois passage of the civil rights law capped a generally successful period of struggle. Illinois's new constitution in 1870 desegregated the militia and required universal public education. Subsequent school laws in 1872 and 1874 clarified and reinforced the responsibility of local officials to provide equal education to all students.[20] In succeeding years African American state legislators fought, albeit unsuccessfully, for bills to suppress mob violence, to prevent racial discrimination by life insurance companies, and to protect and extend the rights of poor and working-class citizens. They succeeded in incorporating the African American militia regiment into the state national guard and in strengthening the civil rights law.[21] These gains were won despite the handicap of a mass base that was smaller in absolute numbers than in Ohio and, more telling, was smaller as a proportion of the total electorate than in either Ohio or Indiana.

African Americans actively worked for the gains they won from state legislatures.[22] Most important, African Americans cast ballots in sufficient numbers to make their votes a prize worth fighting over. Under the leadership of men such as Cincinnati's Peter Clark, Evansville's Charles E. Sheldon, and Cairo's William T. Scott, some African American voters acted independently. In Ohio black Republicans responded to the Democratic victory in 1883 by organizing a network of equal-rights leagues in many of the state's urban communities. The leagues' goals were the repeal of the separate-school law and the anti-intermarriage law, both achieved four years later. Periodic conventions were held in each state, and statewide organizations were established for agitation and lobbying. African Americans wrote letters to African American and European American periodicals, petitioned, caucused, rallied, and marched.[23] The statewide organizational impulse culminated in 1890, when each of the three states created a unit of the National Afro-American League, founded three years before at the initiative of New York editor T. Thomas Fortune. Anticipating the program of the NAACP, the league demanded an end to limitations on voting rights, action to halt racist violence, bans on discrimination in schools and public facilities, and cessation of exploitation of convicts and workers. The state affiliates in Ohio and Indiana soon folded, but the Illinois branch continued to be active through the 1890s.[24] In Ohio the league failed to put down roots because African American leaders did not share the pessimism that motivated Fortune.[25] In a statement that rings only somewhat less true for Indiana and Illinois, David Gerber summarizes the achievements in Ohio that fueled their optimism:

> While there had been no moral revolution accompanying the ame-liorative trend of the 1880s, a high point in the history of racial advancement in Ohio had nonetheless been reached—a high point which, though dependent upon enfranchisement, in an important sense exceeded it as a racial landmark. While obtaining the vote had been vital to the achievement of citizenship and hence of the gains of the 1880s, enfranchisement was an act done for blacks by whites with little reference to black feelings and aspirations. However much moral support blacks had lent the process, they had lacked the power to be among its prime movers; instead, they had been placed in the degrading position of watching and waiting while others determined their fate. In contrast, the achievements of the 1880s had been deeply influenced by black political power and black activities in pursuit of racial welfare. As voters, lobbyists, legislators, and politicians, blacks had proven to be skilled manipulators of the party system and of government, and they had significantly furthered their own advancement.[26]

Despite the effort that underwrote legislative gains and the undeniable legal changes that occurred, in the final analysis African American progress was severely limited. White politicians allowed no more changes in their state's racial status quo than were perceived as necessary to attract or secure black votes. No new state agencies were created to enforce the civil rights or school laws, leaving individuals to depend upon state authorities to act or, in the absence of state action, to pursue their legal rights in the courts at their own expense. This left complainants at the mercy of lawyers and judges. The former sometimes subverted efforts to push forward test cases, and the latter often interpreted the statutes as narrowly as possible. Suits against refusal of service in Indiana restaurants, for example, were deterred by an 1888 ruling that the plaintiff had to prove the owner's responsibility for discriminatory acts by his staff. Indiana's public-accommodations law was such a dead letter that George L. Knox, who as editor of the *Freeman* energetically championed civil rights, refused to serve African American customers in the elite barber shop he operated in Indianapolis.[27] So did George Myers, confidant of power broker Mark Hanna and owner of a first-class Cleveland barber shop. Had Knox and Myers felt that they were required by the authority of their respective states' civil rights laws to serve their fellow African Americans, no doubt they would have done so.[28]

School laws did not produce education for African American children of equal quality with European American students across any of the three states. Ohio came closest. Ohio's 1887 school desegregation law, framed by African American legislator and future AME bishop Benjamin Arnett, brought about rapid and peaceful desegregation in a majority of the state's school districts. Since European American parents would rarely consent to their children's being taught by an African American, the law's implementation also resulted in widespread job losses by African American teachers. These costs were most severe in Cincinnati, where a separate system had flourished since before the Civil War. In a few communities African Americans agreed to retain segregated schools. In others, including Arnett's home town of Xenia, school authorities gerrymandered the city to ensure that segregation was maintained. Washington Court House abandoned its "colored" school, but African American students in its integrated schools were all taught by European American teachers.[29]

Illinois's school laws of 1872 and 1874 mandated local authorities to provide equal education to all students, but, while this required that black students be given equal access to schools, it did not specify that the schools be racially integrated. Thus, by omission rather than by argument, Illinois law accepted the principle of separate but equal, thereby anticipating the doctrine enunciated by the U.S. Supreme Court in *Plessy v. Ferguson* (1896). In districts where there were too few black children to make building a separate school economically feasible, they were integrated into white schools. But where their numbers were greater, locally mandated segregated schools were legal. African American parents who objected to their children's assignment to a separate school could choose between launching a civil suit on grounds of inequality or a political campaign against the offending school board trustees. "Alternatives offered by the Illinois Supreme Court," writes Robert

McCaul, "thus placed the initiative and expense squarely on the blacks and exposed them likewise to the dangers of reprisals from the whites."[30]

Indiana's law allowed separate schools where black numbers made them financially feasible and imposed no requirement that facilities for black children, whether integrated or segregated, be equal to those for whites. Indianapolis built and maintained separate schools, which came closer to the European American standard than elsewhere in the state. The capital city also integrated its high schools. In the southern part of the state, however, high school instruction for African Americans was provided as a meager adjunct to the segregated primary schools. The relatively large number of segregated schools gave employment to African American teachers.[31] Outside of Indianapolis, however, African American teachers taught using facilities and materials that fell below the European American norm. This was not a matter of oversight, but rather a product of judicial action. In an 1884 case brought to the Indiana Supreme Court (*State ex. rel. Mitchell v. Gray*), the justices ruled that an African American parent had no recourse against clearly unequal separate schooling. Recognizing that further appeal was futile, black Hoosiers took no further cases to the state supreme court.[32]

Other active and looming forms of racial prejudice escaped legislative sanction. No law prohibited discrimination in hiring or wage rates, or forced unions to admit blacks. No law banned restrictive covenants or other means to prevent African Americans from moving into European American neighborhoods. The white residents of Washington Court House who lived in the new subdivisions on the town's west side had no need to fear contact with black neighbors. At the other end of the region's urban hierarchy, neither did white Chicagoans living outside that city's new black enclaves. Even if restaurants would agree to serve them, poor black workers could not afford to patronize most such establishments.

At least one African American served in the lower house of each state legislature more or less continuously from the mid-1870s, and some representatives, such as Ohio's Benjamin Arnett and Harry Smith and Illinois's John W. E. Thomas, distinguished themselves.[33] Arnett and Thomas led the fights for their states' civil rights acts, and Smith took the lead in the struggle to strengthen Ohio's civil rights law in 1894 and framed the successful antilynching bill two years later. Even the most energetic and effective African American politicians in the Midwest, however, exercised what influence they possessed on the sufferance of their European American counterparts. Smith's political career, for example, effectively ended after the escalating horrors of lynching during the 1890s drove him to an emotional blast against the false pretenses of American liberty.[34] African American politicians operated within a political structure controlled by European Americans, and that fact strictly limited their options, both of thought and deed. Neither mobilization at the grassroots, action outside the narrow bounds of formal politics, nor coalition with agrarian or urban radicals was conceivable for these upwardly mobile men.[35]

Yet imaginative approaches became more and more necessary as the 1890s waned. In each of the three states Republicans gained the upper hand over their Democratic rivals, and, as their new advantage became clear, Republican politicians lost what interest they once had in bidding for the African American vote.[36] Whether from optimism arising from African American gains, pessimism generated by losses, or mere recognition of their weakening leverage, African American leaders abandoned the initiative and went on the defensive by the turn of the century.[37] Stalemate at the state level, however, did not necessarily imply stasis in local communities. On the contrary, the very weaknesses of African American gains in state capitals, together with the inherent importance of local government, produced continued struggle and conflict in local communities.

AT THE LOCAL LEVEL

Understanding African American struggle and the European American response within local communities requires a broad definition of political conflict, one that transcends the limited terrain of voting and office holding. Conflict took many more forms than formal politics, and, although other struggles often intersected or overlapped with partisan warfare, neither formal competition nor informal strife necessarily determined the outcome in the other realm.[38] African American striving for a better life destabilized midwestern communities through challenges to the distribution of jobs, offices, and schools. Meanwhile, through local experience European American residents came to perceive their African American neighbors as likely transgressors of what whites regarded as community mores.

One way in which such perceptions were shaped was the definition and punishment of deviant behavior. The key actors were local police officers. Since sheriffs, town marshals, and sometimes even constables were elected, they presumably reflected the attitudes of their largely European American constituency. In turn, their actions confirmed and further shaped local perceptions of deviancy. The evidence of police behavior reveals a wide gap between treatment of European Americans and African Americans as well as the application of quite different standards of justice. Despite stipulations in state civil rights laws that prohibited racial discrimination in jury

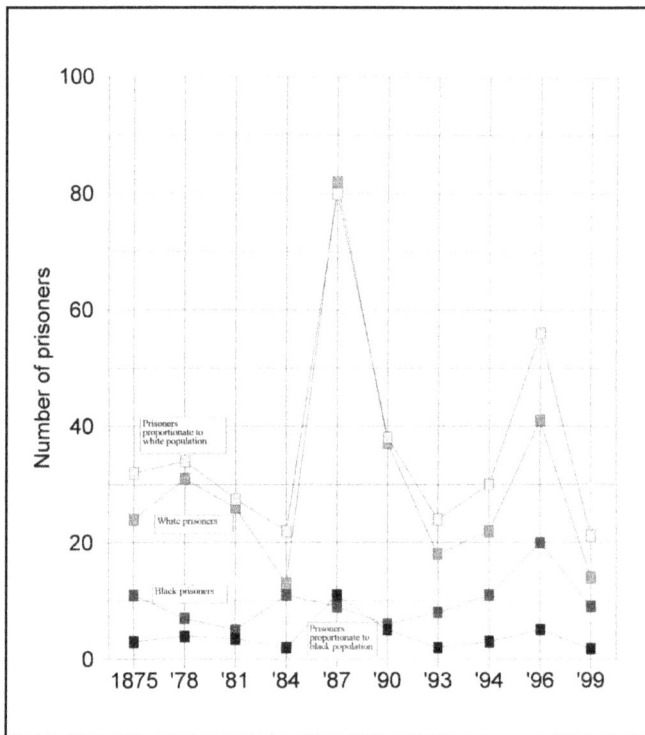

Figure 4.1 Jailings of Blacks and Whites in Fayette County, Ohio, 1875–1899. Source: Fayette County Jail Register, Fayette County Jail, Washington Court House, Ohio

selection, bailiffs called few African Americans for jury duty.[39] African Americans won jobs as police officers in some towns—Crawfordsville, Indiana, and Springfield, Illinois, for example—but across the region they were even scarcer than African American jurors.[40] Furthermore, the region held few African American attorneys. The result was an overwhelmingly white criminal justice system, which applied northern, European American, urban standards of behavior to African American newcomers from largely rural backgrounds. To make matters worse, both antebellum rhetoric emphasizing the degrading effects of slavery and partisan-inspired Democratic racial slanders prepared midwestern whites to perceive African Americans' behavior as characteristically deviant.

In cities African Americans were more likely than European Americans to be arrested for petty crimes: men for "loitering," "disorderly conduct," and "disturbing the peace," and women for prostitution.[41] African Americans held mass meetings to protest police brutality, and sometimes police officers were convicted of criminal charges for such assaults or fined as a result of civil actions.[42] Whites were more often charged with serious crimes than blacks, but African Americans were tried more quickly, convicted more frequently, and received longer sentences for similar offenses.[43] Across Ohio the county jails, which housed those convicted of middle-level offenses as well as offenders who could not afford to pay their fines, consistently held a disproportionate number of African American prisoners over the period from 1872 to 1916.[44]

Washington Court House reflected the general pattern. A sample drawn from the Fayette County jail register during the last quarter of the nineteenth century reveals a pronounced tendency among local police officials to incarcerate African Americans.[45] In figure 4.1, the bottom line indicates the number of arrests of African Americans that would have been proportionate to African American representation in the county population, while the top line shows the same hypothetical number of prisoners for the European American population. The middle two lines reflect the actual numbers of white and black prisoners.

Although the numbers are small, the trends are clear. In all but two of the sampled years (1887 and 1890) African Americans were arrested at a higher rate than their proportion of the population would have predicted. The same pattern appeared in Xenia during 1901–1902.[46] The evidence from these two communities, the only small midwestern towns for which data have been gathered, signify clearly the presence of a perception of excessive African American criminality among local police. Furthermore, while during the 1880s the pattern was mixed, during the 1890s African Americans were consistently overrepresented among Fayette County prisoners, suggesting an intensifying concern with African American criminality.

Of all the issues that embroiled local politics in the Lower Midwest, one stands out, both because of its durability and on account of the intensity of the passions it aroused. That issue was schools. Pressure came from both sides of the color line. African American parents wanted better education for their children, and many of them had pulled up roots in the South and migrated north primarily for that reason.[47] Some European American parents were willing to accept school integration. African American women who grew up in Canton and Cleveland remembered being made to feel no color consciousness—until high school. Then a teacher discouraged career aspirations, and a principal separated a biracial couple on a dance floor.[48] School officials no doubt thought they acted on behalf of color-conscious parents, and it seems that a sufficiently large number of parents to keep local climates highly charged did not want their children attending school with African American children. State laws in Indiana and Illinois provided no resolution, since they left the issue of separate schools to local option. Even in Ohio, where state law after 1887 gave community officials no right to sustain separate schools, the weight of local opinion was sometimes able to prevail in keeping them separate.[49] Given the intensity of parental feeling on the issue, however, and the absence of state machinery beyond the courts capable of enforcing state law, local situations were often unstable. And since town and county officials were the only instruments through which local option could be exercised, the schools issue constantly threatened to infiltrate formal politics. Similarly, political partisanship pervaded decision making regarding schools.[50]

If access to industrial jobs for men, gainful work for women, and home ownership for families made the Lower Midwest a crazy quilt of varying opportunities, schools overlaid on the pattern another layer of complexity. African American children attended the same classes as European American children in some communities in each state, most often in Ohio, least commonly in Indiana.[51] But integration and segregation could coexist, not only within the same local school system, but also within the same school. Within "integrated" schools, African American children were taught in a separate room, known as the "fifth room"; were forced to sit together in the classroom; or were required to use separate drinking cups.[52] Like employment opportunities and residential segregation, the pattern of African American treatment in schools was subject to change. Whether faced with segregated or integrated schools, African American parents demanded better treatment for their children. European American parents pressed back, insisting on further circumscription of African American "privileges." Community leaders considered the condition of their schools an important feature of the face the community presented to the outside world and segregated, desegregated or resegregated them accordingly.

African American parents confronted teachers and administrators singly and collectively to protest discriminatory behavior.[53] In Cairo, before Illinois amended its constitution to allow black children to attend public schools, a group of parents led by an African American teacher, T. J. Shores, marched on one of the schools to demand either access to the white schools or public support for black schools. After separate schools were established in Cairo in accordance with state law, more than 125 African American parents and school children occupied a European American school building to back their demands either to bring the black school closer to white standards or to admit black children to white schools. Their sit-in was successful in that local authorities renovated the existing black elementary school, soon built a second, and then constructed a high school for African American students. The high school became a focus of the African American community and featured the teaching of black history. Among whites, the sit-in created friction that eventually destroyed the Republican coalition, and the daughter of a school board trustee concluded that her black neighbors represented "the most impudent, irrational, unruly race that ever walked the globe."[54]

African Americans also turned to the courts to assert their rights. As historian Morgan Kousser points out, "In an era when black communities were generally small and poor, and before the 1909 founding of the NAACP gave some national co-ordination to the legal struggle for racial equality, blacks were very active in asserting their civil rights through the courts."[55] This was abundantly true of the Lower Midwest, where African Americans launched at least thirty-three cases challenging racial discrimination in schools, two-fifths of all those that Kousser discovered across the United States between 1834 and 1903. The bulk of these appeared during the years between the Civil War and the century's end. Black Ohioans initiated fifteen cases over twenty years beginning in 1871. In Indiana African Americans filed five court challenges before 1884, when an adverse decision closed off all avenues of redress. Six cases were launched in Illinois, capped by the monumental *Bibb* struggle in Alton, which began in 1897 and lasted into the twentieth century. Case titles reflect accurately the local focus of these challenges: *Gibson v. Oxford, Ohio; Jackson v. Felicity, Ohio; Longress v. Quincy, Illinois; McCollum v. Xenia, Ohio; Nelson v. Springfield, Ohio; Peair v. Upper Alton, Illinois; Townsend v. Richmond, Indiana;* and *Taylor v. Centralia, Illinois.*[56]

Black pressure could produce white counterpressure. In the aftermath of passage of Ohio's Arnett Law outlawing separate schools, local school boards "used branch schools, fifth rooms, gerrymandering, organized and unorganized violence, threats, harassment, intimidation, and prolonged legal strategies to keep blacks from integrating Ohio public schools."[57] After the postwar demonstration at a white school in Cairo, school officials revoked T. J. Shores's teaching certificate, and the fury of an aroused European American public opinion drove him from the town.[58] But even when there was no immediate push by African Americans for increased access or better facilities, European American parents exerted pressure of their own. Conflict erupted in Springfield, Ohio, during the early 1880s, involving a demonstration by African American students, a court case (*Gazaway v. White*, 1882), and a referendum.[59] But once the Ohio legislature passed the Arnett Law in 1887, Springfield schools quietly desegregated. Seventeen years later, a white teacher wrote:

> [A]nimosity on the part of the whites toward the colored is strong and growing; and on the part of the colored race there is a growing jealousy of rights, real or supposed. It is manifest everywhere. In the public

schools the separation of colored and white children was abolished twenty [*sic*] years ago; and the plan has been provocative of trouble. Oftentimes white parents refuse to permit their children to sit by the colored in the school room; and, on the other hand, many colored parents are so jealous of their social rights that they object to any approach to a plan of so seating the children in the school room as to bring them in a group by themselves.[60]

When Grace Brewer graduated as the only African American in her class at Vincennes (Indiana) High School, her eight classmates boycotted the occasion.[61] When Charles Bunch at age six began to attend the Washington School in Centralia, Illinois, with five other black pupils, a campaign began to remove them, which was defeated only after African Americans and their European American allies carried the fight to the city council.[62] The longest and most bitter such battle took place in Alton, Illinois, as a result of a decision by city officials to resegregate the schools, which had been integrated for a quarter of a century.[63] Apparently the city fathers hoped to attract more European American migration to the community and felt that all-white schools would serve the purpose. The African American community rallied behind Scott Bibb and his children to fight the case through the courts, a sit-in, and boycott. After an epic struggle that extended over eleven years, seven jury trials, and five state supreme court appeals, and which attracted support for the complainants from across the state, Alton African Americans won their case in the courts. But they lost in Alton, as school officials successfully maintained that the state supreme court judgment applied only to the two Bibb children on whose behalf the case had been brought—who were now too old to attend. Alton schools remained segregated until the 1950s.[64]

Unlike the struggles over schools, in which African Americans usually fought alone against European American officials, labor conflicts forced African Americans to take sides in clashes between two white factions, bosses and workers. The most common such battles took place in coal-mining towns, which were scattered across the southern regions of Ohio and Indiana and the breadth of Illinois. Conflicts raged both in communities that had been created by coal operators to mine newly discovered deposits and in already existing towns. Miners continually attempted to organize, and operators just as often resisted. Mine operators seeking to defeat organizing or striking miners found Emancipation a boon, and soon after the Civil War ended they were recruiting replacements or strikebreakers among the substantial numbers of experienced African American miners in the South. Edna Boysaw, born a slave on a Virginia plantation, told what happened next.

[W]hen Lincoln freed us, we rejoiced, yet we knew we had to seek employment now and make our own way. Wages were low. You worked from morning until night for a dollar, but we did not complain. About 1870 a Mr. Masten, who was a coal operator, came to Richmond [, Virginia] seeking laborers for his mines in Clay County. He told us that men could make four to five dollars a day working in the mines, going to work at seven and quitting at 3:30 each day. That sounded like a Paradise to our men folks. Big money and you could get rich in little time. But he did not tell all, because he wanted the men folk to come with him to Indiana. Three or four hundred came with Mr. Masten. They were brought in box cars. Mr. Masten paid their transportation, but was to keep it out of their wages. My husband was in that bunch, and the women folk stayed behind until their men could earn enough for the transportation to Indiana.

When they arrived about four miles east of Brazil, or what was known as Harmony, the train was stopped and a crowd of white miners ordered them not to come any nearer Brazil. Then the trouble began. Our men did not know of the labor trouble, as they were not told of that part. Here they were fifteen hundred miles from home, no money. It was terrible. Many walked back to Virginia. Some went on foot to Illinois. Mr. Masten took some of them South of Brazil about three miles, where he had a number of company houses, and they tried to work in his mine there. But many were shot at from the bushes and killed. Guards were placed about the mine by the owner, but still there was trouble all the time. The men did not make what Mr. Masten told them they could make, yet they had to stay for they had no place to go.

When her husband was injured in the mine, Edna Boysaw brought her children to Indiana. She supported the family by washing for local families until her husband could return to work, more than a year later. "After the strike was settled," she recalled, "things were better. . . . But the coal operators did not treat the colored folks very good. We had to trade at the Company store and often pay a big price for it." But," she concluded, "we had many white friends and sure was thankful for them."[65]

If the Boysaws' white friends were coal miners, the family's story was probably unusual. The coming of African American strikebreakers or replacements to a coal-mining town was not likely to endear them to European American miners whose jobs were to be given to the newcomers. In many communities, as in Brazil, white miners greeted the arrival of black miners with bullets. Such conflicts punctuated labor history in all three states of the Lower Midwest during the 1870s and 1880s, and continued in Illinois through the 1890s. They created a significant obstacle to attempts by the United Mine Workers of America (UMWA) to construct a powerful and, hence, necessarily interracial, union in the coalfields.[66] In 1895 a well-organized mob of mostly immigrant miners systematically attacked a colony of African American miners and their families in Spring Valley, Illinois, and drove all the residents from their homes. The African Americans had arrived during the previous year to replace striking miners.[67] Bullets also met African American miners at Virden, Illinois, in 1898, and African American strikebreakers fought deadly gun battles with miners at Pana and Carterville in 1899.[68]

In towns and cities with more diversified economies, African American strikebreakers became a target for angry strikers in other industries. African American strikebreakers appeared in metal-trades strikes in Springfield (1886), Fremont (1903), Hanging Rock (1904), and Cleveland, Ohio (1896, 1901). In Chicago they were used to break strikes among longshoremen (1863), meatpackers (1886, 1894, 1904), hotel workers (1887), railroad workers (1894), iron and steelworkers (1898), construction trades (1899, 1900), and teamsters (1905).[69]

The relationship between black and white workers was not always one of competition and conflict. Cooperation sometimes replaced contention.[70] Joint or allied action became most common during the 1880s, in the heyday of the Knights of Labor. Founded in 1869, the Knights' local assemblies spread rapidly across the country during the early years of the 1880s. "The local assembly," stated the model constitution, "is not a mere trade union or beneficial society, it is more and higher. It gathers into one fold all branches of honorable toil, without regard to nationality, sex, creed or color."[71] Sometimes midwestern Knights acted on these principles by organizing integrated local asssemblies. Such an assembly was operating by 1883 in Richmond, Indiana. The European American majority wanted their African American comrades to organize separately, but the latter refused. One refuser was quoted as explaining that "this is the only organization in which we stand on an equal footing with the whites, and it is a big thing." Perhaps the prospect of equality explains why African American membership in the Richmond assembly was growing much faster than the European American.[72] African Americans did organize separate locals in both large and small communities across the Lower Midwest. Chicago had all-black assemblies (of waiters and ham bag sewers), but so did small towns Decatur and Murphysboro. Two African American assemblies operated in Indianapolis, and there was one each in Evansville, Cementville and Terre Haute. African American Knights organized in Cleveland and Columbus, and also in Dayton and Rendville.[73] The Knights declined rapidly after 1886, and the craft unions that outlasted or replaced them were less prone to allow African American membership. Unlike their craft union succes-sors, the Knights were not loath to enter local politics in pursuit of their members' interests.[74] For African American workers, political engagement preceded the Knights' brief but eventful struggle and continued after the organization's decline.

The basic factors shaping local political conflict were the same everywhere throughout the region. African Americans consistently felt grievances stem-ming from discrimination and tried to wield their voting power to obtain satisfaction. Precariously balanced partisan forces produced a Republican need for black votes and a corresponding Democratic need to shake the Republican coalition, either by bidding for black votes or by appealing to racist white Republicans. Gallipolis, Ohio; Evansville, Indiana; and Cairo, Illinois are only three examples of towns in which African American support during the Gilded Age was crucial to Republican control.[75] In this situation, African Americans had three options. First, they could organize within the Republican Party to achieve recognition and redress. This was no doubt the most common course taken.[76] Republican support did pay off in some com-munities. During the late nineteenth century, African Americans elected their own aldermen or city councilors in Oberlin, Urbana, and Xenia, Ohio; and Cairo and Nokomis, Illinois. The large African American voting bloc in Pulaski County, Illinois, regularly elected African Americans as county and city councilmen, city attorney, county coroner, and police magistrate.[77] But even in Chicago, where African Americans made up only 1 percent of the population, enfranchisement quickly produced the city's first African American police officers as well as an all-black fire company.[78] Remaining a nominal or active Republican loyalist seems to have been generally dis-appointing, however, as the GOP rarely rewarded its African American constituents with tangible recognition proportional to their support.[79] The basic reasons why the Republican Party was so stingy when it came to rewarding African American loyalty were, first, that the party could usually depend on African American support and, second, that the Republicans feared leaving themselves vulnerable to the Democrats' race card by making African American appointments. Punishing the Republicans for their stingy patronage was easily achieved when the electorate was as fully mobilized as it typically was during this period, since voters could hurt their party merely by staying home on Election Day. But for African Americans, defeating the Republicans meant placing their fate in the hands of a group of whites who were even less inclined to be sympathetic to their demands, and at the same time infuriating their erstwhile allies, who knew exactly whom to blame for their defeat.

The conditions facing African Americans in local communities across the Midwest varied, of course, both from place to place and over time. At some times and in some places African Americans fought vigorously for their political rights, threatening white Republicans or retaliating for their snubs. Probably most of the time and in most communities African American voters sustained the GOP. When they did so, the label that is often applied to their politics is "accommodationist." The term is useful only if we understand clearly that it refers to a strategy rather than a passive acceptance of marginality. In her study of the African American community in a small town—Geneva, New York—Kathryn Grover explains:

> At different historical moments, Geneva's African Americans con-templated their local situation and took its measure. They continually assessed and reassessed how open or closed local white society was, when it would allow them to take direct political action on their own behalf and when it would not. And when it did not, accommodation became a strategy, not a mindset—a means to an end, not a hapless end in itself. As a racial and statistical minority, for African Americans it was always a question of how much accommodation was necessary in order to live a stable life. At some times, local circumstances and the political climate of the region and country made action to improve the quality and opportunities of life for themselves and their children seem possible. Some sought broader improvement for their neighbors and their race generally. At other times, direct political action seemed only to promise to encumber them further, to heap liability upon funda-mental disadvantage, and accommodation then seemed to be the only logical route to security.[80]

The second option was to abandon the Republican Party for the Democrats, temporarily or permanently. Such a course required considerable personal courage amid the face-to-face relationships of intensely partisan small towns, where political leanings were hard to conceal. Political independence meant either refusing to allow emancipation to guide present choices or revising the Republican version of the history of emancipation, as a black Democrat later described to an interviewer. Attempting to explain why so many blacks voted Republican, William Hubbard said:

> Well, they claim Abraham Lincoln freed them, and Abraham Lincoln didn't free them. They freed theirselves. And one woman told me, said, "Who told you that?" I said, "I can read, Lady." Yeah, I can read. And my mother, she told us that, too, that Abraham Lincoln didn't free the colored people.

Q. What ... how did she explain it, I mean, that they freed themselves?

A. 'Cause they fought, I mean, to get freedom. They fought to get freedom, and they won the battle. If it'd been left to what-you-call-him they wouldn't have won no battle. They'd been still slaves, but they fought to be free.[81]

This avenue led to success on the state level in Ohio in 1883, when the new Democratic governor dispensed more patronage to African Americans than any previous Democratic and most Republican administrations, effectively raising the bar for his Republican successor. In addition, as noted above, the Democratic-controlled legislature enacted a state public-accommodations law.[82] Three years earlier, black voters in Peru, Indiana, had demonstrated the success of swing voting when they helped to elect a Democratic sheriff who far outdid local Republicans in appointing African American deputies and bailiffs and summoning African American jurors.[83] The risks of political independence, however, were clearly shown at the turn of the century in Cairo, Illinois. There, African American voters had sustained Republican hegemony since ratification of the Fifteenth Amendment. After Republicans in 1898 refused to support African American candidates, many black voters cast their ballots for either the Democrats or a local Negro Protective ticket. The Republicans were defeated. When they regained power, Republicans led the campaigns for a new voter registration law that effectively disfranchised many African Americans and a commission form of city government in which at-large voting severely reduced the clout of the remaining African American voters.[84] Whether abandoning the Republicans elected Democrats or not, it had the certain effect—as black Republicans constantly pointed out—of dividing the African American vote and thereby diluting African Americans' already thin influence.[85]

A third option involved declaring independence of both major parties. This course was probably taken even less often than the minority path of voting Democratic. Peter Clark, a longtime Cincinnati activist, in the late 1870s announced his conversion to socialism and advised African Americans to vote for the Ohio Workingman's Party. Shortly afterward, however, Clark returned to the Republican ranks.[86] Third-partyism did achieve one spectacular success on the local level, election of an African American mayor of a northern town. This occurred in 1887 in Rendville, Ohio, a mining community of about 1,000 residents, evenly divided between African Americans and European Americans. J. S. Tuppins was a druggist, born in Xenia, who opened a drug store in Rendville in 1886. More important for his political success, Tuppins helped to organize an African American local of the

Knights of Labor. The next year Tuppins ran as the Union Labor candidate for mayor and was elected.[87] At least one more African American became mayor of Rendville in succeeding years, but by 1891, African Americans had returned to voting Republican.[88] Rendville was clearly a highly politicized community, as it was also the home of Richard L. Davis, the only African American elected to the national executive board of the UMWA in the nineteenth century.[89] But Tuppins's election as a labor candidate had been made possible not only by the organization of local African American voters but also by a unique circumstance, the strength of the Knights of Labor, and after the Knights' rapid decline in the late 1880s that circumstance no longer held.

Formal local politics thus provided African Americans an uncertain path to amelioration of their conditions, but a virtually certain means to annoy or alienate at least one sizable segment of the political community. Democratic anger at African American loyalty to the Republicans appeared in the vehemence of Democratic editors and speakers playing the race card. One particularly caustic practitioner was William C. Gould of Washington Court House, editor during the late 1860s and early 1870s of the local Democratic paper.[90] Democrats also vented their resentment against white Republicans who were, in their view, too friendly to their black allies. George Knox was living in Greenfield, Indiana, during the controversy over African American migration from North Carolina in 1879. He reported that a European American storekeeper who had donated food to migrants arriving in Greenfield found his store burned down.[91] White Republican antagonism manifested itself in the numerous incidents in which African American nominees or candidates were betrayed or scratched from the ticket. In Washington Court House, for example, black and white Republicans put together a biracial slate for local elections in 1872 under the label "Mechanics and Laborers." The African American Masonic leader Alexander Anderson was the only black nominee for a seat on the town council. Anderson lost, however, while most of the rest of his slate swept to victory.[92] Small-town politics in Gilded Age America was a vicious game, to be sure, and African Americans played it as hard as anyone else. African Americans, however, suffered from its treacheries more than other groups because their need for political change was more pressing than the rest. Politics then as always made strange bedfellows, but in the Lower Midwest there was always one political actor with whom few European Americans would freely agree to share a blanket.

At the end of the nineteenth century and during the early years of the twentieth, heightened antagonism between white and black Midwesterners and worsening conditions for African Americans resulted from an interplay between white prejudice and black pressure for change and a similar two-way interaction between national trends and local struggles.[93] As southern white demagogues and northern editors portrayed African Americans as unworthy and disruptive members of the body politic, midwestern whites witnessed at close range in their local communities African Americans' broadly political behavior as strikebreakers, as competitors for office and influence, and as educational warriors. European Americans believed that African Americans should be grateful for past favors, but African Americans who perceived full citizenship as their right and their due saw discrimination in workplaces and schools and government offices as illegitimate restrictions on their freedom. African American struggles for change in a prejudiced white world do not, of course, justify either the European American image of them as a disruptive element or the heightening barriers to black aspirations that flowed from such perceptions. White racism was the cause of both enduring discriminatory practices and the new turn-of-the-century constraints, and European Americans made choices about whom to blame for their troubles. Seeing African Americans as especially disruptive required ignoring or minimizing the divisions and conflict evident among European American capitalists and workers, partisans and factional rivals, and various offenders against assorted local norms. Nor was it the only possible or likely image of blacks. Against it could be set an impression drawn from the quiet, steady work of, for example, many members of the Anderson, Chester, Weaver, and Oatneal families in Washington Court House; the devotion of African American churchgoers; and the associational activity of members of African American voluntary societies. African Americans could equally well be seen as solid contributors to the best aspects of community life. Which image European Americans adopted depended on a choice, for neither was unambiguously true, and each could be accepted only by ignoring some dimensions of African American lives. Hard-working, churchgoing Andersons, Chesters, Weavers, and Oatneals were also political actors. Hard-working, churchgoing Andersons and Chesters were also purveyors of what many whites regarded as vice. White racism is not an historical constant, and has varied in breadth and intensity in response to changing contexts.[94] African American struggles in midwestern localities, while they do not justify its coming, help to explain the gathering storm in the region and the nation.

5

VIOLENCE
Patterns of Attack and Riposte

Rev. Harper preached a sermon on the race war Sunday night.
—Crawfordsville, Indiana, correspondent to the Indianapolis *Recorder,* 1899[1]

There is too much indifference by some of us who are up here in the north, but yet you are not safe up here: if you go too far they would swing you right here in Chicago: they did try to do it some years ago. We are not safe here, although a little more so than our brethren in the southern section of the country.
—Reverdy Ransom, 1896[2]

For so long a time has the black man believed that he is an American citizen that he will not be easily convinced to the contrary. It will take more than the hangings, the burnings and the lynchings, both north and south, to prove it to his satisfaction. He is not so credulous as he was. He is a different man. The American people cannot turn back the tide of years and make him what he was. And so it [is] an entirely new people with whom they have to deal.
—Paul Laurence Dunbar, 1898[3]

Migrants came to the Lower Midwest hoping to find a better life than they left behind in the former slave states. In light of northern whites' sacrifices in the titanic struggle for freedom and the legal and constitutional changes migrants and their European American allies were able to bring about, their hopes seemed at first to be justified. But as the Civil War faded into an increasingly distant past, African Americans came to recognize that state capitals, where the new statutes were hammered out, could not serve as the forge on which European American attitudes were reshaped. Local communities were the true furnaces of racial interaction, and they were as capable of inflaming white prejudices as incinerating them, as efficacious at searing African American aspirations as fueling them.

ATTACK

Studies of racial violence in the United States typically focus upon lynchings. At least part of the reason for this emphasis is that lynching has been thought to be easily defined, as an illegal group action causing the death of a person or persons under the pretext of service to justice or tradition.[4] A recent comprehensive analysis of southern lynching has shown that the number of incidents of whites lynching blacks rose through the 1880s to a peak of nearly one hundred per year in the early 1890s, then declined irregularly over the subsequent third of a century.[5] Nor was the North, including the Lower Midwest, free from vicious mob attacks upon its African American citizens.

How did African American migrants, prospective migrants, and community residents regard racially inspired mob violence? In his autobiographical *Black Boy,* Richard Wright testifies to the chilling effect that news of a lynching could produce:

> What I had heard altered the look of the world, induced in me a temporary paralysis of will and impulse. The penalty of death awaited me if I made a false move and I wondered if it was worth-while to make any move at all. The things that influenced my conduct as a Negro did not have to happen to me directly; I needed but to hear of them to feel their full effects in the deepest layers of my consciousness.[6]

Similarly, Luther Wheeler, born in Cairo, Illinois, in 1914, recalled knowing the precise spot where a lynching had taken place five years before his birth.[7] But a focus on lynching deaths defines too narrowly the threat of white violence to African Americans. For a migrant deciding whether and where to settle or resettle in the Lower Midwest, other forms of antiblack violence could produce an impact similar to that of a completed lynching. For example, a mob attack that failed to kill its victim because of forces beyond the mob's control could signal local white attitudes just as clearly. The scope of an inquiry into European American violence should be broadened beyond lynching for another reason, too. An analysis of lynching that restricts itself to completed lynchings can leave an impression of African Americans only as victims. When prevented lynchings are included in the analysis, however, in particular those averted by African American action, a more rounded picture, one that is capable of incorporating African American agency, comes into view.[8]

Antiblack collective violence in the Lower Midwest included twenty completed lynchings and at least six attempted lynchings, five nonfatal mob attacks, four fatal mob attacks, and five full-scale riots in which mobs took over a large portion of a city and were dispersed only by a significant military force (table A.4).[9] At least one riot occurred in each of the three states:

Akron, Ohio (1900); Evansville, Indiana (1903); Springfield, Ohio (1904 and 1906); and Springfield, Illinois (1908). Chicago experienced recurrent strike-related violence, but in none of the region's other cities that reached 100,000 population by 1910—Cincinnati, Columbus, Cleveland, Dayton, Toledo, and Indianapolis—were any violent incidents reported. Some attacks took place in rural areas, but small towns and small cities were the most common sites of antiblack collective violence.

Historian Fitzhugh Brundage, in an exhaustive study of lynchings in Georgia and Virginia, uses a taxonomy incorporating four types of mob violence to illustrate the complex of actions and motives involved in lynchings. Small mobs of less than fifty participants were either terrorist mobs, which "made no pretense of upholding the law," or private mobs, which "exacted vengeance for a wide variety of alleged offenses." Posses, which could range widely in size, became mobs when they "overstepped their quasi-legal function." Mass mobs, Brundage's fourth category, numbered more than fifty and "punished alleged criminals with extraordinary ferocity and, on occasion, great ceremony."[10] Mass mobs clearly reflected community values in their bloody work, as they operated openly, making no attempt to conceal participants' identity. Posses less clearly represented the will of their communities, and private and terrorist mobs, whose members often masked themselves or operated under cover of darkness, seem not to have considered themselves as unambiguous instruments of community wishes. Georgia represents a Deep South pattern, in which all four types of mobs were active. In Virginia few terrorist mobs or posses appeared, and mob violence was carried out primarily by private and mass mobs. But Virginia was not representative of the border states, for terrorist mobs were more common in Kentucky and Missouri than in the Old Dominion. Most southern lynchings involved whites killing blacks; some were white-on-white murders, and a few were black-on-black, but almost never did blacks participate in lynching whites.[11]

Antiblack violence in the Lower Midwest fits the border state pattern, in which private, terrorist, and mass mobs predominated, whether the attack culminated in a lynching or not. Only one posse-type mob appeared, in the murder of Eli Ladd in Blountsville, Indiana, in February 1890. But at the root of this deadly conflict lay a private feud between Ladd and a friend of the justice of the peace who deputized and led the posse that killed Ladd. Ladd's killing illustrates the difficulty in applying categories to acts of violence, but it also demonstrates the variety of forms that Brundage's categories are designed to convey.[12]

Terrorist violence in the Lower Midwest sometimes occurred for explicitly political reasons. The intertwining of race, politics, and violence is clearly evident in an incident that occurred in the Clinton County, Ohio, hamlet of Sabina during the spring of 1889. Local Republicans were divided by the contest for the party's nomination for state representative. George Slater, an African American, was an active and prominent supporter of one of the candidates, Dr. M. Wilkerson. One night, a group of masked men seized Slater, bound him and hanged him from a tree outside Wilkerson's office. Wilkerson awoke and came to Slater's rescue before he strangled. The mob dispersed when Wilkerson emerged. The masked men were unwilling to attack a prominent European American professional, but they had no scruples about lynching his vocal African American supporter, an act that was clearly intended to intimidate Slater's friends and Wilkerson's backers among the African American community.[13]

Terrorist mobs usually appeared in the Lower Midwest during conflicts between strikers and strikebreakers. One of the best-known examples is the mob of largely immigrant coal miners who attacked a settlement of African American miners and their families at Spring Valley, Illinois, on August 4, 1895. Spring Valley, a company town owned by the Chicago and Northwestern Railroad, had been the scene of struggles between miners and owners since 1889. In that year the owners had locked out the miners, eventually replacing them with Italian, Belgian, French, German, Polish, and other European workers. The new workers went out in 1894 as part of a national coal strike led by the United Mine Workers, but they were defeated. The mine owners now brought in African American miners. The violence in 1895 was provoked by an assault and robbery against an Italian worker. City police arrested five African American suspects. When a mob began to march on the jail, the suspects were freed. But the police then searched the settlement, "the Location," where the African American miners lived, and confiscated weapons. The mob marched on the Location headed by a brass band, stopping on the way to demand of the mine manager that he discharge all the company's black workers. He refused, and the mob then attacked the settlement, driving men, women, and children out of their homes and assaulting them as they fled. The Italian mayor of the town did his best to prevent county officials from interfering with the onslaught. Fortunately, no one was killed. The refugees regrouped in a nearby town, and during the next few days they attempted to gather their belongings from the wrecked settlement. Through the use of terror the mob had tried to achieve a political goal, driving rival workers from their jobs. But the victims' effective regroupment gave the first indication that the mob's goal was not to be achieved.[14]

African American communities across Illinois rallied to the support of the Spring Valley victims. From Peoria, Galesburg, Evanston, Elgin, East St. Louis, Rockford, Moline, and Chicago came resolutions of indignation, angry telegrams to the governor, and offers of material support for the refugees. "Black outrage," concludes historian Caroline Waldron, "forced the state to act." Governor John Peter Altgeld, initially reluctant to jeopardize his support among immigrants and workers, launched an inquiry and offered the use of state troops to county officials. Furthermore, the quick and furious response of the state's African Americans "undermined Spring Valley officials' tacit approval of the violence."[15] Facing the threat of state intervention, town officials were forced to protect black miners as they returned to work several days after the riot. A few days later, two women and a man who had been driven from the Location, accompanied by an African American legislator from Chicago and backed by a legal fund contributed by Chicago's African American community, pressed charges against their attackers. As miners emerged from the mine the next day, ten victims waited with the sheriff to identify rioters. Two dozen were arrested. Eight were convicted of riot and criminal assault and sent to the state penitentiary or reformatory.[16]

Waldron argues that the frustration of the rioters' goal resulted from native whites' prejudice against the unassimilated immigrant miners, and she shows that this outcome was possible because of African Americans' rapid mobilization and effective deployment of the language of citizenship. "Many times," stated the Afro-American League of Illinois, "Afro-American citizens who were bred and born in this country, and who are in every sentiment and action, thoroughly American, are denied the opportunity of earning daily bread while imported aliens are indiscriminately employed in their stead."[17] The African American press played a major role both in linking local communities together and in shaping black protest. Through these means African Americans overcame their initial handicap, the unwillingness of both local and state authorities to assist their cause, and succeeded in negating a well-organized terrorist campaign.[18]

A terrorist purpose sometimes inhered in violence that was initiated and directed for private ends. This was the case in the lynching of Roscoe Parker in West Union, a tiny hamlet in Adams County in southern Ohio, in January 1894. Parker was suspected of the murder of an elderly farm couple. He was taken from jail, over opposition by the sheriff and his deputy, and lynched by a mob that included neighbors of the murdered couple. The lynching took place at a preselected site beside a path leading to an African American rural settlement, where he was hanged and shot. The mob was reported as hanging Parker at that particular spot "to teach the blacks a lesson."[19] Although no one was indicted for Parker's murder, his lynching did have other results. It spurred Harry Smith, editor of the *Cleveland Gazette* and newly elected to the Ohio legislature, to propose an antilynching bill drafted with the help of white civil rights advocate Albion Tourgee. Smith's bill passed two years later. It was the most comprehensive legal attack on lynching ever enacted and eventually served as a model for laws in other states and in the NAACP's campaign for federal legislation.[20]

A terrorist element was largely lacking, however, in the only case of a possible black-on-black lynching in the Lower Midwest during this period. The victim was Peter Betters, a livery stable worker in his late thirties who was believed to have assaulted a sixty-five-year-old African American widow, Martha Wallace Thomas. Betters had previously boarded at Thomas's home in Jamestown, a village near Xenia, Ohio. Betters was jailed, but a small lynch mob of between seven and ten masked persons, said to have been composed of either all African Americans or both African Americans and European Americans, quietly gained entry to the jail through a window about midnight. The lynchers pried open Betters's cell with a crowbar, threatened to shoot him if he gave an alarm, then marched him down the street to the fairground, where he was hanged. Martha Thomas belonged to a well-known local family. Her mother was still living in Xenia, as were her two brothers, and her son worked in nearby Springfield. This was clearly a private lynching carried out to wreak vengeance for a wrong done to a member of an established local African American network. Even so, the choice of such a public site as the fairground suggests that the lynchers intended Betters's fate to serve as a warning to other potential assailants of women.[21]

The lynchers of Peter Betters almost certainly included African Americans, if they did not make up the entire mob. There is no record of a mob composed entirely of whites organizing to avenge an assault against a black person. This and other examples indicate that African Americans were not immune from acting in a violent and illegal manner when they felt justified in doing so. Between 1882 and 1930, 148 African Americans were lynched in the South by mobs that were partially or entirely African American.[22] Such incidents occurred from time to time in the Midwest as well. In 1892 an alleged murderer was lynched in Kansas.[23] A Chicago mob was only prevented by the police from lynching a black informer who had turned in a respected local citizen who had escaped from a Tennessee penitentiary.[24] Some citizens of the black town of Brooklyn, Illinois, were reported in 1903 as attempting to lynch an alleged assailant against an African American woman.[25] Such incidents kindled debate among African Americans. Participants in these debates avoided the gender issues involved when men lynched other men, supposedly in defense of women, and the legitimacy of violence was not at issue either. Such questions did not figure in European American dialogue over lynching—everyone assumed that violence could be justified in certain cases, and no one questioned men's right to act violently—and their absence from both discourses testifies to shared cultural assumptions. Instead, discussions among African Americans turned on matters of race and legality. When they noticed such incidents, northern black newspaper editors sometimes censured African American participation in lynch mobs, pointing out that African Americans could hardly blame European Americans if they engaged in lynching themselves.[26] A report from the grassroots at one site of a black-on-black lynching took a different tack. "Many of the colored people of this place," the correspondent reported from Pine Bluff, Arkansas, "are in favor of heavy punishment being meted out to the guilty parties, while others think it a poor rule that will not work both ways. The whites are not punished for lynching and the colored people had as well go free for the same crime."[27]

According to the NAACP's compilation of newspaper reports, slightly more African Americans (twenty-nine) than European Americans (twenty-six) were lynched in Ohio, Indiana, and Illinois between 1889 and 1918.[28] Yet African Americans never comprised more than 3 percent of the population in any of these states during that period. And the judicial outcome in Spring Valley was infrequently repeated; even when their identities were well known, lynchers were rarely prosecuted and even more rarely convicted. African American participation in lynching indicates that mob violence perpetrated against African Americans did not always function as a means of racial repression, but it should not obscure the fact that mob violence usually was intended to achieve that end.

The ferocity of a European American mob after African American victims and white communities' sanction for that frenzy appeared clearly in a triple lynching in southern Indiana in 1900. The first two lynchings took place in Rockport, a small Ohio River town in Spencer County, upstream from Evansville. In 1900 Rockport's African American population of 564 represented 20 percent of the town's total. On Sunday, December 16, the town was aroused by news of discovery of the body of a young white barber, Hollie Simons. Police suspected two local African Americans, Bud Roland and Jim Henderson. Roland had once worked in Simons's shop as a bootblack, but had been discharged. Roland and Henderson had been seen together near where Simons was attacked, so they were arrested. The decision to arrest Roland and Henderson was taken at a mass meeting, at which, according to the local newspaper, "citizens pledged themselves to stand between the officers and danger of prosecution should any objection be made to searching houses without the legal formality of a writ from the court."[29] A mob gathered around the jail and, when the sheriff attempted to move the prisoners, armed men prevented it. Only the year before, provoked by a wave of lynchings of European Americans, Indiana had passed a law requiring a sheriff to request militia assistance if he had cause to believe that a lynching was afoot and providing for removal from office as a penalty.

The sheriff, however, made no appeal to the governor for military assistance despite the ring of armed men surrounding the jail. At 7:30 P.M. a prearranged signal launched an assault on the jail. The sheriff did not resist the mob, but he refused to relinquish the keys, so a telephone pole was used as a battering ram to open a hole in the wall. Roland was taken out first. With a noose around his neck, he confessed, implicated Henderson and, to everyone's surprise, related that a third African American man, Joe Rolla, was involved. The mob hanged Roland, followed by Henderson, and then headed for the hotel where Rolla worked as a porter. They were met by the hotel staff, who had hidden Rolla upstairs, and who provided an alibi for their colleague.

By Monday morning, Rolla had been arrested, and about 11 A.M. he was taken to Boonville, in neighboring Warrick County. The two county sheriffs, sensing that another mob attack was in the offing, tried to drive the prisoner to Evansville. They were prevented from carrying out their plan, however, by a crowd of Boonville citizens, who insisted that Rolla remain. In midafternoon a mob, evidently made up of Rockportians, marched on the Boonville jail equipped with ropes, crowbars, and a telephone pole. The mob numbered between fifty and seventy-five men, and their progress was watched by "the whole of Boonville and hundreds of Warrick Countians and people from Spencer county."[30] Protesting his innocence, Rolla was taken from the jail and hanged. By this time the governor had ordered troops to Boonville, but Rolla was dead before they left Evansville.

In Rockport and Boonville mob law prevailed, as it did in the South. Bud Roland had no opportunity to defend himself, and his confession was forced, to put it mildly. The mob regarded Roland as debased enough to commit a premeditated brutal murder, yet they killed Henderson solely on his word, and then traveled fifteen miles to lynch Rolla on the same flimsy grounds. The sheriffs of two counties ignored Indiana's newly minted antilynching law and made no serious effort to defend their prisoners.[31] Nor did any European American in the two counties except Rolla's fellow hotel workers attempt to interfere with the mobs' work. In Brundage's taxonomy, these were both mass mobs, operating with the full sanction of the white communities. The crowd of thousands cheered Rolla's murder. The mobs did their work unmasked, yet no charges seem to have been lodged against any participant. A local marshal was quoted as saying that black residents had become "overbearing and lawless," and white citizens were said to have approved the mob killings as a warning to their African American neighbors.[32]

The damage done by the Rockport and Boonville lynchers did not end with the deaths of Roland, Henderson, and Rolla. Instead, the triple lynching inspired civic authorities in other counties in southern Indiana to take action against undesirable elements, who were invariably perceived as African American. Vigilance committees were reported to have formed in Grand View, Enterprise, Tell City, and Leavenworth to drive out "the worst element of negroes." In Evansville, local officials instructed the police to arrest all "strange negroes." If they could not satisfactorily explain their presence in the city, they were to be sentenced to imprisonment at hard labor. The purge was justified by the claim that the city held 2,000 African Americans who refused to work, spent their time in saloons, and sold their vote at election time.[33] The tensions on both sides of the color line generated by such actions contributed to the outbreak of Evansville's bloody race riot two years later.

The role of local white elites in antiblack violence comes into focus in the story of the foiled lynching in Washington Court House in 1894. The immediate sequence of events that produced the tragedy that unfolded there began with a report on October 9 by a fifty-one-year-old European American widow, Mary Parrett Boyd, that she had been raped in her rural home by an African American. Official suspicion turned to William Jasper Dolby, twenty, who lived with his grandmother in the nearby village of Jeffersonville. Dolby had been arrested during the previous summer for disorderly conduct, evidently as a result of an approach made to another European American woman, and had recently completed his sentence in the county jail.[34] A description was circulated, and Dolby was apprehended near Columbus and returned to Washington Court House early on the morning of Tuesday, October 16. In midafternoon of the same day, Boyd came to the jail and, without a police lineup, identified Dolby as her assailant. By that evening, a large crowd had gathered around the jail with the evident intention of lynching Dolby. After darkness fell, Sheriff James F. Cook, a Republican Civil War veteran and longtime county sheriff, asked for military support, and the local militia unit, Company E of the 14th Regiment, Ohio National Guard, mobilized twenty-six men. Their commander ordered the crowd to disperse, and local officials three times declared the crowd to be a riotous assembly, but the mob only increased in size, so Cook telegraphed Governor William McKinley to request more troops. Before dawn on Wednesday, October 17, Companies B and C of the same regiment arrived on a train from Columbus under the regimental commander, Colonel A. B. Coit.[35]

Attention now focused on the county jail and courthouse, the two buildings that occupied the courthouse square in the center of town. The jail, a single-story brick structure, occupied the northwest side of the square, its main door about 70 feet (21 meters) from the nearest entrance to the courthouse. Constructed only ten years before, the square sandstone courthouse stood three stories high, topped by a tower and cupola. Although there were

Figure 5.1 Ohio National Guardsmen form a gauntlet to convey William Dolby from the jail (left) to the courthouse door (center). Photo credit: Ohio Historical Society

entryways on the ground floor, the principal entrances, decorated with tall double oak doors, stood at the top of flights of stone steps and opened into the second story. Officials decided to hold Dolby's trial on Wednesday afternoon in the courtroom on the third floor. A grand jury was hastily empanelled and returned an indictment without the presence of either Mrs. Boyd or William Dolby. The problem now was to bring Dolby from the jail across those seventy feet to the courthouse through a crowd numbering somewhere between 300 and 2,500.

Curious bystanders no doubt made up part of the crowd. Its most active members, in contrast, had a powerful motive to destroy the accused rapist and in addition were accustomed to getting their way. Mary Boyd, as well as being highly regarded personally, was well connected in Fayette County society. She belonged to a family of prosperous farmers, although she herself was not well off, having been widowed during the Civil War decade. Her brother had served as a county commissioner, her son Elmer was an attorney, and one brother-in-law was a wealthy lumber merchant in Washington Court House. Also present, pacing back and forth before the courthouse and announcing to all and sundry what he intended to do with the revolver he carried, was another brother-in-law, Henry Kirk, also a wealthy farmer. During the afternoon, Sheriff Cook later testified, he was approached by "some of the oldest and best men in the county," who inquired "what sort of resistance I would offer if a party would come to take the man from jail." Cook replied that he would protect the prisoner "to the utmost and at all hazards," even if it meant endangering himself.[36] Colonel Coit reported a similar meeting, with the same result.[37] The local Republican newspaper had already added its armload of fuel to the flames by announcing the rape in banner headlines: "SHOULD BE HUNG—MRS. KATE BOYD, AN ESTIMABLE WIDOW LADY—OF PARROTS STATION OUTRAGED BY A YOUNG COLORED FIEND."[38]

Coit tried to solve the problem of moving Dolby to the courthouse by creating a gauntlet formed by a double line of soldiers between the jail door and the courthouse, bayonets pointing outward (figure 5.1). The tactic very nearly failed, as the mob rushed forward when the deputies brought Dolby out of the jail, pushing the soldiers backward. Dolby and an accompanying deputy fell down, and Henry Kirk and other members of the mob seized the prisoner. Several militia officers fought back the would-be lynchers with pistols and sword butts and fists, aided by the bayonets and rifle butts of the troops, until Dolby could be rushed into the courthouse. Henry Kirk's nose was broken by a blow from a rifle butt. The waiting judge, Horatio B. Maynard, conducted a three-minute trial in which William Dolby pleaded guilty to the charge of rape and was sentenced to twenty years at hard labor

Photo credit: Jack Blacker

Figure 5.2 The bullet holes in the courthouse doors.

in the state penitentiary, including an annual ten days in solitary confinement, the maximum legal penalty. Coit rushed downstairs to announce the outcome to the outraged mob in the hope of satisfying their demands. When angry shouts and curses and a volley of rocks met his announcement, he ordered the troops to load their weapons and proclaimed that further attacks would draw fire. Nevertheless, Coit and Cook abandoned their initial plan to convey Dolby to the penitentiary at Columbus on a late-afternoon train, deciding instead to hold out in the courthouse until the arrival of reinforcements.

The troops withdrew inside the courthouse, closing and barricading all the doors but those at the northwest entrance. In early evening, a fire was set at a stable near the courthouse, where the sheriff's horses were stabled, in an attempt to draw the troops out, but Coit and Cook refused to be distracted. Shortly afterward, a group of men and boys began battering at the closed southeast doors with a 20-foot (6.1 meter), 260-pound (118 kilogram) oak timber. When the doors gave way, the guardsmen fired into the besiegers, the mob behind them, and the curious crowd that filled the square (figure 5.2). One teenage boy was killed instantly, four young men were fatally wounded, and more than a dozen other citizens were injured. The guardsmen's volleys broke the spirit of the mob. When reinforcements arrived, Coit marched Dolby to the train behind a wall of troops and conveyed him directly to the penitentiary.

In the riot's aftermath, citizens of Washington Court House clamored for legal retribution against Coit. They found themselves isolated, however, as newspapers across the state denounced the resort to mob law and defended the decision to fire. The local coroner, who was related to both the Boyd family and one of the victims of the shooting, produced a report blaming Coit for the deaths, and the colonel was indicted on three counts of manslaughter. Meanwhile, Coit requested a military court of inquiry, which cleared him of wrongdoing after a ten-day hearing that questioned 167 witnesses. A lengthy trial on the first manslaughter charge resulted in acquittal, after which the state legislature forced the remaining charges to be dropped and reimbursed Coit for his legal expenses. The entire process was extremely frustrating, humiliating, and painful to the local leadership in Washington Court House, especially the legislature's decision to pay Coit's legal bills.[39]

The discomfiture of the local elite was entirely warranted, because participation by some of their members ignited the mob attacks. Fayette County had been the scene of rapes and attempted rapes before October 1894 by both black and white men, yet never before had the crime provoked mob violence.[40] That a lynch mob formed after William Dolby was apprehended seems to have been due primarily to the leadership and example provided by the men of Mary Boyd's prominent family, who sought to turn a private grievance into a public injury, and to punish that injury in the most public possible way. In their plaintive and fulsome protests against the condemnation rained upon their community and the official backing given to Coit, local leaders conveniently ignored the role played by Boyd's family during the afternoon assault. They focused instead upon the small number and rowdy behavior of the rioters who were involved in the evening attack on the southeast doors. Yet the evening's attackers were doing no more than following the example of the consequential and wealthy men who had taken the lead a few hours earlier in attempting to lynch William Dolby. Although members of the local elite may not have been involved in the fatal action, they set in motion the process that led to that end.

Local elites in Washington Court House, however, were not united on the issues at stake. After Dolby's sentencing and before the evening attack, the Presbyterian minister and Elmer Boyd both addressed the mob, beseeching them to disperse. So did Mills Gardner, a leading attorney, former state legislator, Republican presidential elector, and longtime supporter of the local African American community. The county turned on Sheriff Cook, who was trounced in the next election, and on Judge Maynard, who barely won reelection while the rest of the Republican ticket sailed to victory. Harry Daugherty (a local lawyer who was later to become Warren Harding's presidential campaign manager and U.S. attorney general) defended Coit against the manslaughter charge, arousing the bitter opposition of his neighbors. Indeed, two years later Daugherty waged a rugged battle to control the delegation from the congressional district to the Republican national convention on behalf of William McKinley's presidential aspirations, as many Fayette County Republicans still harbored resentment toward the governor who had not only sent the troops but also endorsed the court of inquiry's acquittal of Coit from responsibility for the deaths.[41]

The African American community of Washington Court House, too, may have been divided in its understanding of the meaning of the events of October 16 and 17, 1894. Was the lynch mob a response to a singular act and an attack upon a specific individual, or did it carry implications for all those of dark skin and African descent? Among the wounded from the guardsmen's fusillade was African American Frank Jackson McBride, who was shot in the foot. Possibly a bystander, perhaps an onlooker as firemen doused the stable fire, McBride may have demonstrated by his presence that he did not regard this public area as an unsafe place for him at a time when a white mob was trying to batter down the courthouse doors and lynch another African American man. Or he may have recognized the rioters as a threat and was trying to show that he was not intimidated. The Washington Court House correspondent of the *Cleveland Gazette* completely ignored the violence, as if it had no relevance to the African American world.[42] (In another column, Harry Smith was editorializing on the events in Washington Court House and the official response.)[43] Eugene Chester remained in his hometown throughout the period encompassing the attempted lynching, and John Oatneal decided to settle in Washington Court House in its immediate aftermath.

Many others, however, chose differently. Migrants had been attracted to Washington Court House over the years since the outbreak of the Civil War, but the African American population ceased to grow during the 1890s. Possibly the town became an unattractive place for African Americans for the same reasons that the European American population stabilized, a casualty of the hard times of a depression decade. Or perhaps the severely constricted opportunities for good jobs for black men and women painted the town a less appealing hue in African American eyes, counteracting the beckoning odds of gaining home ownership there. Indeed, during the 1880s the town's African American population, while still growing through inmigration, had expanded more slowly than its European American population. Perhaps the message of persistent official prosecution of African Americans now combined with recognition that the only lynch mob in the town's history had formed to kill an African American—and not a transient African American, but a county resident. Meanwhile, equally serious crimes received routine treatment. There is no evidence that the 1894 mob represented a backlash against African American gains in wealth, status, or influence. Instead, the mob violence appears to have been cut from the same cloth as the day-to-day discrimination African American citizens faced in the job market, but shaped into its peculiar pattern by elite leadership. If a shared motive drove whites and blacks equally from Washington Court House during the 1890s, that stimulus no longer operated after 1900, when the European American population resumed its growth. That African American numbers shrank while white numbers expanded after 1900 indicates that forces operating only or primarily upon blacks were responsible for the exodus. Mob violence was only one of those forces.

Because of foresight on the part of local officials and fortuitous circumstances, the Akron riot in August 1900, like the mob action in Washington Court House, did not include wholesale attacks upon members of the city's small African American population. But it certainly was racially inspired.[44] Its catalyst was the arrest of Louis Peck, an African American local resident, for the attempted rape of a six-year-old European American girl. Peck confessed and pleaded guilty. Anticipating a lynching attempt, Akron police took Peck to Cleveland, bringing along another African American prisoner, as the police expected that "the mob would probably not discriminate in selecting a colored man on whom to wreak their vengeance."[45] A mob gathered before the city hall, which contained the jail, and authorities allowed several impromptu committees drawn from the crowd to search the building. Despite the committees' assurances that Peck was not inside, the mob refused to believe them and attacked the building. Police defended it by firing into the crowd, wounding some rioters and killing two children among the bystanders. The rioters obtained guns from a nearby hardware store and fired a barrage at the building. They then blasted the building with dynamite and set fire to it. Some members of the mob tried to turn its fury toward African Americans, but few were to be seen on the streets. When firemen came to fight the fire in the city hall and an adjoining building, the rioters fired on them to prevent them from succeeding. By the time Ohio National Guard troops arrived (leaving behind their African American cooks), the city hall was gutted by the fire. Local newspapers claimed that the rioters were mostly teenaged boys, but when twenty-one rioters were eventually arrested and charged, the eighteen whose ages were reported averaged thirty-five years. The riot left two dead and at least twenty-five wounded or injured, including three police officers and six firefighters.[46] Although no African Americans suffered from the mob, African Americans could plainly see that a mob that dynamited and burned its own city hall in an attempt to kill a black prisoner, fighting white police and firemen in the process, would not have dealt lightly with any African American who was believed to have transgressed social norms—or perhaps any African American it might have encountered.

The Evansville riot three years later followed Akron's basic pattern, but with a significant twist. Street violence against individual blacks fired African American militancy, which in turn provoked an escalation of European American destructiveness. The result was a longer list of casualties than in Akron.

On July 3, 1903, a gun battle on an Evansville street left a longtime member of the police force, Louis Massey, dead, and his opponent, African American John Tinsley, aka Robert Lee, wounded. Tinsley was thirty-five years old, married, and employed on a street crew. Massey was not the first law officer he had shot; Tinsley had served five and one-half years in prison for shooting a deputy sheriff in Rockport in 1895. He had come to Evansville after being driven from Rockport two years earlier in the racial purge that followed the lynchings of Roland, Henderson, and Rolla.[47] Tinsley was arrested the next day and imprisoned in the city jail. Early in the morning of July 5, a mob made two attempts to break into the jail to lynch Tinsley, but the building's stout doors defeated them. Nevertheless, city officials, fearing further mob action, took Tinsley to Vincennes. No troops were sought, however; despite Akron's example, local authorities no doubt believed that the threat of mob violence would be dissipated by removal of its target. During the afternoon, gangs of whites roamed the streets beating up blacks, and African American families began leaving town. A larger, armed mob attacked the jail that evening, believing that Tinsley was still inside. They were finally persuaded to leave by a committee that conducted a thorough search for Tinsley, when a rumor spread that armed African Americans had shot a European American man. No evidence was ever produced that the man was shot, but an armed detachment of about twenty-five African American men was indeed patrolling the streets. They exchanged fire with the mob before retreating. But before that exchange the rumor of armed blacks was enough to set off the cry, "Let's kill every nigger in town," and the mob turned to Baptisttown, the principal African American neighborhood. Mob attacks on African American property were both random—they marched through Baptisttown firing right and left—and deliberate and selective. They attacked three saloons, which represented the most visible of the few African American businesses. The mob also chose to terrorize the residents of an integrated tenement building, attacked a barber shop, and wrecked a black-owned hotel—after thoughtfully clearing it of whites and crippled persons. Both blacks and whites pillaged hardware stores of their guns, and groups of both roamed the streets, trading shots.

Indiana National Guard troops were mobilized on July 6 to guard the jail, and this set the stage for the last act of the riot. Acting on a rumor that African Americans were sheltered in the jail building and aware that more troops were to arrive soon, the mob gathered again during the evening. The front ranks pressed the line of soldiers and deputies back to the jail walls, and then someone fired a shot. Believing themselves under fire, guardsmen and deputies outside the jail and deputies at the windows poured a devastating fire into the mob. This action finally broke the back of the riot, after nearly forty-eight hours. By the next morning, Evansville was occupied by more than a thousand troops and under martial law. Twelve European Americans had died, and more than thirty others were wounded or injured. African American casualties were not reported. A grand jury laid indictments for rioting or riotous conspiracy against sixty-four men, among whom African Americans were seriously overrepresented (31 percent of those traced in local records). Nine European Americans and four African Americans were convicted; the four blacks served prison terms, but only one white did. The grand jury, backed by local African American ministers, recommended revoking the licenses of African American saloon keepers; in the only policy change flowing from the riot, the Evansville city council hiked saloon license fees generally.[48]

For Evansville's African Americans, the message of the riot was unmistakable. All African Americans were to be punished for the sins of one. The fruits of African American enterprise were to be destroyed, and breaches of the color line were to be closed. Resistance to attack was to be met by increased violence. If anyone failed to understand, the meaning was underlined throughout the rest of the summer by harassment of African Americans and vandalism of black property.[49] No such reminders were necessary, however, as Evansville swiftly shifted in African American eyes from magnet to way station en route to other northern destinations. The African American population declined by one-sixth by 1910, while the

Table 5.1 Percentage African American in Violent Towns

	Towns where violence was reported 1885–1910	Towns where violence was not reported 1885–1910
Mean Percentage African American, 1890		
Ohio	8.0* (5)	3.9* (95)
Indiana	4.8 (6)	3.2 (54)
Illinois	6.4* (8)	2.7* (68)
Mean Percentage African American, 1900		
Ohio	7.5 (5)	3.2 (120)
Indiana	6.2* (9)	2.6* (71)
Illinois	7.3 (8)	3.0 (105)

( ) Number of towns
* Significant at the .05 level
Sources: Table A.4; U.S. census reports, 1890, 1900.

city's European American population continued to grow. African American numbers did not regain their 1900 level for half a century.

Relying on simple tallies of incidents, historians of antiblack violence emphasize differences between the North and the South, where most incidents occurred.[50] In addition to absolute numbers, antiblack violence in the Lower Midwest diverged from southern patterns in three ways. While southern lynchings peaked during the summer months, in the Lower Midwest both lynchings and antiblack violence in general surged in *both* winter and summer (table A.4).[51] Possibly this was because many racial conflicts in the South were sparked by disputes over agricultural work, while most violence in the Lower Midwest took place in towns and cities.[52] Second, a special kind of southern occasion, the "spectacle lynching," was absent from Ohio, Indiana, and Illinois. Spectacle lynchings were "blatantly public, actively promoted" affairs, including "the specially chartered excursion train, the publicly sold photograph, and the widely circulated, unabashed retelling of the event by one of the lynchers."[53] Such affairs evidently constituted too blatant an exhibition of disregard for law for northern state authorities to tolerate. Third, while the number of southern lynchings declined after the early 1890s, there was no letup in the pace of antiblack violence in the Lower Midwest, as the number of incidents during the twentieth century's first decade equaled those of the nineteenth century's last.

Similarities, however, deserve greater emphasis than divergences in regional experience. First, nearly every form of antiblack violence that

121

appeared in the South—indeed, in the Deep South—also broke out in the Lower Midwest: private, posse, terrorist and mass lynch mobs, as well as full-scale race riots. In addition, violence against African Americans was most likely in communities with relatively large African American populations. Although not all differences are statistically significant, the pattern is consistent across all three states (table 5.1).

In the South, the incidence of lynchings increased from county to county along with the proportion of population that was African American, but only up to a point. Southern black-majority counties (54 percent and over) showed the opposite pattern, as the number of lynchings declined as the proportion of African American rose. This relationship is consistent with a view of lynching as a white response to "threats of black competition for greater access to economic, political, or status resources."[54] In the Lower Midwest, no town except Brooklyn contained an African American majority. In nearly all midwestern urban communities African American numbers were so small, and racial prejudice so pervasive, that the possibility of effective economic competition between blacks and whites seems remote. To be sure, African Americans did make progress in wealth and home ownership, albeit slowly. But while such forms of self-improvement may have diluted stereotypes of inferiority, they hardly threatened the dominant position of whites as a group. The readiness of African American workers to break strikes certainly made them unwelcome in many communities, especially coal-mining towns, but the access to jobs thus gained was often temporary and fell far short of constituting a level playing field for job competition.

African American numbers, however, could support other kinds of behaviors capable of forming a perception among at least some whites that their town held "too many blacks," or that the African Americans it held were too disorderly. Political contestation is the most obvious. As we have seen in the previous chapter, African American political maneuvers alienated Republicans and Democrats alike, while African American aggressiveness in launching court challenges to discriminatory practices troubled the waters in various communities. This is not to say that the size of a community's African American population was automatically translated into black political power or influence. Effective mobilization depended upon a combination of various factors, such as leadership and the local balance between parties. But if African American numbers provided a base for struggle among generally voteless black Southerners, they were even more likely to do so for voting black Midwesterners.

Other forms of rivalry that may have played a part in stimulating anti-black violence are sexual competition, and, more broadly, a kind of "forbidden fruit" effect, in which white men announced in riot their disdain for both African Americans and manifestations of an African American culture that they and their fellow white men found all too attractive. Such complex motivations seem to have been at work in the pair of full-scale race riots in Springfield, Ohio, in March 1904 and February 1906. Both riots featured mob attacks on a downtown block of saloons run mostly by African Americans and known as "the Levee."[55] The mob turned to attacking African American homes during the second riot only after authorities had frustrated their attack on the saloons. After the first riot, Springfield officials, like the grand jury in Evansville, sought to close specifically African American–operated saloons, ignoring the city's "white dives," which, as a local newspaper noted, were "equal in viciousness to any the mob's wrath destroyed in the Levee precincts."[56] Both blacks and whites had patronized the Levee saloons before the riot, probably attracted by forms of African American music and dance that seemed exotic in contrast to respectable Victorian culture.

Springfield's riots in 1904 and 1906 made manifest a dimension of antiblack violence that was only latent in Washington Court House. When African Americans entered midwestern towns, they stepped into the midst of an ongoing cultural clash between respectable and disreputable classes. African Americans who found rare opportunity in the vice business—such as King David Anderson and Martha Lawson in Washington Court House—also placed themselves, willingly or not, on the disreputable side. In part, this was a class war, as black elites joined white elites in anathematizing working-class cultural expression.[57] But it was just as much a cultural struggle, since some upper-class and middle-class white men, and a few women of the same classes as well, crossed the lines into enemy territory by patronizing "dives" or finding sexual companions across the color line.

By the analysis presented above, antiblack violence in the Lower Midwest is overdetermined. That is, the factors cited could well have existed generally throughout the region, but the evidence indicates that incidents of antiblack collective violence flared only in some, indeed, in a minority of communities. Some communities avoided violence because the number of African Americans was simply too insignificant to be a threat.[58] (But also the threat or the reality of white violence kept African American numbers small or nonexistent in more communities than has been generally recognized.)[59] As we have seen, a relatively large African American proportion characterized communities where recorded outbreaks of antiblack violence occurred. In those places, "too many blacks" could refer to any or all of a variety of complaints. Too many workers competing for the available jobs. Too many saloonkeepers harboring gamblers and prostitutes and musicians playing crazy music. Too many voters supporting the wrong party. Too many

Table 5.2 Lynching Rates, 1890–1909

	Lynching Victims, 1890–1899	1890–99 African American Population, 1890	Victims per 100,000 Population
Ohio	5	87,113	5.7
Indiana	1	45,215	2.2
Illinois	2	57,028	3.5
Georgia	104	858,815	12.1
Kentucky	66	268,071	24.6
Virginia	27	635,438	4.2
	Lynching Victims, 1900–09	1900–1909 African American Population, 1900	Victims per 100,000 Population
Ohio	1	96,901	1.0
Indiana	5	57,505	8.7
Illinois	5	85,078	5.9
Georgia	99	1,034,813	9.6
Kentucky	41	284,706	14.4
Virginia	12	660,722	1.8

Sources: Table A.4; W. Fitzhugh Brundage, *Lynching in the New South: Georgia and Virginia, 1880–1930* (Urbana: University of Illinois Press, 1993), appendixes A and B; George C. Wright, *Racial Violence in Kentucky, 1865–1940: Lynchings, Mob Rule, and "Legal Lynchings"* (Baton Rouge: Louisiana State University Press, 1990), appendix A.

black men gaining access to white women. Too many black men limiting white men's access to black women. Too many white women gaining sexual access to black men. Too many black men and women having fun. Too many white men and women having fun in their company. The combination of complaints varied in breadth and intensity from community to community, and even in places where grievances were broad and deep, lack of leadership or absence of a precipitating incident may have forestalled violence. An uncommon event, violence required the coming together in precise though varying combinations of a variety of favorable conditions and propelling forces.

Whatever the motives of its perpetrators, antiblack violence in the Lower Midwest flared more commonly than has generally been recognized, and it certainly occurred often enough to loom large in the eyes of its intended targets. Such violence is normally measured by counting the absolute number of incidents or victims. Although historians have always recognized that the great difference in the size of northern and southern African American populations makes this comparison suspect, no one has yet produced a better yardstick.[60] A more precise comparison is presented in table 5.2, using the only available comparative statistics, those for lynchings in Georgia, Virginia, and Kentucky during the 1890s and 1900s.

Kentucky's numbers are higher than those in any other state because they are derived from an unusually thorough search in local newspapers and county histories. George Wright argues that tallies for other southern states would increase if an equally diligent search were conducted, and his point holds as well for the midwestern states.[61]

During the 1890s the lynching rate in the Lower Midwest fell well behind that in Georgia, and even further behind the rate in Kentucky. Ohio's rate of lynchings per 100,000 African American population, however, exceeded that in Virginia, and Illinois's was not far behind. Even more striking, during the first decade of the twentieth century both Illinois and Indiana lynched African Americans at a pace exceeding Virginia's. And Indiana, with 8.7 lynching victims per 100,000 black population, nearly equaled the rate in Georgia (9.6). An important conclusion may be drawn from these comparisons. The incidence of lynching in the states of the Lower Midwest was comparable to rates in some southern states when controlled for size of African American populations. In other words, the smaller absolute number of lynchings is explained by the fact that the Lower Midwest had fewer African Americans to attack. Or, to put the matter another way, white Midwesterners lynched their black neighbors at a rate that would have ranked them comfortably among the states of the South.

The appearance in the urban Lower Midwest of a relatively high level of antiblack collective violence points directly to the unsettled nature of race relations there during the late nineteenth and early twentieth centuries. A society in which relationships of domination and subordination are well entrenched does not require spontaneous extralegal outbursts of violence against the dominated in order to maintain the control of the dominant. Instead, the normal institutions of society do the job, justified in their operation by the society's ruling ideology. Lynchings were virtually unknown, for example, in South Africa under apartheid.[62] In the North after emancipation, however, the institutions that had maintained European American domination over African Americans before the Civil War generally lost their power to do so. Meanwhile, the numbers of African Americans were growing, and they were settling in communities where blacks had hardly been a presence before. No law prevented African Americans from living where they wished, taking any job they were capable of performing, or (except in

Indiana and Nebraska) marrying whomever they pleased. Formally, they stood as equals to every other American. By the 1890s, southern racist ideologues were busy crafting an ideology of black primitivism to rationalize renewed subordination, but the flourishing violence in both the South and the North shows how little they had achieved. Normal measures may have slowed black progress and inhibited black assertiveness, but they had not succeeded in preventing either. As Paul Dunbar wrote in the midst of the Lower Midwest's wave of antiblack violence, African Americans refused to accept that they were less than full citizens.

RIPOSTE

African American responses to European American violence varied over a wide spectrum from place to place, across time, and within African American communities. If Martha Thomas's family and friends took part in hanging Peter Betters, their behavior demonstrates that no universal repugnance to lynching existed among Afro-Midwesterners. All public African American voices, however, unequivocally denounced mob law. The most vocal were the newspaper editors. Their editorials expressed surprise and disgust at the outbreaks of antiblack violence in the Midwest; demanded respect for law; and castigated local, state, and federal officials for failing to protect prisoners and punish rioters.[63] Their sentiments were echoed by ministers, church congregations, and mass meetings, where money was raised to succor victims' families and to support legal action. Sunday school conferences demonstrated the convergence of religious, benevolent, and political activity by publicly censuring mob violence, as did the founding convention of the Indiana State Federation of Colored Women's Clubs.[64] As in other forms of political activity, African Americans were unequivocal in demanding their rights be respected, especially after particularly blatant transgressions. In Illinois, the Spring Valley riot provoked reactions in African American communities across the state. A lynching in Urbana in 1897 had a similar impact in Ohio.

Some editors tried to limit the damage done by white violence to their state's image as a haven for blacks. Harry Smith of the *Cleveland Gazette* consistently attempted to find reasons to distinguish lynching communities invidiously from the rest of Ohio.[65] In a similar vein, George Knox of the *Freeman* and George Stewart of the Indianapolis *Recorder* distanced themselves and other law-abiding African Americans from victims of antiblack violence. The murder of which one lynching victim was accused, wrote Knox, "is a foul blot on the Negro race that only years of atonement and contrition can undo."[66] The lynching of an accused rapist moved Knox to denounce rape and to conclude that the accused man "received his just deserts, but at unauthorized hands."[67] After the Evansville riot, the *Freeman* editor feared that John Tinsley's killing of officer Massey would bias white Indianians against their African American fellow citizens.[68] Stewart responded to the Evansville riot in similar fashion, noting with approval that "Indiana cities and towns are systematically cleaning out the objectionable and indolent negroes."

> The general cry is to "get busy" or move on. We welcome this municipal house-cleaning and feel confident that in the end, the race will be greatly benefited.
>
> The race problem is nothing more or less than a condition in which the better class of whites must unite with the better class of blacks, against the mob-ruling anarchistic class of poor whites and "jim crow" negroes. Government for the people and by the people, demands that this latter element should be improved or subdued.[69]

No editor condoned African American participation in lynching, but editors generally regarded defensive violence in a different light. The *Chicago Defender* is often held up as an exemplar of militant rhetoric in favor of armed self-defense. Long before the *Defender* began publishing in 1905, however, other midwestern editors had established this journalistic tradition. In 1879 one of the first African American papers in the Lower Midwest, the *Indianapolis Leader,* praised African Americans in Bloomington, Indiana, who armed themselves and defied white terrorists. African Americans possessed all the rights of American citizens, the editor emphasized: "There is a class of ignorant roughs in this country who can learn this fact only through the administration of soothing doses of buck shot and minnie balls in copious quantities. If they interfere with you, friends, let them have it; it is what they need."[70] The editors of Chicago's *Conservator* and *Broad Ax* and Indianapolis's *Recorder* published similar sentiments.[71] Shocked by the Urbana lynching, Harry Smith, then serving in the Ohio legislature, agreed: "The use of arms must be resorted to by our people. It is the only remedy."[72] Even George Knox, who usually counseled against resort even to defensive violence, urged acquittal of an Ohio man who had shot and killed two armed white harassers.[73]

Other Afro-Midwesterners probably needed no urging from editors to take up the gun in self-defense. A tradition of armed resistance existed even before there were African American newspapers in the Lower Midwest to report and approve it.[74] During the Cincinnati riots in 1862, armed African

Americans not only defended their own neighborhoods, but also invaded an Irish district.[75] Armed self-defense was reflexive and personal, but it was also collective and deliberate.[76]

Sometimes, however, a resort to armed self-defense did not turn out well, as a case in Fremont, Ohio, in 1902 demonstrated. During a strike at a local factory, three African American strikebreakers who were attacked by a mob fired at their attackers, killing one and wounding two others. The court refused to consider their action as self-defense and convicted at least two of them.[77] Collective self-defense seems to have succeeded, however, in three other instances. In Bloomington, Indiana, in 1879, attempts to terrorize and drive out local African American residents were met with armed defiance. Sympathetic European American residents heard of the intimidation and denounced the terrorists.[78] During the following year, some whites in Aurora, Indiana, tried to maintain the town's lily-white reputation by ordering out of the community six African American workers brought to town by a Cincinnati contractor. Apparently such harassment had always worked before to drive out African Americans from what the *Leader* referred to as a "God-forsaken, devil-ridden, hoodlum sink hole of pauperism and crime," but this time the workers frightened off their attackers by brandishing revolvers.[79]

In Decatur, Illinois, African American residents arrived at armed self-defense after trying other strategies. Decatur African Americans by the early 1890s had mobilized effectively enough to elect a county supervisor and to obtain appointment of two letter carriers and a police officer. They were unable, however, to stop the lynching in 1893 of Samuel J. Bush, an itinerant worker accused of raping two European American women. A mass meeting in the lynching's aftermath debated various strategies before resolving to appeal to local and state officials to punish the mob's leaders, who were well known. Two grand juries, however, refused to return indictments. A year later an African American porter, James Jackson, was arrested and charged with the rape of a European American woman. This time local blacks refused to rely upon local authorities to prevent a lynching. Instead, more than a hundred armed men took over the streets of Decatur each night for three nights, effectively raising the costs of lynching higher than local whites were willing to pay.[80]

Many of the themes of midwestern antiblack violence that I have traced thus far may be found in the region's best-known race riot before World War I, the Springfield, Illinois, riot. But the brutal violence in Lincoln's town also affords a rare opportunity to examine perceptions of such violence by remaining members of a local African American community. According to sociologist Roberta Senechal's fine study, African American progress played a crucial part in provoking the full-scale race riot that occurred on August 14 and 15, 1908. The specific events leading to the riot began on July 4 when Clergy Ballard, a European American mining engineer, was fatally stabbed during a struggle with an intruder in his home. The next morning, Alabamian Joe James, briefly released from jail on a vagrancy charge during Fourth of July celebrations the previous day, was found sleeping off a spree in a yard near the scene of the crime. The police arrested James, but despite threats of lynching from some of Ballard's many friends, no mob material-ized for nearly six weeks afterward. In reporting Ballard's murder, the local press focused on African American crime and the threat of coerced inter-racial sex, since the intruder had first been discovered in the bedroom of Ballard's teenage daughter, and the newspapers assumed that rape was the motive for the intrusion.

On Friday, August 14, the same themes reappeared in inflammatory newspaper reports that Mabel Hallam, the European American wife of a streetcar driver, had been raped by an African American. She identified George Richardson, a construction hand who had been working in her neighborhood, as the assailant. When threats of a double lynching of James and Richardson began to spread, the county sheriff and a local militia com-mander removed the two prisoners from Springfield to Bloomington. To transport James and Richardson out of town speedily, officials canvassed friendly car owners. Harry Loper, a European American restaurant owner who owned a fast, reliable automobile, volunteered to help. As in Akron and Evansville, removal of their initial target failed to pacify the mob. Learning of Loper's role in the escape, the mob attacked his restaurant, sacked it, and burned the offending car. The mob then began assaulting individual African Americans found on the streets. In addition, it targeted Springfield's "Levee," a two-block district of saloons, small restaurants, pawnshops, and cheap boardinghouses on East Washington Street in the downtown area. Moving through the first block, the mob systematically destroyed every African American business while sparing most European American shops. At the beginning of the next block, however, the mob met stiff resistance from the owner of the corner saloon, "Dandy Jim" Smith, and his friends, who fired down from second-floor windows above the saloon. The defenders fatally wounded three rioters before retreating in the face of superior force. The mob wrecked Smith's establishment, then gave the other black busi-nesses on the block the same treatment.

By this time the riot had been going on for three hours, but because of official temporizing sufficient troops had not been mobilized to begin the task of ending it. The rioters moved on from the smashed businesses of the Levee to a larger African American residential district, "the Badlands," where they began to assail and burn African American homes. At about two A.M. on Saturday, the mob encountered Scott Burton, a barber whose shop had been destroyed earlier and who was determined to defend his home. Burton got off at least one shotgun blast before he was seized, hanged, and his body mutilated. Finally, Illinois National Guard troops arrived—white troops, since officials had chosen not to mobilize the forces of the African American Eighth Regiment—and dispersed the mob with a volley.

Despite the presence by the next day of more than 1,400 troops, the mob reassembled during the evening and commenced hit-and-run attacks on African American residential areas that the troops were unable to protect. One group deliberately marched to the home of William Donnegan, a wealthy retired shoemaker who had lived in Springfield since 1845. Donnegan's throat was cut and he was hanged. Throughout the rest of Saturday night, groups of rioters attacked the homes of prosperous and prominent African Americans, including grocer Clarke Duncan and his son Otis, a state government worker and major in the Eighth Regiment. The riot did not end until early Sunday morning. On Monday, 3,700 troops were in the city. By the riot's end, at least twenty-one African American businesses had been damaged or destroyed, and more than forty African American homes were burned.[81]

Springfield's European American elite appear to have condoned the first night's violence, if they did not participate in it. An eyewitness report stated that by the time the first troops arrived, "the better element had almost entirely disappeared from the ranks of the mob," clearly implying that the "better element" had participated in the initial mob action.[82] On Saturday, the local press held that "the riot was an effective and justifiable remedy for black misbehavior."[83] The *Illinois State Journal* editorialized that "[i]t was not the fact of the whites' hatred of the negroes, but of the negroes' own misconduct, general inferiority or unfitness for free institutions that were at fault."[84] Only after Saturday night's violence did white elite opinion conclude that the rioting had gone too far. Elite whites, however, were not sufficiently upset by the events of the riot to ensure that judicial punishment was meted out to those responsible.

Nevertheless, most of the rioters were evidently members of the working class, young men who generally lived some distance from their targets. The mob clearly targeted African American achievers, those who had raised themselves above the level that was felt to be appropriate for blacks. Successful African Americans did not, of course, threaten to displace or even equal prosperous European American professionals or businessmen. But the secure government jobs, although lowly, and the thriving businesses drawing white as well as black trade attracted the rioters' wrath like a lightning rod. So too did African American families living in otherwise all-white neighborhoods. Politics also fuelled the violence, as Springfield African Americans had been able to influence the local scene sufficiently to obtain appointment of a significant share of police officers and firefighters, as well as minor positions on the city payroll. The saloons represented not only racial interzones where African American music and dance brought blacks and whites together in a sexually charged setting. They also served as headquarters for African American political leaders.[85]

Good relations across the color line, including sexual intimacy, also aroused the mob's anger. European Americans who employed or otherwise tried to help African Americans were threatened with reprisals. The mob had at least three reasons to hurt Harry Loper. In addition to his role in spiriting James and Richardson away from a lynching, Loper employed African American waiters in his elegant restaurant. He also opened his restaurant, one of the city's finest, to African American diners. William Donnegan died not only because he was prosperous, but also because his wife was a European American.[86]

The Springfield riot thus shared elements in common with other outbreaks of antiblack collective violence in the Lower Midwest. A unique body of source material, however, allows investigation of one significant dimension of such events that remains obscure in all other outbreaks: the perspective of the African American community. During the 1970s, the Oral History Office at Sangamon State University (now the University of Illinois–Springfield) commissioned interviews with older residents of the Springfield African American community, including some who lived through the 1908 riot, and others who, although they were born or arrived in the capital after the event, were told about it by survivors.[87] Their memories reveal an internal image of the riot that differs significantly from most views of the event adopted by outsiders to Springfield, both African American and European American.

The Chicago *Broad Ax,* in its report on the riot, succinctly outlined the image of the riot held by African Americans outside Springfield and, in part, by European Americans sympathetic to African American grievances.

No pen nor tongue can ever portray the horrors and the suffering which were visited upon the heads of defenseless Negro men, women and children who were peaceable and law-abiding and not guilty of committing any crimes whatever, during the supreme reign of anarchy, mob and lynch law in Springfield—heretofore the fair city, which has the proud distinction of holding within its walls the remains of Abraham Lincoln, whose monument, as it were, was stained with the life blood of some of the Negroes who received their first taste of freedom from the promulgation of his emancipation proclamation.[88]

The dramatic contrast between racist violence and its setting in the hometown of the Great Emancipator of course served the purpose of shaming northern whites. Such a contrast would lose much of its force, however, if one believed that emancipation resulted primarily from the efforts of African Americans themselves, as at least some African American Democrats did.[89] Nevertheless, European Americans generally did hold the conventional view of Lincoln as philanthropist, and the mob's obvious racism therefore chagrined the most liberal whites and provoked some of them into taking a leading part in creating the National Association for the Advancement of Colored People shortly afterward.[90] The view of riot victims as "peaceable and law-abiding and not guilty of committing any crimes whatever" was not, however, accepted by most European American observers. Reformer Graham Taylor expressed a common assumption when he explained the mob's violence as caused by African American "depravity."[91] Even William English Walling, who joined with other liberal whites to assist in founding the NAACP, acknowledged that African Americans had committed crimes, although he argued that African American criminal behavior was not disproportionate to European American crime.[92] But however one viewed black Springfielders' behavior before the riot, on their role during the bloody events a general consensus took shape: They were victims.[93]

Among the African American community in Springfield, in contrast, a different image emerged, flourished, and blossomed in its oral tradition. A few reports at the time noted that "the negroes were desperate, and fought viciously and aggressively";[94] that "in a few cases the Negroes attempted retaliation when opportunity offered."[95] A correspondent for the Indianapolis *Freeman* described the mob in caustic terms as cowards and hoodlums encouraged by police inaction and described Scott Burton as "one poor Negro that gave up his sweet life, but took two of the hoodlums along with him."[96] *Freeman* editor George Knox recognized the possibility of violent retaliation when he deplored vengeance and insisted upon respect for law.[97]

Some survivors of the riot emphasized acts of armed self-defense. Mattie Hale, who lived with her family on a farm on the outskirts of Springfield, recalled African American businessmen, "men of the world, they were rough men . . . gamblers," who could have left, but stayed in town to protect their property.[98] Edith Carpenter's father, grocer Edward White, also stayed.

[M]y father put out the word if they [the mob] bothered him, what he would do to them. I had a sister, that's the . . . oldest sister, and at that time she was living in Chicago and she was expecting a new baby and so my mother had gone to Chicago to be with her until the baby was born. So anyway I guess we must have called long distance and told them about this thing and so my sister's husband got a whole lot of ammunition together, guns, big long guns, and a whole lot of the bullets and everything, and he bundled that stuff up and got it to Springfield and it was taken to my father's store. So he had sent word out and let everybody know that if anybody bothered him, he certainly had everything to do with and I'll let you know they came right straight down that street, so they say, Adams Street; our store was on Adams Street. I'll let you know that they never bothered him, and my father had all day long, he might get a chance to nap a little bit, but all day and all night long, he had a gun on each shoulder and he marched from where our store was on 15th and Adams to our home where we lived at 1312 East Monroe, and that was back and forth all evening. And so, I think somebody said that one time he looked out and saw them coming, I think, and so when they saw him with all his guns, they turned and went the other way.[99]

Others went even further in emphasizing African American agency rather than victimization. Harry Mann, born in Springfield in 1903, heard from his grandfather about the firefight at Dandy Jim Smith's saloon. Smith and his friends "fought and had white folks up on the porches dying and everywhere else. They was hauling them [a]way in the nighttime, the Negroes had killed so many of them. . . . They said they killed an awful lot of them."[100] John Wilson worked at a Springfield coal mine during the riot. He knew personally some of the men who took part in the battle at Smith's and had killed rioters. Wilson also related a story about a white family in his neighborhood whose two sons went downtown during the riot against their mother's wishes and never returned. Afterward, the family disposed of the boys' clothes. Wilson, too, believed that many more European Americans had been killed than appeared in official reports. "[White] people were dead in the streets and in the hallways. At that time we understood there were many."[101] LeRoy Brown, a Springfield native who was in his early twenties at the time of the riot, was acquainted with both Scott Burton and William Donnegan. He also heard that "there were lots of white people killed that night but they carried them out of town and buried them some place."[102]

Albert Harris and Margaret Ferguson also focused on the battle at Smith's saloon and the number of hidden European American fatalities. Harris, another Springfield native, was thirteen years old in 1908. "Dandy

Jim and Andy Gordon, and they were bad men! And they tell me that Dandy Jim and Andy stood upon his platform—I mean his counter—just poured volley after volley with their guns into this mob," Harris recalled. In Dudley's livery stable on East Washington Street, Harris was told, "for three or four days they'd find bodies [of whites] where they had crawled up there and died in his livery stable."[103] Margaret Ferguson was only four years old when the riot occurred, but she accurately described the fray at Smith's. "[T]he blacks did defend themselves," she concluded, "and they did it very well."[104]

In the eyes of the African American community of Springfield, that community was certainly not "defenseless." Nor did the picture of the riot in local oral tradition correspond with the image of blacks as victims that informed the founding of the NAACP. Instead, local citizens focused on their community's success in hurting and killing those who would hurt and kill them. Obviously the tradition of African American agency during the riot took root and thrived among those who stayed in Springfield after the riot. Although Senechal has shown that reports of an African American exodus from Springfield in the riot's wake have been exaggerated, some did leave as a result of the violence.[105] Those who left might have shared a different perspective, and the same is true of those who would have migrated to Springfield but turned elsewhere because of the riot. During the period 1890–1910, the capital city experienced the third largest loss in share of the African American population among Illinois urban places.[106] So the emphasis upon African Americans' killing of whites could have been reflexive and rationalizing, an attempt by longtime Springfield residents to justify to themselves and others decisions to stay in a community that the riot had branded as racist in the eyes of outsiders. Yet some of those who passed on the tradition were not loath to tell how race relations had deteriorated in their community after the riot.[107] In their eyes white oppression formed part of the story, but so too did black resistance.

PART THREE

Moving In and Moving On, 1860–1930

After slowing for a quarter of a century, African American migration into the Lower Midwest quickened during the 1890s and the first decade of the new century. The growing numbers of black Southerners entering midwestern towns may well have provided fuel for the white fears and hatred that produced such brutal results in the wave of mob violence that swept over the region during the same years. The conjoined impact of rising African American migration and swelling European American violence sent the three states on two divergent courses before a new current, the First Great Migration, realigned their paths once again. Migrant choices stemmed, however, from more than their experiences north of the Ohio River. Migrants' southern origins, too, were in flux. As in the Lower Midwest, change in southern states proceeded at disparate speeds, with important consequences for migration.

When the unprecedented numbers of new migrants entered the region during the century's second decade, they found a world that was radically changed from the one that had greeted their predecessors during the Civil War. Agriculture was in decline, with profound implications for the market towns that depended upon a healthy rural hinterland. Industry thrived, and so did cities, and the urban industrial jobs increasingly available for African Americans with the falling-off of European immigration during World War I was a leading cause for the new migrants' presence. The larger African American numbers that already populated the Lower Midwest, a product of the previous half century's migrations, could now provide much more information and support for the newcomers than they themselves had enjoyed. Among the knowledge those reconnaissance parties could pass along was the story of race relations during the previous half century and the conclusions the earlier migrants had drawn from living that history.

6

A TASTE OF LEMON PIE
Urban Experience in the South

I don't want to stay here, life is a burden for us colored folks here on account o[f] no vote, but have to pay tax. Better not accumulate too much here, no matter how hard you work, nor how honest you gets it—well you can't even enjoy it, not speaking of other crimes that they do to the Race down here. Don't put my name on this letter as I will get in serious trouble.
—"Interested Southerner," 1917[1]

Although [the Great MIgration] is the first movement to stir discussion among the masses of Negroes themselves and attract nation-wide attention, it is but the extension and intensification of a steady, less spectacular shift of Negro population which has been in progress since the close of the Civil War.
—T. J. Woofter Jr., 1919[2]

The present migration of Negroes from the South is another chapter in the story of the masses struggling to secure better conditions of living and larger life. This movement northward is vitally changing the South, the North, and the Negroes themselves, North and South.
—George Edmund Haynes, 1918[3]

African American migrants to the Lower Midwest during the seventy years covered by this study came in four distinct waves. The spurt of the Civil War years was followed, as we have seen, by the trickle of the years between the war and 1890. During the twenty to twenty-five years after 1890, a larger human stream flowed across the Ohio and Mississippi rivers, many crossing on the new Ohio River bridges. Finally, a flood of migrants came after 1915 in what we know as the First Great Migration.

All these migrants viewed the Midwest through eyes conditioned by their prior experience in the South. But the South itself changed over the course of the years between the Civil War and the Great Migration. In addition to the political changes of disfranchisement and segregation that powerfully affected black Southerners, the region underwent significant industrialization and urbanization, which also helped to shape the perspective of African Americans. These changes, however, came very unevenly to this large and diverse region, altering some parts of it almost overnight, while others remained fixed in agrarian ways. To understand how southern migrants to the Midwest viewed midwestern cities, we must learn how they perceived southern cities.[4] This chapter represents only a beginning to that important project. In tracing the patterns of African American urbanization in the states that formed the principal sources of migration to the Lower Midwest, it seeks to outline the experiential grounding for migrant perceptions.

SOUTHERN CITIES, FOR AND AGAINST

Historians of African American urbanization in the South between the Civil War and the onset of the First Great Migration disagree about the extent and nature of black urban mobility and its meaning for the mass movement northward after 1915. Some historical studies point to the advantages offered to black Southerners by cities compared to the countryside.

> Cities offered an array of consumption and investment opportunities not available in the countryside; the schools were better and more accessible; housing was better, albeit still poor by some standards; greater variety was available in food and other consumption goods; medical assistance was easier to obtain; churches and other social institutions were more abundant and flourishing. In the city, black people were less exposed to white intimidation, gaining some security from mere numbers. A large, concentrated, [*sic*] black community allowed the emergence of a more complex and developed black community with its own merchants, craftsmen, and professional people. . . . In brief, the cities offered greater material opportunities, and black people responded with a massive migration.[5]

These historians' emphasis on the spread of urbanization in the South and its benefits for African Americans has provided a foundation for others' argument that the First Great Migration to the North consisted largely of urban workers, whose places in southern cities were filled by an offsetting stream of former rural dwellers.[6] According to the "displacement hypothesis" formulated in 1942 by sociologist Lyonel Florant and since adopted by other scholars,

> The flow of population . . . involved two or more segments of migrants: first those who moved from southern farms to southern cities, and second those who moved from southern cities to northern cities. It is evident that a single chain of relatively short moves of this nature would have the same effect on the subsequent distribution of the Negro

population as a single move, either direct or in stages, from a farm in the South to a city in the North.[7]

In this view, southern cities played a key role in adapting agricultural workers to an urban way of life and industrial skills.[8]

Urban historians, in contrast, have strongly emphasized the limited extent of African American urbanization and the constraints on black progress in southern cities. After a surge to the cities in the aftermath of the Civil War, African American urbanization slowed, and for good reason. During the period 1880–1910, "the black presence in the urban South failed to keep up with the overall pace of urbanization. . . . This was due in part to the devastating mortality blacks experienced in the cities, where poverty, filth, and poor health care drove death rates up to more than twice those of whites."[9] During the late nineteenth century, African American population growth lagged behind European American in New South cities such as Atlanta, Raleigh, and Birmingham as well as in older centers such as Richmond, Savannah, and New Orleans.[10] In addition to the disadvantages of urban life itself, the planter elites who controlled southern public affairs made strenuous efforts to keep their labor force immobilized in the countryside.[11] This emphasis on the repellent features of southern cities and the slow pace of southern black urbanization merges smoothly with an older view that migrants generally traveled directly from the rural South to the urban North. Perhaps the first, though by no means the last, observer to articulate this perception was NAACP executive secretary James Weldon Johnson, who wrote after two visits to the South during the height of the Great Migration, "I think that most of these people [the northern migrants] have come from the rural districts of the South rather than from the cities. . . ."[12] Novelist Richard Wright agreed. "Perhaps never in history," he wrote in 1941, "has a more utterly unprepared folk wanted to go to the city."[13]

In the same letter in which he reported his impressions, Johnson admitted, "I found no means of getting at definite figures and I have found no means of doing so since that time."[14] Since the Great Migration no one else has been able to "get . . . definite figures," and therein lies the root of interpretive divergence. In order to understand the origins and experiences of northern migrants, we need a tally of the sequence of moves made during his or her lifetime by every northern migrant, or at least a representative sample. For comparison, we should have a similar tally for every nonmigrant. Such records, of course, do not exist. In their absence, we must build from the ground up as well as generalize from the top down. In particular, we must examine subregions of the South to assess the applicability of statements about the region in its entirety. As an analyst of African American

139

urbanization wrote nearly a century ago, "what is in some degree true of the South as a whole is not true of most of its parts."[15]

The principal source of African American migrants to Ohio, Indiana, and Illinois throughout the years from the Civil War to the Great Depression was what the U.S. Census Bureau calls the East South Central region. This region includes two Upper South states with relatively diversified economies (for the South), Kentucky and Tennessee, and two Lower South cotton states, Alabama and Mississippi. By 1910 the Lower Midwest was home to approximately 87,000 African American migrants from the east south central states, and no other southern region contributed anywhere near as many. Twenty years later, three times that number had settled in the Lower Midwest.[16]

MOBILITY IN FOUR STATES

Migration north was only one option available to African American residents of Kentucky, Tennessee, Alabama, and Mississippi. In addition to staying put and moving to other rural areas within the region, they could travel to a regional town or city or migrate to another southern region to the east or south (Florida received substantial inmigration)[17] or farther west. Their large patterns of mobility therefore form the necessary context for understanding the specific choice to move north.

Black Kentuckians entered the Civil War decade as the most urbanized in the region. As a result of the common slave state practice of discouraging African American urbanization, however, Kentucky blacks in 1860 were a less urban population than whites. Both black and white urbanites were concentrated in Louisville, which in both cases held about half of the state's urban population.[18] A substantial though unknown number of black Kentuckians left the state during the chaos of the Civil War, most traveling to areas just across the Ohio River in Ohio, Indiana, and Illinois.[19]

The war years and the quarter century that followed witnessed the strongest urban movement of black Kentuckians before the Great Depression. Two characteristics of this transition are particularly salient in attempting to understand the migrants' perceptions. First, it took place both within and beyond Kentucky's borders. Within Kentucky, the black urban population quintupled, as the rate of African American urbanization far surpassed the European American pace. Second, both within Kentucky and in the northern states to which Kentuckians moved, their setting of choice was small and midsize towns and cities, not the large cities with their relatively ample African American communities. Louisville's African American population

Table 6.1 Principal Destinations of African American Migrants within and from the East South Central States, 1860–1930

	1860–1890	1890–1910	1910–1930
Kentucky	(1) Small & midsize towns in Kentucky (2) Small & midsize towns in Lower Midwest	Large cities in Lower Midwest	Large cities in Lower Midwest
Tennessee	(1) Southwest (2) Midsize towns in Tennessee (3) Small & midsize towns in Lower Midwest	(1) Southwest (2) Large cities in Lower Midwest	(1) Large cities in Lower Midwest (2) Large cities in Tennessee
Alabama	Southwest	(1) Southwest (2) Towns & cities in Alabama	Large cities in Lower Midwest
Mississippi	(1) Southwest (2) Small towns in Mississippi	(1) Southwest (2) Small towns in Mississippi	(1) Large cities in Lower Midwest (2) Southwest

Note: Urban size descriptions refer to a national, not state, urban hierarchy. "Small" denotes towns of 2,500–9,999 population; "midsize" refers to places of 10,000–99,999; and "large" indicates cities of 100,000 and more.

growth now lagged behind the pace of black urbanization for the state.[20] So did Cincinnati's on the other side of the Ohio (as chapter 1 showed). Whether they remained within Kentucky or left the Bluegrass State, African American migrants were exploring new options in the hopeful aftermath of Emancipation. Small-town life was novel, however, only in the sense that it offered an experiment in freedom within a largely white world. As an urban setting tightly enmeshed within an agrarian economy and culture, the small town also represented continuity with rural experience.

White Kentuckians had no intention of allowing black hopes and aspirations, whether utopian or prudent, to come to fruition. During the postwar years whites attempted to halt black progress by inaugurating a reign of terror through both legal and extralegal means.[21] After 1890 the pace of black urbanization in Kentucky slowed drastically, while the rate of outmigration accelerated.[22] The migration stream, which during 1860–1890 had divided among towns on both sides of the Ohio River, now flowed mostly north. But it no longer fed midwestern towns and villages. Now it flooded into the large cities of Ohio and Indiana, which it had previously bypassed.[23] Significantly, Louisville's African American community showed no corresponding gain, growing no faster than the statewide rate of population increase. It was not cities as such that now attracted Kentucky's migrants; it was *northern* cities.

The pattern set around the turn of the century held during the years of the Great Migration (1910–1930), as black urban growth in Kentucky dwindled even further, while migration to northern metropolitan centers continued to grow (tables 6.1 and A.5).

The course of African American urbanization in Tennessee generally followed the pattern in Kentucky. As in Kentucky, African Americans were a less urban population than European Americans in 1860, but African Americans urbanized more rapidly during the succeeding three decades. Unlike in Kentucky, however, urban places within their home state represented a more popular choice than outmigration. African American urban growth in Tennessee took place across the urban hierarchy, but most rapidly at the top. As in Kentucky, mobile African Americans seem to have regarded urban places with hope in the post–Civil War years.

Urban dreams fared only somewhat better in Tennessee than in Kentucky. White terror, disfranchisement, and segregation destroyed many of the gains of the Civil War period. Although urban migrants found greater access to education, solidarity, and some degree of security, their employment prospects offered "little improvement over the rural life they had left behind. The range of job opportunities was somewhat greater, but unemployment, higher costs, and crowded living conditions endured well into the twentieth century."[24] As a result, death rates for urban blacks were significantly higher than for whites.[25] After 1890 the urban stream dwindled within the Volunteer State, while the volume of outmigration swelled (tables 6.1 and A.5). Those migrating to the Lower Midwest joined Kentuckians in turning toward metropolitan centers. Kentucky, a slightly more urban state than Tennessee by 1890, became a stepping stone for Tennesseeans moving north.[26] Within Tennessee a pyramidal urban system on the northern model failed to develop by 1910. Instead, its urban hierarchy exhibited a dumbbell shape, with Nashville and Memphis at the top, a host of villages at the bottom, and very little in between. In Middle Tennessee, African Americans left rural areas in greater numbers than European Americans, but poor job prospects in Nashville diverted them to other destinations.[27] As a result, Nashville's black population grew at less than the statewide urban rate during 1890–1910, but in Memphis the black population grew faster, partly as a result of migration to this dynamic cotton and lumber market from the mid-South region, including Arkansas and Mississippi.[28] Substantial migration to the largely rural Southwest meant that Afro-Tennesseans' mobility split into rural and urban streams, with the latter, whether headed for in-state or northern destinations, mostly flowing to large cities. Nonmetropolitan urban places played a lesser role.

During the Great Migration years, the rate of urban migration in Tennessee rose, while in Kentucky it continued to decline. Even as black urbanization surged in Tennessee, however, it fell well behind the quickening pace of outmigration from the Volunteer State. Memphis itself no doubt became a final destination for some, while for others, such as the young Richard Wright, it served as a way station on the road north.[29] After 1910 metropolitan migration became the norm for long-distance Tennessee migrants. A narrow path led to Memphis and Nashville, but a broad highway beckoned to Chicago, Indianapolis, Dayton, Toledo, and Cleveland.

In general, the migration patterns of Alabama and Mississippi were distinct from the Upper South pattern in both direction and timing before the Great Migration years. Neither Alabama nor Mississippi witnessed significant African American urbanization during the Civil War or postwar years to 1890. In both states the volume of outmigration consistently exceeded the size of the urban stream from the outset, and continued to do so until the eve of the Great Depression. During the late nineteenth century, migration from Alabama and Mississippi flowed westward rather than northward or cityward, reflecting the aspirations of Deep South farmers for rural independence.[30] Their decisions contrasted with those of Tennesseans, who launched parallel urban and southwestern expeditions, and even more with Kentuckians, whose principal destinations had always been northward and urban.[31] Nevertheless, the pace of African American urbanization within Alabama did not fall far behind the rate of outmigration during the half century after 1860, and a small portion of the outmigration probably went to urban destinations in the Upper South and Lower Midwest. Still, in 1910, black Alabamians were no more urban than their white counterparts, despite the well-known mushroom growth of black urban population in the Birmingham region. Birmingham by 1910 also did not dominate its state's urban hierarchy as Memphis and Nashville did Tennessee's. Black urbanites in Alabama were spread more evenly among urban places of various sizes. After 1910 outmigration, now primarily to northern metropolitan centers such as Chicago, Gary, East Chicago, Akron, Cleveland, and Youngstown—but also to the Upper South—doubled the quickening pace of urban mobility within Alabama (tables 6.1 and A.5).

Mississippi, too, witnessed a minor spurt of African American urban movement within the state's truncated urban system. During 1860–1890 black Mississippians urbanized at double the rate of whites, and during the ensuing twenty years an even larger number moved townward. African American urbanization within Mississippi, however, paled in comparison to the concurrent movement westward, and after 1910 it virtually faded away altogether (tables 6.1 and A.5). Furthermore, in 1910 black Mississippians were still less urban than whites, and even after 1910 the southwestern branch of their migration stream continued to grow, uniquely among east south central states. Their change of direction toward northern cities during the Great Migration therefore appears to represent a more radical departure from their past experience than was the case for African Americans in any other of the east south central states.

Several general conclusions may be drawn from this survey of African American migration patterns in the east south central region. First, for African Americans collectively, urbanization within the region appears as an alternative that was often tried and nearly as often rejected. For Kentuckians and Tennesseans, city life's testing time was the Civil War and postwar years. For Mississippians, southern urbanism shone brightest as an alternative around the turn of the century. Black Alabamians moved townward in ever-increasing numbers until the Great Depression, but the number of those who chose to leave the state altogether grew even faster. White Southerners, in suppressing black opportunity in their cities, restricted the possibilities for urban growth in their region.[32] Frustrated in the South, black Southerners found urban opportunity elsewhere.

In one important sense, the urban experience tried and rejected in the South prepared black Southerners for the urban experience they would encounter in the North. In most cases, the first urban place—and perhaps also the second and third—in which migrating African Americans settled after leaving the farm was a small or midsized town. This was true whether the migrant was a Kentucky or Tennessee migrant during the Gilded Age or an Alabamian or Mississippian moving at the turn of the century. Such places, with their close economic and social ties to a rural hinterland and their dependence upon agricultural cycles, allowed a gradual transition from rural roots to urban ways.[33]

What proportion of outmigrants was exposed to urban life varied from state to state. Figures 6.1 to 6.4 compare the size of the black urban populations of the East South Central states with the volume of outmigration in each of the four decades between 1890 and 1930.

These comparisons do not provide a perfect test of the likelihood of migrants' exposure to urban life in the South prior to emigration, since a migrant could have moved into a southern town or city after one census and then moved out of the state before the next census. Some migrants traveled through more than one of the region's states. The comparison does, however, furnish a rough comparative index to the likelihood of substantial exposure to urban life in the South. The probability of an emigrant's having lived in a southern town before emigration was clearly greatest in Kentucky and

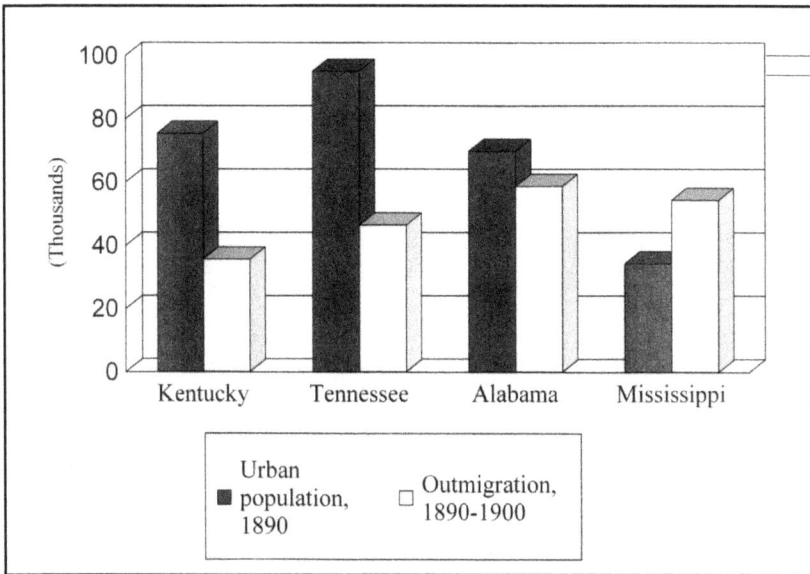

Figure 6.1 Black Urban Populations within and Estimated Gross Outmigration from the East South Central States, 1890–1900. *Sources:* U.S. Bureau of the Census, *Negro Population in the U.S., 1790–1915* (Washington, DC: Government Printing Office, 1918), table 9; W. E. Vickery, *The Economics of the Negro Migration, 1900–1960* (New York: Arno, 1977), table 37

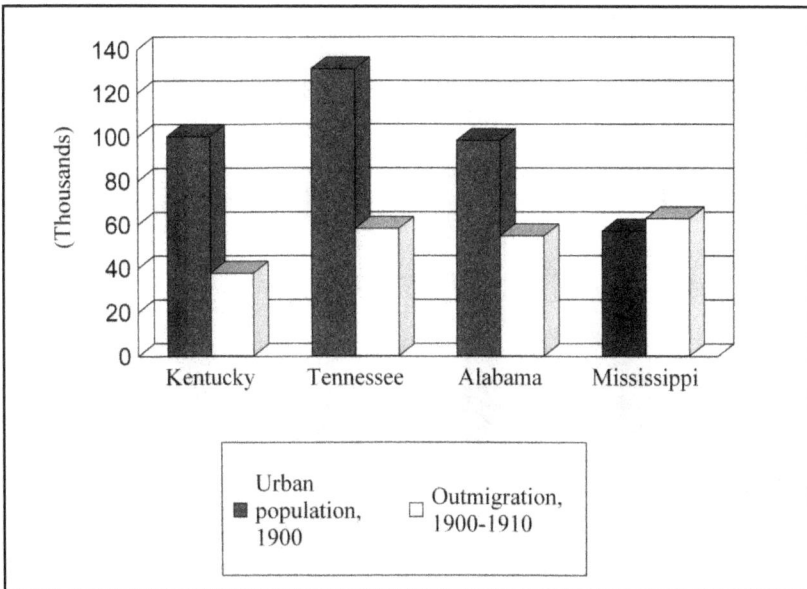

Figure 6.2 Black Urban Populations within and Estimated Gross Outmigration from the East South Central States, 1900–1910. *Sources:* U.S. Bureau of the Census, *Negro Population in the U.S., 1790–1915* (Washington, DC: Government Printing Office, 1918), table 9; W. E. Vickery, *The Economics of the Negro Migration, 1900–1960* (New York: Arno, 1977), table 37

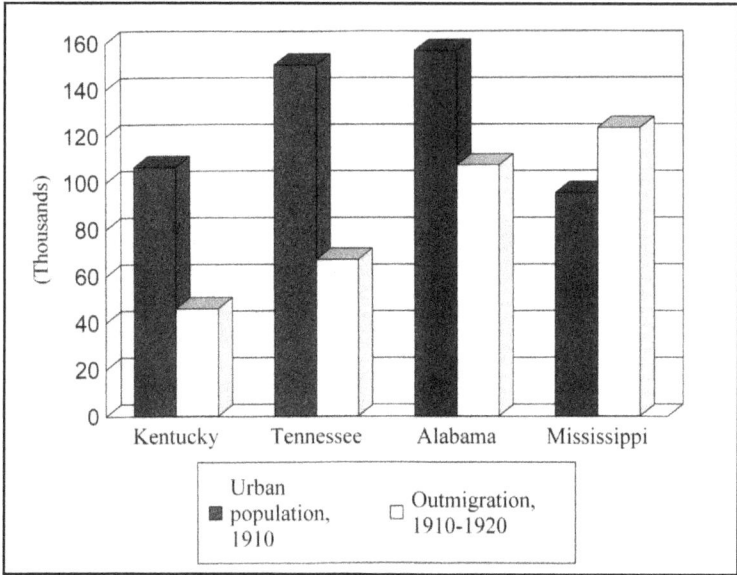

Figure 6.3 Black Urban Populations within and Estimated Gross Outmigration from the East South Central States, 1910–1920. *Sources:* U.S. Bureau of the Census, *Negro Population in the U.S., 1790–1915* (Washington, DC: Government Printing Office, 1918), table 9; W. E. Vickery, *The Economics of the Negro Migration, 1900–1960* (New York: Arno, 1977), table 37

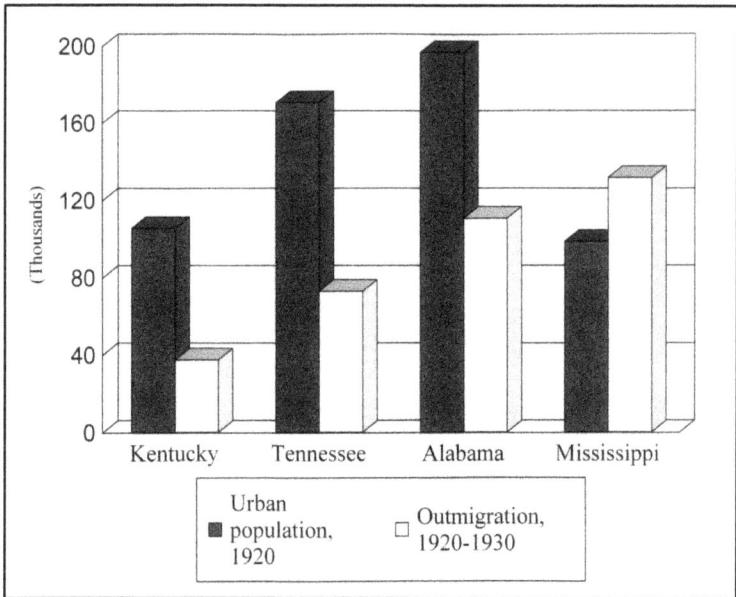

Figure 6.4 Black Urban Populations within and Estimated Gross Outmigration from the East South Central States, 1920–1930. *Sources:* U.S. Bureau of the Census, *Negro Population in the U.S., 1790–1915* (Washington, DC: Government Printing Office, 1918), table 9; W. E. Vickery, *The Economics of the Negro Migration, 1900–1960* (New York: Arno, 1977), table 37

Tennessee throughout the entire period and in Alabama during the decades 1900–1910 and 1920–1930.

In Mississippi, in contrast, the volume of outmigration consistently exceeded the prior size of the state's urban population. Compared to migrants from the other east south central states, migrants from Mississippi, it seems, were least likely to have experienced urban life in their home state before migrating north.

URBANITY'S FRUITS

For the East South Central region as a whole, the process of urbanization over the entire period 1860–1930 means that increasing numbers of potential migrants were exposed to urban life in the South, even despite the swelling volume of outmigration. The approximately 50,000 black urbanites in 1860 grew to about 570,000 in 1920, while the urban proportion of the African American population rose from one in thirty to nearly one in four. During the 1870s the ratio of emigrants to urban dwellers was about even. In the 1920s, in contrast, there were five black urbanites for every three emigrants.[34] The lives of individual migrants reflected these large-scale changes in the South. Born in Huntsville, Alabama, a town of about 8,000, in 1916, Mrs. Jimmie D. Smith moved with her family to Chattanooga (population 58,000) shortly afterward. In 1923 her father, a boilermaker, migrated with his family to Muncie, Indiana, a somewhat smaller industrial center than Chattanooga.[35] Jack Emmett Martin was born in 1884 in McMinnville, a tiny (1,244) village near Chattanooga, but moved to Nashville, where

Table 6.2 Southern Migrant Oral History Interviewees' Birth Community Size by Period of Migration (in percentages)

	1859–1889	1890–1915	1916–1930
100,000 or more	0.0	4.8	3.4
25,000–99,999	0.0	9.5	10.3
10,000–24,999	2.7	0.0	0.0
2,500–9,999	5.4	14.3	17.2
Rural	91.9	71.4	69.0
Total	100.0	100.0	99.9*
N	37	21	29

* Does not equal 100.0 because of rounding

Source: Oral history respondents (see appendix C).

Table 6.3 Migrant Oral History Interviewees' Last Southern Community Size by Period of Migration (in percentages)

	1859–1889	1890–1915	1916–1930
100,000 or more	0.0	0.0	4.1
25,000–99,999	18.2	12.5	4.1
10,000–24,999	9.1	50.0	74.5
2,500–9,999	0.0	18.8	9.2
Rural	72.7	18.8	8.2
Total	100.0	100.1*	100.1*
N	11	16	98

* Does not equal 100.0 because of rounding

Source: Oral history respondents (see appendix C).

his father worked for a short time as a schoolteacher. In 1890 the family migrated to Springfield, Illinois, and Martin found rare white-collar work as a clerk in a brickyard. Even while he worked in Springfield, however, fondness for the countryside may have led the family to settle in Rochester, a village a few miles outside the Illinois capital.[36] The increasing likelihood of urban origins was reflected in the backgrounds of midwestern migrants, revealed in their oral histories (table 6.2).

During the late nineteenth century, virtually all migrants originated in the rural South. By the Great Migration period, that number had declined to seven out of ten. The second-largest category, where one out of six were born, was the smallest urban places, those below 10,000 population. Most migrants, however, did not remain in the countryside until they moved north (table 6.3). Whereas during the late nineteenth century nearly three-quarters made their last southern stop in a rural neighborhood, during the years 1890–1915 less than one-fifth did so. By the Great Migration years, less than one-tenth were leaving for the North from the countryside.

These conclusions are based on small numbers, which are not derived from a representative sample of migrants. The numbers provide, however, the only evidence that has been compiled tracking migration sequences over the entire period from the Civil War to the eve of the Great Depression. On the one hand, the slow pace of African American urbanization in the South is reflected in the fact that the proportion of migrants who were born in urban settings is not large, even during the period 1916–30 (31 percent). For comparison, in 1910, 41 percent of Afro-Kentuckians and 32 percent of Tennesseans lived in urban communities, although the numbers were considerably smaller for Alabama (17 percent) and Mississippi (9 percent).[37] On the other hand, although a majority of migrants continued into the Great Migration years to begin their lives in rural areas of the South, the flow to the Lower Midwest did draw disproportionately from southern urban dwellers. The typical migrant was born in the countryside and moved to one or more southern towns and cities during his or her lifetime. As the years went by, migrants became more and more likely to have encountered an urban world first in the South, even if they originated in the most rural states. Those who moved from southern farms to southern cities were often the same people who later moved from southern cities to northern cities.

This survey of migration patterns should resolve scholarly disagreement by providing chronological depth and spatial breadth to generalizations about the African American urban experience in the South. The willingness of black Southerners in the east south central states to try their fortunes in southern cities suggests hopes and beliefs that southern urban life offered something better than could be found in cotton and tobacco fields. Individuals and families acting on those aspirations formed a pattern of collective experimentation following emancipation, in which southwestern migration, urbanization, and northern migration all figured at various times in the four states.[38] Or, to change the metaphor, the African American army sent forth from its rural southern base various reconnaissance parties to explore the available options. Some southern cities, such as Memphis, proved sufficiently satisfactory to be worth holding and reinforcing. The majority of southern cities, however, turned out to be no less hazardous to the lives and welfare of African Americans than the countryside. By 1915, then, the army began to turn northward in force, executing in two massive movements during the twentieth century the transfer of much of its body to northern cities. In at least the formative stage of that transition, southern towns and cities played the same role as northern nonmetropolitan urban places. It was in fact the same part that nonmetropolitan urban places played in the concurrent but more protracted European American urban migration, as a bridge to the metropolis.

What about the lemon pie? During the First Great Migration, a Mississippi migrant to Chicago told an interviewer that urban black Southerners responded more readily than rural ones to the lure of the northern metropolis. "If you have never eaten lemon pie," he explained, "you don't know how fond you may be of it. After you have tasted it, it's different."[39]

THE ADVANCE GUARD
ARRIVES

Many were drawn to Sangamon county by the hope that they might in her fertile soil and liberal public sentiment, find the fullest opportunity for race development. Subsequent events have proved that this hope was unfounded.
—W. T. Casey, Springfield, Illinois, 1926[1]

Madison [Indiana] was like Jim Crow, just like in the South. You accepted it. You had to. There was nothing else you could do. You resented it, but you accepted it—or you left. So we left.
—Evan Guess, 1998[2]

Migration has been the great weapon of the Negro against oppression and distress.
—W. E. B. Du Bois, 1905[3]

During the two decades bracketing the turn of the twentieth century, African Americans flowed into the Lower Midwest. Larger numbers moving into the region from the South distinguished this period from the years 1867–1890. The region's pull reached deeper into the South, beyond the border states that had provided most of its previous migrants. Within Ohio, Indiana, and Illinois, too, African Americans were on the move, forsaking their rural neighborhoods for urban destinations. In Ohio and Indiana interstate and intrastate migration streams converged upon metropolitan centers, bypassing or abandoning the small and midsize towns that had attracted the bulk of mobile African Americans during the years before 1890. This metropolitan shift foreshadowed a similar change in direction that would later occur in Illinois. Since the Civil War at least, African Americans moving into and within the Lower Midwest had proceeded with a mixture of hope and caution. As new transportation links multiplied their options and better communications widened their field of knowledge, they faced changing situations in both their old and new homes with the same prudent disposition.

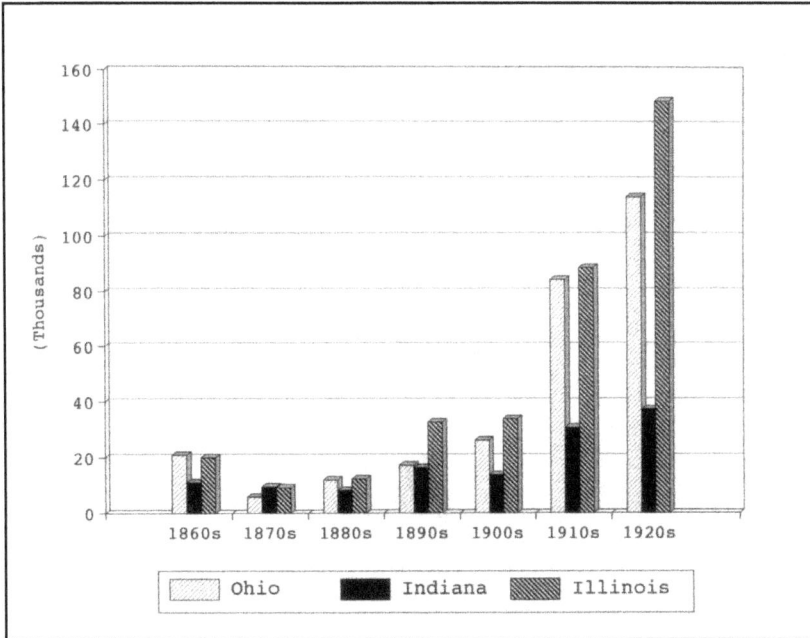

Figure 7.1 Estimated Gross Black Migration into the Lower Midwest, 1860–1930. *(Note:* Migration data are for "nonwhites," but virtually all nonwhites in these states during this period were black.) *Sources:* Michael P. Johnson, "Out of Egypt: the Migration of Former Slaves to the Midwest during the 1860s in Comparative Perspective," in *Crossing Boundaries: Comparative History of Black People in Diaspora,* ed. Darlene Clark Hine and Jacqueline McLeod (Bloomington: Indiana University Press, 1999), 229; W. E. Vickery, *Economics of the Negro Migration, 1900–1960* (New York: Arno, 1977), table 39

NEWCOMERS

The 1890s were a turbulent decade for the country as a whole, but black Southerners emerged from these years as a people who lost the most.[4] Economic depression gripped the nation for five bitter years beginning in 1893. Hard times for farmers provoked the rurally inspired movement that eventuated in the Populist Party. Although Populism gained its greatest grassroots strength in the South, the movement never managed to blend the divergent perspectives of black and white farmers. Following the example of laws mandating separate railway accommodations, segregation legislation spread across the South from the late 1880s, accelerating after the Supreme Court in the *Plessy* decision (1896) gave federal sanction to the new Jim Crow order. The triumph in 1890 of the Mississippi Plan for constitutional disfranchisement produced a similar model for southern elites to employ in

151

banishing virtually all African Americans from the political arena. Through a host of symbolic gestures, white Northerners and Southerners celebrated the reconciliation of the formerly warring sections, and as an integral part of that process white mainstream popular culture demeaned and caricatured African Americans.[5] Such messages were reinforced by racially based arguments justifying the extension of American control over the Hawaiian Islands and the Philippines. In 1898 the editor of Springfield's *Illinois Record* wrote that "at no time since the war of [']61 has the prejudice cropped out against the American Negro more than it has today. It comes from the school door and the battle field, from the work shop and the coal fields, from church and state."[6]

During the 1890s the tide of African American migration to the three states of the Lower Midwest, which had been at ebb for more than two decades, began to rise. Between 1890 and 1910 Ohio received an estimated gross migration of about 43,000, which at least equaled and probably exceeded the total of the previous three decades. Indiana's total of about 30,000 inmigrants also probably equaled or bettered its numbers for 1860–1890. As novel as these increases were, they were dramatically overmatched by the gathering wave of migration to Illinois. The Prairie State, which in 1890 held the smallest proportion of African American population among the three, attracted about 67,000 migrants over the next twenty years, which represented one and one-half times its total for the entire period between 1860 and 1890 (figure 7.1).

Most of the rising numbers of migrants traveling to the Lower Midwest came from familiar sources. The Upper South continued to furnish the bulk of travelers moving into the region. Indeed, the two states of Kentucky and Tennessee still ranked as the chief sources of African American newcomers to each of the three midwestern states. Together, Kentuckians and Tennesseans provided volumes of the new arrivals ranging from more than one-third (to Illinois during the 1890s) to six-sevenths (to Indiana during the 1900s). With them came West Virginians and North Carolinians into Ohio from the east and Missourians into Illinois from the west.

Alongside the familiar accents, however, new voices revealed that the magnetism of the Midwest was beginning to draw migrants from more distant sources. During the 1890s about 300 Georgians joined the approximately 500 who lived in Ohio in 1890. Twenty years later, the 1890 numbers had more than tripled. Similarly, the 400 South Carolina–born Ohioans, whose population had remained stable throughout the late nineteenth century, grew into 1,100 by 1910. Indiana began to attract more Georgians and Alabamians. Illinois's newcomers became not only much more numerous but also more diverse in their backgrounds. Previously tiny populations doubled (Louisianians), tripled (Arkansans and South Carolinians), qua-drupled (Georgians), or increased sevenfold (Texans). More sizable groups at the period's beginning also grew substantially. The 900 Alabamians of 1890 became 3,200 by 1910, while 1,400 Mississippians multiplied to 4,600 during the same period.[7]

In emigrating from Mississippi, a state whose European American elites took the lead in crushing black aspirations, African Americans made a political statement. The "consistent pattern of black outmigration" from a state that "permitted blacks few other avenues of protest" meant that "black Mississippians exercised the ultimate freedom—the freedom to move, to search elsewhere for the political and economic opportunities, the human dignity, and the personal security they could not find at home."[8] Similarly, the advance of segregation and disfranchisement in North Carolina, capped by the bloody Wilmington riot of 1898, produced a volume of emigration in the century's first decade that was nearly as large as the better-publicized exodus between 1910 and 1920.[9] In Kentucky, the pace of outmigration—surges during the 1870s and 1890s, separated by a lull during the interven-ing decade and followed by an ebb during 1900–1910—closely paralleled the chronological pattern of lynchings of African Americans.[10]

The expansion of the railway network, which proceeded apace across the country during the 1880s and was especially rapid in the South, meant that those who wished to escape Dixie now found mobility somewhat less challenging than before. Increased circulation of northern African American newspapers such as the *Cleveland Gazette* and the Indianapolis *Freeman* brought news of the North to southern readers, while growing literacy increased their numbers.[11] Would-be migrants not only could learn in northern newspapers of the advantages of the North, but also could identify towns in which violence broke out.[12] In addition, the steady growth of northern African American communities expanded the foundations for chain migration in the form of more potential informants for would-be migrants and more providers of material assistance for actual ones. Step migration became less critical as a result, so that the proportion of migrants who traveled directly from their southern starting place to their final north-ern destination more than quadrupled, to a total of about 37 percent, com-pared to the period 1860–1890 (table 1.1).

The lessening likelihood of step migration was also related to changes in the balance between the sexes in the migration stream: "Men were more likely than women to work their way north gradually, picking up a few dollars and some encouragement from friends along the way."[13] Women, in con-trast, more commonly traveled from southern point of departure to northern destination in a single trip. This was certainly the case among migrants to the Lower Midwest. During the entire period 1860–1930, 56 percent of female oral history subjects, but only 44 percent of males, made the journey in a single jump, and the same proportion held during the shorter period between 1890 and the onset of the Great Migration.[14] Therefore, as the sex composition of the migration shifted from largely male to a more balanced ratio, the frequency of step migration was reduced accordingly.

The sex ratio of the migration stream did change in this way during the post–Civil War migration. During the 1870s, as we have seen, far more men than women migrated into the Lower Midwest (figure 1.1). Ohio and Indiana received more than 200 male migrants for every hundred females, and Illinois's ratio, while lower, was still very high at about 150. In the 1880s, however, more women entered the migration stream to each of the three states. This "men first, women later" pattern reflected a variety of situations, not merely the familiar image of married men venturing forth, then returning for their wives. Some of the complexities are illustrated by the experience of the Bragg-Tate family of Granger County, Tennessee, and Portland, Indiana. Tolbert Bragg was born in slavery in 1836. He married a woman who had at least one child by a previous marriage, but she died in Tennessee. In 1881 Bragg and the children, all boys, loaded their belongings on a two-horse wagon and set off over the mountains for the North, settling in Portland, a county seat of about 3,000 population in east central Indiana. One of the young men who accompanied him, stepson Preston Tate, who was in his late twenties at the time of migration, returned repeatedly to Tennessee during the next few years, to restore his health and to court Mary (Mollie) Emily Eaton. In 1884 Preston and Mollie married in Tennessee, then returned to Portland, where they lived for a time with Tolbert Bragg before purchasing land for a home of their own, which Preston Tate built himself, room by room. On their nuptial journey they took the train.[15]

The "men first, women later" pattern is, of course, a common one in migrations. It characterized successive stages of the westward movement in the United States. African American migration from St. Helena Island, Georgia to New York City was pioneered by men, with women following as the number of Islanders in Harlem increased and transportation facilities improved. By the early 1930s, female Islanders in the metropolis finally outnumbered males.[16] Various factors explain the pattern, including the kinds of jobs available in newer versus older settlements; the presence of family members to protect girls and women from sexual harassment; and the need for female networks to provide support for individual women. The forms of support furnished by female networks could include information, encouragement, child care, swapping of household goods, and, perhaps most crucially, assistance with childbirth at a time when most women gave birth at home with help from a midwife and a circle of female friends.[17] A migrant group's typical cycle therefore featured an early phase in which men dominated the migration stream and step migration was common. During the second phase of the cycle, more women entered the stream as migrant populations at the destination grew and provided bigger anchors for migration chains, female networks formed and expanded, and single-jump journeys accordingly became more prevalent.

Such a cycle played itself out during the 1870s and 1880s. The burst of new migrants in the 1890s signaled the beginning of a fresh cycle of African American migration to the Lower Midwest, one that, like the previous cycle, would unfold over roughly the next two decades. The sex ratio of the migration stream, instead of declining as it would have done if the previous cycle had continued, instead remained at about the same level across the region as a whole. In this early phase of a new migration cycle, three factors kept the proportion of women higher than during the 1870s migration: larger populations in midwestern destinations produced by the 1860–1890 migration, hence more opportunities for chain migration and female network formation; better transportation options; and the fact that the bulk of the 1890s migration hailed from nearby states of the upper South, which also facilitated travel. The second stage of this new cycle, the "women later" phase, was signaled by a falling sex ratio (indicating more women arriving) in each of the three states after 1900.

Although single-jump migrations became more prevalent among the 1890–1910 migrants than among their predecessors, newcomers after 1890 did not necessarily arrive less well informed about their destinations or with less support than before. Sixty percent of migrants still made at least one stop on their way, and more than one-quarter of the total stopped both during migration in the South and at least once in the North before reaching the final destination. Family remained a key part of the migration process, as many migrants followed relatives to their destination or traveled in the company of kin. John Lucas, for example, was brought to Muncie at the age of three years by his mother, who was joining John's father. Mr. Lucas, a former Kentucky farmer, had worked in a factory in Peru, Indiana, before he was alerted by a family friend to better opportunities in Muncie's factories.[18] Following the lead of Bertha Craig's father, six or seven families moved from the Campbellsville, Kentucky, area to Petersburg, Illinois, during the century's first decade.[19] More African American newspapers published in the Lower Midwest, more settled migrants to write letters, and more literate southerners to read them all lessened the need for movement to be gradual as a means of gaining information about potential destinations. Finally, most migrants' origins in nearby states meant greater opportunities to learn about the Midwest through a variety of means, from newspapers and letters to personal visits back and forth.

White oppression in the South, including violence or the threat of violence, clearly played a part in stimulating the new wave of African American migration.[20] Writing from Glasgow, Kentucky, to his sister in Indiana, William Mace expressed a feeling that was no doubt shared by many: "I tell you now the people[,] the colored[,] are very much oppressed by the whites here in this country & as for my part I am going out of them shooting down bla[c]k men on the streets like dogs[.] I shall stay in no such a country. . . ."[21] Bruce Hayden grew up in Fulton, Kentucky, a small town in one of the state's most virulent lynching counties. By the age of nine he had witnessed "three or four" lynchings. The last one was in 1899, when he watched a mob of drunken whites dragging a black man down the street and lynching him in the "Jockey Yard," a horse-trading market. Myria Hayden decided on the spot that she did not want her children to see another lynching—or become a victim of one—so she packed a few belongings and left for Illinois with Bruce and his brother and sister. Her destination was Du Quoin, where her brother had established himself.[22] Across the South, African American outmigration increased from county to county as the incidence of lynchings rose.[23] Southern lynchings of African American victims peaked in the early 1890s at more than one hundred annually.[24] Yet the correlation between southern lynchings and midwestern migration is not perfect. Migration into the region continued strongly after 1900, indeed more powerfully than during the 1890s, while the frequency of lynchings declined, both in the South as a whole and in Kentucky, the Lower Midwest's most prolific source of African American migrants.[25] The rising trend of lynchings may have stimulated the onset of the new cycle of migration in the late 1880s and early 1890s, but less dramatic forces must have operated to prolong the cycle.[26]

Swings in the southern economy also show only a partial relationship to the flow of migration into the Lower Midwest. To be sure, the South was generally depressed during the 1890s. But so was most of the nation, including the Lower Midwest. The only economic bright spot in the Lower Midwest during that depression decade shone in east central Indiana, where the discovery in 1886 of an immense natural gas field brought to the area a countercyclical boom, which lasted for the next fifteen years. Gas-boom towns such as Anderson, Marion, and Muncie profited from hard times elsewhere, as they lured factories with promises of cheap or free fuel and other inducements.[27] Stimulated by rising cotton prices, the southern economy flourished after the end of the 1890s depression. From an average of seven cents a pound in the 1890s, cotton rose to an average of more than ten cents between 1900 and 1915, on the way to an unheard-of 25 cents during 1916–1920.[28] Not only European Americans prospered. African American farm ownership in the South climbed steadily to an all-time high in 1910, narrowing the enormous gap between black and white property holding.[29] Yet the new current of African American migration to the Lower Midwest continued to flow steadily through bad times and good.

NEW AND OLD CHOICES

New arrivals in Ohio, Indiana, and Illinois during the twenty years after 1890 found populations in flux, and their own mobility added new colors to the kaleidoscopic changes underway. Each state suffered net losses of native-born whites (Indiana during the 1890s was an exception, thanks to the gas boom) while gaining new accessions of foreign-born.[30] The bleeding of sons and daughters from midwestern farms turned into a hemorrhage, and diminishing opportunities in the agricultural lands to the west that had attracted previous generations of outmigrants channeled some of the rural outflow into the region's towns and cities, where it merged with the immigrant inflow.[31] The urban world expanded accordingly, as towns and cities multiplied and filled. By 1910, urbanites comprised 40 percent of Indiana's people, 55 percent of Ohio's, and 60 percent of Illinois's (tables A.6–A.8).

Black Buckeyes and Hoosiers led the rural outflow, but their paths carried many of them to different destinations than their white counterparts. Rural depopulation was even more rapid among African Americans in the two states than among European Americans. But while European American populations swelled across the urban hierarchy, the growth of African American populations was generally restricted to the big cities.

In Ohio, towns in the lowest size category (2,500–9,999), which included Washington Court House, in the aggregate suffered an absolute loss of African American citizens, while welcoming large numbers of incoming European Americans. Towns and cities between 25,000 and 99,999—Springfield's class—also recorded a shrinkage of their aggregate African American population between 1890 and 1910, while their European American numbers grew. Among nonmetropolitan places, African American expansion took place only in midsize places (10,000–24,999), but in these towns as well there was a distinct difference between black and white trends. While African American numbers grew at well below the statewide rate of black population growth (18 percent to 29), European American populations grew faster than the statewide white rate (83 percent to 31). Only in the five cities that exceeded 100,000 population by

1910—Cincinnati, Cleveland, Columbus, Dayton, and Toledo—did African American numbers increase faster than European American (225 percent to 147). Even so, the rapid growth in African American numbers at the top of the urban hierarchy could not offset retarded growth or loss at other levels, so that the overall rate of African American urbanization fell behind the European American pace (62 percent to 81). Nevertheless, the flood of migrants to the largest cities left African Americans in 1910 significantly more concentrated in the Buckeye State's metropolitan centers (43 percent to 29). This spread represented a definite change from the pattern of 1890, when there had been little difference between the metropolitan presence of African American and European American populations. These currents defined a metropolitan shift in Ohio, a decided change in the direction of African American mobility and one that was quite distinct from the pattern of European American movement.

Afro-Indianans executed a similar, and similarly distinct, metropolitan shift in the decades around the turn of the century. In contrast to Ohio, African American numbers increased at every level of the urban hierarchy, and at the higher levels (10,000 and above) they grew faster than the statewide rate of black population growth. But in every tier below the top, European American populations grew faster, tripling the African American growth rate at the lowest level and nearly matching that record in towns of 10,000 or more. Only in Indianapolis did African American numbers expand faster than European American (139 percent to 120). As in Ohio, African Americans' more rapid growth at the top level failed to offset the European American advantage in every other size category, leaving the statewide rate of European American urbanization higher (98 percent to 69.5). As in Ohio, nevertheless, the African American rush to the top of the urban hierarchy widened the gap between African American and European American metropolitan proportions. White Buckeyes and Hoosiers were collectively ascending their states' urban ladders step by step. Their black counterparts leaped directly to the top.

While drastic change characterizes African Americans' locational choices in Ohio and Indiana, continuity with Gilded Age patterns defines Illinois. As we have seen, Illinois during the twenty years after 1890 attracted nearly as many African American migrants as did Ohio and Indiana together. Yet those who moved within the Prairie State followed the paths taken by those who came before. In further contrast to the behavior of mobile African Americans in its sister states, black Illinoisans traced much the same routes as white ones. Certainly this was true for both the countryside and the proliferating number of nonmetropolitan urban places (i.e., everywhere but Chicago). In each urban tier, the rate of African American population growth virtually equaled the European American rate. As far as destination size was concerned, in the aggregate African American and European American choices were virtually the same. Only because of a higher African American growth rate in Chicago (209 percent to 97) did African American urbanization for the state as a whole spurt ahead of the European American rate. Despite this performance, by 1910 Chicago held almost identical proportions of the two populations (39 percent of European Americans and 40 percent of African Americans). No African American metropolitan shift occurred in Illinois.[32]

The contrast between the Prairie State and its neighbors to the east is even more striking when set beside the fact that Illinois by 1910 had begun to attract more migrants from the Deep South.[33] While its sources of African American migration changed more, migrants' locational choices within the state changed less. Even the destinations chosen by new migrants from the Deep South illustrate the theme of continuity in Illinois's migration flow. In 1900, for example, only 1,148 of the 3,116 Mississippi-born blacks living in Illinois resided in Chicago. The percentage of Mississippi-born blacks living in Chicago (36.8 percent) was virtually the same as the percentage of all black Illinoisans residing in the Windy City (35.4 percent). Alabama-born blacks were more likely to be Chicago residents in 1900 (1,181 of 2,387, or 49.5 percent), but one-half of former Alabamians still lived elsewhere in the state.[34] Changing sources did not alter the pattern of locational choices. Indeed, as we shall see, the origins of the new Deep South migrants to Illinois help to explain the continuity in their destination choices within Illinois.

The currents described above set the central problem of this book. Why did mobile African Americans in Ohio and Indiana carry out such a dramatic, novel, and distinctive shift to the largest cities of their region? Why did their counterparts in Illinois make different choices? The previous chapters have described how African American Midwesterners came to the nonmetropolitan communities of the region and what they found and what they did there. The remainder of this chapter and the one to follow will focus on the choices to abandon small towns and cities in favor of metropolitan destinations. Answers suggested to this question by previous writing that touches on the question are incomplete because no study has been framed in such a way as to provide a full answer. In their pathbreaking general histories of African Americans in Indiana and Ohio, respectively, Emma Lou Thornbrough and David Gerber suggest that catalysts affecting both blacks and whites caused the change: mechanization of agriculture and increasing costs of land and equipment, "the increasing marginality of the family farm within the larger economy," and "superior opportunities for education, recreation and social life" in the cities.[35] While these factors may have contributed in some way to African Americans' new locational choices, logically they cannot by themselves explain them. Such conditions affected both blacks and whites, and the metropolitan shift, as we have seen, was a distinctively African American movement. Therefore some agent or combination of agents operating uniquely or with significantly greater force upon African Americans must have been responsible.[36]

Sociologist James Loewen has put forward an explanation that pertains specifically to African Americans. European Americans in nonmetropolitan communities throughout the northern and western United States, he shows, began after 1890 an uncoordinated but effective campaign to drive African Americans from their towns and cities, through violence and other forms of intimidation and harassment. Soon after, new suburbs surrounding metropolitan cities also closed themselves to would-be African American residents.[37] But in Illinois the number of "sundown towns"—towns that did not allow African Americans to remain overnight—was rapidly growing during the years 1890–1910, and that did not stop African American migrants from continuing to populate the state's nonmetropolitan communities.

To compound the interpretive problem, the extremely low rate of rural population growth in Illinois indicates that rural outmigration was taking place in the Prairie State as in its sisters to the east, so the same forces pushing members of farm families off the land in Ohio and Indiana must have been operating there, too. And whatever appeal Cincinnati, Cleveland, Columbus, Dayton, Toledo, and Indianapolis possessed, Chicago, the regional metropolis, must have manifested in abundance. Yet no African American metropolitan shift occurred in Illinois before 1910. No one has attempted to explain why Afro-Illinoisans at the turn of the century did not make the same locational choices as their counterparts in Ohio and Indiana, because until now no one has noticed the contrast. But whatever explanation is formulated to understand the distinctive choices made by the latter must also encompass the different decisions made by the former.

EXPLAINING CHANGE AND CONTINUITY

Understanding the choices that created the metropolitan shift in two states and deferred it in a third requires reconstructing the perceptions of both migrants and nonmigrants toward two kinds of places: the nonmetropolitan urban places that repelled African Americans and the metropolitan communities that attracted them. Both must be taken into account, and both were changing as the nineteenth century gave way to the twentieth. But only one published source of which I am aware portrays migration during this period from a midwestern small town to a large city from the perspective of the migrant. This is the autobiography of George L. Knox, barbershop owner and publisher of the Indianapolis *Freeman,* who moved in 1884 from Greenfield, Indiana, a town of about three thousand, to Indianapolis. Knox's memoir takes the form of a classic nineteenth-century rags-to-riches story in which the honest and industrious protagonist (Knox) overcomes all obstacles thrown in his way. Living in Greenfield since 1865, Knox built a thriving barbering business and become deeply involved in Republican Party politics. In his words, Knox left Greenfield solely because "I had outgrown the town."[38] His biographer points to another factor that probably also influenced Knox, although mentioning it would have blunted the thrust of Knox's narrative. In 1879, in the midst of the uproar over a supposed African American exodus from North Carolina to Indiana, Knox took charge of providing for a small party of North Carolinians who arrived unexpectedly in Greenfield. For this he was vilified for several years afterward by the local Democratic newspaper editor, who called unsuccessfully for a boycott of Knox's shop. In addition, he was repeatedly threatened with violence because of his race and politics, although Knox gloried in relating how former enemies became friends after closer acquaintance.[39] For George Knox, then, economic aspirations and political conflict seem to have figured in the decision to migrate. To acknowledge the latter's part in his decision, however, would have deflected the upward curve of his life that Knox wrote his book to trace.

Oral history evidence is scarce for the years around the turn of the century, since the ex-slave narratives generally reflect earlier migrations, while most of those who were interviewed in community oral history projects during the 1970s and 1980s took part in the larger mass movement after 1915. None of the extant migrant interviews, whether of interregional or intraregional migrants, articulate the perceptions or considerations upon which the crucial decision was based. Census data, however, contain considerable information bearing upon both individual and aggregate mobility. When this evidence is interrogated carefully, patterns emerge from which perceptions may be inferred.

First, who went to the cities? Given the conjunction of metropolitan growth and nonmetropolitan stagnation, it seems likely that the metropolitan migration stream was composed of both intrastate and interregional migrants, with most of the latter, of course, coming from the South. If only or mostly interregional migrants streamed to the large cities, then the lower levels of Ohio's urban hierarchy would not have lost population, and the black populations of nonmetropolitan places in both Ohio and Indiana would have grown because of the arrival of rural intraregional migrants.

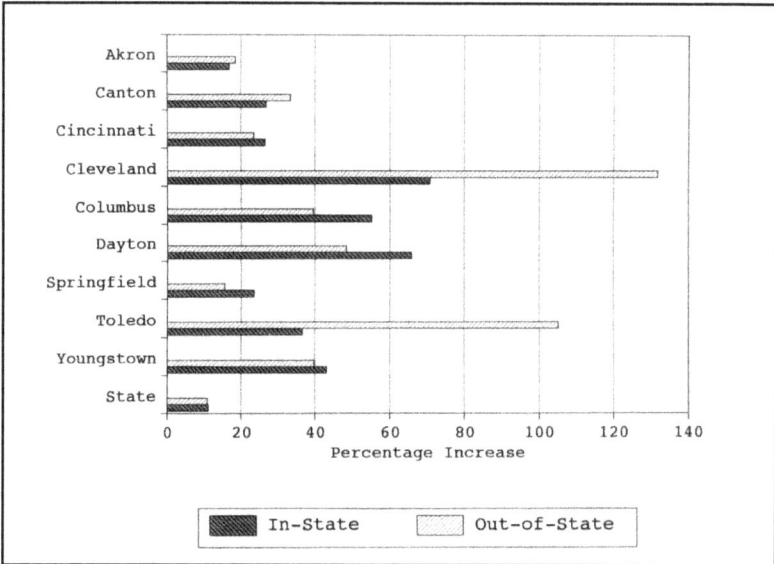

Figure 7.2 African American Population Growth by Origin, Ohio Cities, 1890–1900. *Sources: Population of the United States at the Eleventh Census: 1890, Part I* (Washington, DC: Government Printing Office, 1895), tables 28–31; *Twelfth Census, 1900, Vol. I: Population, Part I* (Washington, DC: Government Printing Office, 1901), 702–29.

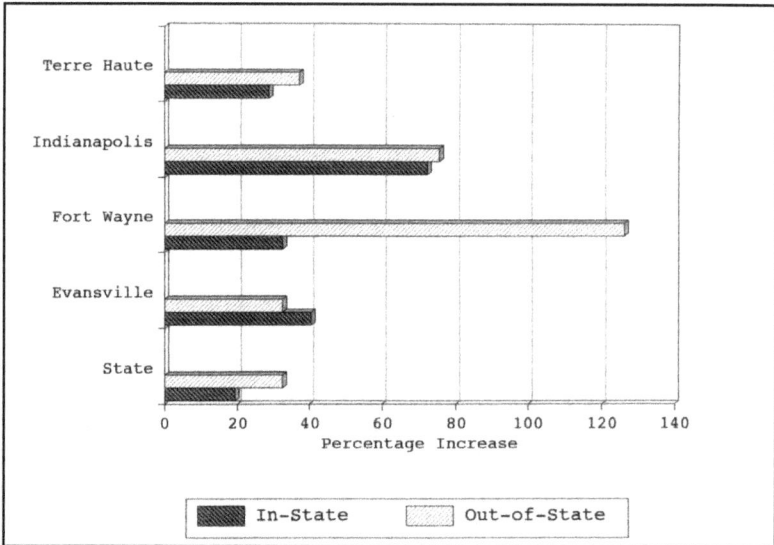

Figure 7.3 African American Population Growth by Origin, Indiana Cities, 1890–1900. *Sources: Population of the United States at the Eleventh Census: 1890, Part I* (Washington, DC: Government Printing Office, 1895), tables 28–31; *Twelfth Census, 1900, Vol. I: Population, Part I* (Washington, DC: Government Printing Office, 1901), 702–29.

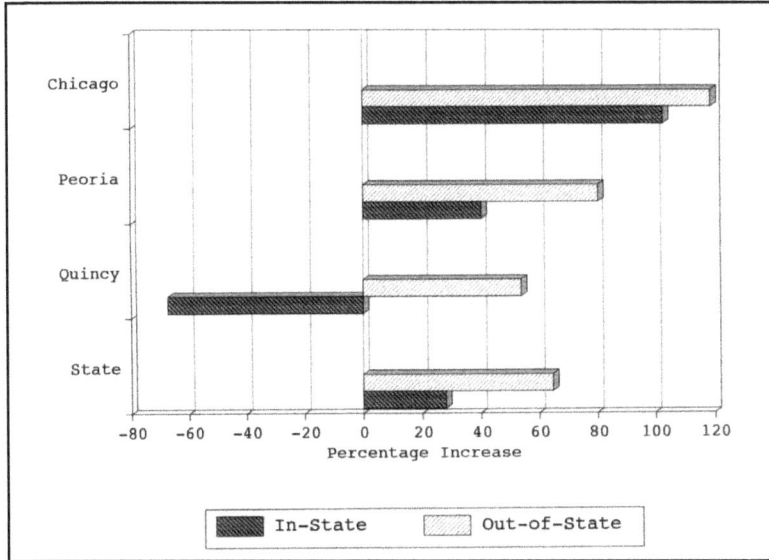

Figure 7.4 African American Population Growth by Origin, Illinois Cities, 1890–1900. *Sources: Population of the United States at the Eleventh Census: 1890, Part I* (Washington, DC: Government Printing Office, 1895), tables 28–31; *Twelfth Census, 1900, Vol. I: Population, Part I* (Washington, DC: Government Printing Office, 1901), 702–29

By the same token, if only intrastate migrants from rural areas and small and midsize urban communities traveled to the big cities, then the incoming migrants would have more than taken their places in nonmetropolitan communities. Empirical evidence to confirm these suppositions and to trace city-to-city variations is available for the decade of the 1890s (figures 7.2–7.4; the 1910 census did not contain information on origins of urban populations).[40]

In Ohio, all nine cities for which origins information is available attracted both intrastate and interstate migrants. This may be seen by comparing each city's rate of increase of Ohio-born population with the statewide rate. Northern cities were generally unhealthy places for African Americans, in whose polluted, poorly serviced and poverty-stricken environments black populations had difficulty in reproducing themselves.[41] Therefore, it seems likely that the cities' rates of natural increase were not higher than the statewide rate, and in fact were probably lower. So any city's growth in Ohio-born population in excess of the state rate represents a minimum estimate of inmigration from within the state. The estimate should be considered as a minimum also because some of each city's increase in population born outside the state represented newcomers to the city who had moved there from elsewhere in Ohio after emigrating from their state of birth. Each city, then, drew from both intrastate and interstate migration streams, although they varied considerably in the volume of each and the relation each stream bore to the other. Of the five metropolitan centers of 1910, Columbus and Dayton were more likely to attract intrastate than interstate migrants, while Cleveland, Toledo, and Cincinnati exerted a stronger attraction for interstate travelers. (Cincinnati's ratio of interstate to intrastate increase, 1.8 to 1, is masked in figure 7.3 because of its large out-of-state population in 1890, which reduces the percentage increase.) The 1890s, however, represented the slower of the two decades for African American inmigration to Ohio. Indiana and Illinois, which experienced more dramatic spurts of inmigration during the decade, provide a better window on the process.

As in Ohio, both short- and long-distance travelers fed the growth in Indiana cities. Both Terre Haute and Fort Wayne showed greater appeal to interstate than intrastate movers, but the numbers were small in both cases.[42] In Evansville the unique excess of in-state over out-of-state growth probably reflects the poor treatment and restricted opportunities afforded African Americans in a city that before 1890 had been a powerful magnet for migration.[43] Even before the 1903 riot, newcomers to the state were beginning to bypass the Ohio River city. In contrast, Indianapolis continued to attract a large migration stream composed of both intrastate and interstate movers, nearly two of the latter for every one of the former. The large percentage increases among both sets of travelers suggests that Indiana's metropolitan shift was caused both by veteran Hoosiers who had renounced alternative settings and by newcomers unwilling to try their luck in smaller urban places.

Population movements were more volatile in the three Illinois cities for which origins data are available, mainly because of Quincy. The years 1890–1910 were not kind to Quincy, which fell behind the rate of urban population growth in Illinois and lost ten percent of its African American citizens. During the 1890s the Mississippi River city suffered an exodus of its Illinois-born that could not be offset by a feeble inflow of interstate migrants. Peoria also lagged behind the statewide rates of urban growth for both total and African American populations, the latter contributed to by slow growth rates in the 1890s for both Prairie State and out-of-state citizens. Chicago attracted more than four interstate migrants for every native Illinoisan, but the doubling in size of the latter group indicates that the Windy City appealed to both types of migrant. Across the region metropolitan migration, whether or not it was accompanied by stagnation elsewhere in a state's urban hierarchy, resulted from choices made by both native Midwesterners and newcomers.

Who were the intrastate migrants? To put the question another way, was outmigration from small towns and midsize cities selective of African Americans compared to European Americans, or among African Americans? If outmigration was selective among blacks and whites, was it selective in the same way for both? Linkage of the 1890 census reconstruction for Washington Court House to the 1900 census and comparison of the 1900 census samples for the two Springfields to the 1910 census make possible an analysis of migration selectivity at the individual level in two decades.[44] Unfortunately, Washington Court House during the 1890s does not make a good laboratory in which to examine interracial differences in migration selectivity, since the lack of growth in both its black and white populations suggests parallel outmigrations. Divergence between black and white migration patterns appeared only after 1900, when European American population growth resumed but African American did not. But Washington Court House during the 1890s provides the only small-town laboratory available in which to test for migration selectivity among its African American residents.

Given the flat population numbers for both groups, it should not be surprising that there was no statistically significant difference between rates of disappearance (the percentage who did not appear in the 1900 census) for blacks and whites.

	African Americans	*European Americans*
Men	29.8	34.3
N	114	907
Women	45.5	38.4
N	44	440

Among both populations, neither age, region of birth, occupational category, nor property holding consistently predicted disappearance (tables A.9–A.10). Age (the young were more likely to leave and the old to die) and region of birth (southern-born were more likely to leave than northern-born) influenced European American men's disappearance rate, but did not significantly affect women's. No variable effectively shaped African American choices to leave. The most tenable conclusion is that outmigration during the 1890s took from Washington Court House a cross-section of both its European American and African American residents.

Springfield, Ohio, provides a better case study of mobility, for the growth of the industrial city's African American population lagged well behind its European American population during the decade that encompassed Springfield's race riots. Among the 1900 sample, African Americans disappeared from census records at a significantly higher rate than European Americans.[45]

	African Americans	European Americans
Men	69.6	57.8
N	270	187
Women	75.7	59.3
N	243	214

The industrial city experienced more population turnover overall than Washington Court House, although at least part of the difference is caused by the method of reconstructing the 1890 census for the smaller town. But the wider gap between African American and European American disappearance rates in the Miami Valley city points to the impact upon mobility of Springfield's race riots of 1904 and 1906, which were far more destructive and pogrom-like than the focused mob violence in the town on Paint Creek.[46]

As in Washington Court House, no background characteristic consistently influenced the likelihood of departure from Springfield among African Americans of either sex (tables A.11–A.12). The impulse to leave was general. Interracial contrasts underline this point. The youngest and the oldest European Americans were significantly more likely to disappear from the records, but probably for different reasons. The rate for those over fifty years of age no doubt was boosted by death, while those under thirty usually vanished from the records because they moved on (some young women also could not be found because of name changes following marriage). The reason why age did not affect the African American disappearance rate is that both men and women in their forties were somewhat more likely than their European American counterparts to leave, and men and women in their thirties were much more likely to do so, producing a more even distribution of disappearances by age among African Americans than among European Americans. The contrast is indicative of unfulfilled aspirations. Despite the presence of a structure of economic opportunity in the industrial city, African Americans in the phase of their life cycle when European Americans were settling down in Springfield and raising families were leaving instead. Among European American women, marriage and home ownership significantly reduced the likelihood of departure, but this was not the case for African American women. Except for the greater stability of African American men who had lived in Springfield since at least 1880, the African American exodus took from the city a cross-section of its citizens.

Springfield, Illinois, too, makes a good laboratory to examine outmigration from midwestern towns. During the decade in which its bloody riot occurred, the growth of its European American population far outpaced the African American rate. In this the Illinois capital was atypical of Illinois nonmetropolitan urban communities, where black and white populations generally grew in tandem, but representative of such places in Ohio and Indiana. African American mobility was more complex in the Illinois Springfield than in either of the other case study towns examined. African American women were significantly more likely to disappear from census records between 1900 and 1910 than their European American counterparts, but men were not.[47]

	African Americans	European Americans
Men	68.6	63.9
N	283	180
Women	71.6	58.3
N	215	223

If the sample is representative, then the slow growth during the riot decade was disproportionately caused by women's greater propensity to leave.

Several attributes conditioned European American male mobility (table A.13). Southern birth, renting, and arrival since 1880 all predisposed white men to vanish from the records by 1910. Among African American men, in contrast, the impulse to leave was general. African American women's disposition to leave, however, responded to variation in age, marital status, renting, and persistence, while European American women's was conditioned only by age (table A.14). Among the under-fifties, young women of both groups were significantly more likely to vanish from the records than older ones. African American single women, renters, and newcomers were the most mobile members of their sex. But among the most mobile groups of African

American women, an equally significant difference appears in comparisons with the same set of European American women. African American young women, singles, renters, and newcomers were all much more likely to leave than their European American counterparts. Part of the difference between female African American and female European American mobility was caused by the fact that the ranks of the former included more women in their twenties, renters, and newcomers (although not more singles), but the fundamental dividing line was racial.

In Washington Court House, the foiled lynching of 1894 does not appear to have disproportionately propelled African Americans from the town, since European Americans showed an equal propensity to leave during the depressed decade of the 1890s. The unequivocally racist mob violence in the two Springfields during the following decade, in contrast, stimulated an African American exodus. Female outmigration from Springfield, Illinois, during its riot decade was selective of those with the shallowest roots in the community, but across all three case-study communities, the best answer to the question of which men and women left is that the impulse was common. Outmigration from such places was usually not very selective. Age, family ties, sectional origins, placement within the stunted African American occupational hierarchy, home or property ownership, and local roots exerted no consistent influence upon the propensity to leave. Eugene Chester, who left his birthplace in midlife and took his "famous smile" to Columbus, was representative of adult African Americans who abandoned midwestern nonmetropolitan places after years of striving and failing to get ahead.

From the perspective of migration theory, this result is not surprising. The most powerful generator of selectivity is distance between origin and destination. As distance increases, potential migrant populations become more differentiated according to their ability to learn about possible destinations and to afford the travel necessary to reach them.[48] For residents of urban places in the Lower Midwest, information about potential destinations, especially the region's largest cities, was easily obtained through a variety of means: newspapers, correspondence, or friends and relatives living there. Indeed, for many an opportunity for personal inspection was only a short train ride away. So was a permanent move. Before George Knox moved from Greenfield to Indianapolis, he had carefully prepared the ground with repeated visits.[49] Eugene Chester's move from Washington Court House to Columbus was no doubt the result of more than twenty years of train trips back and forth to the state capital on Columbus and Cincinnati Midland Railway coaches. When discriminatory treatment or restricted opportunities blunted aspirations, or when white violence threatened the security of oneself or one's family, anyone was likely to leave. In some cases such decisions

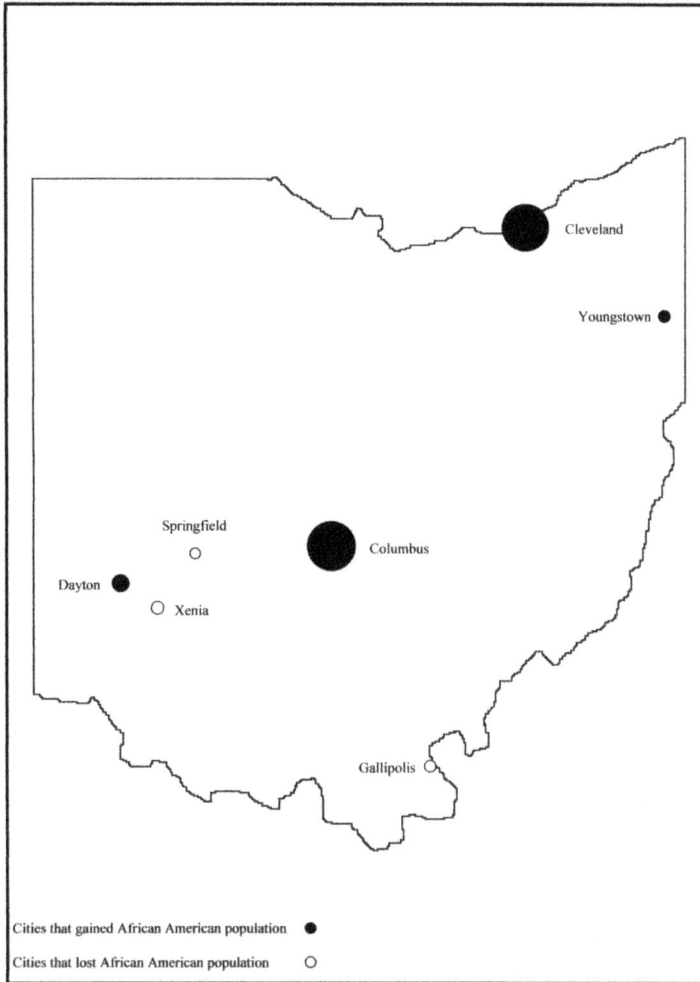

Figure 7.5 Gainers and Losers of African American Urban Population Share in Ohio, 1890–1910.

may have been the product of impulse or a single event, but for others they were the fruit of long years of experience and frustration—plus greening pastures elsewhere.

Finally, what factors governed the locational choices that brought African Americans to large cities in Ohio and Indiana but did not bring about the same result in Illinois? In Ohio a clear-sighted appreciation of the reality of and the potential for white violence played a significant part in shaping the new pattern of African American mobility. Every community experiencing an incident of antiblack collective violence lost share of the black urban population.[50] But not only did African Americans leave places where violence occurred, they also left the *kinds* of places—rural areas and small and mid-size towns and cities—in which lynchings, attempted lynchings, and race riots were taking place.[51] Furthermore, they traveled to precisely the kinds of places that were not only peaceful at the moment, but also where they would be most likely to find security in numbers, cities with large African American populations.[52] Akron and Dayton provide an instructive contrast. Both were among Ohio's most rapidly industrializing cities. Both may have offered opportunities to blacks in unskilled factory work. But Akron's small African American community in 1890, only 451 persons, gave less protection against the race riot that broke out there in 1900 than would have been the case in Dayton, where the black community was more than four times bigger. Dayton made a major gain in its share of the state's urban black population between 1890 and 1910; Akron lost share. Even Cincinnati, in relative decline economically but still sheltering Ohio's largest African American community, increased its share of urban black population, dramatically reversing the trend of the previous thirty years.[53] Of the five cities containing Ohio's largest African American communities in 1890, three—Columbus, Cleveland, and Dayton—ranked among the major gainers in black population share over the next twenty years. A fourth, Springfield, the scene of vicious race riots in 1904 and 1906, was among the major losers (figure 7.5).[54]

More than the negative factor of white violence and discrimination, however, drove African American migration across Ohio at the turn of the century. While distinctive, the pattern of African American migration was not totally different from that of European Americans.[55] Both segments of Ohio's population began to shift from the southwestern quadrant of the state to the rapidly industrializing northeast. Booming industrial towns exerted as strong a pull on black migrants as did places with large African American populations, and most of the former were located north of Columbus and east from Toledo.[56] But in pursuing industrial opportunity, African Americans made their choices incorporating racial criteria. Bypassing violent Akron, they traveled instead to tranquil Toledo, Elyria, Lorain, Canton, Cleveland, and Youngstown.[57]

The African American metropolitan shift in Ohio illustrates clearly the intermixture in black migrants' choices of racial and economic factors. Black Ohioans were pushed toward the cities by a wave of intolerance and racially motivated violence, which temporarily drowned their hopes of integration into American society on terms of equality. Increasingly barred from skilled occupations, they sought out the industrial jobs that were becoming increas-

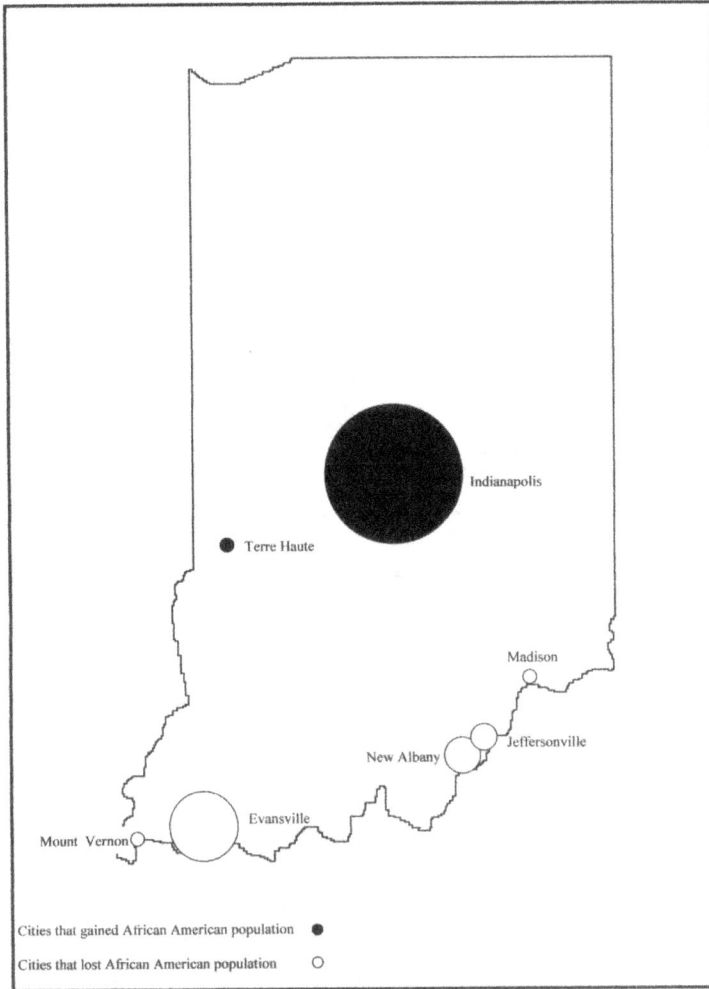

Figure 7.6 Gainers and Losers of African American Urban Population Share in Indiana, 1890–1910.

ingly plentiful in northeastern Ohio cities, even though informal (and illegal) barriers to access to public facilities were being raised there as well as in other regions of the state.[58] Growing concentrations in Ohio cities in turn created opportunities for African American entrepreneurs to find markets within the African American community.[59] The movement cityward thus laid the foundations for the emergence of a new urban African American society and culture.

Such a culture was also beginning to appear in Indianapolis, the principal beneficiary of African American mobility in the Hoosier State. Holding

Figure 7.7 Mothers and babies at the Flanner House tuberculosis clinic, which was added by 1919 to the social settlement's range of activities for the rapidly growing African American community of Indianapolis. *Credit:* Indiana Historical Society (A70)

only one-third of Indiana's black urban population in 1890, the capital city attracted more than three-fifths of the state's black urban growth over the subsequent twenty years. There was a regional dimension to African American mobility, as all five of the towns that suffered major losses in black urban share were Ohio River towns, while both of the two major gainers were located in the central part of the state (figure 7.6).[60] But its most striking aspect was the supersession of the pattern of dispersion that had characterized the previous thirty years by consolidation at the top of the state's urban hierarchy.

The racial distinctiveness of that pattern of concentration suggests that something more than economic motives was at work, and that possibility is strengthened by the contrast between these years and the 1860–1890 period, when black and white urban migrations flowed along parallel paths. Such parallelism did not end after 1890, as the force of dynamic local economies continued to draw African American migrants.[61] In the Hoosier State, more rural and less industrialized than Ohio, factory towns did not exert the strong pull on both African American and European American migration

172

that they did in the Buckeye State. But unlike in 1860–1890, the movement of 1890–1910 was more than a labor migration.

Black urban share tended to fall in communities that experienced antiblack violence, but the correlation is not statistically significant. This is not conclusive, however, on the direction or strength of the relationship between these variables. Of the eight communities where antiblack collective violence was reported, data are not available on African American population for three (because they were below 2,500 total population in 1890). Of the remaining five, three (Evansville, Lebanon, and Vincennes) lost black urban population share.

Unlike in 1860–1890, the size of towns' African American population at the period's outset shows a positive and significant correlation with black urban growth during the years 1890–1910.[62] This correlation, however, is entirely the product of the mass movement to Indianapolis. With the Hoosier capital excluded from the analysis, in fact, the correlation turns strongly negative.[63]

What were the sources of the Hoosier capital's attraction? If population growth is an indicator of economic health, Indianapolis's economy was expanding rapidly during these years, as the capital increased its share of the state's total urban population (from 18 to 20 percent). Its share of Indiana's African American urban population expanded much more rapidly, from 32 percent in 1890 to 45 percent by 1910. Indianapolis's attraction cannot be explained by specifically industrial opportunities, since the capital's proportion of Indiana manufacturing workers actually declined (from 18 to 17 percent). The most likely explanation combines the repulsive power of violence and the appeal of a new kind of community. Evansville offers a revealing comparison. In 1890 Indianapolis's African American population of 9,133 was of course Indiana's largest, but second-place Evansville, with 5,553, also held a substantial number. By 1900, Afro-Evansvillians had created an impressive array of community institutions, and they enjoyed as well close proximity to the Kentucky origins from which many of them had come.[64] Further development of an African American urban culture in Evansville was severely hindered, however, by the race riot of 1903, which evidently convinced many residents, as well as potential migrants, that other cities offered safer environments. In stark contrast to its rapid growth during the late nineteenth century, Evansville's black population dropped by 15 percent between 1900 and 1910. As incentives to migration, a dense community life and many potential links for chainmigration gave way before racist violence.

In addition to a larger and equally clustered African American population, Indianapolis could offer even an even more extensive institutional

Figure 7.8 In 1913 the Senate Avenue YMCA in Indianapolis was able to attract members of the local and national African American elite to the opening of its new building, including George L. Knox, longtime publisher of the Indianapolis *Freeman* (far left), entrepreneur and philanthropist Madame C. J. Walker, and Booker T. Washington. *Credit:* Madame C. J. Walker Collection (C2137), Indiana Historical Society

network. The capital alone had a social settlement for African Americans, Flanner House (founded in 1898; figure 7.7), and the largest African American YMCA in the United States (Senate Avenue, founded in 1902; figure 7.8).[65] Furthermore, Indianapolis had witnessed no lynchings or race riots since 1876, and the sheer size and clustering of its African American community may well have promised security in numbers to those who perceived the vulnerability of African Americans in smaller communities.

These quantitative changes are consistent with a qualitative change in African Americans' perceptions of the array of potential destinations that the state presented to them. During the 1860s through the 1880s, dispersion across a rapidly expanding urban hierarchy suggests an attitude of optimism about whites' willingness to grant equal access to new opportunities. The subsequent pattern of consolidation in the state's largest city implies a growing pessimism about the prospects for equal opportunity in local white worlds, but also hints at a recognition of the possibilities created by an emerging African American urban culture. The novelty of what was

Figure 7.9 Olivet Baptist Church, Chicago, ca. 1903. *Credit:* Chicago Daily News Collection DN-0000183, Chicago Historical Society

being constructed in the capital's African American community, centered on Indiana Avenue to the north and west of downtown Indianapolis, cannot be overemphasized. Like other northern cities, Indianapolis was beginning to combine the African American numbers and density of a southern city with the relative freedom of the North. The larger economy and society within which black Hoosiers functioned was of course still controlled by racist whites. Yet within the larger white world, African Americans were coming to learn that some northern cities better combined safety, economic opportunity, and community life than any other setting in the United States.

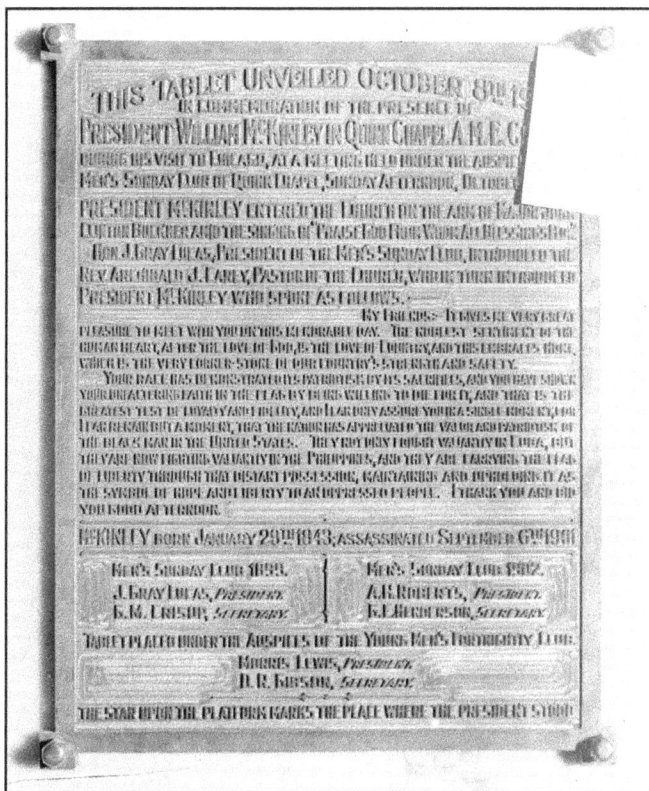

Figure 7.10 A tablet commemorating President McKinley's reelection campaign visit to Quinn Chapel, AME, in Chicago in 1900. *Credit:* Chicago Daily News Collection DN-0000173, Chicago Historical Society

That lesson was slow in bringing African American migrants to the midwestern metropolis of Chicago, but perhaps that was because migrants were careful to distinguish between cities with histories of antiblack violence and those relatively free of such attacks. In 1890 Chicago already held the region's largest African American community, more than 14,000. That community tripled in size over the following twenty years, which gave Chicago the largest share increase of any Illinois urban place.[66] Before investigating why more migrants were not attracted to Chicago, it would be worthwhile to ask why the Windy City drew as many as it did. Migrants' choice of Chicago was probably conditioned in several ways by past migrations. Chicago's larger black settlement created by its Gilded Age migrations formed the necessary base for migration chains that channeled new interstate migrants to the Windy City. Information passed by former migrants and other newspapers

Figure 7.11 Two African American policemen among eight new hires by the Chicago police department in 1903. *Credit:* Chicago Daily News Collection DN-0003344, Chicago Historical Society

played a larger role during this period than the famous Chicago *Defender,* which was not founded until late in the period (1905), struggled to survive during its early years, and did not begin to advocate northern migration until 1916.[67] The sheer size of Chicago's black community facilitated development of the infrastructure for an African American urban community. This was manifested in Chicago's uniquely large and expanding network of African American institutions: churches, fraternal societies, welfare institutions, and businesses.[68] By the turn of the century Chicago's largest African American congregations, in Olivet Baptist Church and AME Quinn Chapel, had built impressive edifices (figure 7.9). President William McKinley's visit to Quinn Chapel during the heat of the 1900 presidential election testified to the influence of a concentrated black vote in a key urban center (figure 7.10). So did the hiring of African American policemen (figure 7.11).

Only Chicago had a black-run hospital, the Provident, founded in 1891, and later a black bank, the Binga Bank, established in 1908. In 1900 the Rev. Reverdy C. Ransom founded the Institutional Church and Social Settlement, which offered African Americans a wide range of social and

Figure 7.12 The Rev. Reverdy C. Ransom and Mrs. Ransom in 1903 on the steps of the Institutional Methodist Church, which he founded three years before as Chicago's first settlement house for African Americans. *Credit:* Chicago Daily News Collection DN-0000555, Chicago Historical Society

educational activities as well as support services (figure 7.12).[69] Chicago's first black-owned silent movie theater, Mott's Pekin Temple, opened in 1905. But even when movie houses in African American neighborhoods were white-owned—as most were—African American pit orchestras framed films with blues and jazz.[70] Chicago's burgeoning community life pulled African Americans to the Windy City during a period when the city's share of overall urban growth in Illinois was falling, a result of suburbanization in the metropolitan area as well as rapid urban growth elsewhere in the state.[71] Furthermore, Chicago's industries, which in 1890 already employed nearly three-quarters of the state's manufacturing workers, created jobs far more rapidly during the new century's first decade than any other urban place.[72]

Chicago's manifold advantages, however, did not produce an African American metropolitan shift in Illinois during the period when one was taking place in Ohio and Indiana. Despite its record of growth, Chicago's appeal to mobile African Americans in its state was comparatively weaker than that of the major cities of its sister states to migrants within those states. Beginning with more than two-fifths of Illinois's African American urban population in 1890, the Windy City drew 58 percent of the state's urban increment over the next twenty years. Indianapolis, meanwhile, began with a smaller proportion (32 percent) but attracted a larger slice of Indiana's increase (64 percent). Ohio's five largest cities also absorbed much more of their state's urban black population growth (76 percent) than their proportion in 1890 warranted (46 percent).

One dimension of Chicago life that could not have attracted migrants was freedom from white mob violence, since the Windy City witnessed more bloody outbreaks than any other place in the Midwest. European American mobs attacked African American workers during a packinghouse strike in 1894, construction workers' strikes in 1899 and 1900, another stockyard strike in 1904, and a lengthy teamsters' strike in 1905 (table A.4).[73] Academic distinctions between labor violence on one hand and racial violence on the other probably held little meaning for African American migrants, who could see who was doing the attacking and who was attacked. Across the state, a majority of the places where antiblack violence flared lost share of the state's African American urban population.[74] Cairo, which experienced the largest loss of African American urban share, amply demonstrates the power of interracial friction to repel. A completed lynching in 1909 and a failed one in the following year climaxed twenty years of worsening race relations in the river city.[75]

No regional redistribution of the Prairie State's African American population occurred during 1890–1910. While Chicago in the north gained, so too did Danville in central Illinois and East St. Louis in the south (figure 7.13). Meanwhile, the major losers could be found in every region, from Galesburg in the north through Quincy, Jacksonville, and Springfield in the central part of the state to Cairo, deep in "Egypt." Outside Chicago, economically thriving towns and cities exerted the most powerful pull on the black migration flow.[76] Both commercial and industrial centers drew African American migrants. Nearly as strong as the tug of prosperity was the repellent power of large African American concentrations, just as in the late nineteenth century. Mob violence also repelled black migrants, but Chicago's example kept them from seeking security in numbers. The complex

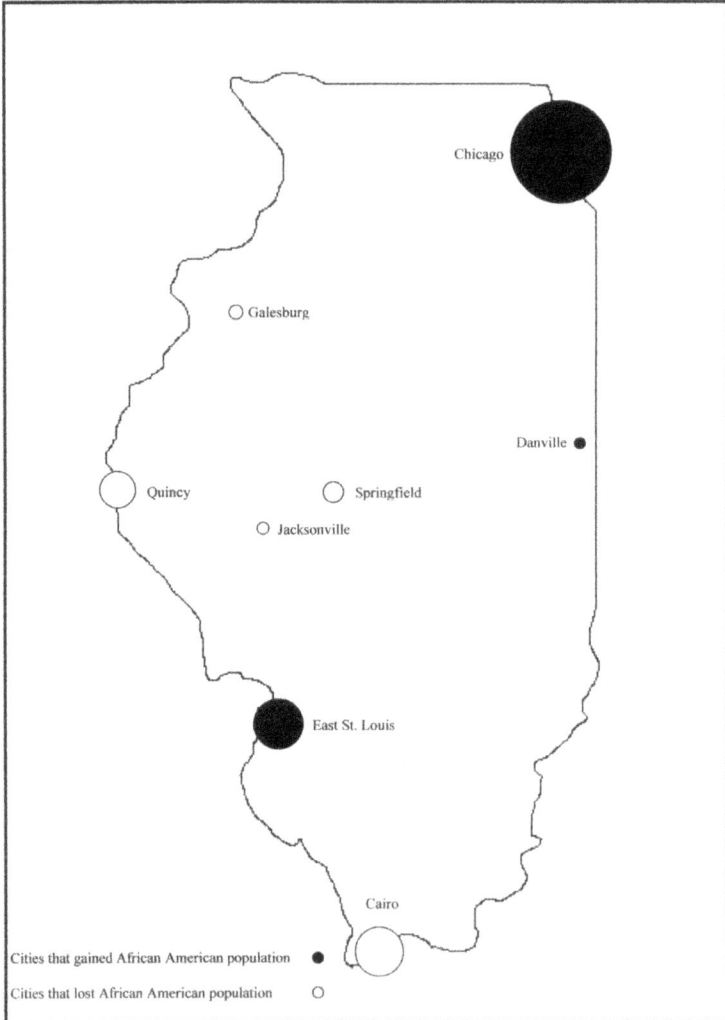

Figure 7.13 Gainers and Losers of African American Urban Population Share in Illinois, 1890–1910.

flows of African American mobility in Illinois can best be characterized as a labor migration responding effectively to changing opportunities. An indicator of this fact is that white migration flowed in parallel channels. Where differences in the two currents appeared, antiblack violence bore the responsibility. But, ironically, white violence in the Windy City helped to keep the two streams flowing side by side by offsetting Chicago's other attractions for black migrants.

Violence thus played a significant part in channeling African American migration during the two decades around the turn of the twentieth century. This should not come as news. If white brutality played a part in convincing migrants to leave the South, they were likely to be alert to the possibility of similar threats in their new homes. In Ohio and Indiana, where attacks on African Americans took place only in nonmetropolitan places, white violence helped to turn the flow toward the largest cities, in which African Americans expected to find security in numbers. In Illinois, white violence in Chicago contributed largely to preventing a similar metropolitan shift from occurring. Lynchings, attempted lynchings, and race riots were extraordinary events that only appeared at specific times in only a few of the hundreds of urban places in the Lower Midwest. Yet such outbreaks were also "normal" in the sense that they represented an extension of the everyday forms of discrimination through which European Americans protected their privilege and power. White violence sprang from complex roots: rivalry over limited goods, envy of real and imagined African American characteristics, and resentment of African American gains. Migration, too, responded to complex, though less dramatic, patterns of historical flow, especially swirling economic currents.

One such ordinary change was the increased presence of females in the migration stream. The hypothetical link between growing female numbers and a cityward alteration in direction is the presumed greater availability of jobs for women that comes with increased city size.[77] Springfield, Ohio, and Springfield, Illinois—towns of more than 30,000 population in 1900—presented a somewhat more diverse range of opportunities for African American women's gainful employment than Washington Court House, whose population numbered only about 5,000 in 1890. When African American women in the South were widowed and made their own locational choices, they "turned to service jobs as the means to support themselves and those jobs were overwhelmingly located in cities rather than the countryside."[78] If women did generally choose larger urban destinations, then their growing numbers in the migration streams to Ohio and Indiana may help to explain the metropolitan shift in those states. The effect of growing numbers of female migrants could only have been partial, however, since it would have influenced only the course of interstate migration, and, as we have seen, both intrastate and interstate migrants were responsible for the metropolitan shift. Women's contribution to metropolitan mobility will be explored further in chapter 8. At this point I merely note that, if women's choices did tend to deflect interstate migration in a cityward direction, then in Illinois those decisions were also affected by other factors, which induced a different course.

A final "ordinary" factor that assists greatly in explaining the deferral of Illinois's metropolitan shift is the prior urban experience, or lack of it, of its migrants. As we have seen, Illinois was distinguished during the 1890–1910 period by the large size of its African American migration stream and as well by the larger presence within that stream of travelers from the Deep South.[79] Ohio and Indiana, in contrast, continued to draw more heavily from the border states and other northern states. Deep South migrants, as chapter 6 demonstrated, were generally less likely than those from the Upper South to have experienced urban life in the South before migration, due to the retarded pace of urbanization in their states of origin. Migrants from Kentucky and Tennessee, for example, enjoyed greater opportunity to acclimate themselves to urban life before they moved north than Alabamians, and a great deal more such opportunity than Mississippians. This process of urban "seasoning" prepared border-state migrants to continue further up the urban ladder when they crossed the Ohio River and chose Cincinnati, Cleveland, Indianapolis, or Toledo. But the larger presence in Illinois's migration stream of Deep South migrants, whether from Alabama, Louisiana, Arkansas, Mississippi, or other states, meant that the Prairie State received a larger component of migrants who were coming straight from cotton fields. Their choices of nonmetropolitan destinations in Illinois mirrored the choices that border state migrants to the North had made in prior years, sometimes south of the Ohio River and sometimes north: to make the movement from rural to metropolitan settings gradually, turning themselves into urbanites step by step as they moved to larger and larger towns and cities.

The twenty years after 1890 should be understood as a period of transition in the history of African American migration and urbanization in the Lower Midwest. More migrants entered the region, but not as many as were to come during the two decades to follow. More travelers from the Deep South came, but, again, not as many as were to arrive afterward. Women made up a larger part of the migration stream than during the 1870s and 1880s, but they were to contribute an even larger proportion during the 1920s. A metropolitan shift began to occur, but only in two of the three states. Continuation of these trends, however, should not be taken to indicate that the entire process was an inexorable one, pushed ahead solely or even primarily by forces external to the Lower Midwest. Instead, the transitions that took place *within* the region influenced the greater changes that were to follow.

8

NEW BLACK WORLDS

[A]t one time, you didn't have anything to choose here in Canton, wasn't nothing here anyway. Now you say why did they come here. Well, if you, if you notice maybe it just a little bit I said a little bit better than Mississippi.
—Kathleen Borboza, Canton, Ohio, 1970s[1]

My youngest brother was about four or five months old [in 1929]. My oldest brother was four, and I was two. My mother put all three of us on her hip and came north because she had a sister and two brothers that had already left Mississippi and had been writing to her constantly about the improvements in the quality of life for black people in Chicago. She had been, of course, trying to get my father interested, but my father had all this time been in Mississippi and had all his roots in Mississippi, and he wanted to remain there in Mississippi. . . .
It must have been hard for an eighteen-year-old woman—with three children—to leave her husband like that. Not that there was any conflict between them, except that she wanted to leave the South—and I thank God that she did!
—George Johnson, Chicago, 1990s[2]

A bout half a century after substantial African American migration to the Lower Midwest began, everything changed overnight—or so it seemed. Suddenly in the middle of the 1910s a leaderless African American army began to pour into the region, and its advance continued relentlessly for a decade and a half. African American arrivals had never gone unnoticed by their European American neighbors, but the large numbers traveling into the region after 1915 turned up the volume and heightened the intensity of public discussion among whites and blacks alike.[3] Unnoticed in the clamor were important continuities between previous and present migrations. Undaunted by the criticism directed their way and the obstacles placed in their path, African American migrants continued to travel to destinations new and old where they found the best opportunities and the fewest difficulties in pursuing them.

THE FLOOD

During the second year of the Great War, several factors converged to stimulate the First Great Migration of black southerners to the North. Against a background of stiffening barriers of legal segregation in the southern states, disastrous flooding and the spread of the boll weevil pushed African Americans from the South. The war cut off the torrent of European immigration that had raged since the end of the depression of the 1890s, and American preparedness campaigns, soon followed by involvement in the war, left factories hungry for workers. In 1910, 89 percent of African Americans lived in the South; by 1930 migration lowered that figure to less than 79 percent.[4] By bringing masses of African Americans out of the South and into northern metropolitan centers, placing them in industrial jobs, and regaining their right to vote, the Migration represented a "watershed" in African American history.[5]

Appreciation of the First Great Migration as a turning point, however, should not be allowed to blind us to significant continuities between this and previous migrations.[6] In fact, the mass movement of the years between 1915 and the eve of the Great Depression should be seen as the product of a long period of experimentation with various alternative options. As we have seen in chapter 6, mobile African Americans in the east south central states had tried both migration to the Southwest and urban migration within their region at the same time when they were testing the possibilities in the Lower Midwest. Such collective experimentation with conditions in other southern or western states and southern cities typified African American life in the South as a whole before World War I. In further testimony to continuity, the tide that flowed into the North after 1915 had already begun to rise in the years around the turn of the century. Estimates of gross migration, rather than the more commonly employed net projections, show that

> even without the stimulus of World War I, significant Negro out-migration [from the South] would probably have occurred. . . . If 1900–10 rates had applied to 1910–20 populations, 79 percent of the gross out-migration to all states and 42 percent of the gross out-migration to non-southern states that did occur in 1910–20 would have taken place anyway. . . . In sum, the main impact of World War I was not in accelerating the rate of gross out-migration of nonwhites from southern states. Rather it was to shift the direction of that outflow towards non-southern states.[7]

Another element of continuity lies in the fact that the displacement farther south of the sources of northern migration that so many have identified with the Great Migration—from the border states to the Deep South—actually began much earlier, during the 1890s at the latest.[8] Migration to the Lower Midwest should be understood, then, as one among several mobility strategies adopted by black Southerners. Their choices of which one to use at a particular time were conditioned by a changing complex of factors, which included access to information and the availability and cost of transportation, both of which were affected by distance between origin and destination. In addition, conditions at the place of origin and at various potential destinations also figured in the calculations of potential travelers. Individual and family decisions had to take these shifting structural factors into account.

The story of Alonzo Parham, who came with his family to Chicago in 1923 at the age of twelve, illustrates some significant features of movement during the Great Migration. Parham's family had farmed in Fulton County, Georgia, but the spread of the boll weevil threatened their livelihood. His father found work in a small town in Virginia, first in a coal mine and then aboveground, and asked his wife to bring their three children and join him. But when Mrs. Parham discovered that the town contained no facilities for the children's further schooling, she refused. The family then followed Mr. Parham's brother to Chicago, blazing a trail to the Windy City for other Fulton County families who came later. Their mobility demonstrated both step migration in Alonzo's father's case—from rural Georgia to small-town Virginia to midwestern metropolis—and chain migration, both in joining Alonzo's uncle and in creating a pathway for others. The Parhams' story also illustrates the common "men first, women later" pattern and the characteristic single-jump movement of women. Economic opportunity was necessary but not sufficient to channel their movement: also foremost was educational latitude. The Parham family's concern for education paid off when Alonzo, who graduated as an honor student from Chicago's Wendell Phillips High School, was nominated to the U.S. Military Academy at West Point by U.S. Congressman Oscar DePriest.[9] DePriest himself was a migrant who left Alabama with his family during the Kansas Exodus and then moved from Salina, Kansas, to Chicago in 1889. His career depended on the political mobilization of both men and women in the Southside to wield the strength that migration had forged. In fact, DePriest's breakthrough election as Chicago's first black alderman in 1915 rested upon the metropolitan mobility of the pre–Great Migration years. The Great Migration itself created the conditions that made possible his election to Congress.[10]

The Midwest, which had shown a weaker attraction than the Northeast during the years 1890–1910, now emerged as the prime regional magnet for southern migrants.[11] Ohio's 84,000 African American newcomers during the decade of the Great War more than tripled the previous historically high numbers of 1900–1910. During the twenties the numbers grew by half again to establish a new record high. In Indiana migrant numbers doubled, to more than 30,000, during the war decade, and then grew to 37,000 in the twenties. Illinois's migrant numbers multiplied more than twice during 1910–1920 over the previous high, and during the postwar decade reached nearly 150,000. By 1930 Illinois, which seventy years before had held the smallest African American population of the three states, contained the largest at about 329,000. Ohio's was now second at 309,000, while Indiana lagged far behind with about 112,000.

Ohio's African American migrants participated in a much larger migration to the Buckeye State, which recorded net gains of both native- and foreign-born whites between 1910 and 1930. Although European immigration to the United States dwindled, first because of the war and later as a result of the restrictive federal legislation of the 1920s, all three states continued to attract more foreign-born travelers than they lost. Indiana and Illinois, however, perpetuated the post–Civil War pattern of net losses among native-born whites.[12] African American numbers were usually dwarfed by the European American inflows, but their higher rate of mobility meant that their percentage of each state's population grew. By 1930, African Americans made up 4.6 percent of Ohio residents, 4.3 percent in Illinois, and 3.5 percent in the Hoosier State.

Georgians, Alabamians, and Mississippians now flocked to the Lower Midwest, their unfamiliar accents making their numbers seem even larger than they were and their arrival a more novel event than the earlier migrations from those states warranted. One such traveler was Sallie Hopson, who departed Macon County, Georgia, in 1917, in company with her mother and sister. They took the Central of Georgia to Atlanta, then changed to the Louisville & Nashville to Cincinnati. The trip to Cincinnati took "about two days and one night, with lunch basket and extra cover to keep warm when the train got chilly."[13] Going on from Cincinnati to Cleveland, their ultimate destination, required at least one more change of train. Illinois's Deep South migrants far outnumbered travelers from the state's traditional sources in the Upper South, but large numbers of Kentuckians and Tennesseans continued to flow to Ohio and Indiana alongside the newcomers from the Deep South.

Migration from the Deep South was facilitated by completion of the southern railroad network and improvement in train schedules. Only 9,000 phantom miles of mostly unusable line at the close of the Civil War, the southern network expanded to nearly 35,000 miles over the last third of the nineteenth century. In 1893 travel by rail from Selma, Alabama, to Toledo, Ohio, required a scheduled time terminal-to-terminal of more than thirty-one hours. By 1930 the same trip still required two changes, in Birmingham and Cincinnati, but the total time fell to just over twenty-five hours. A trip from Clarksdale, Mississippi, to Chicago via Memphis on the Yazoo and Mississippi Valley Railroad (the "Yellow Dog") and the Illinois Central now took only eighteen hours and twenty minutes, compared to an even thirty scheduled hours in 1893.[14]

Wherever they originated, the bulk of the migrants followed the Hopsons' example in choosing a large midwestern city. Across the region, more than five-sixths of the growth in the African American population occurred in the fifteen cities that reached 100,000 total population by 1930. In Ohio and Indiana the migrants of 1910–1930 followed paths well worn by the migrants who had preceded them since 1890. In Illinois African American travelers executed the metropolitan shift that their predecessors had chosen not to undertake.

It cannot be emphasized enough that the African American metropolitan transition in the Lower Midwest was part and parcel of a sweeping process of urbanization that changed the face of the nation. During the first two decades of the twentieth century,

> radical changes in transportation and communication slowed down the subdivision of metropolitan hinterlands and the multiplication of service centers. Higher-order settlements began to capture market areas once controlled by lower-order settlements, while activities and services tended to reconcentrate in but a few high-order centers.[15]

But African Americans did more than participate in America's metropolitan movement: they led the way.

Just as the first stage of Ohio's metropolitan shift had been a distinctively African American movement, so too was its continuation after 1910. The rate of growth of African American populations in the largest cities dwarfed the rate for whites, raising the proportion of black Ohioans in its big cities above two-thirds, compared to less than two-fifths for whites (table A.15). The African American share of population in those cities more than doubled. Interstate migration certainly contributed to the metropolitan shift, but so too did intrastate mobility, as both rural areas and the smallest towns (under 10,000 population) either lost population or showed a growth rate so anemic as to indicate significant outmigration. Geraldine Moreland typified Ohio's intrastate migrants. Born in Cambridge, Ohio (population 8,000 in 1900), she moved to Toledo before the Great War in search of bet-

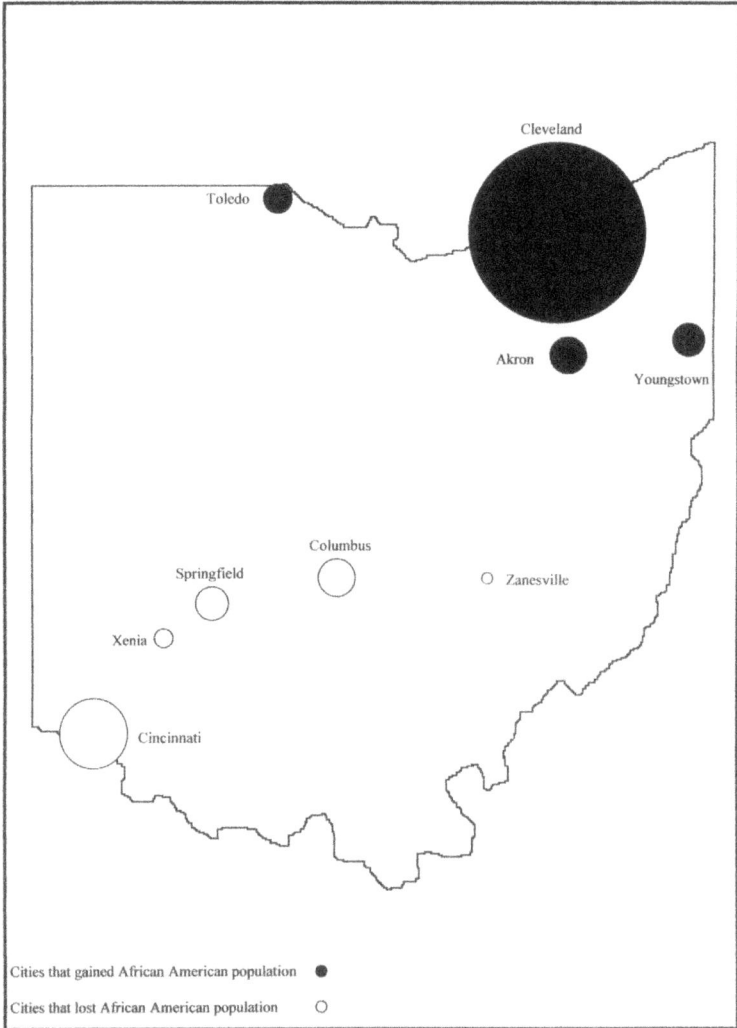

Figure 8.1 Gainers and Losers of African American Urban Population Share in Ohio, 1910–1930.

ter employment opportunities.[16] In contrast to the preceding period, African American migration during 1910–1930 now showed no particular attraction to cities having large African American populations. Instead, black migration flowed in a channel parallel to white migration, only running more strongly to the same destinations.[17]

In moving to Ohio cities during the First Great Migration, African Americans chose carefully among the available alternatives. Despite their large African American communities at the beginning of the period, both

Cincinnati and Columbus failed to attract enough new migrants to retain their share of the state urban black population. The relative fading of Cincinnati's and Columbus's attraction in the eyes of black migrants from the South is powerfully indicative of choices made, since the main rail lines draining the Lower South, such as the Southern Railway and Louisville & Nashville systems, terminated in Cincinnati, requiring transfers to lines to northeastern Ohio cities, most of which ran through Columbus.[18] The cities that gained most were northeastern industrial cities, even Akron (figure 8.1).[19]

During this period, the contrast between Akron and Springfield as African American migrant destinations shows how in migrant eyes the memory of past violence interacted with present opportunity. Both Akron and Springfield had experienced major race riots, and both had lost share of Ohio's black urban population during 1890–1910 despite Akron's dynamic industrial scene.[20] During the second decade of the new century, Akron became the state's fastest-growing city because of its booming rubber factories, and the city's industrial expansion made it a powerful magnet for both black and white movers.[21] Even if black workers were restricted, as at Firestone, to unskilled jobs handling raw materials, the dramatic expansion of rubber production created hundreds of jobs for migrants.[22] Springfield, however, experienced a slight industrial decline compared to other Ohio cities and became a less attractive destination for both African American and European American migrants.[23] By 1930 Akron's African American population, which had been one-seventh the size of Springfield's in 1910, had surpassed that of the Miami Valley city. With white violence a receding threat, industrial opportunity beckoned African Americans to Ohio's northeastern urban complex. A pattern of urban mobility first cut by violence was reconfigured by economic opportunity.

While industrial dynamism was the primary force in channeling African American migration during the era of the First Great Migration, it was not migration's only magnet. This is clearly shown by the case of Cleveland, by far the most powerful attraction in the state. With ten percent of Ohio's black urban population in 1910, Cleveland attracted one-third of the increase in that population during the next twenty years. Yet Cleveland expanded its share of the state's adult manufacturing workers only slightly (by less than 1 percent) during that period, and actually suffered a loss of about the same magnitude in its share of Ohio's total urban population. Cleveland's loss of total urban share is somewhat misleading, since its suburbs, such as East Cleveland and Cleveland Heights, were gaining share, but the contrast between the city's powerful attraction for blacks and its less intense magnetism for whites still requires explanation. Black migrants congregated in Cleveland in part because they were prevented by white pressure from moving to many of its growing suburbs, but in addition the city possessed a positive appeal in African American eyes. During the years between 1915 and 1920, Cleveland's appeal was burnished by African American breakthroughs into the industrial jobs that had previously been filled by immigrants.[24] Although Cleveland's share of Ohio's industrial jobs did not expand dramatically, the number of its factory jobs that were open to African American workers increased. But in addition to a thriving industrial base, Cleveland by 1920 had become the site of the largest African American community in Ohio. To be sure, at 34,000 that community was considerably smaller than Chicago's Bronzeville or New York's Harlem, but it was still bigger than anything Ohio had seen before. Its size and forced compactness made possible the creation and elaboration of a network of black institutions: churches, businesses, fraternal societies, social welfare organizations such as the Phillis Wheatley Association, and cultural institutions such as Karamu House. Though late in development because of the relatively small size of Cleveland's pre–Great Migration black population, these institutions nonetheless formed the essential fabric of an African American urban community. That community attracted black migrants not so much because of the security from white violence it could provide as because it offered the positive values of an urban cultural life.[25] The attraction of such a community brought more migrants to the Forest City during the twenties than during the previous decade despite a slowing pace of job openings.[26]

Indiana experienced even more dramatic changes in its economy and society during the 1910s and 1920s than the Buckeye State. Agricultural modernization throughout the period and agricultural depression during the 1920s cut a swath through its rural population and sideswiped the small towns and cities that depended upon farm business. A winnowing-out process occurred in the urban hierarchy, as towns either grew rapidly or stagnated. Evansville, Gary, Fort Wayne, and South Bend joined Indianapolis in the ranks of cities boasting more than 100,000 population, and the northern location of three of the four newcomers exemplified the pattern of change in the state's economy. Indiana's zone of dynamic growth centered upon the railroad lines that crossed the state's northern region, passed through the Calumet in its northwestern corner, and converged in Chicago. The zone's defining characteristic was industrial expansion.[27] Eight more cities joined the four of 1910 between 25,000 and 100,000 population, but others did not grow to replace them in the classes below 25,000. In fact, both size categories below 25,000 suffered an absolute loss of population (table A.16).

African American migration added to the complexity of change in Indiana, as the state received two distinct migration streams. A traditional current from the Upper South states, mainly Kentucky and Tennessee,

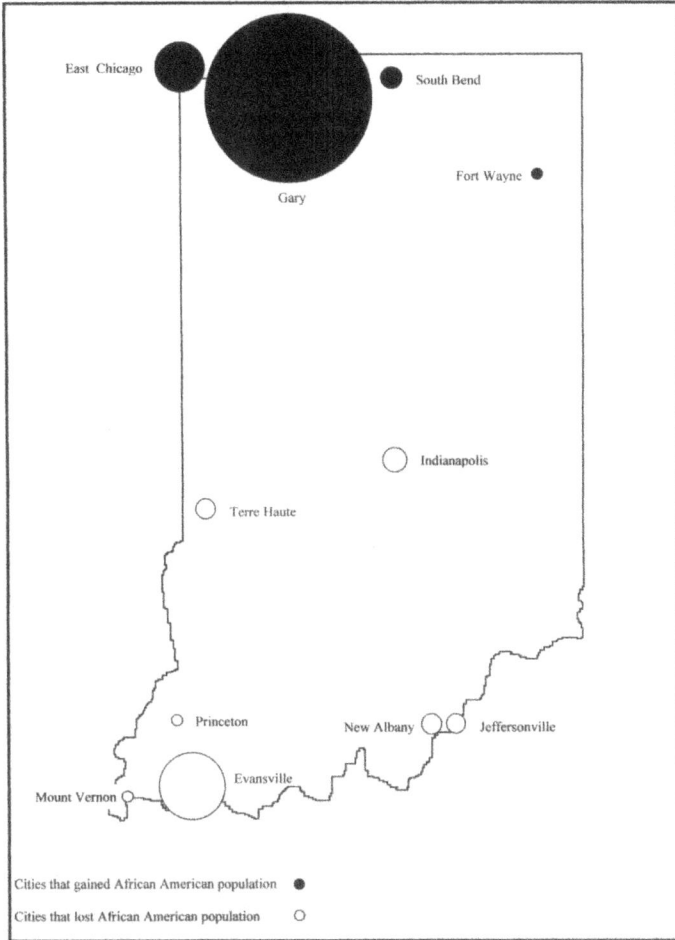

East Chicago

South Bend

Fort Wayne ●

Gary

Indianapolis

Terre Haute

Princeton

New Albany Jeffersonville

Evansville

Mount Vernon

Cities that gained African American population ●

Cities that lost African American population ○

Figure 8.2 Gainers and Losers of African American Urban Population Share in Indiana, 1910–1930.

continued to flow, with many of its migrants ending up in Indianapolis.[28] Meanwhile a new stream from the Deep South, which had traditionally supplied few migrants to the Hoosier State, began to swell during the 1910s and crested during the 1920s, pumping thousands of newcomers into the burgeoning industrial cities of the Calumet region (figure 8.2).[29] For the entire period 1910–1930, the Deep South stream exceeded the flow from the Upper South by roughly a 4:3 ratio.[30] The impact of this new flow was so powerful that, despite doubling its African American population, Indianapolis lost two percentage points from its share of the state's black urban population (from 45 to 43 percent). The modern steel city of Gary, which had begun to rise from the sand dunes of the Lake Michigan shore only in 1906, became Indiana's most powerful magnet for African American migrants, whose numbers increased Gary's black population from 383 in 1910 to 17,922 by 1930 and its share of the urban black population from virtually nothing to nearly 17 percent.[31] Other powerful magnets included East Chicago, South Bend, and Fort Wayne.

To a considerable extent, African American migration in Indiana during 1910–1930 flowed parallel to European American. Both flows were strongly attracted to the most dynamic industrial towns and cities.[32] White mobility, like black, was divided into two streams. The thriving industrial cities of the Calumet drew immigrants from Mexico as well as a current of southern and eastern European immigrants, the latter interrupted by World War I and then squeezed off by the immigration legislation of the 1920s. Urbanization elsewhere in the state was fuelled by native-born whites leaving the state's rural areas and small towns. Yet there was also a difference.[33] African Americans' abandonment of the lower ranges of the urban hierarchy occurred somewhat faster than European Americans', and their concentration in the upper range was correspondingly more rapid. By 1930, two-thirds of black Hoosiers lived in cities having more than 100,000 population, compared to less than one-quarter of whites. In part, African Americans' consolidation in the larger cities represented a continuation of the metropolitan shift that had begun in the late nineteenth century. Of the sixty towns reporting black population in 1890, the African American percentage shrank during the ensuing forty years in nearly two-thirds. But the rest of the African American metropolitan movement resulted from the new stream flowing from the Deep South to the booming industrial cities of the Calumet.

Largely because of the boom in the Calumet, economic opportunity became the principal force behind African American migration in Indiana during the Great Migration years. After the Evansville riot of 1903, no further lynchings, attempted lynchings, or race riots were reported in Indiana until 1930, despite the rise of the Ku Klux Klan to political influence during the early 1920s.[34] Blacks tended to leave towns that had experienced violence during 1885–1910, but such places were usually economic laggards as well.[35] Indianapolis's African American urban culture attracted migrants, most of whom were Kentuckians and Tennesseans, who were more likely than Deep South migrants to have kin or friends among those already settled in the capital city. Indianapolis failed to draw new Deep South migrants because in the years after 1910 the capital city's economy was not growing as fast as the Calumet's industrial prodigies. In addition, the Mississippians, Alabamians, Arkansans, and Georgians who peopled the Calumet cities had established no substantial beachheads in the capital city. Nearby Chicago, in contrast, had begun to attract significant numbers of Deep South migrants since the 1890s.[36]

The choices made by Indiana's African American migrants during the Great Migration years resembled in some ways those made by their predecessors during the 1860–1890 period. In both cases, many migrants chose rapidly growing local economies in communities where few or no African Americans had lived before. But as a result of choices made during the intervening period, the array of possibilities had changed markedly, and this made the nature and meaning of the new migrants' choices different, too. During 1860–1890 a relatively small migration stream dispersed across a large number of small urban places. During 1910–1930, in contrast, a very large stream (for Indiana) funneled into a very few urban places, which already were, or rapidly became, large cities. Blacks' quest for economic opportunity was a constant across all three periods, and to a considerable extent the structural changes in the state's economy can explain the northward shift in black Hoosiers' center of gravity.

But structural economic changes cannot entirely explain the concurrent shift up the state's urban hierarchy, because there were small cities with buoyant industrial economies that did not attract a corresponding share of African American migrants. Examples include Anderson and Muncie, two gas-belt towns that maintained or rebuilt an industrial base after the gas ran out. Both gained a significant share of manufacturing workers during 1909–1929—no small feat considering the dramatic gains made by the cities of the Calumet region—yet failed to secure a similar share of African American migrants.[37] Neither city was likely to attract many Deep South migrants given the largely Upper South origins of their African American residents, but they could reasonably have expected to draw more migrants from the still sizable Kentucky-Tennessee migrations.[38] Yet Fort Wayne and South Bend, industrial cities with 1910 black populations of comparable or smaller size than Anderson and Muncie, captured much larger shares of post-1910 migrants.[39] The principal difference between the two sets of cities is the larger size of the former two in 1910: Fort Wayne held a total population of nearly 64,000 and South Bend nearly 54,000, compared to Anderson's less than 23,000 and Muncie's 24,000. This comparison indicates that by the century's second decade African American migration had gained momentum toward large cities.

That momentum probably derived partly from a recognition of the dangers of smaller places, formed during the violent years around the turn of the century. Any preference for large cities over small towns on grounds of safety did not, however, operate independently of the quest for economic

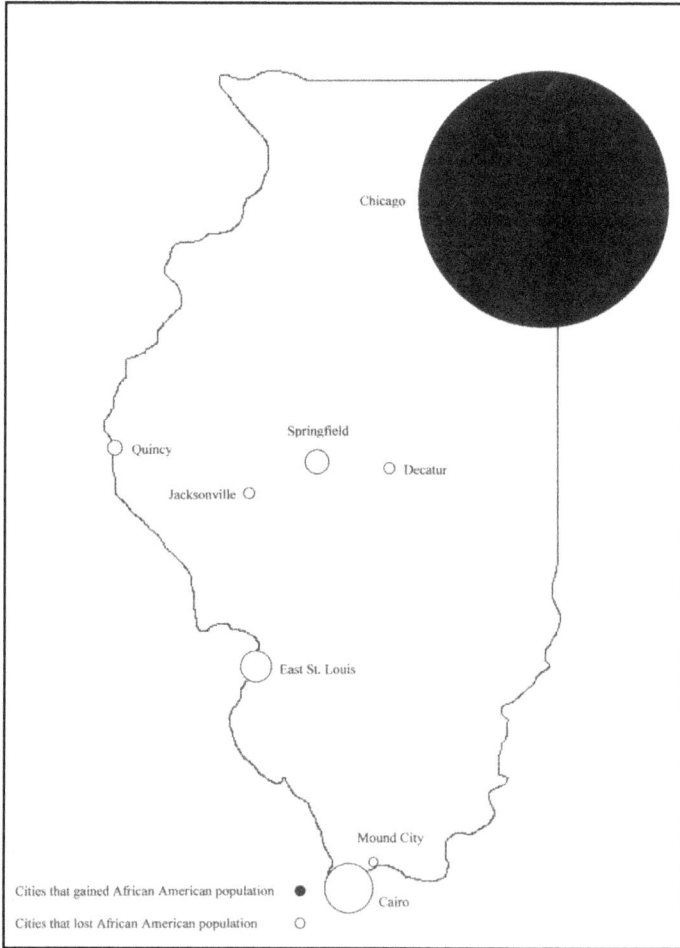

Figure 8.3 Gainers and Losers of African American Urban Population Share in Illinois, 1910–1930.

opportunity. Evansville's huge loss occurred because the city was neither thriving industrially, prospering economically, offering blacks access to industrial jobs, nor regarded by African Americans as a safe place to live.[40] When deciding among peaceful, prosperous, and industrially dynamic communities, however, city size seemed to matter to many migrants. The wind that drove migrants' boats toward such large ports gained strength from their prior experience in the South. As chapter 6 demonstrated, those who traveled north during the Great Migration years were more likely than their predecessors to have lived in an urban community—most likely a small one—in the South. Having set their feet on the lower rungs of the urban ladder, they were now willing, like their European American counterparts, to climb higher.

In Illinois the Great Migration accompanied, and helped to bring about, a delayed metropolitan shift. Between 1910 and 1930 the Prairie State's African American population tripled, and nearly seven-eighths of the growth took place in Chicago (figure 8.3). Meanwhile, Illinois villages and towns saw African American population increases lag behind the European American rate (table A.17). In some Illinois towns, such as Belleville, Bloomington, Cairo, Jacksonville, Mattoon, Monmouth, Mound City, Metropolis, and Quincy, African American populations suffered absolute declines. Both intrastate travelers leaving such communities and interstate migrants fueled Chicago's gain. By the eve of the Great Depression, Chicago and Peoria—the only two cities over 100,000—held nearly three-quarters of the state's African Americans, compared to one-half of the European American population.

What caused both those who had experienced life in Illinois and new-comers to the state to bypass the smaller urban communities whose appeal had persisted undiminished since the Civil War? No factor can be eliminated at the outset, but neither did a single force cause Illinois's metropolitan shift.[41] Urban places that suffered the greatest losses in share of the state's African American urban population tended to rank among the most economically and industrially stagnant communities. A significant exception is Decatur, whose buoyant economy rode a strong industrial current, but where a lynching had taken place in 1893. Evidently the lynching, and perhaps a tense racial atmosphere that followed, blinded potential settlers to the town's appeal—or its racial politics meant that jobs in Decatur's booming factories were not open to blacks.[42] Chicago, however, defeats any attempt to place simple economic opportunity at the heart of migrant choice. During the century's second and third decades, Chicago suffered the state's largest decline in both share of total urban population and share of manufacturing workers.[43] Of course, the city of Chicago's relatively poor performance economically and industrially did not mean that metropolitan Chicago was suffering, since many of the thriving places—communities such as Cicero, Evanston, Oak Park, Maywood, Winnetka, and Wilmette—occupied Chicago's suburban fringe. But it was the city of Chicago that attracted so many African American migrants despite falling behind other towns' rate of demographic and industrial expansion. Within Chicago the expansive years of industrial jobs opening for African American workers between 1915 and 1920 were followed by periods of hard times during the recession

Table 8.1 The Spread of All-White Towns

	Ohio			
	1860	1890	1910	1930
Towns of 2,500 or more population	35	100	139	173
Towns reporting no blacks	1	4	4	10
Percentage	2.9	4.0	2.9	5.8

	Indiana			
	1860	1890	1910	1930
Towns of 2,500 or more population	15	60	88	95
Towns reporting no blacks	0	5	3	18
Percentage	0.0	8.3	3.4	18.9

	Illinois			
	1860	1890	1910	1930
Towns of 2,500 or more population	33	76	144	192
Towns reporting no blacks	4	5	12	34
Percentage	12.1	6.6	8.3	17.7

Source: Study data

of 1920–21 and in the latter half of the 1920s. Poverty-level wages for a majority of employed African American workers required families to find a second source of income.[44]

White violence played a part in causing the metropolitan shift, but it was not a simple role. Incidents of antiblack public violence tended to discourage black population growth or even reverse it in communities where mob brutality occurred, such as Decatur, Danville, Pana, Belleville, Cairo, and Springfield. Residents left, and would-be migrants were repelled. But Chicago's appeal survived the deaths of 23 of its African American citizens and injury to at least 342 others in the state's biggest race riot, in the summer of 1919.[45] Corneal Davis, whose family had decided to leave Vicksburg, Mississippi, after the lynching of Corneal's boyhood friend, arrived in Chicago in August 1919, in the immediate aftermath of the Chicago riot.[46] And the bloody race riot in East St. Louis in July 1917, which left even more African American dead, cannot be wholly blamed for the city's loss of black urban share, at 3 percent the second largest in Illinois.[47] East St. Louis also fell behind the rate of total urban population growth and lost share of industrial workers.[48]

One factor in the choices made by Illinois migrants during the period 1910–1930 was new restrictions on their freedom of access. This is shown by the growing number and proportion of Illinois towns in which no African Americans were reported by the census. Particularly noteworthy is the fact that this represented a reversal of a trend apparent during the late nineteenth century, when the percentage of "all-white" towns fell (table 8.1). Between 1890 and 1910 the percentage of towns having no reported African American residents rose only slightly from its 1890 nadir, but during the next twenty years that percentage increased rapidly, until by 1930 it represented more than one-sixth of all urban places. Between 1860 and 1930, the number of African Americans in Illinois multiplied more than forty times over, yet at the onset of the Great Depression the proportion of the state's urban places in which African Americans could be found was lower than on the eve of the Civil War.[49]

African American residents had never been reported in some Illinois towns, such as Beardstown in Cass County, and among whites oral tradition cited informal intimidation as the means of keeping such communities "lily-white."[50] The increase in the number of "all-white" communities after 1910, however, reflected two new developments, heightened pressure on African Americans to leave independent towns and white suburbanization.[51] Lily-white small towns scattered throughout the state, many of them with stagnant populations, were joined by rapidly growing communities in the Chicago suburban fringe, such as Des Plaines, Highwood, Lansing, Lemont, Lyons, Riverdale, Villa Park, West Chicago, and Westmont. African Americans were not absent from the metropolitan periphery: The all-black suburban town of Robbins was incorporated in 1917; Evanston increased its share of black urban population between 1910 and 1930; and other suburban towns, such as Maywood, Highland Park, and Chicago Heights, made substantial gains in black population.[52] But whether through restrictive covenants, intimidation, or white violence, blacks were shut out of a growing number of suburban communities. The same trend appeared in Ohio and Indiana, in both of which the number and proportion of "lily-white" towns reached a new peak in 1930.[53]

Just as European American hostility blocked African American access to new suburban communities, the same force repelled residents and turned away potential newcomers from non-metropolitan urban places in general. As the case studies in chapters 2 and 3 demonstrate, despite better opportunities for home ownership than in large cities, small towns and small cities offered few remunerative jobs for African American men or women. Apart from ownership of a small home, property accumulation was painfully slow. Such day-to-day discrimination operated in nonmetropolitan towns in all three states, but before 1910 several factors had slowed Afro-Illinoisans' response to it. Repeated mob violence in Chicago had vividly demonstrated the presence of white hostility in the prairie metropolis (while the metropolitan centers of Ohio and Indiana were relatively peaceful). The substantial numbers of Deep South migrants who began coming to Illinois in the 1890s generally left rural backgrounds and used a stay in a small town or small city as "seasoning" to urban life before venturing to the big city. By the 1910s, then, two lessons were probably learned: first, how to adapt to urban life, and, second, that no midwestern community of any size was immune from mob violence.

Once these lessons were learned, the pull of Chicago's attractions could finally exert maximum force. The choice of Chicago as a destination reflects the possibility of African American community building, an opportunity to develop black churches and fraternal societies and black businesses—in short, the institutional infrastructure for an African American urban culture.[54] Chicago became an urban black community—or rather interlocking communities, the Southside and the West Side—of unprecedented size, wealth, and diversity.[55] Unlike small towns and small cities on the Illinois prairies, Chicago offered a variety of choices, of church, of workplace, of social circle, options that were not available in smaller places. Furthermore, the diversity of a large African American community allowed greater scope for retention of southern culture than was possible where a black community might represent a larger proportion of the whole, but be smaller in numbers, more homogeneous, and more exposed to white oversight.[56]

One Chicago migrant's reflections upon the contrasts between Chicago and his Mississippi origins also illustrate some reasons why the Windy City was preferred over smaller northern urban places. Born about 1901, Junius Gaten came to Chicago before World War I with his aunt and uncle. Although he lived in a neighborhood that was at first largely white, he remembered both a segregated world in Chicago and the joys of a rich African American community life. He reminisced about black nightclubs, theaters, ballrooms, businesses, and fraternal societies. The issue in Mississippi was not, Gaten said, simply a matter of survival.

> I didn't come out of a lazy family. I came out of a family in the South that had everything they needed 'cuz they worked like hell for it. We never seen a hungry day. Plenty to eat, plenty of everything, chickens, cows, hogs, pigs, anything. What you didn't have was freedom that you had here. If you would go to town, you'd better get out from there before the sun started to goin' down. You don't want to be caught back up in there. Anyway in a way we didn't see—we in our towns was quiet. We didn't have any nightclubs,

any cabarets. When I got to be a young man, we saw the bright lights as you call them. And I enjoyed that.

In Chicago, Gaten recalled,

> We had the Pithians, Attamatocks Club, the Odd Fellows Clubs, the Elks, we had the Masonics. We all had dance halls and entertainment of all kind[s]. So we enjoyed life.... You see, life was not easy, but coming from the South where you was burdened down, you were afraid to talk, you afraid to say this, if you was on the sidewalk white folks come by, you got to get off, get in the mud. Here we had a little freedom. And it meant so much just to be free and to be able to make your own living and spend your money like you see fit.[57]

As historian Grace Hale notes, "By the 1910s and 1920s, the urban North had become the promised land for African American migrants from the South not because it promised a time or place of racial ease but because it held out the promise of racial agency."[58] That promise shone brightest in the big cities, where African American numbers created the greatest distance between blacks and whites while holding out the prospect of political influence in the larger community. Chicago drew African American migrants, not only because it was the midwestern metropolis, but also because it was a *black* metropolis.

FROM THE TRICKLE TO THE FLOOD

The argument presented thus far depends upon certain assumptions about the efficiency of communications, between North and South and within the North. Migrant flows to some kinds of destinations and away from others correspond to specified sets of characteristics of urban places, such as the occurrence or nonoccurrence of violence, economic prosperity or slump, industrial dynamism or stagnation, and large or small African American populations. Some of these correspondences can be explained by the experience of residents within a community, but the redirection of mobility by those who never had such exposure requires us to assume that such migrants learned about both chosen and rejected communities, directly or indirectly, from those who did. Similarly, a persistent characteristic of the migration process, such as the refusal to avoid towns containing large proportions of European immigrants, holds analytical meaning only if we can assume that the migrants knew in advance of the immigrant presence and decided to move in regardless.[59] The issue of communications in turn raises the question of the influence of the pre–Great Migration migration—"the trickle"—upon the Great Migration, "the flood."

"Even though the [late nineteenth-century] migration streams were relatively small compared to later periods," write Daniel Johnson and Rex Campbell, "they may have served a very important function, i.e., they developed pathways and linkages that served as mechanisms for facilitating and even encouraging later movements."[60] Historians who have examined specific southern origins or northern destinations emphasize continuity between the trickle and the flood, manifested in personal links between earlier and later migrants.[61] During the Great Migration, investigators sent into the South by the U.S. Department of Labor's Division of Negro Economics reported that letters from previous migrants operated powerfully to instigate emigration.[62] A survey of Virginia farm families in the late twenties found that 75 percent had offspring living in the North, usually in cities.[63] When whites in East St. Louis charged that blacks had flooded the city in the months before the 1917 riot, the railway station manager pointed out that what was mistaken for crowds of arrivals were actually large welcoming committees, averaging ten or twelve for each passenger.[64] Migrant oral histories provide abundant evidence for chain migration, as migrants rarely arrived at their midwestern destination without some prior personal link. Even the minority who came friendless usually possessed information about the place.[65] Furthermore, various studies comparing migrants with nonmigrants have shown that migrants were more likely to be literate.[66] Nevertheless, both contemporaries and later historians believed that migrants arrived in northern cities uninformed and unprepared for urban life.[67] Before concluding that information networks constituted a structural component of African American migration to the Lower Midwest, further evidence is required.[68]

The 1890, 1900, and 1930 censuses reported state-of-birth statistics for larger cities, from which the origins of African American residents of those cities may be derived.[69] Because it contained a larger number of sizable cities than its sister states to the west, Ohio furnishes the best laboratory in which to study continuity of migration patterns, from which the efficacy of communications may be inferred. A comparison of the share held by cities of migrants from each source reveals that large migrant groups in each city in 1930 were generally already overrepresented in that city as early as 1900 (table A.18). Columbus presents the most striking example. The 1,060 West Virginians living in the capital city on the eve of the Great Depression represented a substantial increase over the 324 who had been living there thirty years before. So did the 3,409 Virginians, compared to 1,266 in 1900, and the 2,310 North Carolinians, whose numbers had increased from 250 in 1900. In part these concentrations reflect the channeling effect of railway lines. The principal lines connecting Virginia, West Virginia, and North Carolina with Ohio—the Baltimore & Ohio, the Chesapeake & Ohio, and the Norfolk & Western—all ran through Columbus. But choices still had to be made, since all three lines also ran to Cincinnati, the B & O to Akron, and the C & O to Toledo.[70] In all of these cities Virginians, West Virginians, and North Carolinians were underrepresented in 1930. How did prospective migrants in Virginia, West Virginia, and North Carolina come to choose Columbus over Cincinnati, Akron, Toledo, and other cities, if not through the influence of communication with previous travelers?

Similar patterns of continuity appear in concentrations of Deep South migrants as well. Tiny colonies of South Carolinians in Youngstown (14) and Cleveland (43) in 1900 nevertheless represented significant clusters in light of the scattered distribution of their 437 fellow Palmetto Staters across Ohio. By 1930 these clusters had grown into much larger settlements, 963 and 3,509, respectively, and the two northeast industrial cities still held significant shares of the greatly augmented number of South Carolina migrants to the Buckeye State (11,831). Similarly, Toledo's distinctive cluster of Mississippians in 1930 (936) grew from a small but equally special 1900 cohort of seventeen.[71]

Communication created city-specific migration streams among the six major groups of Ohio's black migrants during the Great Migration period. Cleveland was a mecca for five of the six state groups—Georgians, Alabamians, Tennesseans, South Carolinians, and Mississippians—and was shunned only by Kentuckians, who settled instead in Cincinnati and the Miami River Valley cities of Springfield and Dayton. Georgians, besides Cleveland, were significantly overrepresented in 1930 only in Akron and Cincinnati. Alabamians generally migrated to the northeastern cities, except Toledo. Tennesseans, in contrast, generally preferred Toledo and Dayton along with Cleveland and avoided Akron, Youngstown, and Columbus. South Carolinians liked Cleveland and Youngstown, but they shunned Toledo along with the Miami Valley cities. Mississippians chose Cleveland and Toledo, and were underrepresented in Akron, Cincinnati, Columbus, and Springfield.

Communication networks, of course, can only partially explain the channels cut by mobile African Americans, for as important as the amount of information transmitted is its content. To place communication in context it may be helpful to follow the choices of one state cohort across forty years of migration. In 1890 only 474 Georgia-born African Americans lived in Ohio, and in 1900 there were 847. By 1930 their number had mushroomed

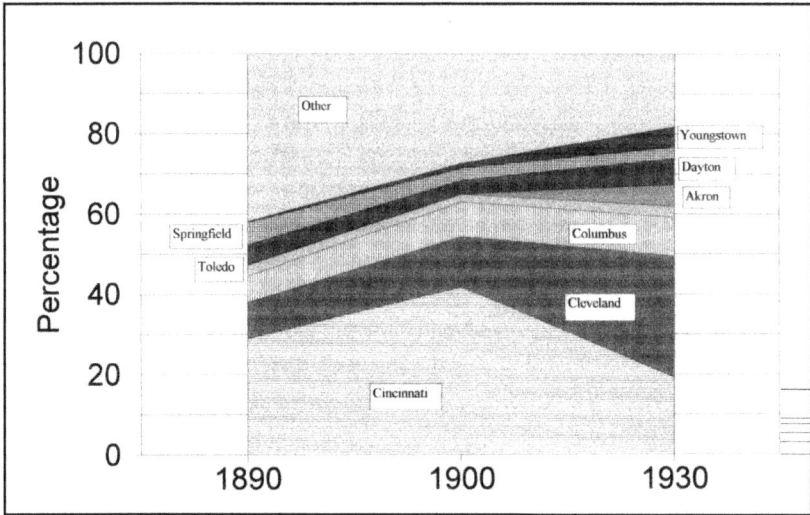

Figure 8.4 City Choices of Georgia-born Ohioans, 1890–1930.
Sources: Eleventh Census, 1890, Part I (Washington, DC: Government Printing Office, 1895), Tables 28–31; *Twelfth Census, 1900, Vol. I: Population, Part I* (Washington, DC: Government Printing Office, 1902), 702–29; U.S. Bureau of the Census, *Negroes in the U.S., 1920–1932* (Washington, DC: Government Printing Office, 1935), 24, 28–31, 34–36

to 48,847. Yet Georgians' locational choices remained remarkably consistent, as can be seen in the regular proportions attracted to Springfield, Dayton, Toledo, and Columbus (figure 8.4). When they were not, the changes can be explained by factors already noted. Cincinnati, which held Ohio's largest African American community in 1890, increased its share during the 1890s as African Americans sought security in numbers from the wave of white violence breaking over the state, then lost share as the state's economic and industrial heartland moved north. Closer to that beating commercial heart, Youngstown and Akron attracted more travelers from Georgia during the Great Migration. Cleveland's African American community grew based on its industrial strength, and maintained its appeal based on the promise of its new black urban world. Collectively, these large cities attracted more and more Georgians away from smaller centers as the years went by.

The migrants of the Lower Midwest's trickle years thus appear to have played a crucial role in channeling the flood. They were the reconnaissance parties, exploring the new territory and reporting what they found to their friends and relatives in the South, who in turn passed on their reports to others. Their letters and visits, and the newspapers they supported, furnished the means by which prospective migrants learned that there were few jobs for them in the North until the immigrants stopped coming. Or that small towns could be not only unwelcoming but violently hostile. Or that a new world, beset by old dangers but also pregnant with novel possibilities, awaited them in the region's metropolitan centers.

METROPOLITAN MAGNETS

To understand fully the implications of metropolitan choices, a searchlight must be thrown onto the dangers and possibilities latent in large midwestern cities. Whether in Chicago's stockyards, Gary's steel works, Akron's rubber factories, or Cleveland's foundries, big cities after 1915 offered jobs for African American men. In fact, the Midwest led the nation in opening factory jobs to African Americans.[72] The new availability of industrial work in cities reversed patterns of decline in black occupational opportunity since the late nineteenth century, when immigrants squeezed African Americans out of trades, such as barbers and waiters, which they had previously dominated.[73] Factory work, while rarely skilled or open to advancement, at least provided regular pay in good times, a chance to change disagreeable jobs, and relief from the close personal scrutiny by whites common in the South.[74] In addition, the expansion of African American communities offered new opportunities, however limited, for black entrepreneurs.[75]

Premature death constituted the principal danger of black metropolitan life. Northern cities were historically unhealthy places for African Americans, the number of deaths commonly exceeding births.[76] In midwestern rural areas and small towns, African American death rates, while higher than those of European Americans, generally seem to have been lower than those prevailing in metropolitan places.[77] For some migrants, the decision to move cityward, either from the rural South or from a smaller northern community, no doubt shortened their lives.

The second major danger facing African Americans entering the city was the pressure on family life caused by loss of control over their habitat. Chances for home ownership were severely diminished in metropolitan places compared to nonmetropolitan communities. The 1920 census reported rates of black homeownership in southern states ranging from 14.5 percent in Georgia to 41.2 percent in Virginia, and averaging around 20 percent.[78] As we have seen, the percentage of African Americans living in family-owned homes stood at 23 and 37 percent in the two 1900 Springfield samples, and reached as high as 48 percent in Washington Court House in the same year. A sample drawn from the 1920 census in Muncie, Indiana, found 32 percent of adult African Americans living in family-owned homes.[79] In contrast, only 17 percent of African American homes in

Indianapolis, 9.5 percent in Gary, and 7.4 percent in Chicago were owned in 1920. In the South, too, the proportion of black homeowners tended to fall as city size increased.[80] To move cityward was to reduce one's chances of becoming a homeowner and thereby to exert the most fundamental form of control over one's surroundings.

One of the most serious aspects of the situation was restriction of the parts of the city in which African Americans could live, i.e., the creation of "the ghetto." White terrorism and restrictive covenants kept African Americans confined to an area that expanded, but expansion never came quickly enough to alleviate overcrowding. Meanwhile, European Americans moved out of neighborhoods that had initially been racially mixed. Because of the overwhelming demand for housing in a limited area, African American families typically paid higher rents than European Americans would have paid for the same accommodations. Overcrowded quarters, together with city officials' reluctance to provide urban services to African American neighborhoods, as well as police action in pushing city vice districts into those same neighborhoods, of course contributed mightily to the notoriously high African American metropolitan death rates. In addition, high rents took back from African American families at least part of the higher wages they gained by moving north and cityward.[81]

At the time, many commentators, both European American and African American, blamed the difficulties African Americans faced in northern cities on the migrants themselves. In white eyes, "the Negro problem" had moved north.[82] Sober scholarly reflection leads to a significantly different view. "[T]he situation in the city," as sociologist Charles Tilly points out, "rather than the fact of moving, shook Negro family life in the time of the great northward migration."

> The distinction may seem academic: the impact of any move on the individual always includes the differences in living conditions between the origin and the destination. Yet it matters a great deal. For in the one case we might conclude that as migration slowed down and the immediate shock of moving faded, the troubles of Negro families would disappear. In the other case, we could hardly expect much improvement until the opportunities open to Negro men and women in the big city changed.[83]

As subsequent history has shown, those opportunities did not change for a very long time.

One opportunity that big cities did offer in contrast to smaller urban places was jobs for women. Women's gainful work furnished a way of coping with the high rents African American families had to pay, as well as the low wages relative to whites that were paid to black workers. Most of these jobs were in domestic service, but some were in factories.[84] In contrast, most small towns and small cities provided little opportunity for African American women beyond domestic work, and perhaps not much even of that. In Evansville African American women's only "industrial" work took place in a cigar factory.[85] Oral history respondents in Springfield, Illinois, agreed that African American women who wanted better jobs than domestic service had to leave.[86] The contrast between African American women's opportunities for gainful work in larger and smaller urban places may have been, at least in part, a function of numbers. Even if large cities held the same proportion of families who could afford to hire a maid, nurse, or laundress, the proportion of the population that was African American was often smaller in such places than in lesser urban communities, and the supply of African American domestic help accordingly restricted. Big-city work opportunity for women in turn spurred migration and helps to explain the ongoing metropolitan shift in all three states.[87]

More than the huge numbers of migrants during the World War I decade signaled the onset of a new cycle of migration. In all three states of the Lower Midwest, the sex ratio of the migration stream rose, indicating a greater infusion of men than women. This occurred most dramatically in Ohio, where industrial opportunity played such a large part in drawing travelers to the dynamic northeastern cities. Then during the twenties the migrant sex ratio fell, to parity in Indiana and below parity (i.e., more women than men) in Ohio and Illinois (figure 1.1).[88] Among midwestern cities after 1890, a rising proportion of women in the migrant stream over a twenty-year period usually accompanied growth in the city's share of its state's African American urban population.[89] That is, the proportion of women migrants grew just when a city's migration stream expanded.

Women's role in metropolitan growth may be seen in the histories of individual cities of the Lower Midwest (figure 8.5).[90] The long-term trend over the years between 1890 and 1930 was for sex ratios to fall from high levels. That is, cities in 1890 generally contained more African American males than females, but over the next forty years more women than men came. By 1930 the four largest African American communities—Chicago, Cleveland, Cincinnati, and Indianapolis—were near parity. The principal deviations from this long-term trend appear in the dynamic northeastern Ohio industrial cities—Akron, Toledo, Cleveland, and Youngstown—during the 1910–1920 decade. During the twenties, women dominated the migration stream in every city, bringing down sex ratios across the top range of each state's urban hierarchy.

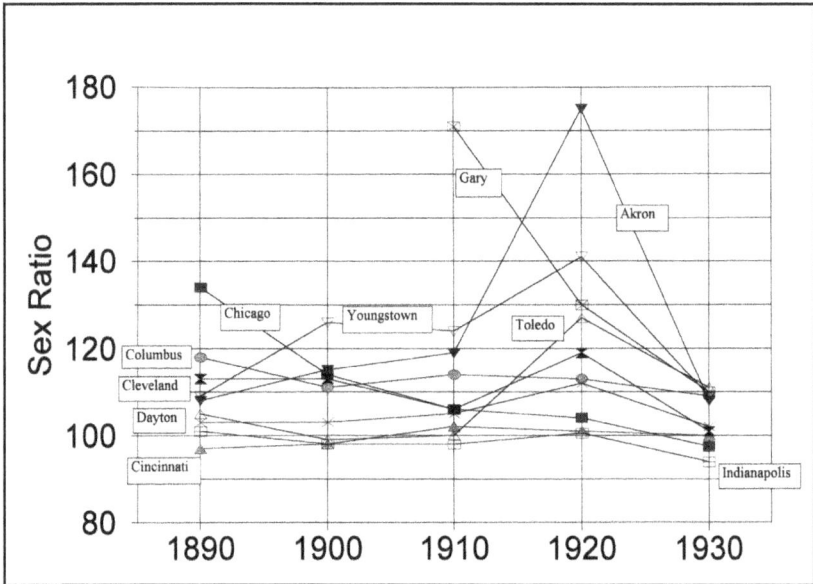

Figure 8.5 The Changing Sex Balance in Large Midwestern Cities, 1890–1930. *Sources:* U.S. Bureau of the Census, *Negro Population 1790–1915* (Washington, DC: Government Printing Office, 1918), p. 156; *Negroes in the U.S., 1920–32* (Washington, DC: Government Printing Office, 1935), p. 85

These temporal and geographic variations between men and women strongly suggest that migration was a gendered experience at the African American grassroots.[91] In each of the three cycles of migration between the Civil War and the onset of the Great Depression, men led the way. Although across the seventy-year period men did move cityward, they were more likely to stop in rural areas during the post–Civil War years and in smaller centers. When women came north in rising numbers relative to men during the 1880s, the migration as a whole was too small to have much impact in redirecting the flow toward the big cities. Women did cause such an impact in Ohio and Indiana, however, during the new century's first decade. Women's effect on the path of midwestern migration became apparent once again during the 1920s, when their locational choices contributed to the continuing metropolitan channeling in Ohio and Indiana and the new cityward direction in Illinois.

In conclusion, the choices that brought African American migrants to midwestern cities were not simple ones. They were based on a multitude of sometimes conflicting incentives, which reinforces the point that choice operated at the heart of the movement. Personal and collective histories, both in the South and in the North, weighed heavily in shaping locational decisions. So too did present opportunities, the information networks that carried news of dangers and possibilities, and the transportation systems that conveyed the migrants themselves. Metropolitan migration was both racially tinged and shaped by structures common to blacks and whites alike.

ALTERNATIVES

Even in the face of the metropolitan transition underway across the region after 1910, some small cities continued to draw African American migrants. Their magnetism, continuing in some states and renewed in others, indicates that the appeal of metropolitan centers, while broad, was not universal. Furthermore, some migrants who were classed by the census as metropolitan residents in fact were seeking lifestyles as close as possible to a small-town model.

In Ohio towns and cities with more than 10,000 but less than 100,000 population enjoyed healthy growth during the twenty years after 1910. Communities in the lower part of this range gained European American population faster than the statewide rate, and the more populous small cities actually grew more rapidly than Ohio's biggest cities (table A.15). Yet healthy as were the increases in European American populations, African American populations in both size categories expanded at more than double the European American rate. The proportion of black Ohioans who lived in towns in these brackets fell only because of the concomitant rush to the cities. Black mobility to these midsized cities reversed the pattern of 1890–1910. Having avoided such communities around the turn of the century, migrants were now returning to them.

Intrastate migrants moving step by step up the urban hierarchy certainly contributed to this growth in midsize cities, but so too did interstate travelers. During the Great Migration, Alabamians and Georgians made up the largest groups of migrants to the Buckeye State. In 1930, virtually all of the Georgia-born and Alabama-born blacks living in Ohio had migrated to the state during the previous thirty years. They were more likely to be living in the state's seven largest cities (Akron, Cincinnati, Cleveland, Columbus, Dayton, Toledo, and Youngstown) than were U.S.-born blacks as a whole (79 percent and 76 percent respectively, compared to 67 percent), but one-fifth of black Georgians and nearly one-quarter of black Alabamians were living in smaller places.[92]

In Indiana and Illinois, African American population growth in the growing numbers of second-tier cities (25,000–99,999) kept pace with European American increases. Indiana's second-tier cities actually increased their share of the state's African Americans, probably because they drew from the devastated rural areas, villages, and small towns. Data are not available to assess definitely the distribution of interstate and intrastate migrants among Indiana urban places, however. In Illinois it is possible to estimate the proportion that migrants from Mississippi, the state's most prolific source of inmigrants during the period 1910–1930, contributed to the total who settled in nonmetropolitan communities. That proportion, between 27 and 38 percent, somewhat exceeds the proportion that black Mississippians comprised of the total African American migration stream to the Prairie State.[93] It follows, then, that Mississippians did not concentrate in Chicago, instead continuing to divide between metropolitan and nonmetropolitan destinations.

Possible factors to explain small cities' appeal to African Americans include the familiarity of a small-town environment to those who had never lived in a large city and a more relaxed pace of life. Some would-be migrants who wrote from the South to the Chicago *Defender* indicated that they preferred small towns.[94] "I don[']t care for the large city life," a barber wrote from Starkville, Mississippi. "I rather live in a town of 15 or 20 thousand."[95] Phoebe Mitchell Day, born in Springfield, Illinois, worked for two years in Chicago before returning to Springfield to stay. "I've always been used to a small city, and I never was really happy living in Chicago," she recalled.[96]

For those migrants attracted by newly opening industrial jobs, these could be found in small cities as well as large ones.[97] In Ohio African Americans were drawn to the fast-growing industrial cities of Barberton, East Cleveland, Elyria, Massillon, Niles, and Warren in the booming northeastern part of the state, as well as to Middletown near Cincinnati; these cities held 1930 populations ranging from 16,000 to 41,000.[98] Every Indiana small city that gained a significant share of the state's African American urban population was a thriving industrial community. These included former gas-belt cities Anderson and Muncie, northern manufacturing centers Elkhart and Kokomo, and East Chicago and Hammond in the Calumet region. In Illinois rapidly growing industrial activity helps to explain the appeal of Chicago's western suburb Maywood and Rockford farther west. Meanwhile, however, other lusty industrial small cities, such as Ohio's Norwood and Illinois's Cicero, Blue Island and Granite, stoutly resisted any larger African American presence.[99] And African American migrants poured into other small cities where the pull of new industrial opportunities was weaker, such as Cleveland Heights, Ohio, and Evanston, Illinois.

Greater opportunity for a more extensive range of personal contacts with other community residents may have offered to African Americans an opportunity to dispel racial stereotypes, which in the early twentieth century were uniformly negative. When an African American doctor moved into an all-white neighborhood in Canton, Ohio, he and his family had "problems. People didn't want them. . . . But after they got to know them they accepted them."[100] But the author of an intensive study of African American life in the small-town North argues that racial stereotypes were never completely shaken off. The white community in Monroe, Michigan "assumed some level of responsibility for *its* blacks. But having an identity in Monroe only mollified and did not defuse or nullify the effects of the more powerful social identities," that is, the negative stereotypes (emphasis in original).[101] Nevertheless, in contrast to the impersonal contacts of large cities, African American residents may have found establishing an individual identity less difficult in smaller urban settings.

The findings from the three case study communities examined thus far indicate that greater opportunity for home ownership distinguished smaller from larger cities during the years around the turn of the century. This factor and others may be tested for the Great Migration era by a close scrutiny of a fourth case-study community, Muncie, Indiana. In 1880 Muncie was only slightly larger than Washington Court House, but it held a much smaller African American community. Discovery of an immense natural gas field in northeastern Indiana in 1886 changed everything for Muncie, as for other gas-boom towns. Natural gas supplies and other inducements enticed glass and metal works to the "Magic City," and their presence allowed Muncie to escape the effects of the severe depression of the 1890s. In fact, Muncie's European American population expanded by 85 percent during the depression decade, and its African American community also experienced healthy growth (77 percent). Drawn by the gas boom–induced prosperity, Alexander Kelley and his wife Belle came to Muncie from Indianapolis in 1886. Both had been born in slavery, Alexander in 1855 in North Carolina, and Belle two years later in Kentucky. In 1873, Alexander reported, his mother "decided to take me farther west where I would have better advantages." In Indianapolis Alexander learned to cook and worked as a hotel chef. Belle, meanwhile, had traveled to Indianapolis with her parents. She and Alexander met and married in the capital city, then moved to Muncie. Belle worked as an "expert housekeeper," and Alexander found a position as chef in the Kirby House Hotel, where he cooked for many years.[102] Their grand-daughters still lived in Muncie in 2001.

The local economy slumped after the gas ran out in 1901, but Muncie reindustrialized during the second decade of the century.[103] By that decade's conclusion, Muncie was a diversified industrial city. Its best-known works, the Ball Brothers Glass Manufacturing Company, had been for two decades the nation's leading maker of glass fruit jars, but the town also held other significant glass factories such as the Hemingray Company, which made insulators for the rapidly expanding electrical industry. In addition, foundries and other metalworks and a recently built Chevrolet assembly plant figured large on the local industrial scene. Muncie now held more than 36,000 citizens, and during the period of impressive growth since 1880, its African American population had grown faster than the European American, to a total of 2,054 in 1920. At 5.6 percent, the proportion of African Americans in Muncie's population exceeded that in New York, Chicago, Cleveland, or Detroit.[104]

Interviewed in 1980, a black migrant to Muncie who had worked in one of the city's foundries recalled, "You could always get a job in Muncie when you couldn't get a job any place else. Used to be plenty of work here in the factories and the foundaries [*sic*]. . . ."[105] Most African American men worked in unskilled jobs in metalworks, with another substantial group in glass factories. A few blacks managed to find skilled work as machinists. About one in ten women workers also filled industrial jobs, all in glassworks.[106] One reason for African Americans' presence in Muncie's factories may have been that they allowed employers to carry out the shopworn tactic of creating ethnic divisions among their work forces, a trick that would otherwise have been impossible to pull off in a town that attracted few European immigrants.

As well as jobs, African American migrants found integrated schools, buses, and streetcars, although no white-run restaurants would allow them to eat on the premises and theaters seated blacks only in the balconies, forms of discrimination that continued at least into the 1930s. Some parks and swimming pools were closed to blacks. Oral history interviewees reported that African Americans were not hired as clerks in stores or waiters in restaurants.[107] The glass workers' union excluded African Americans. Despite African Americans' long and now substantial presence in Muncie, as late as 1920 a local newspaper seemed to regard them as an alien element. The *Muncie Evening Press* carried a regular "Colored News" column that reported local events, illnesses and recoveries, and comings and goings. In every respect but the names of its subjects, the "Colored News" column was identical to the paper's "Society" column, but the two features never appeared on the same page.[108] The public sector, however, told a different story. At least in part because of black Muncie's increasing political weight, before 1900 an African American had been appointed to the fire department, another to the post office, and a third to the police force.[109]

Muncie also seems to have been free from antiblack collective violence. Its relatively tranquil racial atmosphere may have been particularly important in bolstering Muncie's appeal to African Americans during its industrial slowdown in the first decade of the century, a period when violence flared in other communities such as Evansville, while black migrants continued to flow into Muncie. Muncie's proportion of black population grew even during the 1920s, when it was a stronghold of the Ku Klux Klan.[110] Some of the Muncie interviewees recalled witnessing Klan meetings or having personal acquaintance with Klansmen, but none recalled any incidents of Klan-inspired violence against blacks.[111] And if their memories are accurate, black Munsonians took the Klan's antics in stride. "The Klan was active in 1920," reported Henry Sims. "They used to assemble right down here on Broadway. There was an auditorium there and a rink. They'd use the skating rink and things. And they'd use that to meet there. But, the Klan never did anything around here. Had a parade."[112]

African American residences clustered in three of Muncie's nine wards, but the clusters were generally racially integrated. Three-fifths of the members of a sample drawn from the 1920 census manuscripts lived in households that had at least one European American neighbor, and one-quarter lived in households having two European American neighboring families.[113]

Muncie's African American community was both knit together by a vigorous associational network and linked to developments in the larger African American world. By 1903, when the community numbered a little over 700, one African Methodist Episcopal and one Baptist church were holding services, and they were joined within a decade by a Methodist Episcopal congregation. A Masonic lodge and its associated Eastern Star chapter for women, lodges of the Knights of Pythias and the Odd Fellows, together with local societies, were also functioning by 1903.[114] By 1918 the small circle of African American businessmen had established a local branch of Booker T. Washington's National Negro Business League, and a chapter of the National Association for the Advancement of Colored People was active by 1920, only eleven years after the founding of the national organization.[115]

Although their industrial jobs were routinized, closely supervised, and allowed little scope for advancement, Muncie's housing market afforded color-blind opportunity for African American families to own their own homes. The African American home ownership rate (32 percent) was lower than the European American rate (43 percent), but the difference is entirely accounted for by differences in age, origin, and, most important, persistence within the community. Because more African Americans than European Americans were newcomers to Muncie, they had not had as much time to accumulate the price of a home. And time within the community mattered, because for both men and women persistence was the most powerful predictor of home ownership.[116] Like the two Springfields before 1900, Muncie before 1920 offered a structure of opportunity for home ownership, with the advantages for family life that control over one's immediate environment allowed.

Alexander and Belle Kelley made up one set of home owners. In 1920 they were living in Whitely, a racially integrated working-class neighborhood that held Muncie's principal African American community, situated near the metalworks where many local men were employed. Alexander was cooking at the General Motors plant, one of the very few African Americans employed there. Also living in the Kelleys' mortgaged home was their married son James, who was working as a busboy at the Kirby House Hotel, Alexander's longtime employer; married daughter Beulah; and Beulah's husband, James Taylor, a Tennessee migrant who worked as a fireman at a foundry. Down the street lived James Blackburn, who, like Alexander and Belle Kelley, had been born in the South on the eve of the Civil War. James and his wife, Lula, had migrated from North Carolina to Indiana between 1899 and 1903, arriving in Muncie before 1910.[117] Both were listed in the census as unable to read or write, but all six of their children living at home or nearby were literate; one son worked in a foundry, another as a hotel porter. The Blackburns, too, owned a mortgaged home.[118] For both longtime Munsonians the Kelleys and the more recently arrived Blackburns, persistence in Muncie paid off in home ownership. The Kelley home provided family-controlled housing for five adults, a foundation and nexus of mutual support for workers holding jobs at the bottom of the local occupational ladder that few African Americans were allowed to climb.

Migrants to metropolitan cities sought similar benefits in black suburbs. Whether built by European American developers, one of the few African American construction companies, or the owner himself or herself with assistance from family and friends, homes could be acquired in the suburbs for much less than in the central cities.[119] In Evanston north of Chicago, Cleveland's Chagrin Falls Park, Cincinnati's Lincoln Heights, and in many other communities in these and other midwestern cities, African American suburbanites sought the same combination of semirural setting, small-scale development, and proximity to metropolitan jobs that attracted European Americans to city fringes. Evanston offered mainly domestic and service jobs in the Chicago metropolitan area rather than industrial work, but by 1920 black Evanstonians had achieved a home ownership rate of 31 percent, nearly the same as their counterparts in Muncie.[120] The small group of middle-class African Americans who populated the Chicago suburb of Morgan Park did even better, owning nearly half of their homes.[121] Suburban settings that attracted migrants were diverse, including industrial satellites, clusters of domestic service workers in wealthy white suburbs, and all-black residential communities.[122] Some, such as migrants to Evanston, came directly from the South, stopping in Chicago no longer than necessary to change trains. Others, such as residents of Chagrin Falls Park and Lincoln Heights, tasted city life before escaping to the suburbs.[123] In the suburbs they could gather extended families, engage in home food production to cushion unstable employment, and build community institutions: "By 1920, fully one-fourth of the nation's African American YMCAs and YWCAs were located in suburbs."[124] Their homes may have been simple, and city services deficient or missing altogether, but African American suburbanites managed to recreate desired elements of familiar settings and were able to gain a valued measure of control over their surroundings.

Suburbs attracted about 15 percent of the African American population growth in northern metropolitan centers between 1910 and 1940, or about 285,000 people.[125] Between 1910 and 1930, about 16 percent of the increase in African American population in the Lower Midwest took place in small towns and small cities.[126] These figures suggest that a significant proportion of the migrants to, among, and within Ohio, Indiana, and Illinois during the Great Migration years, perhaps as many as one in four, settled away from the burgeoning central cities. Together with the evidence concerning urban experience in the South, migration sequences, and changing patterns of locational preference, such decisions reveal that the bright lights of Chicago and other metropolitan centers were refracted through the migrants' own backgrounds and dispositions.

CONCLUSION

We found a little more freedom in Toledo, Ohio than in Camden, Arkansas.
—Welton Barnett, Toledo, 1976[1]

In the very process of being transplanted, the Negro is becoming transformed.
—Alain Locke, 1925[2]

All those who have studied African American migration agree that the mobility choices made by several hundred thousand ordinary people in the aggregate produced a profound impact upon the history of the United States in the twentieth century. Culture, politics, and urban geography were all reshaped in significant ways.[3] The migrants did change their own situation, and for many of them the alteration was for the better.[4] In changing their own lives, they also transformed both the places they entered and the places they left.[5]

This book has attempted to define the outlines of the age of the village for African Americans and to estimate the impact of their nonmetropolitan experience upon their metropolitan era. I hope it will lay to rest any doubts that African Americans did have their own age of the village, an intervening stage between the rural world in which most lived at the Civil War's onset and the metropolitan society that encompassed the vast majority at the beginning of the twenty-first century. To be sure, the small-town period for African Americans represented a much more compressed part of their history than it did for European Americans. On the other hand, it lasted longer than most have previously recognized. In the Lower Midwest, the eve of the Great Depression found numbers ranging from one-fifth in Ohio to one-quarter in Indiana and Illinois still living in nonmetropolitan urban places (tables A.15–A.17). Furthermore, a minority of those normally counted as part of metropolitan populations found or created settings within the world of the large cities that nurtured as much as possible the lifestyle of the small town.

African Americans found some aspects of small-town society appealing, which explains why a significant minority continued to reside there or tried to recreate it in alien environments. But a majority of black Midwesterners rejected it for the quite different world of the big city. Explaining their decisions requires consideration of four major variables, which varied from state to state as well as evolving over time. Economic change channeled both black and white migrations into, out of, and within the Lower Midwest. In African American as in European American mobility, women's relative presence or absence within a migration stream affected the direction of the stream: The larger the proportion of women, the more likely the stream flowed to big cities. The emergence of metropolitan black communities of unprecedented size, wealth, and diversity increasingly attracted African American travelers, both from the South and from smaller communities in the Midwest. Migrants' prior experience, whether in a rural or urban setting, in the South or the North, powerfully influenced their choice of destination.

The answer to my initial question about whether the bullet holes in the courthouse doors at Washington Court House offered an explanation for the decline of African American nonmetropolitan populations is yes and no. Antiblack collective violence did play a role in convincing African Americans that their future lay elsewhere, but it is only one part of a much larger and more complex story. Seen from an African American perspective, the Lower Midwest was a violent place, and most of the attacks between 1885 and 1910—all of those that occurred in Ohio and Indiana—took place in small towns and midsize cities. But such violence was reported in only a small minority of towns, and some black residents chose to stay even in towns where a mob had gathered or a lynching was organized, while other African Americans decided to move to such places, including even young, newly married couples, such as John and Victoria Oatneal in Washington Court House. One factor that may have played a large part in such decisions was the greater ease of acquiring ownership of a family home in smaller urban communities. Access to home ownership was offset, however, by the limited range of job opportunities, especially for women. Therefore, as women came to fill a larger place in the migration stream from the South, the flow was nudged cityward.

Classic migration theory distinguishes between "push" and "pull" factors, but today, migration scholars recognize that these categories are interdependent. A "push" may only become strong enough to propel migration when a "pull" becomes sufficiently attractive to offer a reasonable alternative, and the same holds true in reverse for a "pull" factor.[6] The locational choices of African American migrants in the Lower Midwest from the Civil War to the Great Depression fit comfortably within this new perspective. Nonmetropolitan communities in the Midwest became attractive destinations during the Civil War and the postwar years because they offered the appeal of a prosperous urban setting in a nonsouthern state, yet one tightly bound to familiar agricultural cycles, and in a climate and topography similar to those of the border states from which most migrants originated. For some, the decision to settle in a nonmetropolitan community paid off, especially when compared to the worsening racial atmosphere in the South. For many others, however, the restricted job opportunities and the threat of violence in small towns and midsize cities burnished the appeal of a larger African American urban community. Their decisions to move cityward augmented the size, widened the range of backgrounds, and amplified the economic, social, and cultural resources of metropolitan African American populations. Meanwhile, migrants from the Deep South began to join the migration stream, mainly to Illinois and the Calumet region of Indiana. At first, they followed the earlier path of their border state predecessors to nonmetropolitan communities, before joining the latter in turning cityward during the twentieth century's second decade. By the time cessation of European immigration and multiplying wartime needs opened industrial jobs to African Americans on a large scale, many migrants from the South had already tasted urban life in either the South or the North—or both. For them, the immediate "push" came, not from cotton, sugar, or tobacco fields, but from smaller black communities under constant white surveillance, and the relevant "pull" emanated from metropolitan black communities so large as to enjoy an unprecedented degree of autonomy from white control. The appeal of formerly attractive small towns and midsize cities in both the South and the North diminished relative to the magnetism of the new African American metropolitan culture.

If one term had to sum up why African Americans rejected the midwestern small towns and cities to which they were initially attracted, I think the best one would be "variability," both geographic and temporal. Small towns and small cities were unpredictable places, precisely because they were white worlds. Some small-town environments were unquestionably hospitable to some, most, or perhaps even all of their African American residents. Testimony to this effect is not hard to find. The sterling example of racial egalitarianism is Covert Township, Michigan, where radical white abolitionists and black settlers determined on equality established during the Civil War decade an atmosphere of racial harmony that persisted through the nineteenth century's end.[7] Although individual whites in Monroe, Michigan, acted out their prejudices toward blacks, the courts evidently dealt fairly.[8] During the 1860s Steubenville, Ohio enjoyed a well-deserved reputation for racial tolerance.[9] Orphaned in the tiny hamlet of

Ellettsville, Indiana, Jeremiah Jackson received indispensable help from his European American neighbors, which allowed him to become the first African American graduate of the Indiana University School of Medicine. Throughout his many years as a physician in Evansville, Jackson returned regularly to Ellettsville for ceremonial occasions.[10] In Tuscola, Illinois, Bruce Hayden passed the civil service examination with flying colors to become the first African American letter carrier. Disappointed whites were appalled that the postmaster would even consider appointing "a nigger on the post office," but the postmaster replied, according to Hayden, that "you had no business letting a nigger get smarter than you." Hayden held the job for thirty-two years.[11] Even in Springfield, Illinois, Phoebe Mitchell Day, who lived through the 1908 riot, reported of her co-workers in the state office building, her white neighbors, and nurses who cared for her at the local hospital, "they all treated me lovely."[12]

Small towns and small cities differed from each other. Some treated African Americans comparatively well, while others barred them completely. European Americans pondering a move had to consider only the general economic condition of a prospective destination, but African Americans' prospects depended as well upon the local racial atmosphere. Tuscola was good to Bruce Hayden's family, but when he moved sixty miles west to Springfield, he found it a terribly prejudiced town.[13] Worse, a single community's racial atmosphere could change almost overnight. By the 1880s Steubenville's reputation for tolerance had begun to tarnish, and when new roller-skating rinks opened, their proprietors refused to admit African Americans.[14] Black Altonians no doubt thought their schools were safely integrated until local officials decided to resegregate them. No one was prepared for the lynchings and race riots that boiled up like summer tornadoes in midwestern communities. When one's family's welfare depended on the goodwill of individual European Americans, and one's safety rested upon the attitudes of a small European American community, it must have been disconcerting to watch individual moods and the communal temper shift in response to stimuli emanating from mysterious local or extralocal sources. European Americans in large cities may have been equally unpredictable, but spatial differentiation of residential, commercial, and industrial zones, de facto residential segregation, and congregation of African Americans limited daily interaction with whites, while larger African American populations provided greater security in numbers.

The role played by nonmetropolitan urban communities in channeling African American migration restores to the European American residents of those communities a degree of agency that is often missing in histories of the small town. Instead, small towns are commonly seen as victims of inexorable forces of centralization.[15] By making their towns inhospitable places for African Americans, whether through unwillingness to share well-paying occupations, segregation of theaters and restaurants, or mobs and lynchings, European Americans injured their communities economically and culturally. They needed people, as their editors incessantly proclaimed, to support local markets. The worst of them, the sundown towns and suburbs that succeeded in driving out all African Americans or banning them from entering, fostered—and sometimes continue to foster—prejudice, paranoia, and parochialism.[16] In addition, nonmetropolitan communities in the Lower Midwest could have nourished, instead of persecuting, the creators and purveyors of new musical and cultural modes. By encouraging the interpenetration of African and European styles, small towns could have put themselves in the vanguard of cultural change in modern America instead of the rear guard. Had they done so, they might have escaped the overblown but deeply hurtful indictments by modernist intellectuals during the twenties.[17]

If white racism had been tempered, even the great numbers of migrants who came during the First Great Migration could have been absorbed into the growing populations of the nonmetropolitan urban communities of the Lower Midwest. This can be demonstrated by estimating the size of the influx to metropolitan centers beyond what would have occurred if African American urban population growth had been spread evenly across the urban hierarchy of each state. Population growth thus attributable to the African American metropolitan shift amounts to about 27,000 in Indiana and 82,000 in Ohio during the period 1890–1930, and approximately 77,000 in Illinois during 1910–1930.[18] During the corresponding periods, the white nonmetropolitan population of Indiana grew by roughly 500,000, that of Ohio by 900,000, and that of Illinois by more than 800,000.[19] This means that in every state, if nonmetropolitan towns had maintained the attraction they had held for African Americans before the metropolitan shift, African American newcomers would have represented less than 10 percent of the actual growth in European American population such places sustained. This fact implies that rather than structural conditions in play across midwestern urban systems, forces within communities played the key role in channeling African American migration. African Americans whose achievements fell short of their aspirations within nonmetropolitan towns and cities left, not because the communities were faltering, but because they were not prospering within them.[20]

In considering the full sweep of African American migration to the Lower Midwest from the Civil War to the eve of the Great Depression, it is hard to escape the conclusion that the movement was for the most part a deliberate and orderly one. This view contrasts, of course, with a common image of headlong flight from southern oppression. It differs as well from the portrait of a black exodus from the vicious prejudice of northern communities—sundown towns and suburbs—recently painted by James Loewen.[21] Such images figure large because of the dramatic conventions of literary representation or, in Loewen's case, the need to evoke full sympathy for the victims of white racism to support a praiseworthy call for reform. In other words, it makes a much better story than a gradual transition governed by sober consideration of available alternatives. But the facts that the flood of the Great Migration years was preceded by a half century trickle; that migrants from the Deep South began to enter the region in significant numbers at least twenty years before the major movement erupted; that personal communication between earlier and later migrants played a large part in channeling migration flows; that mass migration to the metropolitan North was only one among an array of strategies for dealing with oppression; and, most important, that migration responded to identifiable disappointments, dangers, and opportunities, all argue for placing African American migration firmly within the picture painted by modern historians of human mobility.[22] As one such historian writes of late nineteenth-century migrants in general, "Rarely [did they] leave home without a clear idea of where they were going and how they would get there."[23]

Finally, the findings of this study are consistent with the view that African American experience since the Civil War produced a new race consciousness by the 1920s.[24] Among intellectuals the new perception appeared in the concept of the New Negro, and among the masses it underlay the outpouring of support for Marcus Garvey's black nationalism.[25] Little race consciousness seems to be evident in the locational choices made by the first wave of migrants to the Lower Midwest, those who came between 1860 and 1890, but their experience in small towns and small cities probably contributed significantly to the process of forming such an outlook. It did so negatively, by demonstrating durable white hostility to black achievement. But the nonmetropolitan experience also contributed positively to formation of racial consciousness, by introducing migrants from diverse backgrounds to each other and by providing the setting in which they created, in cooperation with their new acquaintances, the institutional sinews of community.[26] By the twentieth century's second and third decades, the unprecedented African American worlds in metropolitan centers exerted a powerful magnetism, in part by exhibiting wider opportunities for community building. Even those who sought to recreate a small-town lifestyle in metropolitan suburbs clustered with other African Americans. Garveyism attracted mass support in the Midwest: in Cleveland, in Gary, and in Chicago, despite a feud between Garvey and the *Defender*'s Robert Abbott.[27] In light of three factors—the treatment African Americans received in midwestern urban worlds; the convergence in metropolitan destinations of people from various origins; and the vision of a vibrant African American urban culture emerging in such cities as Chicago, Cleveland, and Indianapolis—such a perceptual change seems quite likely. Just as African American migrants altered their new environment, the Midwest changed its new African American citizens.

Table A.1 Blacks and Whites in Ohio's Urban Hierarchy, 1860–1890

1860						
Size Category	Places 1860	1890	Whites	Percent of Whites	Blacks	Percent of Blacks
100,000+	1	2	157,313	6.9	3,731	10.2
25,000–99,999	1	7	42,618	1.9	799	2.2
10,000–24,999	3	14	50,872	2.2	1,531	4.2
2,500–9,999	30	77	134,953	5.9	4,998	13.6
Rural			1,908,082	83.2	25,614	69.8
Total urban			385,756	16.8	11,059	30.2
Total			2,293,838		36,673	

1890						
Size Category	Whites	Percent of Whites	Percent Change	Blacks	Percent of Blacks	Percent Change
100,000+	543,542	15.3	245.5	14,644	16.9	292.5
25,000–99,999	336,149	9.4	688.7	13,515	15.6	1,591.5
10,000–24,999	192,854	5.4	279.1	6,301	7.3	311.6
2,500–9,999	353,831	9.9	162.2	16,232	18.7	224.8
Rural	2,131,783	59.9	11.7	35,989	41.5	40.5
Total urban	1,426,376	40.1	269.8	50,692	58.5	358.4
Total	3,558,159		55.1	86,681		136.4

Sources: Joseph C. G. Kennedy, *Population of the United States in 1860* (Washington, DC: Government Printing Office, 1864), 373–95; *Population of the United States at the Eleventh Census: 1890, Part I* (Washington, DC: Government Printing Office, 1895), 451–85.

Table A.2 Blacks and Whites in Indiana's Urban Hierarchy, 1860–1890

Size Category	Places 1860	1890	Whites	Percent of Whites	Blacks	Percent of Blacks
			1860			
100,000+	0	1	—	0.0	—	0.0
25,000–99,999	0	3	—	0.0	—	0.0
10,000–24,999	3	10	41,529	3.1	1,220	10.7
2,500–9,999	12	46	59,810	4.5	1,510	13.2
Rural			1,237,661	92.4	8,698	76.1
Total urban			101,339	7.6	2,730	23.9
Total			1,339,000		11,428	

Size Category	Whites	Percent of Whites	Percent Change	Blacks	Percent of Blacks	Percent Change
			1890			
100,000+	96,282	4.5	N/A	9,133	20.3	N/A
25,000–99,999	109,416	5.1	N/A	6,916	15.4	N/A
10,000–24,999	137,989	6.5	232.3	5,926	13.2	385.7
2,500–9,999	208,420	9.7	248.5	6,591	14.7	336.5
Rural	1,585,687	74.2	28.1	16,649	36.8	91.4
Total urban	552,107	25.8	444.8	28,566	63.2	946.4
Total	2,137,794		59.6	45,215		293.3

Sources: Joseph C. G. Kennedy, *Population of the United States in 1860* (Washington, DC: Government Printing Office, 1864), 113–28; *Population of the United States at the Eleventh Census: 1890, Part I* (Washington, DC: Government Printing Office, 1895), 451–85.

Table A.3 Blacks and Whites in Illinois's Urban Hierarchy, 1860–1890

1860

Size Category	Places 1860	1890	Whites	Percent of Whites	Blacks	Percent of Blacks
100,000+	1	1	111,214	6.5	958	12.6
25,000–99,999	0	2	—	0.0	—	0.0
10,000–24,999	2	18	27,502	1.6	261	3.4
2,500–9,999	19	55	101,459	6.0	1,255	16.4
Rural			1,464,148	85.9	5,154	67.6
Total urban			240,175	14.1	2,474	32.4
Total			1,704,323		7,628	

1890

Size Category	Whites	Percent of Whites	Percent Change	Blacks	Percent of Blacks	Percent Change
100,000+	1,084,998	28.9	875.6	14,271	25.0	1,389.7
25,000–99,999	69,856	1.9	N/A	2,635	4.6	N/A
10,000–24,999	273,461	7.3	894.3	11,165	19.6	4,178.8
2,500–9,999	234,426	6.2	131.1	5,806	10.2	362.6
Rural	2,093,135	55.7	43.0	23,151	40.6	349.2
Total urban	1,662,741	44.3	592.3	33,877	59.4	1,269.3
Total	3,755,876		120.4	57,028		647.6

Sources: Joseph C. G. Kennedy, *Population of the United States in 1860* (Washington, DC: Government Printing Office, 1864), 88–101; *Population of the United States at the Eleventh Census: 1890, Part I* (Washington, DC: Government Printing Office, 1895), 451–85.

Table A.4 Antiblack Collective Violence in the Lower Midwest, 1885–1910

Date	Victim	Place	Population at Most Recent Census
June 19, 1885	Henry Howard lynching	Coshocton Coshocton Co. Ohio	3,044
July 13, 1885	Frank Wallace (attempted lynching)	Marion Grant Co. Indiana	3,182
January 18, 1886	Holly Epps lynching	Vincennes Knox Co. Indiana	7,680
June 13, 1887	Peter Betters (possible black-on-black lynching)	Jamestown Greene Co. Ohio	877
March/April 1889	George Slater (attempted lynching)	Sabina Clinton Co. Ohio	Unknown
February 8, 1890	Eli Ladd lynching	Blountsville Henry Co. Indiana	<2,500
January 14, 1892	Henry Corbin lynching	Oxford Butler Co. Ohio	1,922
June 3, 1893	Samuel Bush lynching	Decatur Macon Co. Illinois	16,841
January 12, 1894	Roscoe Parker lynching	West Union Adams Co. Ohio	825
February 5, 1894	Frank Hall (attempted lynching)	Lebanon Boone Co. Indiana	3,682
April 15, 1894	Seymour Newlin lynching	Rushsylvania Logan Co. Ohio	497
July–August 1894	Attacks on black strikebreakers at stockyards	Chicago Cook Co. Illinois	1,099,850

Table A.4 *continued*

October 17, 1894	William Dolby attempted lynching	Washington C. H. Fayette Ohio	5,742
August 21, 1895	Noah Anderson lynching	New Richmond Clermont Co. Ohio	2,379
August 4–5, 1895	Black strikebreakers at coal mines shot	Spring Valley Bureau Co. Illinois	3,837
June 4, 1897	Charles Mitchell lynching	Urbana Champaign Co. Ohio	6,510
October 13, 1898	Black strikebreakers at coal mines shot	Virden Macoupin Co. Illinois	1,610
November 7, 1898	George Stewart lynching	Lacon Marshall Co. Illinois	1,649
April 10, 1899	5 blacks killed 7 blacks wounded	Pana Christian Co. Illinois	5,077
June 30–September 17, 1899	6 blacks killed	Carterville Williamson Co. Illinois	<2,500
1899 (n.d.)	Attack on black strikebreakers at sewer construction site	Chicago Cook Co. Illinois	1,099,850
April–Fall 1900	Violence against black strikebreakers in building-trades strike	Chicago Cook Co. Illinois	1,099,850
August 1900	Riot after black suspect taken from city	Akron Summit Co. Ohio	42,728
December 16, 1900	Bud Rowland Thomas Henderson lynchings	Rockport Spencer Co. Indiana	2,882
December 17, 1900	John Rolla lynching	Boonville Warrick Co. Indiana	2,849

Table A.4 *continued*

February 26, 1901	George Ward lynching	Terre Haute Vigo Co. Indiana	36,673
November 20, 1902	James Dillard lynching	Sullivan Sullivan Co. Indiana	3,118
April 26, 1903	Unknown lynching and mob attack on construction workers	Thebes [Santa Fe] Alexander Co. Illinois	417
June 6, 1903	David Wyatt lynching	Belleville Saint Clair Co. Illinois	17,484
July 5, 1903	John Tinsley aka Robert Lee attempted lynching, then riot	Evansville Vanderburgh Co. Indiana	59,007
July 23, 1903	J. D. Mayfield [Metcalf?] lynching	Danville Vermillion Co. Illinois	16,354
March 7, 1904	Richard Dixon lynching and riot	Springfield Clark Co. Ohio	38,253
June–August 1904	Attacks on black strikebreakers in stockyards	Chicago Cook Co. Illinois	1,698,575
April–May 1905	Attacks on blacks during teamsters' strike	Chicago Cook Co. Illinois	1,698,575
February 1906	Riot after black suspect taken from town	Springfield Clark Co. Ohio	38,253
April 30, 1907	Six black men beaten by mob	Greensburg Decatur Co. Indiana	5,034
August 15–16, 1908	Scott Burton William Donnegan	Springfield Sangamon Co. Illinois	34,159
November 3, 1909	William James lynching	Cairo Alexander Co. Illinois	12,566

Table A.4 *continued*

January 11, 1910	Hosen Taborn Harry Taborn Alexander Jenkins attempted lynching	Vienna Johnson Co. Illinois	<2,500
February 18, 1910	John Pratt attempted lynching	Cairo Alexander Co. Illinois	14,548

Sources: Chicago Tribune, January 1 (or near) issue, 1886-1911; NAACP, *Thirty Years of Lynching in the United States, 1889–1918* (New York, 1919); David A. Gerber, *Black Ohio and the Color Line, 1865–1915* (Urbana: University of Illinois Press, 1976); David A. Gerber, "Lynching and Law and Order: Origin and Passage of the 1896 Ohio Anti-Lynching Law," *OH* 83 (Winter 1974): 33–50; Emma Lou Thornbrough, *The Negro in Indiana before 1900: A Study of a Minority* (1957; reprint, Bloomington: Indiana University Press, 1993), 276–87; U.S. census reports, 1880–1910; Charles Branham, "Black Chicago: Accommodationist Politics Before the Great Migration," in *The Ethnic Frontier: Essays in the History of Group Survival in Chicago and the Midwest*, ed. Melvin Holli (Grand Rapids, MI: Eerdmans, 1977), 211–62; John H. Keiser, "Black Strikebreakers and Racism in Illinois, 1865–1900," *JISHS* 65 (Autumn 1972): 313–26; R. R. Wright Jr., "The Negro in Times of Industrial Unrest," *Charities* 15 (1905): 70–73; Victor Hicken, "The Virden and Pana Mine Wars of 1898," *JISHS* 52 (Summer 1959): 263–78; Caroline Waldron, "'Lynch-law Must Go!': Race, Citizenship, and the Other in an American Coal Mining Town," *JAEH* 20 (Fall 2000): 50–77; Felix L. Armfield, "Fire on the Prairie: The 1895 Spring Valley Race Riot," *JIlH* 3 (Autumn 2000): 185–200; William M. Tuttle Jr., *Race Riot: Chicago in the Red Summer of 1919* (1970; reprint, Urbana: University of Illinois Press, 1996), 112–23; Marilyn Kaye Howard, "Black Lynching in the Promised Land: Mob Violence in Ohio, 1876–1916" (Ph.D. diss., The Ohio State University, 1999); *Cyclone and Fayette Republican* (Washington Court House, OH), April 3, 1889; *Indianapolis Star*, May 1–2, 1907; *Hillsboro* (OH) *Gazette*, July 31–August 14, 1903; *Hillsboro* (OH) *News-Herald*, July 30–August 13, 1903; local newspapers in or near communities where incidents occurred.

Table A.5 Outmigration in the East South Central States, 1860–1930 (in hundreds)

	1860–1890	1890–1910	1910–1930
Kentucky			
Urban increment (net)	607	314	99
Outmigration (gross)	442*	733	834
To Ohio, Indiana, & Illinois	225*	455	545
Tennessee			
Urban Increment (net)	866	549	897
Outmigration (gross)	581*	1,045	1,401
To Southwest	231*	307	87
To Kentucky	57*	142	117
To Ohio, Indiana, & Illinois	62*	226	617
Alabama			
Urban increment (net)	514	870	1,118
Outmigration (gross)	645*	1,133	2,183
To Southwest	225*	333	143
To Mississippi	226*	318	131
To Tennessee & Kentucky	53*	108	408
To Ohio, Indiana, & Illinois	6*	43	672
Mississippi			
Urban increment (net)	267	612	384
Out–migration (gross)	573*	1,168	2,552
To Southwest	354*	703	747
To Tennessee & Kentucky	104*	239	408
To Ohio, Indiana, & Illinois	5*	49	662

* 1870–1890

Notes: "Southwest" includes Arkansas, Louisiana, Oklahoma, and Texas.

The outmigration estimates refer only to those born within each state. Since they do not include residents of each state who were born in other states, they must be regarded as minima.

Sources: Joseph C. G. Kennedy, *Population of the United States in 1860* (Washington, DC: Government Printing Office, 1864), 8, 181–83, 270, 467; *Population of the United States at the Eleventh Census: 1890, Part 1* (Washington, DC: Government Printing Office, 1895), 451–85; *Thirteenth Census, 1910, Vol. 2: Population* (Washington, DC: Government Printing Office, 1913), 60–62, 752–55, 1060–61, *Vol. 3: Population* (Washington, DC: Government Printing Office, 1913), 762–64; William Edward Vickery, *The Economics of the Negro Migration, 1900–1960* (New York: Arno, 1977), tables 34, 37, 49, 50, 52.

Table A.6 Blacks and Whites in Ohio's Urban Hierarchy, 1890–1910

1890

Size Category	Places 1860	1890	Whites	Percent of Whites	Blacks	Percent of Blacks
100,000+	2	5	543,542	15.3	14,644	16.9
25,000–99,999	7	9	336,149	9.4	13,515	15.6
10,000–24,999	14	23	192,854	5.4	6,301	7.3
2,500–9,999	77	102	353,831	9.9	16,232	18.7
Rural			2,131,783	59.9	35,989	41.5
Total urban			1,426,376	40.1	50,692	58.5
Total			3,558,159		86,681	

1910

Size Category	Whites	Percent of Whites	Percent Change	Blacks	Percent of Blacks	Percent Change
100,000+	1,342,827	28.8	147.1	47,545	42.7	224.7
25,000–99,999	381,664	8.2	13.5	11,625	10.4	-14.0
10,000–24,999	353,510	7.6	83.3	7,409	6.6	17.6
2,500–9,999	504,142	10.8	42.5	15,703	14.1	-3.3
Rural	2,072,754	44.5	-2.8	29,170	26.2	-18.9
Total urban	2,582,143	55.5	81.0	82,282	73.8	62.3
Total	4,654,897		30.8	111,452		28.6

Sources: Population of the United States at the Eleventh Census: 1890, Part 1 (Washington, DC: Government Printing Office, 1895), 451–85; *Thirteenth Census, 1910, Vol. 1: Population* (Washington, DC: Government Printing Office, 1913): 191, 201, *Vol. 3: Population* (Washington, DC: Government Printing Office, 1913): 418–25, 504–11, 566–72.

Table A.7 Blacks and Whites in Indiana's Urban Hierarchy, 1890–1910

Size Category	Places 1860	1890	Whites	Percent of Whites	Blacks	Percent of Blacks
			1890			
100,000+	1	1	96,282	4.5	9,133	20.3
25,000–99,999	3	4	109,416	5.1	6,916	15.4
10,000–24,999	10	20	137,989	6.5	5,926	13.2
2,500–9,999	46	63	208,420	9.7	6,591	14.7
Rural			1,585,687	74.2	16,376	36.4
Total urban			552,107	25.8	28,566	63.6
Total			2,137,794		44,942	

Size Category	Whites	Percent of Whites	Percent Change	Blacks	Percent of Blacks	Percent Change
			1910			
100,000+	211,780	8.0	120.0	21,816	36.2	138.9
25,000–99,999	235,288	8.9	115.0	10,035	16.6	45.1
10,000–24,999	330,900	12.5	139.8	8,953	14.8	51.1
2,500–9,999	317,058	12.0	52.1	7,621	12.6	15.6
Rural	1,544,935	58.5	-2.6	11,895	19.7	-27.4
Total urban	1,095,026	41.5	98.3	48,425	80.3	69.5
Total	2,639,961		23.5	60,320		34.2

Sources: Population of the United States at the Eleventh Census: 1890, Part 1 (Washington, DC: Government Printing Office, 1895), 451–85; *Thirteenth Census, 1910, Vol. 1: Population* (Washington, DC: Government Printing Office, 1913): 191, 201, *Vol. 3: Population* (Washington, DC: Government Printing Office, 1913): 418–25, 504–11, 566–72.

Table A.8 Blacks and Whites in Illinois's Urban Hierarchy, 1890–1910

Size Category	Places 1860	1890	Whites	Percent of Whites	Blacks	Percent of Blacks
1890						
100,000+	1	1	1,084,998	28.9	14,271	25.0
25,000–99,999	2	11	69,856	1.9	2,635	4.6
10,000–24,999	18	20	273,461	7.3	11,165	19.6
2,500–9,999	55	112	234,426	6.2	5,806	10.2
Rural			2,093,135	55.7	23,151	40.6
Total urban			1,662,741	44.3	33,877	59.4
Total			3,755,876		57,028	

Size Category	Whites	Percent of Whites	Percent Change	Blacks	Percent of Blacks	Percent Change
1910						
100,000+	2,139,057	38.7	97.1	44,103	40.4	209.0
25,000–99,999	418,046	7.6	498.4	16,216	14.9	515.4
10,000–24,999	318,474	5.8	16.5	12,696	11.6	13.7
2,500–9,999	513,304	9.3	119.0	12,523	11.5	115.7
Rural	2,138,081	38.7	2.1	23,511	21.6	1.6
Total urban	3,388,881	61.3	103.8	85,538	78.4	152.5
Total	5,526,962		47.2	109,049		91.2

Sources: Population of the United States at the Eleventh Census: 1890, Part 1 (Washington, DC: Government Printing Office, 1895), 451–85; *Thirteenth Census, 1910, Vol. 1: Population* (Washington, DC: Government Printing Office, 1913): 191, 201, *Vol. 3: Population* (Washington, DC: Government Printing Office, 1913): 418–25, 504–11, 566–72.

Table A.9 Who Left? Men Living in Washington Court House, Ohio, in 1890 Who Did Not Appear in the 1900 Census

	African Americans		European Americans	
	Percent	N	Percent	N
Age				
Under 21	75.0	4	52.6	76
21–29	22.2	18	34.8	141
30–39	22.6	31	22.7	181
40–49	26.7	30	29.2	168
50 and over	38.7	31	42.9	226
Region of Birth				
South	27.4	73	51.4	72
North	34.1	41	32.7	663
Foreign	—	—	38.6	57
Occupational Category				
High white collar	—	—	35.0	60
Low white collar	33.3	3	29.3	222
Blue collar skilled	40.0	20	38.5	182
Blue collar semiskilled				
& unskilled	25.8	66	33.6	122
Persistence*				
Present in 1880	53.1	64	56.8	481
Total	29.8	114	34.3	907
Mean Assessed Wealth, 1890				
Present in 1900	$ 83	74	$ 1,075	485
Absent in 1900	$ 80	33	$ 894	256

* Since the 1890 census was reconstructed by linking the 1889–90 city directory to the 1880 and 1900 censuses, the reconstruction contains no one who was absent in both 1880 and 1900.

Chi-square is valid and significant at the .05 level for no variables among African Americans and among European Americans for Age and Region of Birth.

Source: Reconstructed census for Washington Court House, OH, 1890, linked to 1880 and 1900 censuses

Table A.10 Who Left? Women Living in Washington Court House, Ohio, in 1890 Who Did Not Appear in the 1900 Census

	African Americans		European Americans	
	Percent	N	Percent	N
Age				
Under 21	28.6	7	43.4	53
21–29	66.7	6	44.0	84
30–39	40.0	10	35.1	74
40–49	72.7	11	37.0	100
50 and over	20.0	10	35.7	129
Region of Birth				
South	42.3	26	48.3	29
North	50.0	18	37.2	392
Foreign	—	—	44.4	18
Occupational Category				
Low white collar	0.0	1	27.8	18
Blue collar skilled	50.0	2	35.7	14
Blue collar semiskilled				
& unskilled	100.0	1	71.4	7
Persistence*				
Present in 1880	71.4	28	57.9	292
Total	45.5	44	38.4	440
Mean Assessed Wealth, 1890				
Present in 1900	$ 141	24	$ 750	266
Absent in 1900	$ 205	20	$ 453	166

* Since the 1890 census was reconstructed by linking the 1889–90 city directory to the 1880 and 1900 censuses, the reconstruction contains no one who was absent in both 1880 and 1900.

Chi-square is not valid and significant at the .05 level for any variable among either African Americans or European Americans.

Source: Reconstructed census for Washington Court House, OH, 1890, linked to the 1880 and 1900 censuses

Table A.11 Who Left? Men Living in Springfield, Ohio, in 1900 Who Did Not Appear in the 1910 Census

	African Americans		*European Americans*	
	Percent	N	Percent	N
Living Arrangements				
Living alone	55.6	18	0.0	1
Living with nuclear or extended family	65.2	187	56.4	165
Living with nonfamily				
Boarders/roomers	87.3	55	72.2	18
Servants	71.4	7	—	—
Other	100.0	3	66.7	3
Age				
21–29	74.0	96	64.9	57
30–39	71.4	56	45.5	44
40–49	55.4	56	46.3	41
50 and over	74.2	62	70.5	44
Marital Status				
Single	75.6	78	61.8	55
Married	65.3	170	53.3	120
Widowed or divorced	85.7	21	81.8	11
Region of Birth				
South	74.4	160	62.5	8
North	63.6	107	56.8	148
Foreign	0.0	1	58.6	29
Occupational Category				
High white collar	100.0	1	22.2	9
Low white collar	75.0	12	57.9	38
Blue collar skilled	69.6	46	56.7	90
Blue collar semiskilled & unskilled	68.4	190	58.8	34
Home Owned or Rented				
Owned	60.0	45	51.4	70
Rented	72.2	212	61.6	112
Persistence				
Present in 1880	56.3	48	55.4	56
Newcomer since 1880	72.5	222	58.8	131
Total	69.6	270	57.8	187

Chi-square is valid and significant at the .05 level among African Americans for Persistence and among European Americans for Age.

Source: Sampled manuscript U.S. census schedules for Clark County, OH, 1900, linked to the 1880 and 1910 censuses

Table A.12 Who Left? Women Living in Springfield, Ohio, in 1900 Who Did Not Appear in the 1910 Census

	African Americans		European Americans	
	Percent	N	Percent	N
Living Arrangements				
Living alone	70.0	10	75.0	4
Living with nuclear or extended family	74.2	194	56.6	196
Living with nonfamily				
Boarders/roomers	66.7	9	87.5	8
Servants	88.9	27	100.0	2
Other	100.0	3	100.0	4
Age				
21–29	75.0	92	75.8	62
30–39	81.5	54	43.6	78
40–49	69.8	43	60.5	43
50 and over	75.9	54	64.5	31
Marital Status				
Single	79.2	48	74.4	39
Married	71.9	146	53.4	146
Widowed or divorced	83.3	48	67.9	28
Region of Birth				
South	73.5	113	33.3	9
North	78.0	127	61.4	176
Foreign	—	—	53.6	28
Occupational Category				
Low white collar	75.0	4	64.3	14
Blue collar skilled	80.0	10	53.8	13
Blue collar semiskilled & unskilled	82.8	64	77.8	9
Home Owned or Rented				
Owned	70.5	61	47.4	76
Rented	75.3	146	63.8	127
Persistence				
Present in 1880	63.6	33	62.5	32
Newcomer since 1880	77.6	210	58.8	182
Total	75.7	243	59.3	214

Chi-square is valid and significant at the .05 level for no variables among African Americans and among European Americans for Age, Marital Status, and Home Owned or Rented.

Source: Sampled manuscript U.S. census schedules for Clark County, OH, 1900, linked to the 1880 and 1910 censuses

Table A.13 Who Left? Men Living in Springfield, Illinois, in 1900 Who Did Not Appear in the 1910 Census

	African Americans		*European Americans*	
	Percent	N	Percent	N
Living Arrangements				
Living alone	78.6	14	100.0	4
Living with nuclear or extended family	64.6	206	60.4	154
Living with nonfamily				
Boarders/roomers	76.7	43	81.8	22
Servants	87.5	16	—	—
Other	100.0	3	—	—
Age				
21–29	68.7	83	68.3	41
30–39	64.5	76	62.3	53
40–49	68.5	54	66.7	39
50 and over	72.9	70	59.6	47
Marital Status				
Single	71.6	74	70.0	50
Married	64.5	169	61.3	119
Widowed or divorced	77.8	36	63.6	11
Region of Birth				
South	68.8	186	90.9	11
North	66.7	93	66.4	110
Foreign	100.0	4	51.9	54
Occupational Category				
High white collar	—	—	50.0	12
Low white collar	75.0	16	64.3	42
Blue collar skilled	68.8	32	63.0	46
Blue collar semiskilled & unskilled	67.3	223	61.5	65
Home Owned or Rented				
Owned	60.2	88	56.4	94
Rented	70.1	174	72.3	83
Persistence				
Present in 1880	55.8	43	43.6	39
Newcomer since 1880	70.8	240	69.5	141
Total	68.6	283	63.9	180

Chi-square is valid and significant at the .05 level for no variables among African Americans and among European Americans for Living Arrangements, Region of Birth, Homeownership, and Persistence.

Source: Sampled manuscript U.S. census schedules for Sangamon County, IL, 1900, linked to the 1880 and 1910 censuses

Table A.14 Who Left? Women Living in Springfield, Illinois, in 1900 Who Did Not Appear in the 1910 Census

	African Americans		*European Americans*	
	Percent	N	Percent	N
Living Arrangements				
Living alone	93.8	16	100.0	8
Living with nuclear or extended family	66.7	168	56.4	204
Living with nonfamily				
Boarders/roomers	100.0	12	75.0	4
Servants	83.3	18	50.0	4
Other	0.0	1	66.7	3
Age				
21–29	80.5	77	67.3	55
30–39	56.1	41	50.0	74
40–49	69.2	39	44.2	43
50 and over	72.4	58	72.5	51
Marital Status				
Single	86.5	37	64.3	42
Married	63.7	113	52.7	131
Widowed or divorced	76.9	65	68.0	50
Region of Birth				
South	70.6	126	57.1	21
North	72.4	87	57.3	150
Foreign	100.0	2	60.8	51
Occupational Category				
Low white collar	—	—	63.6	11
Blue collar skilled	90.0	10	60.0	15
Blue collar semiskilled & unskilled	82.3	62	57.1	14
Home Owned or Rented				
Owned	61.3	80	55.9	111
Rented	77.7	112	62.1	103
Persistence				
Present in 1880	42.9	28	55.6	36
Newcomer since 1880	75.9	187	58.8	187
Total	71.6	215	58.3	223

Chi-square is valid and significant at the .05 level among African Americans for Age, Marital Status, Home Owned or Rented, and Persistence, and among European Americans for Age.

Source: Sampled manuscript U.S. census schedules for Sangamon County, IL, 1900, linked to the 1880 and 1910 censuses

Table A.15 Blacks and Whites in Ohio's Urban Hierarchy, 1910–1930

	1910					
Size	Places			Percent		Percent
Category	1910	1930	Whites	of Whites	Blacks	of Blacks
100,000+	5	8	1,342,827	28.8	47,545	42.7
25,000–99,999	9	18	381,664	8.2	11,625	10.4
10,000–24,999	23	33	353,510	7.6	7,409	6.6
2,500–9,999	102	114	504,142	10.8	15,703	14.1
Rural			2,072,754	44.5	29,170	26.2
Total urban			2,582,143	55.5	82,282	73.8
Total			4,654,897		111,452	

	1930					
Size		Percent of	Percent		Percent of	Percent
Category	Whites	Whites	Change	Blacks	Blacks	Change
100,000+	2,448,058	38.7	82.3	211,464	68.4	344.8
25,000–99,999	708,830	11.2	85.7	29,564	9.5	154.3
10,000–24,999	500,786	7.9	41.7	15,396	5.0	107.8
2,500–9,999	573,866	9.1	13.8	15,538	5.0	-1.0
Rural	2,099,596	33.2	1.3	37,342	12.1	2.8
Total urban	4,231,540	66.8	63.9	271,962	87.9	230.5
Total	6,331,136		36.0	309,304		177.5

Sources: Thirteenth Census, 1910, Vol. 1: Population (Washington, DC: Government Printing Office, 1913): 191, 201, *Vol. 3: Population* (Washington, DC: Government Printing Office, 1913): 418–25, 504–11, 566–72; *Fifteenth Census, Vol. 3, Part 1* (Washington, DC: Government Printing Office, 1932): 491–98; *Statistical Abstract of the U.S., 1931*, 13.

Table A.16 Blacks and Whites in Indiana's Urban Hierarchy, 1910–1930

1910

Size Category	Places 1910	Places 1930	Whites	Percent of Whites	Blacks	Percent of Blacks
100,000+	1	5	211,780	8.0	21,816	36.2
25,000–99,999	4	12	235,288	8.9	10,035	16.6
10,000–24,999	20	17	330,900	12.5	8,953	14.8
2,500–9,999	63	61	317,058	12.0	7,621	12.6
Rural			1,554,935	58.5	11,895	19.7
Total urban			1,095,026	41.5	48,425	80.3
Total			2,639,961		60,320	

1930

Size Category	Whites	Percent of Whites	Percent Change	Blacks	Percent of Blacks	Percent Change
100,000+	707,964	22.7	234.3	74,194	66.2	240.1
25,000–99,999	448,615	14.4	90.7	19,866	17.7	98.0
10,000–24,999	232,399	7.5	-29.8	5,264	4.7	-41.2
2,500–9,999	294,016	9.4	-7.3	3,722	3.3	-51.2
Rural	1,433,142	46.0	-7.2	8,936	8.0	-24.9
Total urban	1,682,994	54.0	53.7	103,046	92.0	112.8
Total	3,116,136		18.0	111,982		85.6

Sources: Thirteenth Census, 1910, Vol. 1: Population (Washington, DC: Government Printing Office, 1913): 191, 201, *Vol. 3: Population* (Washington, DC: Government Printing Office, 1913): 418–25, 504–11, 566–72; *Fifteenth Census, Vol. 3, Part 1* (Washington, DC: Government Printing Office, 1932): 715–19; *Statistical Abstract of the U.S.*, 1931, 13.

Table A.17 Blacks and Whites in Illinois's Urban Hierarchy, 1910–1930

			1910			
Size	Places			Percent		Percent
Category	1910	1930	Whites	of Whites	Blacks	of Blacks
100,000+	1	2	2,139,057	38.7	44,103	40.4
25,000–99,999	11	22	418,046	7.6	16,216	14.9
10,000–24,999	20	34	318,474	5.8	12,696	11.6
2,500–9,999	112	134	513,304	9.3	12,523	11.5
Rural			2,138,081	38.7	23,511	21.6
Total urban			3,388,881	61.3	85,538	78.4
Total			5,526,962		109,049	

		1930				
Size		Percent of	Percent		Percent of	Percent
Category	Whites	Whites	Change	Blacks	Blacks	Change
100,000+	3,219,466	44.3	50.5	236,940	72.0	437.2
25,000–99,999	965,009	13.2	130.8	36,589	11.1	125.6
10,000–24,999	464,724	6.4	45.6	16,115	4.9	26.9
2,500–9,999	651,114	9.0	26.8	14,392	4.4	14.9
Rural	1,966,018	27.1	-8.0	24,936	7.6	6.1
Total urban	5,300,343	72.9	56.4	304,036	92.4	255.4
Total	7,266,361		31.5	328,972		201.7

Sources: Thirteenth Census, 1910, Vol. 1: Population (Washington, DC: Government Printing Office, 1913): 191, 201, *Vol. 3: Population* (Washington, DC: Government Printing Office, 1913): 418–25, 504–11, 566–72; *Fifteenth Census, Vol. 3, Part 1* (Washington, DC: Government Printing Office, 1932): 628–35; *Statistical Abstract of the U.S., 1931*, 12.

Table A.18 Pathways for the Great Migration

City	Percentage residing in city of all native-born blacks in Ohio	
	1900	1930
Akron		
All states	0.5	3.7
Pennsylvania	2.1	5.8
Alabama	0.6	7.1
Georgia	0.0	5.4
Cincinnati		
All states	15.0	15.5
Georgia	41.8	19.2
Mississippi	38.2	12.5
Tennessee	37.8	15.3
Kentucky	37.4	33.4
Alabama	36.1	18.0
South Carolina	23.3	17.5
Indiana	21.9	14.5
Cleveland		
All states	6.0	23.2
Pennsylvania	20.0	27.4
South Carolina	12.6	29.7
Georgia	12.5	30.3
Tennessee	8.8	31.1
Alabama	7.8	31.9
Mississippi	6.8	40.3
Columbus		
All states	8.5	10.6
West Virginia	13.9	24.2
Virginia	12.7	24.5
North Carolina	11.4	23.2
Dayton		
All states	3.5	5.5
Indiana	8.6	11.4
Tennessee	6.0	8.5
Kentucky	5.6	11.8
Toledo		
All states	1.7	4.3
Alabama	3.3	2.5
Mississippi	3.2	12.3
Indiana	3.2	8.0
Tennessee	2.1	8.3
Youngstown		
All states	0.9	4.7
Pennsylvania	10.2	13.3

Table A.18 *continued*

South Carolina	3.2	8.1
Virginia	2.3	8.7
North Carolina	0.1	7.6
Alabama	0.4	7.5

Sources: Twelfth Census, 1900, Vol. 1: Population, Part 1 (Washington, DC: Government Printing Office, 1902), 702–29; *U.S. Bureau of the Census, Negroes in the U. S., 1920–1932* (Washington, DC: Government Printing Office, 1935), 24, 28–31, 34–36.

APPENDIX B

Histories of African American Life in Northern Nonmetropolitan Communities,* 1860–1930, and Oral History Collections Consulted

HISTORIES OF AFRICAN AMERICAN LIFE IN NORTHERN NONMETROPOLITAN COMMUNITIES, 1860–1930

Illinois

Bigham, Darrel E. *On Jordan's Banks: Emancipation and Its Aftermath in the Ohio River Valley.* Lexington: University Press of Kentucky, 2006. Also includes towns in Ohio, Indiana, and Kentucky.

Carlson [Portwood], Shirley J. "Black Migration to Pulaski County, Illinois, 1860–1900." *Illinois Historical Journal* 80 (Spring 1987): 37–46.

———. "Family and Household in a Black Community in Southern Illinois." *International Journal of Sociology of the Family* 18 (Autumn 1988): 203–14.

Cha-Jua, Sundiata Keita. *America's First Black Town: Brooklyn, Illinois, 1830–1915.* Urbana and Chicago: University of Illinois Press, 2000.

———. "'Join Hands and Hearts with Law and Order': The 1893 Lynching of Samuel J. Bush and the Response of Decatur's African American Community." *Illinois Historical Journal* 83 (Autumn 1990): 187–200.

———. "'A Warlike Demonstration': Legalism, Violent Self-help, and Electoral Politics in Decatur, Illinois, 1894–1898." *Journal of Urban History* 26 (July 2000): 591–629.

Cromwell, Janet Andrews. "History and Organization of the Negro Community in Champaign-Urbana, Illinois." MA thesis, University of Illinois (Sociology), 1934.

Dorsey, Curtis. "Black Migration to Waukegan and the Conditions Encountered up to 1933." MA thesis, Northeastern Illinois University, 1974.

Hays, Christopher K. "The African American Struggle for Equality and Justice in Cairo, Illinois, 1865–1900." *Illinois Historical Journal* 90 (Winter 1997): 265–84.

———. "Way Down in Egypt Land: Conflict and Community in Cairo, Illinois, 1850–1910." PhD diss., University of Missouri–Columbia, 1996.

* "Nonmetropolitan" is defined as having more than 2,500 and less than 100,000 population in 1930.

Portwood, Shirley J. "The Alton School Case and African American Community Consciousness, 1897–1908." *Illinois Historical Journal* 91 (Spring 1998): 2–20.

———. "'We Lift Our Voices in Thunder Tones': African American Race Men and Race Women and Community Agency in Southern Illinois, 1895–1910." *Journal of Urban History* 26 (September 2000): 740–58.

Walker, Juliet E. K. "The Achievement of a Dream." Chap. 8 in *Free Frank: A Black Pioneer on the Antebellum Frontier.* Lexington: University Press of Kentucky, 1983.

Wheeler, Joanne. "Together in Egypt: A Pattern of Race Relations in Cairo, Illinois, 1865–1915." In *Toward a New South? Studies in Post-Civil War Southern Communities,* edited by Orville Vernon Burton and Robert C. McMath, 103–34. Westport, CT: Greenwood Press, 1982.

Indiana

Blocker, Jack S., Jr. "Black Migration to Muncie, 1860–1930." *Indiana Magazine of History* 92 (December 1996): 297–320.

———. "Wages of Migration: Jobs and Homeownership among Black and White Workers in Muncie, Indiana, 1920." In *The African Diaspora: African Origins and New World Identities,* edited by Isidore Okpewho, Carole Boyce Davies, and Ali A. Mazrui, 115–38. Bloomington: Indiana University Press, 1999.

Rotman, Deborah L.; Mancini, Rachel; Smith, Aaron; and Campbell, Elizabeth. *African-American and Quaker Farmers in East Central Indiana: Social, Political, and Economic Aspects of Life in Nineteenth-Century Rural Communities: Randolph County, Indiana.* Muncie, IN: Ball State University Archaeological Resources Management Service Report #51, July 17, 1998.

Vincent, Stephen A. *Southern Seed, Northern Soil: African-American Farm Communities in the Midwest, 1765–1900.* Bloomington and Indianapolis: Indiana University Press, 1999.

Michigan

Cox, Anna-Lisa. *A Stronger Kinship: One Town's Extraordinary Story of Hope and Faith.* New York and Boston: Little, Brown and Company, 2006.

DeVries, James E. *Race and Kinship in a Midwestern Town: The Black Experience in Monroe, Michigan, 1900–1915.* Urbana: University of Illinois Press, 1984.

Jelks, Randal M. "Making Opportunity: The Struggle against Jim Crow in Grand Rapids, Michigan, 1890–1927." *Michigan Historical Review* 19 (Fall 1993): 23–48.

Wheeler, James O., and Stanley D. Brunn. "Agricultural Ghetto: Negroes in Cass County, Michigan, 1845–1968." *Geographical Review* 59 (July 1969): 317–29.

———. "Negro Migration into Rural Southwestern Michigan." *Geographical Review* 58 (April 1968): 214–30.

Sawyer, Marcia Renee. "Surviving Freedom: African-American Farm Households in Cass County, Michigan, 1832–1880." PhD diss., Michigan State University, 1991.

New Jersey

Crew, Spencer R. *Black Life in Secondary Cities: A Comparative Analysis of the Black Communities of Camden and Elizabeth, N. J., 1860–1920.* New York and London: Garland Publishing, 1993.

New York

Armstead, Myra B. Young. *"Lord, Please Don't Take Me in August": African Americans in Newport and Saratoga Springs, 1870–1930.* Urbana and Chicago: University of Illinois Press, 1999.

Grover, Kathryn. *Make a Way Somehow: African-American Life in a Northern Community, 1790–1965.* Syracuse: Syracuse University Press, 1994. Geneva.

Sernett, Milton C. "On Freedom's Threshold: The African American Presence in Central New York, 1760–1940." *Afro-Americans in New York Life and History* 19 (January 1995): 43–91.

Ohio

Goings, Kenneth W. "Blacks in the Rural North: Paulding County, Ohio, 1890–1900." PhD diss., Princeton University, 1977.

———. "Intra-group Differences among Afro-Americans in the Rural North: Paulding County, Ohio, 1860–1900." *Ethnohistory* 27 (Winter 1980): 79–90.

Rhode Island

Armstead, Myra B. Young. *"Lord, Please Don't Take Me in August": African Americans in Newport and Saratoga Springs, 1870–1930.* Urbana and Chicago: University of Illinois Press, 1999.

ORAL HISTORY COLLECTIONS

Manuscript Collections

Black Middletown Project. Archives and Special Collections, Bracken Library, Ball State University, Muncie, IN.

Black Oral History of Canton, Ohio. Stark County District Library, Canton, OH.

Chicago Historical Society, Chicago, IL.

Chicago Migrant Interviews, National Urban League Papers. Manuscript Division, Library of Congress, Washington, DC.

Crawfordsville Black Oral History Project. William Henry Smith Library, Indiana Historical Society, Indianapolis, IN.

Illinois Writers Project Collection. Vivian G. Harsh Research Collection, Chicago Public Library, Chicago, IL.

Muncie Black History Project. Archives and Special Collections, Bracken Library, Ball State University, Muncie, IN.

Ohio Historical Society, Columbus, OH.

Oral History Collection, Toledo-Lucas County Public Library, Toledo, OH.

Oral History of the Champaign-Urbana Black Community. Douglass Branch Library, Champaign, IL.

Oral History Office Collection, University of Illinois–Springfield Archives, Brookens Library, University of Illinois–Springfield (formerly Sangamon State University), Springfield, IL.

Oral History Research Center, Indiana University, Bloomington, IN.

St. James AME Church (Cleveland) Oral History Project. Western Reserve Historical Society, Cleveland, OH.

Published Collections

The American Slave: A Composite Autobiography. Edited by George P. Rawick. 41 vols. Westport, CT: Greenwood Press, 1972–79.
Volume 6, "Indiana Narratives"
Series 2, Volume 16, "Ohio Narratives"
Supplement, Series 1, Volume 5 of *The American Slave*

Wallis, Don. *All We Had Was Each Other: The Black Community of Madison, Indiana: An Oral History.* Bloomington and Indianapolis: Indiana University Press, 1998.

Black, Timuel D., Jr. *Bridges of Memory: Chicago's First Wave of Black Migration: An Oral History.* Evanston and Chicago: Northwestern University Press and DuSable Museum of African American History, 2003.

APPENDIX C

Migrant Oral History Interviews

Migration is an extremely complex process, but the tools with which we try to understand it are primitive.[1] The first blunt instrument to hand is always the census, which is essential in measuring volumes of movement from one set of places to another. Indispensable as it is for analyzing migration patterns, however, the use of census data leaves serious gaps in our knowledge of the perceptions, values, and motivations of migrants. At the same time, it tends to homogenize and to simplify the migrant experience.

The flattening effect of statistical data can occur across both space and time. Using the common state-of-birth method, an increase between censuses in the number of Mississippi-born persons, say, in Illinois leads too easily to a conclusion that such migrants traveled directly from Mississippi to Illinois in a one-step, long-distance migration rather than using multiple steps, through, perhaps, Tennessee, Kentucky, and even Indiana or Missouri. In the former case, migration seems to result from a single decision, a choice between Mississippi and Illinois; in the latter, migration is produced by a series of decisions made at different times and perhaps for different reasons. Furthermore, when census data for large cities show increases in the numbers of persons from predominantly rural states, we tend to characterize their movement as rural-to-urban mobility, and to portray the decisions behind the migration in those terms. But again, a longitudinal perspective may show earlier movements to urban places of smaller or even similar size as the census destination.[2] If such movements are not noted, mobility from rural to urban environments may be characterized as a more abrupt transition than it actually was. Compression of migration in space or time heightens the historian's temptation to produce simple, monolithic explanations for choices that were in fact complex and various.

Oral history evidence offers the possibility of providing detailed information about the movements of individuals and families from one place to another, both the movements that were captured by the census and those that were not, the latter left unrecorded because they occurred between censuses or because the census failed to enumerate the persons concerned. Furthermore, oral history can convey information on the subjective side of the migration experience, affording the investigator an opportunity to share the perspective of the migrant. For these reasons, oral history can and should be used to supplement quantitative evidence on migration.

To explore the African American migration experience, I sought out oral histories in published works and archives.[3] I found tapes or transcripts of interviews with migrants in two kinds of sources. A prolific source was the multivolume collection of ex-slave interviews edited by George Rawick.[4] In three volumes containing interviews with ex-slaves living in Ohio or Indiana, I found usable information on about forty migrants who traveled from the South to each state during the period of my study. Since the Federal Writers' Project (FWP) focused on the slavery experience, information on migration was usually slender. Nevertheless, the transcripts often contained useful biographical data and sometimes included reflections on the migration experience as well. The second type of source was archived collections of interviews with African American residents of various communities, which added another 234 migrants to Ohio, Indiana, and Illinois, including a handful of intraregional migrants.[5] Most of these interviews were conducted during the 1970s and 1980s, although I found in the records of the National Urban League (NUL) reports of interviews made during the early years of the First Great Migration. This second type of record was generally more ample in the information it provided on both the process of migration and migrants' perceptions of their experience.

For the historian of migration, these materials present an opportunity to correct the defects of the census, so long as certain limitations are kept in mind. The problems of the ex-slave interviews are well known from the extensive debates over slavery that have gone on among historians over the past thirty-five years, for which the Rawick collection has provided much of the tinder. Many of the respondents were too young during slavery times to have experienced much of the peculiar institution, the selection criteria are unknown and the geographic distribution of the interviewees was not the same as that of the slave population, many of the interviewers were unsympathetic or uncomprehending, and many of the respondents were too old at the time of the interview to remember much of slavery.[6] Some of these problems are less severe, however, for the historian who wishes to use the FWP interviews to understand migration. Migration was a more recent experience in the respondents' lives than slavery, and it was more likely to have occurred in adulthood.[7] For the ex-slaves, migration north took place at a median age of twenty years.[8] Although the FWP collection yields less information on migration than on slavery, what it does provide may be more reliable.

The archived interviews from the 1970s and 1980s also have limitations. Their principal focus was usually life in the local African American community rather than migration, although information about community life can be revealing about the migrants' reception in and adjustment to their new homes. Reasons for selection of the respondents are unknown. For interviewees providing information during the 1970s or 1980s about their lives before 1930, migration was a distant memory. In comparison to the ex-slave narratives, the recent interviews have both a liability and some advantages. Migration typically occurred at an earlier point in the respondent's life than it did for the ex-slaves; median age at migration for the respondents was fifteen years.[9] On the other hand, their interviewers were more likely to be African Americans, and the interviewing protocols were more sophisticated. Additionally, migration was not for most as temporally distant an experience as slavery.[10]

The advantages and disadvantages of the interviews in the NUL collection are virtually a mirror image of those of the 1970s–1980s interviews. All of the early interviews took place in Chicago, while only one of the later ones did. All of the respondents were adults who had very recently migrated, so the migration experience was quite fresh in their minds, and that experience represented the primary focus of the reports. While the interviews often contain useful information on the migrants' southern context, however, basic background information such as age and place of birth is missing. Information is rarely presented verbatim. These lacunae, together with the short time span of the interviews, emphasize the need to gather oral histories from as many sources as possible.

Clearly the ex-slave interviews and the archived interviews "represent" the African American migration experience to the Lower Midwest only in the sense that they are the only firsthand testimony on that experience I have been able to locate. They should not be treated as a random sample in a statistical sense. To be used effectively, they must be placed in context. In relation to the temporal flow of African American migrants from the South to the Lower Midwest, the interviewees' experience does seem broadly to reflect the overall pattern (table C.1).

Table C.1 Pace of Oral History Interviewees' Migration (in percentages)

	Interviewees	*All "Nonwhite" Migrants*		
		Ohio	Indiana	Illinois
1860–1869	10	8	9	5
1870–1879	2	2	7	3
1880–1889	4	4	6	4
1890–1899	2	6	13	9
1900–1909	8	9	11	10
1910–1919	45	30	24	26
1920–1929	29	41	30	43
Total	100	100	100	100
N	260	279,975	126,592	343,980

Note: Estimates for 1860–1869 are for net migration, while those for 1870–1929 are for gross migration.

Sources: Study data; Michael P. Johnson, "Out of Egypt: The Migration of Former Slaves to the Midwest during the 1860s in Comparative Perspective," in *Crossing Boundaries: Comparative History of Black People in Diaspora,* ed. Darlene Clark Hine and Jacqueline McLeod (Bloomington: Indiana University Press, 1999), 223–45; William Edward Vickery, *The Economics of the Negro Migration, 1900–1960* (New York: Arno, 1977), table 39.

Table C.2 Origins of Oral History Interviewees (in percentages)

	Interviewees	*All "Nonwhites" Born Out of State, 1930*		
		Ohio	Indiana	Illinois
Kentucky	34	13	33	7
Tennessee	20	9	18	14
Virginia	10	7	1	2
Georgia	10	23	6	10
North Carolina	7	5	1	1
Alabama	6	16	8	10
Mississippi	4	4	10	20
South Carolina	2	6	1	2
Missouri	2	**	2	6
Arkansas	2	2	4	6
West Virginia	2	2	**	**
Total	99*	87	84	78
Total N	166	207,900	76,300	253,700

* Does not equal 100 because of rounding

** Less than 1 percent

Sources: Study data; Everett S. Lee et al., *Methodological Considerations and Reference Tables,* vol. 1 of *Population Redistribution and Economic Growth, United States, 1870–1950,* ed. Simon Kuznets and Dorothy Swaine Thomas, 3 vols. (Philadelphia: American Philosophical Society, 1957–64), 310, 311, 332.

Table C.3 Oral History Interviewees' Community of Residence in the Urban Hierarchy (in percentages)

| | *Interviewees* | *All African Americans* | | |
Population		Ohio	Indiana	Illinois
100,000+	54	68	66	72
25,000–99,999	27	10	18	11
10,000–24,999	11	5	5	5
2,500–9,999	5	5	3	4
Rural	3	12	8	8
N	283	309,304	111,982	328,972

Sources: Study data; *Fifteenth Census, Vol. 3, Part 1* (Washington, DC: Government Printing Office, 1932), 491–98, 628–35, 715–19.

The migrations of every decade between 1860 and 1930 are reflected in the interviews, and in roughly similar proportions to the actual flow. The only decade to be seriously underrepresented by the migrant interviews is the 1890s, but the balance between the "trickle" before 1916 and the "flood" afterward is about the same for the respondents as for the general migrant population.

The geographical origins of the respondents, known of course from their self-reports, appear at first glance to be less reflective of the main migrant stream, with a disproportionate number from the Upper South states (table C.2).

The actual distribution, however, is more balanced. A large number of interviews of migrants to Canton, Ohio, and to Chicago from National Urban League collections did not include information on place of birth; most of the Urban League respondents, however, reported their last southern residence in Mississippi, and most of these were almost certainly native Mississippians. The distribution of respondents' communities of residence at the time of their interview generally corresponds to the representation of African Americans across the urban hierarchies of their states at the study's conclusion in 1930 (see table C.3). There is, however, some clustering in nonmetropolitan urban places, especially those between 10,000 and 100,000 population. While this distribution makes them somewhat less representative of the overall migration stream, it makes their evidence about their community experience of particular interest to this study.

NOTES

INTRODUCTION

1. In 1980 the census recorded five hundred African Americans in Washington Court House, representing about 4 percent of a town population that had more than tripled over the past century. U.S. Bureau of the Census, *1980 Census of Population*, vol. 1, part 37, table 15.

2. "The significance of urbanization to the political modernization of Negroes," political scientist Martin Kilson writes, "cannot be overemphasized; it afforded them the quality of social organization and institutional differentiation or specialization without which effective political development is impossible." Martin Kilson, "Political Change in the Negro Ghetto, 1900–1940s," in *Key Issues in the Afro-American Experience*, ed. Nathan I. Huggins, Martin Kilson, and Daniel M. Fox (New York: Harcourt Brace Jovanovich, 1971), 28. In light of the evidence of pre- and postemancipation political organization and activity in the rural South recently cited by Steven Hahn, Kilson's claim must be regarded as an overstatement. Nevertheless, Hahn agrees that urban migration significantly advanced African American political mobilization. Steven Hahn, *A Nation under Our Feet: Black Political Struggles in the Rural South from Slavery to the Great Migration* (Cambridge, MA: Belknap Press of Harvard University Press, 2003).

3. Jack S. Blocker Jr., *"Give to the Winds Thy Fears": The Women's Temperance Crusade, 1873–1874* (Westport, CT: Greenwood Press, 1985).

4. David A. Gerber, *Black Ohio and the Color Line, 1865–1915* (Urbana: University of Illinois Press, 1976), 30–32, 271–79; Emma Lou Thornbrough, *The Negro in Indiana before 1900: A Study of a Minority* (1957; reprint, Bloomington: Indiana University Press, 1993), 228–30.

5. Missouri had a larger gross inmigration than Indiana, but I consider it a southern state because of its history of slavery.

6. William E. Vickery, *The Economics of the Negro Migration, 1900–1960* (New York: Arno, 1977), tables 6 and 39.

7. Raymond A. Mohl, "City and Region: The Missing Dimension in U.S. Urban History," *JUH* 25 (November 1998): 3–21. A regional study of urbanization, on which my approach is modeled, is Edward K. Muller, "Selective Urban Growth in the Middle Ohio Valley, 1800–1860," *GR* 66 (1976): 178–99. For a pioneering attempt to define the intersection in the Midwest of place and race, see Gerald Early, ed., *Black Heartland: African American Life, the Middle West, and the Meaning of American Regionalism* (St. Louis: Washington University, 1997), especially James H. Madison, "Is There A Black Heartland? Questions of Place and Race in Midwestern History," 50–64. I know of only two regional studies of African American migration, both of which deal with the Civil War decade: Michael P. Johnson, "Out of Egypt: The Migration of Former Slaves to the Midwest during the 1860s in Comparative Perspective," in *Crossing Boundaries: Comparative History of Black People in Diaspora*, ed. Darlene Clark Hine and Jacqueline McLeod (Bloomington: Indiana University Press, 1999), 223–45; and the work of Leslie A. Schwalm, "Northern Encounters with Emancipation: Gender, Race and Migration in the American Civil War," paper presented at the conference Race, Ethnicity, and Migration: The United States in a Global Context, University of Minnesota, Minneapolis, November 2000, and "'Overrun with Free Negroes': Emancipation and Wartime Migration in the Upper Midwest," *CWH* 50 (June 2004): 145–74.

8. The best-known examples of single-place studies of African American migration are Peter Gottlieb, *Making Their Own Way: Southern Blacks' Migration to Pittsburgh, 1916–30* (Urbana: University of Illinois Press, 1987), and James R. Grossman, *Land of Hope: Chicago, Black Southerners, and the Great Migration* (Chicago: University of Chicago Press, 1989). See also Shirley J. Carlson, "Black Migration to Pulaski County, Illinois, 1860–1900," *IHJ* 80 (Spring 1987): 37–46, and Jack S. Blocker Jr., "Black Migration to Muncie, 1860–1930," *IMH* 92 (December 1996): 297–320. The shortage of studies on a higher than local level helps to explain why, as sociologist Stewart Tolnay notes, "the general subject of how black southern migrants selected their destinations has not been explored thoroughly." Stewart Tolnay, "The African American 'Great Migration' and Beyond," *AnRS* 29 (2003): 217.

9. Daniel M. Johnson and Rex. R. Campbell, *Black Migration in America: A Social Demographic History* (Durham, NC: Duke University Press, 1981), 68. See also Spencer R. Crew, *Black Life in Secondary Cities: A Comparative Analysis of the Black Communities of Camden and Elizabeth, N.J., 1860–1920* (New York: Garland, 1993), 68–69.

10. The percentage of the African American population living in the South, which had fallen by 3.8 percent during the 1910s and by 6.5 percent during the 1920s, decreased by only 1.7 percent during the 1930s. Johnson and Campbell, *Black Migration in America*, 73.

11. For a listing of historical studies on African American life in northeastern nonmetropolitan communities, see appendix B.

12. Kenneth L. Kusmer, "The Black Urban Experience in American History," in *The State of Afro-American History: Past, Present, and Future*, ed. Darlene Clark Hine (Baton

Rouge: Louisiana State University Press, 1986), 91–122.

13. For Illinois, see Sundiata Cha-Jua, *America's First Black Town: Brooklyn, Illinois, 1830–1915* (Urbana and Chicago: University of Illinois Press, 2000); "'Join Hands and Hearts with Law and Order': The 1893 Lynching of Samuel J. Bush and the Response of Decatur's African American Community," *IHJ* 83 (Autumn 1990): 187–200; "'A Warlike Demonstration': Legalism, Violent Self-help, and Electoral Politics in Decatur, Illinois, 1894–1898," *JUH* 26 (July 2000): 591–629; and Shirley J. Portwood, "The Alton School Case and African American Community Consciousness, 1897–1908," *IHJ* 91 (Spring 1998): 2–20; "'We Lift Our Voices in Thunder Tones': African American Race Men and Race Women and Community Agency in Southern Illinois, 1895–1910," *JUH* 26 (September 2000): 740–58. For Indiana, Stephen A. Vincent, *Southern Seed, Northern Soil: African-American Farm Communities in the Midwest, 1765–1900* (Bloomington and Indianapolis: Indiana University Press, 1999), and Darrel E. Bigham, *We Ask Only a Fair Trial: A History of the Black Community of Evansville, Indiana* (Bloomington: Indiana University Press, 1987), stand out.

14. I initially made a tentative selection of Muncie in the expectation that its prominence as a result of the Lynds' attention would have generated a useful set of studies of its African American residents. That hope turned out to be unfounded until the publication in 2004 of the innovative ethnographic study *The Other Side of Middleton: Exploring Muncie's African American Community*, ed. Luke Eric Lassiter, Hurley Goodall, Elizabeth Campbell, and Michelle Natasya Johnson (Walnut Creek, CA: AltaMira Press, 2004). A closer look, however, revealed a rich collection of oral histories of its African American community plus good grounds for comparison in its rising curve of African American population growth, industrial economy, and less violent history of race relations.

15. Jan Lucassen and Leo Lucassen, "Migration, Migration History, History: Old Paradigms and New Perspectives," in *Migration, Migration History, History: Old Paradigms and New Perspectives*, ed. Jan Lucassen and Leo Lucassen (Berne: Peter Lang, 1997), 21.

16. Introductions to the concept of mental maps may be found in Roger M. Downs and David Stea, *Maps in Minds: Reflections on Cognitive Mapping* (New York: Harper & Row, 1977), and Peter Gould and Rodney White, *Mental Maps*, 2nd ed. (Boston: Allen & Unwin, 1986). Theoretical discussions include Reginald G. Golledge, "Human Wayfinding and Cognitive Maps," in *Wayfinding Behavior: Cognitive Mapping and Other Spatial Processes*, ed. Reginald G. Golledge (Baltimore: Johns Hopkins University Press, 1999), 5–45, and Steffen Werner, Bernd Krieg-Brückner, and Theo Herrmann, "Modelling Navigational Knowledge by Route Graphs," in *Spatial Cognition II: Integrating Abstract Theories, Empirical Studies, Formal Methods, and Practial Applications*, ed. Christian Freksa, Wilfried Brauer, Christopher Habel, and Karl F. Wender (Berlin: Springer-Verlag, 2000), 295–316. For empirical studies by geographers, see Jennifer Morris, *Mental Maps of Victoria*, Monash Publications in

Geography No. 8 (Melbourne: Monash University, 1974), and John R. Clark, *Turkish Cologne: The Mental Maps of Migrant Workers in a German City,* Michigan Geographical Publications No. 19 (Ann Arbor: University of Michigan, 1977). For a recent attempt to reconstruct the mental maps of residents of antebellum southern small towns, see Lisa Tolbert, *Constructing Townscapes: Space and Society in Antebellum Tennessee* (Chapel Hill: University of North Carolina Press, 1999).

17. Werner, Krieg-Brückner, and Herrmann, "Modelling Navigational Knowledge," 297; Golledge, "Human Cognitive Maps," 45.

18. This conclusion is based on reading transcripts and listening to tapes of the several hundred oral history interviews of African American migrants to, and community residents within, the Lower Midwest collected for this study. The collections are listed in appendix B.

19. For an attempt to answer similar questions for immigrants, see Caroline Golab, *Immigrant Destinations* (Philadelphia: Temple University Press, 1977).

20. Tolnay, "African American 'Great Migration,'" 218.

21. George C. Wright, *Racial Violence in Kentucky, 1865–1940: Lynchings, Mob Rule, and "Legal Lynchings"* (Baton Rouge: Louisiana State University Press, 1990), 10.

22. W. Fitzhugh Brundage, *Lynching in the New South: Georgia and Virginia, 1880–1930* (Urbana: University of Illinois Press, 1993), 159.

23. Stewart E. Tolnay and E. M. Beck, *A Festival of Violence: An Analysis of Southern Lynchings, 1882–1930* (Urbana: University of Illinois Press, 1995), 255.

24. James W. Loewen, *Sundown Towns: A Hidden Dimension of American Racism* (New York and London: New Press, 2005). Sundown towns and suburbs are those communities that do not allow African Americans to remain within their boundaries after sunset. Loewen finds such communities, in startlingly large numbers, located across the country, but nearly all are located outside the Deep South. Violence directed against African American "interlopers" or potential interlopers, Loewen argues, has been a common means for making and keeping such towns lily-white.

25. Brundage, *Lynching in the New South,* chaps. 6–8; Wright, *Racial Violence in Kentucky,* chaps. 5–6. Brundage explores one incident of resistance in "The Darien 'Insurrection' of 1899: Black Protest during the Nadir of Race Relations," *GHQ* 74 (July 1990): 234–53. See also W. Fitzhugh Brundage, "Review Essay: Mob Violence North and South, 1865–1940," *GHQ* 75 (Winter 1991): 748–70. A study that focuses on African American response in the North is Cha-Jua, "'A Warlike Demonstration': Legalism, Violent Self-Help, and Electoral Politics in Decatur, Illinois, 1894–1898."

26. Tolnay and Beck, *Festival of Violence,* 232.

27. Nell Irvin Painter, *Exodusters: Black Migration to Kansas after Reconstruction* (1977; reprint, Lawrence: University Press of Kansas, 1986); Robert G. Athearn, *In Search of Canaan: Black Migration to Kansas, 1879–80* (Lawrence: Regents Press of Kansas, 1978); Carter Woodson, *A Century of Negro Migration* (New York: Association for the Study of Negro Life and History, 1918), 126, 130.

28. Lyonel C. Florant, "Negro Internal Migration," *ASR* 7 (December 1942): 782.

29. A considerable literature could of course be cited here, but I will refer only to the work that has most strongly influenced my thinking: R. F. Atkinson, *Knowledge and Explanation in History: An Introduction to the Philosophy of History* (Ithaca, NY: Cornell University Press, 1978).

30. Malcolm Chapman, *The Celts: The Construction of a Myth* (London: Macmillan, 1992), 76.

31. The most prominent works include: David Roediger, *The Wages of Whiteness: Race and the Making of the American Working Class* (London: Verso, 1991), and *Towards the Abolition of Whiteness: Essays on Race, Politics, and Working Class History* (London: Verso, 1994); Alexander Saxton, *The Rise and Fall of the White Republic: Class Politics and Mass Culture in Nineteenth-Century America* (London: Verso, 1990); and Grace Elizabeth Hale, *Making Whiteness: The Culture of Segregation in the South, 1890–1940* (New York: Vintage, 1998). For a recent overview and critique of the literature, see Peter Kolchin, "Whiteness Studies: The New History of Race in America," *JAH* 89 (June 2002): 154–73.

CHAPTER ONE

1. Frederick Douglass to Montgomery Blair, September 16, 1862, in *The Life and Writings of Frederick Douglass,* 5 vols., ed. Philip S. Foner (New York: International Publishers, 1952), 3: 284.

2. Quoted in Allison Davis, Burleigh B. Gardner, and Mary R. Gardner, *Deep South: A Social Anthropological Study of Caste and Class* (Chicago: University of Chicago Press, 1941), 342.

3. Austin Andrews, interview, no date, BOHCO.

4. Michael P. Johnson, "Out of Egypt: The Migration of Former Slaves to the Midwest during the 1860s in Comparative Perspective," in *Crossing Boundaries: Comparative History of Black People in Diaspora,* ed. Darlene Clark Hine and Jacqueline McLeod (Bloomington: Indiana University Press, 1999), 231.

5. Christopher K. Hays, "The African American Struggle for Equality and Justice in Cairo, Illinois, 1865–1900," *IHJ* 90 (Winter 1997): 265.

6. Johnson, "Out of Egypt," 229.

7. Ibid. For a thorough description of the Civil War's impact on both shores of the Ohio River, see Darrel E. Bigham, *On Jordan's Banks: Emancipation and Its Aftermath in the Ohio River Valley* (Lexington: University Press of Kentucky, 2006), chaps. 3–4.

8. Johnson, "Out of Egypt," 229.

9. Adah Isabelle Suggs, interview, no date, *AS,* vol. 6: 189–91. For other examples of family migration, see undated interviews of George Taylor Burns, Matthew Hume, Henry Clay Moorman, and Billy Slaughter, in *AS,* vol. 6: 39, 109–10, 140,

178–79; and Bell Kelley and Joseph Ringo in *AS, Supplement, Series 1,* vol. 5: 106, 431. David A. Gerber, *Black Ohio and the Color Line, 1865–1915* (Urbana: University of Illinois Press, 1976), 30–31.

10. Bigham, *On Jordan's Banks,* 101–102.

11. Jennie Elizabeth Oggs, "Jacksonville, Illinois (Early History)," Negro in Illinois File, IWP.

12. Shirley Carlson [Portwood], "Family and Household in a Black Community in Southern Illinois," *IJSF* 18 (Autumn 1988): 205–206.

13. Johnson, "Out of Egypt," 230.

14. William Nelson, interview, no date, *AS, Series 2,* vol. 16: 76.

15. David A. Hall, interview, August 16, 1937, *AS, Series 2,* vol. 16: 41. See also the undated interviews with William Emmons and Virginia Washington, *AS, Supplement, Series 1,* vol. 5: 329–30, 458–60, and with John Henry Gibson, *AS,* vol. 6: 97.

16. Gerber, *Black Ohio,* 29–32; Bigham, *On Jordan's Banks,* 68.

17. *Orville Artis Memoir* (Springfield, IL: Sangamon State University, 1985). The interview was conducted in Springfield in May 1974.

18. Emma Lou Thornbrough, *The Negro in Indiana before 1900: A Study of a Minority* (1957; reprint, Bloomington: Indiana University Press, 1993), chap. 2; Gerber, *Black Ohio,* 14–19; Edgar F. Raines Jr., "The American Missionary Association in Southern Illinois, 1856–1862: A Case History in the Abolition Movement," *JISHS* 65 (Autumn 1972): 258; Wilhelmena Robinson, "The Negro in the Village of Yellow Springs, Ohio," *NHB* 29 (February 1966): 103–104, 110–12; Richard R. Wright Jr., "The Economic Condition of Negroes in the North: II. Negro Rural Communities in Indiana," *SW* 37 (1908): 159–72.

19. For a narrative of one midwestern township where blacks and whites during the 1860s created a durable tradition of equality, see Anna-Lisa Cox, *A Stronger Kinship: One Town's Extraordinary Story of Hope and Faith* (New York and Boston: Little, Brown and Company, 2006).

20. Eric Foner, *Reconstruction: America's Unfinished Revolution, 1863–1877* (New York: Harper & Row, 1988), 8; Marion B. Lucas, *A History of Blacks in Kentucky,* vol. 1: *From Slavery to Segregation, 1760–1891* (N.p.: Kentucky Historical Society, 1992), 160, 166.

21. Nell Irvin Painter, *Exodusters: Black Migration to Kansas after Reconstruction* (1977; reprint, Lawrence: University Press of Kansas, 1986), chap. 19; Robert G. Athearn, *In Search of Canaan: Black Migration to Kansas, 1879–80* (Lawrence: Regents Press of Kansas, 1978).

22. Athearn, *In Search of Canaan,* 209–23; Thornbrough, *Negro in Indiana,* 214–24.

23. William Cohen, *At Freedom's Edge: Black Mobility and the Southern White Quest for Racial Control, 1861–1915* (Baton Rouge: Louisiana State University Press, 1991), 92.

24. Farah Jasmine Griffin, *"Who Set You Flowin'?" The African American Migration Narrative* (New York: Oxford University Press, 1995), 3.

25. Mrs. Preston, interview, no date, *AS*, vol. 6: 153–54.

26. Thomas Lewis, interview, October 4, 1937, *AS*, vol. 6: 123–24.

27. Kisey McKimm, interview June 9, 1937, *AS, Series 2*, vol. 16: 65.

28. Watt Jordan, interview, no date, *AS, Supplement, Series 1*, vol. 5: 396.

29. John William Matheus, interview, July 8, 1937, *AS, Series 2*, vol. 16: 72–73.

30. Preston, interview.

31. McKimm, interview.

32. Jordan, interview.

33. Matheus, interview.

34. For a conceptual and methodological discussion, see Dennis Conway, "Step-Wise Migration: Toward a Clarification of the Mechanism," *IMR* 14 (1980): 3–14.

35. Jacqueline Jones notes a greater tendency of male migrants to "work their way north gradually, picking up a few dollars and some encouragement from friends along the way before breaking out of the South altogether." Jacqueline Jones, *Labor of Love, Labor of Sorrow: Black Women, Work, and the Family from Slavery to the Present* (New York: Basic Books, 1985), 159.

36. Kenneth W. Goings, "Intra-Group Differences among Afro-Americans in the Rural North: Paulding County, Ohio: 1860–1900," *Eh* 27 (Winter 1980): 81–82.

37. Elizabeth Russell, interview, no date, *AS, Supplement, Series 1*, vol. 5: 183, 186.

38. William Williams, interview, August 13, 1937, *AS, Series 2*, vol. 16: 115. For similar stories, see Rev. Charles Williams, interview, no date, *AS, Supplement, Series 1*, vol. 5: 468–72; Charles H. Anderson, interview, no date, *AS, Series 2*, vol. 16: 4.

39. Marc Fried, "Deprivation and Migration: Dilemmas of Causal Interpretation," in *On Understanding Poverty*, ed. Daniel P. Moynihan (New York: Basic Books, 1969), 134–35.

40. During the second half of 1886, the *Cleveland Gazette* had correspondents in three West Virginia and two Kentucky towns, plus one each in Maryland, Tennessee, Georgia, Mississippi, Arkansas, and Texas. Contrast this with the number of communities represented by correspondents in the following northern states: Pennsylvania, eighteen; New York, nine; Indiana, five; Illinois, three. *Cleveland Gazette*, June 26–December 26, 1886. For an emphasis on the importance of illiteracy in deterring migration, see Robert Higgs, *Competition and Coercion: Blacks in the American Economy, 1865–1914* (Chicago: University of Chicago Press, 1977), 120.

41. For an example of early northern correspondence, see *Arkansas Freeman* (Little Rock), October 5, 1869.

42. Studies emphasizing restricted communication as a factor in maintaining distinct northern and southern unskilled labor markets include Gavin Wright, *Old South, New South: Revolutions in the Southern Economy since the Civil War* (New York: Basic

Books, 1986), chap. 3; Warren C. Whatley and Gavin Wright, "Black Labor in the American Economy since Emancipation: What Are the Legacies of History?" in *The Wealth of Races: The Present Value of Benefits from Past Injustices,* ed. Richard F. America (New York: Greenwood Press, 1990), 67–90; Joshua L. Rosenbloom, *Looking for Work, Searching for Workers: American Labor Markets during Industrialization* (Cambridge: Cambridge University Press, 2002), 174–77.

43. Suzanne Model, "Work and Family: Blacks and Immigrants from South and East Europe," in *Immigration Reconsidered: History, Sociology, and Politics,* ed. Virginia Yans-McLaughlin (New York: Oxford University Press, 1990), 138.

44. John F. Stover, *The Railroads of the South, 1865–1900: A Study in Finance and Control* (Chapel Hill: University of North Carolina Press, 1955).

45. Edward L. Ayers, *The Promise of the New South: Life after Reconstruction* (New York: Oxford University Press, 1992), 137–46.

46. *Travelers' Official Railway Guide for the United States and Canada* (June 1893), timetables for the East Tennessee, Virginia and Georgia; Queen & Crescent; Cincinnati, Hamilton & Dayton; Yazoo & Mississippi Valley; and Illinois Central railroads.

47. Painter, *Exodusters,* esp. 200; Athearn, *In Search of Canaan;* Arvarh E. Strickland, "Toward the Promised Land: The Exodus to Kansas and Afterward," *MHR* 69 (July 1975): 376–412; Cohen, *At Freedom's Edge,* chap. 7.

48. Cohen, *At Freedom's Edge,* 169–70 and appendix B, esp. table 17.

49. Everett S. Lee et al., *Methodological Considerations and Reference Tables,* vol. 1 of *Population Redistribution and Economic Growth, United States, 1870–1950,* ed. S. Kuznets and D. S. Thomas, 3 vols. (Philadelphia: American Philosophical Society, 1957–64), 310–11, 332.

50. J. Morgan Kousser, *The Shaping of Southern Politics: Suffrage Restriction and the Establishment of the One-Party South, 1880–1910* (New Haven, CT: Yale University Press, 1974).

51. William Cronon, *Nature's Metropolis: Chicago and the Great West* (New York: W. W. Norton, 1991).

52. Daniel Nelson, *Farm and Factory: Workers in the Midwest, 1880–1990* (Bloomington: Indiana University Press, 1995), vii.

53. Lee et al., *Methodological Considerations and Reference Tables,* 135–39, 190–91; Clifton J. Phillips, *Indiana in Transition: The Emergence of an Industrial Commonwealth, 1880–1920* (Indianapolis: Indiana Historical Bureau and Indiana Historical Society, 1968), 323–24; John H. Keiser, *Building for the Centuries: Illinois, 1865 to 1898* (Urbana: University of Illinois Press, 1977), 9–10.

54. Nelson, in *Farm and Factory,* 10, argues that "the Midwest would have no surplus of underemployed farmers until well into the twentieth century." This may be true for the Midwest as a whole, but the consistent pattern of outmigration by native-born whites seems to indicate otherwise for Ohio, Indiana, and Illinois.

55. George W. Knepper, *Ohio and Its People* (Kent, OH: Kent State University Press, 1989), chap. 12; Emma Lou Thornbrough, *Indiana in the Civil War Era, 1850–1880* (Indianapolis: Indiana Historical Bureau and Indiana Historical Society, 1965); Phillips, *Indiana in Transition;* Keiser, *Building for the Centuries,* 11–12; Cronon, *Nature's Metropolis.*

56. Michael E. McGerr, *The Decline of Popular Politics: The American North, 1865–1928* (New York: Oxford University Press, 1986), chap. 2.

57. Painter, *Exodusters,* 250–55; Athearn, *In Search of Canaan,* 208–24; Cohen, *At Freedom's Edge,* 188–97; Joseph H. Taylor, "The Great Migration from North Carolina in 1879," *NCHR* 31 (January 1954): 18–33; Frenise A. Logan, "The Movement of Negroes from North Carolina, 1876–1894," *NCHR* 33 (January 1956): 45–65.

58. Paul Kleppner, *The Cross of Culture: A Social Analysis of Midwestern Politics, 1850–1900* (New York: Free Press, 1970); Richard Jensen, *The Winning of the Midwest: Social and Political Conflict, 1888–1896* (Chicago: University of Chicago Press, 1971); Melvyn Hammarberg, *The Indiana Voter: The Historical Dynamics of Party Allegiance during the 1870s* (Chicago: University of Chicago Press, 1977).

59. Paul Kleppner, "Greenback and Prohibition Parties," in *History of U.S. Political Parties,* ed. Arthur M. Schlesinger Jr., 4 vols. (New York: Chelsea House, 1973), 2: 1549–81.

60. Jack S. Blocker Jr., *"Give to the Winds Thy Fears": The Women's Temperance Crusade, 1873–1874* (Westport, CT: Greenwood Press, 1985).

61. Jack S. Blocker Jr., *American Temperance Movements: Cycles of Reform* (Boston: Twayne, 1989), chap. 3.

62. Herbert G. Gutman, "Reconstruction in Ohio: Negroes in the Hocking Valley Coal Mines in 1873 and 1874," *LH* 3 (Fall 1962): 243–64.

63. Ronald L. Lewis, "Job Control and Race Relations in the Coal Fields, 1870–1920," *JES* 12 (1984): 35–64; Herbert G. Gutman, "The Negro and the United Mine Workers of America: The Career and Letters of Richard L. Davis and Something of Their Meaning: 1890–1900," in *The Negro and the American Labor Movement,* ed. Julius Jacobson (Garden City, NY: Doubleday, 1968), 49–127; Herbert Hill, "Myth-Making as Labor History: Herbert Gutman and The United Mine Workers of America," *PCS* 2 (Winter 1988): 132–200; John H. Keiser, "Black Strikebreakers and Racism in Illinois, 1865–1900," *JISHS* 65 (Autumn 1972): 313–26; Warren C. Whatley, "African American Strikebreaking from the Civil War to the New Deal," *SSH* 17 (Winter 1993): 525–58. For first-person narratives of African American families involved in strikebreaking in coal mines, see Sarah Mann, interview, June 16, 1937, *AS, Series 2,* vol. 16: 70; Royal Allen Jones, interview, no date, *AS, Supplement, Series 1,* vol. 5: 394; Mrs. Edna Boysaw, interview, no date, *AS,* vol. 6: 23–24. Some midwestern employers had recognized the strikebreaking opportunities presented by black freedom even earlier. In 1863 African Americans had been used to break longshoremen's strikes in Chicago and Cleveland. Philip S. Foner, *Organized Labor and the Black Worker, 1619–1973* (New

York: Praeger, 1974), 14.

64. Paul Avrich, *The Haymarket Tragedy* (Princeton: Princeton University Press, 1984); James Green, *Death in the Haymarket: A Story of Chicago, the First Labor Movement and the Bombing That Divided Gilded Age America* (New York: Pantheon, 2006).

65. Almont Lindsey, *The Pullman Strike: The Story of a Unique Experiment and of a Great Labor Upheaval* (Chicago: University of Chicago Press, 1942).

66. Gerber, *Black Ohio*, 3–9.

67. Thornbrough, *Negro in Indiana*, 68.

68. Quoted in V. Jacque Voegeli, *Free but Not Equal: The Midwest and the Negro during the Civil War* (Chicago: University of Chicago Press, 1967), 170.

69. Ibid., 119–33, 160–66.

70. Roger D. Bridges, "Equality Deferred: Civil Rights for Illinois Blacks, 1865–1885," *JISHS* 74 (Summer 1981): 83.

71. Ibid., 83–84. The new constitution, however, was not adopted.

72. Gerber, *Black Ohio*, 27–29; Thornbrough, *Negro in Indiana*, 185–86.

73. Voegeli, *Free but Not Equal*, 60–64.

74. Ibid., 119.

75. Bridges, "Equality Deferred"; Robert L. McCaul, *The Black Struggle for Public Schooling in Nineteenth-Century Illinois* (Carbondale: Southern Illinois University Press, 1987), 41–43.

76. Thornbrough, *Negro in Indiana*, 235.

77. Ibid., 323–32; John Roy Squibb, "Roads to Plessy: Blacks and the Law in the Old Northwest, 1860–1896" (PhD diss., University of Wisconsin–Madison, 1992), 95–100.

78. Gerber, *Black Ohio*, 36.

79. Voegeli, *Free but Not Equal*, chaps. 7–9; Gerber, *Black Ohio*, 32–40; Thornbrough, *Negro in Indiana*, chaps. 7, 9; Bridges, "Equality Deferred"; Foner, *Reconstruction*, 26–28; Bigham, *On Jordan's Banks*, 87–100; Sundiata Keita Cha-Jua, *America's First Black Town: Brooklyn, Illinois, 1830–1915* (Urbana and Chicago: University of Illinois Press, 2000), 80.

80. Voegeli, *Free but Not Equal*, 177.

81. Gerber, *Black Ohio*, 38–39.

82. Ibid., 182.

83. Leon F. Litwack, *Trouble in Mind: Black Southerners in the Age of Jim Crow* (New York: Knopf, 1998), xiii. See also Gerber, *Black Ohio*, 41–42; David A. Gerber, "Peter Humphries Clark," in *Black Leaders of the Nineteenth Century*, ed. Leon Litwack and August Meier (Urbana: University of Illinois Press, 1988), 183; Foner, *Reconstruction*, 26–27; Grace Elizabeth Hale, *Making Whiteness: The Culture of Segregation in the South, 1890–1940* (New York: Vintage, 1998), 13–16.

84. Glenda E. Gilmore, *Gender and Jim Crow: Women and the Politics of White*

Supremacy in North Carolina, 1896–1920 (Chapel Hill: University of North Carolina Press, 1996), 5.

85. The data set for this analysis includes all towns in each state that reached 2,500 population by 1890 and for which the requisite data are available for both 1860 and 1890. The sources are published census data on town populations and are cited in tables A.1–A.3. Since I am interested in explaining migrant choices, I employ as the dependent variable a measure of the relative attractive power of all urban places in each of the three states across the period 1860–1890. I compute the change in each town's percentage share of the state's African American urban population by subtracting its share at the beginning of the period from its share at the period's end. The same procedure will be used in later chapters for the periods 1890–1910 and 1910–1930. This measure of course includes population changes resulting from both net migration and net natural increase. Probably most of the urban population changes in the African American population of the Lower Midwest during the years between the Civil War and the eve of the Great Depression did result from shifts in the flow of migration. But in fact no measure of net natural increase on the level of the local community is available; therefore, the two components of population change cannot be separated in any study of local destination choices. The same procedure is used to calculate each town's change in share of its state's total urban population.

Using the census for historical analysis of African American migration presents problems as well as opportunities. First, the census missed African Americans in large numbers. Black numbers seem to have been undercounted by at least 15 percent in late nineteenth-century censuses. Worst in this regard were the census counts of 1870 and 1890 in the South, but blacks, including even property holders, were missed in the North as well. See John B. Sharpless and Ray M. Shortridge, "Biased Underenumeration in Census Manuscripts: Methodological Implications," *JUH* 1 (1975): 409–39; Jack S. Blocker Jr., "Bias in Wealth and Income Records: An Ohio Case Study," *HM* 29 (Winter 1996): 25–36. This is not a problem, however, for a study comparing distribution of African American populations among communities so long as it can be assumed that undercounting was either consistent across communities or randomly distributed across them.

Another problem is that the census gives us only a snapshot of mobility, hiding from view many intercensal moves and intermediate stops between census locations. The only resolution to this problem is tracking individual or family movements, for which the best source is migrant oral histories.

86. The black populations of Cincinnati and Cleveland increased by 10,114, while the number of rural dwellers expanded by 10,375. Indianapolis acquired 8,635 new African American citizens, while rural Indiana added 7,951. Chicago gained 13,613 African Americans, but rural Illinois increased by 17,997. Since the larger rural populations in each state grew more than the metropolitan populations through natural

increase, the number of *migrants* who chose large cities was no doubt larger in Ohio and Indiana, but probably not in Illinois.

87. Gerber, *Black Ohio*, 271–72; Thornbrough, *Negro in Indiana*, 228–30. Exodusters who remained in Kansas are reported to have settled in rural areas and small towns. Athearn, *In Search of Canaan*, 171.

88. In this study, "metropolitan" is used to designate the largest cities within a regional hierarchy. In a national urban hierarchy, such cities would be classified according to central-place theory as second- or third-order places. For the period 1860–1930, a population size of 100,000 has been used as an arbitrary cutoff between metropolitan and nonmetropolitan urban places.

89. Although our figures are not comparable, Michael Wayne's research suggests a similar pattern of dispersion among African Americans who migrated to Canada West (Ontario) in the years before the Civil War. Michael Wayne, "The Black Population of Canada West on the Eve of the American Civil War: A Reassessment Based on the Manuscript Census of 1861," *HS/SH* 28 (November 1995): 476–77.

90. The most recent, and perhaps most sophisticated, presentation of this argument is in William J. Collins, "When the Tide Turned: Immigration and the Delay of the Great Black Migration," *JEH* 57 (September 1997): 607–32. A more recent study of African American and European immigrant adult males in northern urban communities in 1920, however, concludes that the two groups did not appear to compete for the same jobs. Stewart E. Tolnay, "African Americans and Immigrants in Northern Cities: The Effects of Relative Group Size on Occupational Standing in 1920," *SF* 80 (December 2001): 598.

91. In none of the three states was there a statistically significant correlation between change in African American urban population share, 1860–1890, and the percentage of foreign-born white population in 1870. The analysis included forty-four towns and cities in Ohio, twenty-four in Indiana, and twenty-eight in Illinois. Analyzing sixty-nine cities over the period 1890–1950, Collins uses estimated African American migration rates as his dependent variable and the rate of foreign-born inmigration as an independent variable ("When the Tide Turned," 626). I chose the proportion of immigrants because I believe this, rather than the rate of inmigration, would have been likely to matter more to an African American potential migrant.

Comparing two New Jersey towns during the late nineteenth century, Spencer Crew finds that African American occupational opportunities were better in Elizabeth, which held a larger immigrant population than Camden. Spencer Crew, *Black Life in Secondary Cities: A Comparative Analysis of the Black Communities of Camden and Elizabeth, N.J., 1860–1920* (New York: Garland, 1993), 93–95, 112.

92. Figures 1.2–1.4 show the relative size of gains and losses for all towns and cities that experienced a change in African American urban population share of more than 1 percent.

93. This conclusion is based on correlation analysis comparing towns' changes

between 1860 and 1890 in African American and European American urban population share. These patterns are complicated in Illinois and Ohio by extreme outliers, the
largest cities. In Illinois, Chicago is an outlier primarily because of its extraordinary
gain in share of the state's total urban population (18.6 percent). The share change
of most communities fluctuated within the range +1 to −1 percent. With Chicago
excluded from the analysis, however, the correlation between change in black urban
share and change in total urban share becomes even more strongly positive ($r = +.54$,
$p < .001$). In Ohio, Cincinnati is an extreme outlier primarily because of the opposite
situation, its huge loss in share of the state's total urban population (20.5 percent).
When Cincinnati is excluded, the correlation between change in black urban share and
change in total urban share remains positive, but becomes nonsignificant ($r = +.18$, $p >$
.10). Cleveland is another outlier because of its large gain in share of Ohio's total urban
population (6.75 percent). With Cleveland excluded, the correlation between change in
black urban share and change in total urban share becomes strongly positive ($r = +.51$,
$p < .00001$).

94. New Albany dropped from 12 percent to less than 4 percent of Indiana's urban
population. Cincinnati fell from more than 40 percent to 20 percent of Ohio's.

95. George C. Wright, *Racial Violence in Kentucky, 1865–1940: Lynchings, Mob Rule,
and "Legal Lynchings"* (Baton Rouge: Louisiana University Press, 1990), demonstrates
the forms and scope of white terrorism in Kentucky, the state that provided by far the
largest number of Gilded Age migrants to the Lower Midwest.

96. They were Cairo, Illinois (35.7 percent); Xenia, Ohio (25.6 percent); and
Gallipolis, Ohio (20.9 percent).

97. Hermann R. Muelder, "Galesburg: Hot-Bed of Abolitionism," *JISHS* 35
(1942): 216–35.

CHAPTER TWO

1. "Seek Their Rights," clipping from *Daily Inter Ocean*, October 21, 1895, Negro
in Illinois File, IWP.

2. *The Freeman* (Indianapolis), February 10, 1894.

3. Pauli Murray, *Proud Shoes: The Story of an American Family* (New York: Harper
& Row, 1956), 25.

4. Emma Lou Thornbrough, *The Negro in Indiana before 1900: A Study of a Minority*
(1957; reprint, Bloomington: Indiana University Press, 1993); David A. Gerber, *Black
Ohio and the Color Line, 1860–1915* (Urbana: University of Illinois Press, 1976).

5. A later chapter will analyze the place of African Americans within the social
structure of the fourth case study community, Muncie, after the onset of the Great
Migration.

6. *Fayette County Herald*, November 5, 1874; *Cyclone* (Washington Court House,

OH), July 4, August 15, 1888.

7. Jack S. Blocker Jr., "Market Integration, Urban Growth and Economic Change in an Ohio County, 1850–1880," *OH* 90 (Autumn 1981): 298–316; *Eleventh Census, 1890, Vol. 5: Agriculture* (Washington, DC: Government Printing Office, 1895), 172–73, 223–24; *Twelfth Census, 1900: Agriculture, Part 1* (Washington, DC: Government Printing Office, 1902), 112–13, 292–93, and *Part 2,* 178–79; *Twelfth Census, 1900: Manufactures, Part 2* (Washington, DC: Government Printing Office, 1902), 691; *Thirteenth Census, 1910, Vol. 7: Agriculture* (Washington,DC: Government Printing Office, 1913), 322, 331, 340. In 1900 Washington Court House held a total population of 5,742.

8. The statistical descriptions and analyses that follow are based upon the U.S. federal census manuscript population schedules for 1860, 1870, 1880, and 1900 for Fayette County. Quantitative statements made about Washington Court House population in 1860, 1870, 1880, and 1900 are based on examination of the entire population. The census schedules for 1890 were destroyed. An attempt has been made, however, to reconstruct as much as possible of the 1890 census through use of a city directory published in 1890—which, perhaps significantly, did not distinguish persons by "color" or "race"—the county tax assessment list for 1890, and the manuscript census schedules for 1880 and 1900. Persons whose names appeared in the directory or tax list were manually linked backward to the 1880 census and forward to the 1900 census. This procedure produced a list of 1,391 names, which was incorporated into an SPSS file with background characteristics from the census schedule(s), tax list, and directory. This probably represents a little less than one-half the adult population of Washington Court House in 1890. These data will be referred to as the "1890 census reconstruction." Since to join this file a person had to appear in at least two lists, in 1890 and either 1880 or 1900, the reader should keep in mind that this population was distinguished by its persistence in Washington Court House.

9. Columbus's, Cincinnati's, and Cleveland's African American population shares ranked well behind Washington Court House, at 6, 4, and 1 percent, respectively.

10. Among African Americans, 83.8 of males and 84.7 percent of females lived with at least one other family member, compared to 88.5 percent of males and 91.1 percent of females among European Americans. The difference among males was caused by a larger percentage of African American boarders, and among females by a larger percentage of African American servants. The percentages are lower when children are excluded from the analysis.

11. U.S. federal census manuscript schedules, Fayette County, Ohio, 1860–1880. All statements made about geographic persistence and mobility in the case study communities are based on nominal record linkage between census schedules. The linkage was done manually using information on name, sex, "color," age, place of birth, and relations to other household members. Only definite matches were considered to reflect persistence. Manual linkage was preferred to computer linkage precisely because the

former allowed consideration of both contextual clues and more extensive background information.

12. There were seventeen Ohio-born persisters among a total 269 African American adults, and 335 Ohio-born persisters out of 1,756 European American adults.

13. Among African American adult female newcomers since 1870, 76 percent lived with another family member in 1880, compared to 86.5 percent among European American adult female newcomers. Among African American adult male newcomers, 73 percent lived with family, compared to 78 percent for European American adult male newcomers.

14. The occupational categories used in table 2.1 are the same employed with the 1900 census in Olivier Zunz, *The Changing Face of Inequality: Urbanization, Industrial Development, and Immigrants in Detroit, 1880–1920* (Chicago: University of Chicago Press, 1982). See appendix 3.

15. The most common occupation of African American girls and women in 1880, domestic servant, was not likely to appear in the city directory, which was intended to list only those perceived as household heads and their spouses. A listing based on a directory therefore drastically understates the actual extent of labor force participation by African American girls and women.

16. Women holding or seeking gainful occupations, according to census designations, included 34 of 115 adult African American women (29.6 percent) and 143 of 801 European American women (17.8 percent).

17. A study of Xenia, Ohio, in 1902 found a more diversified occupational structure for African American women than Washington Court House. Most notably, 17 women worked as teachers, 5 percent of the 333 women who reported gainful occupations. The largest occupational groups were laundresses (26 percent), day workers (24 percent), cooks (10 percent), and domestic servants (10 percent). Despite the greater diversity in Xenia, a significant number of young women were unemployed and living at home, many of whom had attended high school and some of them high school graduates, because they were trying to avoid domestic service. Richard R. Wright Jr., *The Negroes of Xenia, Ohio: A Social Study*, Bulletin of the U.S. Department of Labor, No. 48 (September 1903), 1023–30. At 8,696 population in 1900, Xenia was larger than Washington Court House, with a larger African American population (1,991).

18. Frenise A. Logan, "The Economic Status of the Town Negro in Post-Reconstruction North Carolina," *NCHR* 35 (October 1958): 448–60.

19. This is exactly what a U.S. Department of Labor researcher found in Xenia, Ohio, twelve years later: "[T]here is as yet no large and successful venture outside of the lines of business with which the Negro slave was familiar." Wright, *Negroes of Xenia,* 1027.

20. Jack S. Blocker Jr., "Bias in Wealth and Income Records: An Ohio Case Study," *HM* 29 (Winter 1996): 25–36.

21. See the use of the concept of "opportunity structure" in Theodore Hershberg, Alan

N. Burstein, Eugene N. Ericksen, Stephanie W. Greenberg, and William L. Yancey, "A Tale of Three Cities: Blacks, Immigrants, and Opportunity in Philadelphia, 1850–1880, 1930, 1970," in *Philadelphia: Work, Space, Family, and Group Experience in the 19th Century,* ed. Theodore Hershberg (New York: Oxford University Press, 1981), 461–91.

22. James E. DeVries, *Race and Kinship in a Midwestern Town: The Black Experience in Monroe, Michigan, 1900–1915* (Urbana: University of Illinois Press, 1984), 147.

23. James Gregory notes that studies comparing the economic status of blacks and whites typically ignore migration and regional origin. James Gregory, *The Southern Diaspora: How the Great Migrations of Black and White Southerners Transformed America* (Chapel Hill: University of North Carolina Press, 2005), 379n26.

24. The phrase is David Roediger's. See *The Wages of Whiteness: Race and the Making of the American Working Class* (London: Verso, 1991).

25. The power of "whiteness" may be quantitatively demonstrated by a stepwise multiple-regression analysis in which the variable "color" is allowed to compete freely with the variables "persistence," "age," and "origin." For males, color is the most powerful variable in explaining variation in wealth holding in 1890, and persistence the second most powerful, adding about half as much as color to the (weak) explanatory power of the model. R^2 for the model with two variables is .018. For females, age was the most powerful variable, but color added about one-third as much. R^2 for this model with two variables is .04. The other variables were not related to wealth holding at the .05 level of significance (also known as the .95 level of confidence).

26. *Twelfth Census, 1900: Vol. 2, Population, Part 2* (Washington, DC: Government Printing Office, 1902), 719.

27. Richard Harris, "Self-Building in the Urban Housing Market," *EG* 67 (January 1991): 1–21. For oral history accounts of black migrants who built their own homes, see Tolbert Bragg and Preston Tate (both of Portland, Indiana) and Charles Green and Dulcinda Baker Martin (Springfield, Ohio), interviews, *AS, Supplement, Series 1,* vol. 5: 20–21, 220–21, 351, 416, and Julia Williams, interview, June 10, 1937, *AS, Supplement, Series 2,* vol. 16: 107.

28. John Bodnar, Roger Simon, and Michael P. Weber, *Lives of Their Own: Blacks, Italians, and Poles in Pittsburgh, 1900–1960* (Urbana and Chicago: University of Illinois Press, 1982), 153–54. For a different view, see Daniel D. Luria, "Wealth, Capital, and Power: The Social Meaning of Home Ownership," *JIH* 7 (Autumn 1976): 261–82. In arguing that home ownership did not confer social power or lead to occupational advancement, Luria does not deny that workers sought home ownership.

29. Richard Harris, "Working-Class Home Ownership in the American Metropolis," *JUH* 17 (November 1990): 47. Economic historians William Collins and Robert Margo agree that home ownership can be an important determinant of living standards. William J. Collins and Robert A. Margo, "Race and Home Ownership: A Century-Long View," *EEH* 38 (2001): 68–92.

30. African Americans in Xenia, Ohio, in 1902 had a family home ownership rate

of 63.5 percent. Wright, *Negroes of Xenia*, 1033. Stephen A. Vincent reports that those who moved from Indiana rural communities to small villages and towns in Hamilton and Rush counties achieved a home ownership rate of about 50 percent in the latter settings. Stephen A. Vincent, *Southern Seed, Northern Soil: African American Farm Communities in the Midwest, 1765–1900* (Bloomington and Indianapolis: Indiana University Press, 1999), 146.

31. Daniel McLean, the longtime president of the Peoples' and Drovers' Bank until his death in the 1880s and one of the town's wealthiest citizens, was very active in land speculation. So was Madison Pavey, president in 1889–90 of the only other bank in Washington Court House, the Merchants' and Farmers' Bank. See R. L. Polk & Co., *Directory for Washington C. H., 1889–90* (Washington Court House, OH: Sandy Fackler, 1995); Fayette County Auditor's Tax Duplicate, 1870, 1880, 1890.

32. DeVries, *Race and Kinship in a Midwestern Town*, 247.

33. All biographical data for this chapter come from the following sources, which will normally not be cited individually. U.S. federal manuscript censuses, 1860–1880, 1900, 1910; Fayette County, OH, Auditor's Tax Duplicate, 1870, 1880, 1890; Sandy Fackler, *Fayette County Chronicle: A Collection of Genealogical and Historical Records*, 2 vols. (Washington Court House, OH: Author, 1987), vol. 2; Guardianships, Fayette County, 1863–1879, OHS; monument placement and inscriptions, Washington Court House Cemetery; Maude Post Rankin, *Washington Court House Cemetery*, typescript, Carnegie Public Library, Washington Court House, OH; William H. Parham and Jeremiah A. Brown, *An Official History of the Most Worshipful Grand Lodge of Free and Accepted Masons for the State of Ohio* (1906), 79–80; B. E. Kelley, *Down Through the Golden Years* (1974; a collection of newspaper articles, in the Carnegie Public Library, Washington Court House, OH), 875–76; *R. L. Polk & Co.'s Directory for Washington C. H. 1889–90*; *Washington C. H. and Fayette County Directory, 1906–07* (Columbus, OH: R. L. Polk & Co., 1906); *Washington Court House and Fayette County Directory* (Washington Court House, OH: Herald Publishing, 1913); Fayette County Jail Registers, 1870–99, Fayette County Jail; *Ohio State Register*, May 14, 1868; *Fayette County Herald*, August 1, 1872; the *Cyclone* (alternately the *Cyclone & Fayette Republican*, Washington Court House, OH), various dates; Ohio Annual Conference, A.M.E. Church, *1880, 1890, 1902, 1903, 1904, 1906, 1907, 1911, 1912;* "Autobiographic Sketch of the New Second Baptist Church, 828 Columbus Avenue, Washington Court House, Ohio," typescript, Carnegie Public Library, Washington Court House, OH; Add Burnett, *Remember?*, typescript, Carnegie Public Library, Washington Court House; May M. Duffee, *As I Remember: Washington Court House and My Autobiography* (Wilmington, OH: Wilmington Publishing, 1953), 66–69; Sandy Fackler, *The Fayette Connection* 5 (Fall 1985); Frank M. Allen, ed., *History of Fayette County, Ohio* (Indianapolis: B. F. Bowen & Co., 1914); Ohio Auditor of State, *Special Enumeration of Negroes Emigrating to Ohio between 1861 and 1863*, OHS.

34. Sharon Ann Holt, *Making Freedom Pay: North Carolina Freedpeople Working for*

Themselves, 1865–1900 (Athens: University of Georgia Press, 2000), xix.

35. U.S. federal manuscript census of free population, Granville County, NC, 1860.

36. Gerber, *Black Ohio and the Color Line,* 28–30.

37. Ohio Auditor of State, *Special Enumeration of Negroes Emigrating to Ohio between 1861 and 1863.*

38. The 1870 census described Whiteman as "black," while the other household members were listed as "mulatto."

39. Steven Ruggles, "The Origins of African American Family Structure," *ASR* 59 (February 1994): 136–51.

40. Michael J. Doucet and John C. Weaver, "Material Culture and the North American House: The Era of the Common Man, 1870–1920," *JAH* 72 (December 1985): 568–69.

41. Jack S. Blocker Jr., "Building Networks: Cooperation and Communication among African Americans in the Urban Midwest, 1860–1910," *IMH* 99 (December 2003): 371–78.

42. The crusade in Washington Court House is described in detail by a leading participant in Matilda Gilruth Carpenter, *The Crusade: Its Origin and Development at Washington Court House and Its Results* (Columbus, OH: W. G. Hubbard & Co., 1893). For a history of the movement at the local, state and national levels, see Jack S. Blocker Jr., *"Give to the Winds Thy Fears": The Women's Temperance Crusade, 1873–1874* (Westport, CT: Greenwood, 1985).

43. Jack S. Blocker Jr., "Artisan's Escape: A Profile of the Postbellum Liquor Trade in a Midwestern Small Town," *EEBH* 12 (1994): 335–46.

44. The jail register has been examined for the years 1870–1875, 1878, 1881, 1884, 1887, 1890, 1893, 1894, 1896, and 1899, in addition to the records of the Fayette County Court of Common Pleas, 1868–1874, and a local newspaper that for a time printed reports of arrests, *Fayette County Herald,* May 21–July 30, 1868.

45. Blocker, "Artisan's Escape."

46. William Cronon, *Nature's Metropolis: Chicago and the Great West* (New York: W. W. Norton, 1991), chap. 5.

47. Doucet and Weaver, "Material Culture," 574–76.

48. Blocker, "Artisan's Escape."

49. The most extended account of Andersonville is a retrospective newspaper article in Kelley, *Down Through the Golden Years,* 875–76.

50. I cannot prove that Dora Anderson was the one who paid for King's monument. The circumstantial evidence points that way, however. She received or inherited the family property, and her sister Emily (who seems to have used "Emma") appears to have died only two years after Dora. If it were Emma who was responsible for King's marker, she would presumably also have purchased a more impressive monument for her sister. Emma was also under ten years old and about twenty years younger than Dora when

King and Emily separated. Possibly King bought the monument himself in a final flamboyant gesture. But since he seems to have generously provided for Dora when the marriage broke up, I surmise that he would have willed his remaining property to her and her sister.

51. Burnett, *Remember?*

52. It is possible that Lewis Chester was the first Granville Countian to travel to Washington Court House, as there was a Chester family, perhaps headed by a brother of Lewis, in that county in 1860.

53. Burnett, *Remember?* See also Duffee, *As I Remember,* 66. Duffee was born in 1880, and remembered Eugene and his sisters more than forty years after they had left Washington Court House.

54. For a survey of the complex and neglected topic of cemetery segregation, see Angelika Krüger-Kahloula, "On the Wrong Side of the Fence: Racial Segregation in American Cemeteries," in *History and Memory in African American Culture,* ed. Geneviève Fabre and Robert O'Meally (New York: Oxford University Press, 1994), 130–49.

55. Burnett, *Remember?*

56. A biographical sketch is in *Cleveland Gazette,* November 11, 1899.

57. Burnett, *Remember?*

58. African American lawyers found it impossible to establish themselves even in the much larger black community of Evansville, Indiana. Darrel E. Bigham, *On Jordan's Banks: Emancipation and Its Aftermath in the Ohio River Valley* (Lexington: University Press of Kentucky, 2006), 203.

59. Widows, widowers, and divorced persons were much more common among adult blacks in Xenia, Ohio, in 1900 than among whites nationally. Disproportionate numbers of widowed or divorced persons were also present among African Americans in Farmville, Virginia, and Sandy Spring, Maryland. Wright, *Negroes of Xenia,* 1019. Patterns of marital status in Springfield, Ohio, and Springfield, Illinois, exhibited a slight tendency in the same direction, but the differences between African Americans and European Americans in these two communities were not statistically significant.

60. Crude birth and death rates were calculated for three-year periods straddling or close to census years. The periods used were 1879–1881, 1889–1891, and 1898–1900. The number of white births per 1,000 population was 22.5, 19.2, and 15.9; the number of black births was 21.0, 14.9, and 16.4. The number of white deaths per 1,000 population was 7.8, 7.9, and 7.5; the number of black deaths was 8.3, 13.5, and 12.2. Figures were obtained from the annual volumes of *Ohio Statistics,* published by the office of the Ohio secretary of state. Higher death rates for African Americans were also the norm in Evansville, Indiana. Darrel E. Bigham, *We Ask Only a Fair Trial: A History of the Black Community in Evansville, Indiana* (Bloomington: Indiana University Press, 1987), 50. Stewart Tolnay points out in his study of the African American family that death was the most common form of marriage disruption. Stewart Tolnay, *The Bottom*

Rung: African American Family Life on Southern Farms (Urbana and Chicago: University of Illinois Press, 1999), 96–98.

61. African American men made up 13 percent of the males twenty years and over in Washington Court House in 1900, but represented 33 percent of the widowers.

62. Sundiata Cha-Jua refers to saloon ownership as "the pillar of the nascent Black petty bourgeoisie." Sundiata Cha-Jua, *America's First Black Town: Brooklyn, Illinois, 1830–1915* (Urbana and Chicago: University of Illinois Press, 2000), 165, 188.

63. A different and, in my view, overly benign portrait of the saloon is in Madelon Powers, *Faces along the Bar: Lore and Order in the Workingman's Saloon, 1870–1920* (Chicago: University of Chicago Press, 1998). A more accurate picture of saloon violence, focusing on a small midwestern city, is in Brian Butler, *An Undergrowth of Folly: Public Order, Race Anxiety, and the 1903 Evansville, Indiana Riot* (New York: Garland, 2000), chap. 5, and a recent study of saloon behavior in the Midwest emphasizes how "manly competitition" could lead to violence. Elaine Frantz Parsons, *Manhood Lost: Fallen Drunkards and Redeeming Women in the Nineteenth-Century United States* (Baltimore and London: Johns Hopkins University Press, 2003), 63–64.

64. Butler, *An Undergrowth of Folly,* 120.

65. Blocker, *"Give to the Winds Thy Fears,"* 109.

66. Jack S. Blocker Jr., "Consumption and Availability of Alcoholic Beverages in the United States, 1863–1920," *CDP* 21 (Winter 1994): 631–66.

CHAPTER THREE

1. Charles Green, interview, no date, *AS, Supplement, Series 1,* vol. 5: 351.

2. Reverend Harry Mann Memoir, April 8, 1974, OHUIS, 24.

3. Mrs. Mary Blue Wynne, interview, January 15, 1987, SJOHP.

4. Edwin Smith Todd, *A Sociological Study of Clark County, Ohio* (Springfield: Springfield Publishing, 1904); city directories, 1870, 1892–93, 1901. In both 1890 and 1900, African Americans made up 11.1 percent of Springfield's population.

5. Todd, *Sociological Study,* 12, 38–44; *Twelfth Census, 1900, Vol. 1: Population, Part 1* (Washington, DC: Government Printing Office, 1902), 702–29. Todd lists Tennessee and North Carolina as principal origins of African American migrants, but these were much less significant than Kentucky and Virginia.

6. The analysis that follows employs a stratified random sample drawn from the 1900 U.S. federal manuscript census schedules for Clark County, Ohio. The sample was stratified to reflect the distribution of both European American and African American populations among Springfield's six wards and twenty-nine census enumeration districts. A quota was set for each enumeration district according to its proportion of the total European American population. To select European American members of the sample, in each enumeration district research assistants began at a line number selected

at random. If the entry at that line number was listed as "white" and twenty-one years of age or over, that person was taken for the sample. If not, the researcher moved up the page until someone was found who fit these criteria. We then skipped ahead eighty-five lines and repeated the procedure, moving alternately up and down the page if the initial entry did not qualify. After filling the sample quota for each enumeration district, we moved on to the next district. This procedure produced a sample of 187 men and 214 women, representing in total 1.2 percent of the European American population. This sample was designed to be accurate within a margin of error of ±.05 at the .95 level of confidence in estimating the proportion of the population living in family-owned homes. For sixteen cases, data were missing on home ownership. As a result, the sample should be considered as accurate within a margin of error of ±.06 at the .95 level of confidence.

To select the African American sample members, we simply moved through the entire census schedule for Springfield, selecting every fifth person designated as "black" or "colored" or "mulatto" who was listed as twenty-one years of age or older. This yielded a sample of 270 men and 243 women, which represents 12.1 percent of the African American population (probably about one-quarter of the adult population). Data were missing on homeownership for forty-nine cases. In estimating the proportion of the total population living in family-owned homes, this sample size should be accurate within a margin of error of ±.05 at the .95 level of confidence.

The percentage of adult women living with at least one other nuclear or extended family member was 79.8 percent for African Americans and 91.6 for European Americans. Among European American men, 88.2 percent lived with another family member.

7. Among African American adult female newcomers since 1880, 79 percent lived with another family member in 1900, compared to 91 percent among European American adult female newcomers. Among African American adult male newcomers, 68 percent lived with family, compared to 86 percent for European American adult male newcomers. Given the longer time period for families to form than in Washington Court House (twenty years versus ten), this evidence for family migration is not as strong. The male-female comparison, however, is not affected by the differing periods used to measure persistence.

8. The index of segregation measures how much greater a proportion of African Americans than European Americans would have to move in order to achieve an equal distribution among wards. It is calculated according to the formula in Charles M. Dollar and Richard J. Jensen, *Historian's Guide to Statistics: Quantitative Analysis and Historical Research* (New York: Holt, Rinehart & Winston, 1971), 125–26. The index for Washington Court House in 1900 is 29, for Springfield, Ohio, 14, and for Springfield, Illinois, 35. Comparable indexes for three southern cities in 1900 show that Richmond, Virginia, was more segregated than any of the northern communities; Louisville, Kentucky, was at about the level for Washington Court House, and New

Orleans was slightly higher than Springfield, Ohio. Zane L. Miller, "Urban Blacks in the South, 1865–1920: An Analysis of Some Quantitative Data on Richmond, Savannah, New Orleans, Louisville, and Birmingham," in *The New Urban History: Quantitative Explorations by American Historians,* ed. Leo F. Schnore (Princeton, NJ: Princeton University Press, 1976), 201.

9. Todd, *Sociological Study,* 90.

10. Ibid., 67.

11. Nineteen of twenty machinists were white, but seven of fifteen iron molders and two of four undifferentiated molders were black. The occupations of barber, teamster, and waiter were dominated by African Americans.

12. Todd, *Sociological Study,* 95.

13. Except older southern-born African American women. In the analysis of home ownership in the 1900 samples for the two Springfields, 1880 had to be taken as the base year because of the missing 1890 manuscript census schedules.

14. The procedure used was logistic regression, employing a maximum likelihood ratio. Logistic regression is the appropriate tool when analyzing problems in which the dependent variable, in this case home ownership, is measured at the nominal level. Home ownership as a nominal variable is dichotomous ("yes" or "no"). The analysis of wealth holding in Washington Court House employed ordinary least squares regression, since the dependent variable, assessed wealth, was measured at the ratio level. For an introduction to logistic regression, see Thomas J. Archdeacon, *Correlation and Regression Analysis: A Historian's Guide* (Madison: University of Wisconsin Press, 1994), chap. 14.

15. Again, a stepwise logistic regression program was used. The complete model with the two variables "persistence" and "color" produced a Cox and Snell R^2 of .074. Color contributed nearly as much as persistence to this coefficient. Among all women, color was not a factor in home owning, only persistence and age, in that order.

16. *Cleveland Gazette,* June 26, 1886.

17. Roberta Senechal, *The Sociogenesis of a Race Riot: Springfield, Illinois, in 1908* (Urbana: University of Illinois Press, 1990), chap. 2; Edward J. Russo, *Prairie of Promise: Springfield and Sangamon County* (Woodland Hills, CA: Windsor, 1983), chaps. 2–3.

18. Senechal, *Sociogenesis of a Race Riot,* chap. 2; *Twelfth Census, 1900, Vol. 1: Population, Part 1,* 651–53; *Thirteenth Census, 1910: Vol. 3, Population* (Washington, DC: Government Printing Office, 1913), 504.

19. Among the African American newcomers since 1880, 77 percent of the women and 71 percent of the men were living with at least one other nuclear or extended family member in 1900. The comparable figures for European Americans were 92 percent for women and 83 percent for men.

The analysis to follow is based on a stratified random sample drawn so as to reflect the distribution of populations among Springfield's seven wards and eighteen enumeration districts. The samples of African Americans and European Americans were drawn in the same manner as in Springfield, Ohio. The European American sample produced a file of 403 cases, 180 men and 223 women. This represents 1.3 percent of the European American population in 1900. The sample was designed to be accurate within a margin of error of ±.05 at the .95 level of confidence when estimating the proportion of the adult population living in family-owned homes. Despite missing data on home ownership for twelve cases, the sample does meet that criterion. The African American sample numbers 498, 283 men and 215 women, or 22 percent of Springfield's African American population, and probably close to half of its adult African American population. To estimate the proportion of the adult population living in family-owned homes, a sample of this size should be considered accurate with a margin of error of ±.05 at the .95 level of confidence. The accuracy of the estimate is not affected by missing data on home ownership for 44 cases.

20. Leota Harris Memoir, February 5, 1975, 2 vols., OHUIS. Quotation is from vol. 1: 14.

21. Clarence Liggins Memoir, March 8, 1974, OHUIS.

22. Eighty-five percent of African American men and 87 percent of women were newcomers since 1880, compared to 78 percent of European American men and 84 percent of women.

23. Senechal, *Sociogenesis of a Race Riot,* 16–17, 66–68.

24. Ibid., 63.

25. *Twelfth Census, 1900: Vol. 2, Population, Part 2* (Washington, DC: Government Printing Office, 1902), 714.

26. The only exceptions were older southern-born African American newcomers of both sexes.

27. Leota Harris Memoir, 1: 13–14; 2: 111–112.

28. Emma Lou Thornbrough, *The Negro in Indiana before 1900: A Study of a Minority* (1957; reprint, Bloomington: Indiana University Press, 1993); David A. Gerber, *Black Ohio and the Color Line, 1865–1915* (Urbana: University of Illinois Press, 1976); Allan H. Spear, *Black Chicago: The Making of a Negro Ghetto, 1890–1920* (Chicago: University of Chicago Press, 1967), chap. 2; Kenneth L. Kusmer, *A Ghetto Takes Shape: Black Cleveland, 1870–1930* (Urbana: University of Illinois Press, 1976), chap. 4; Darrel E. Bigham, *We Ask Only a Fair Trial: A History of the Black Community of Evansville, Indiana* (Bloomington: Indiana University Press, 1987), 54–56; Nancy Bertaux, "Structural Economic Change and Occupational Decline among Black Workers in Nineteenth-Century Cincinnati," in *Race and the City: Work, Community, and Protest in Cincinnati, 1820–1970,* ed. Henry Louis Taylor Jr. (Urbana: University of Illinois Press, 1993), 126–55. In contrast, studies of rural blacks have usually focused on property holding. See Kenneth W. Goings, "Blacks in the Rural North: Paulding County, Ohio, 1860–1900" (PhD diss., Princeton University, 1977), which emphasizes limited black achievement; and Johnetta Y. Jones, "Black Land Tenancy in Extreme Southern Illinois, 1870–1920," in *Selected Papers in Illinois History, 1980* (Springfield:

Illinois State Historical Society, 1982), 41–51, and Shirley J. Carlson, "Black Migration to Pulaski County, Illinois, 1860–1900," *IHJ* 80 (Spring 1987): 37–46, both of whom report African American progress in rural Pulaski County. Stephen A. Vincent, *Southern Seed, Northern Soil: African-American Farm Communities in the Midwest, 1765–1900* (Bloomington and Indianapolis: Indiana University Press, 1999), traces declining opportunities in agriculture in two rural Indiana settlements.

29. *Twelfth Census, 1900: Vol. 2, Population, Part 2,* 736; Robert G. Barrows, "A Demographic Analysis of Indianapolis" (PhD diss., Indiana University, 1977), 248–49; Kusmer, *A Ghetto Takes Shape,* chap. 4; Berteaux, "Structural Economic Change"; Spear, *Black Chicago,* 29–41.

30. The correlation is not perfect. In tiny Brooklyn, Illinois, a dormitory town for the metro-east industrial region across the Mississippi River from St. Louis, only 18 percent of African Americans lived in family-owned homes in 1910, a lower rate than in Washington Court House and the Springfields ten years before, although still marginally higher than any of the large cities. In Evansville, Indiana, a city of 59,000 in 1900, black home ownership stood at 9 percent. Sundiata Keita Cha-Jua, *America's First Black Town: Brooklyn, Illinois, 1830–1915* (Urbana and Chicago: University of Illinois Press, 2000), 169–70; Bigham, *We Ask Only a Fair Trial,* 69.

31. Suzanne Lebsock, *The Free Women of Petersburg: Status and Culture in a Southern Town, 1784–1860* (New York: W. W. Norton, 1984), 104. Paul Lammermeier found that women owned nearly one-half of the black-owned real estate in Cincinnati in 1870. Paul Lammermeier, "The Urban Black Family of the Nineteenth Century: A Study of Black Family Structure in the Ohio Valley, 1850–1880," *JMF* 35 (August 1973): 444. Loren Schweninger also finds across the South in 1870 that although there were fewer women property holders, their average holdings often exceeded men's. Loren Schweninger, *Black Property Owners in the South, 1790–1915* (Urbana: University of Illinois Press, 1990), 193–94. Allison Dorsey reports that women in postbellum Atlanta were slower than men to accumulate wealth, based on an examination of those reported with $1,000 or more in taxable property. However, she does not examine the incidence of female property holding or women's share of community wealth. Allison Dorsey, *To Build Our Lives Together: Community Formation in Black Atlanta, 1875–1906* (Athens: University of Georgia Press, 2004), 43. Women's primacy in African American property holding could not have been predicted by studies of African American women which focus on their extremely limited occupational opportunities. Jacqueline Jones, *Labor of Love, Labor of Sorrow: Black Women, Work, and the Family from Slavery to the Present* (New York: Basic Books, 1985), chap. 5; Darlene Clark Hine, "Black Migration to the Urban Midwest: The Gender Dimension, 1915–1945," in *Hine Sight: Black Women and the Reconstruction of American History* (Bloomington: Indiana University Press, 1994), 87–107.

32. Marjorie Abel and Nancy Folbre, "A Methodology for Revising Estimates: Female Market Participation in the U.S. before 1940," *HM* 23 (Fall 1990): 167–76.

33. In the late twentieth century, urban places of different size continued to vary in the risks and opportunities they presented to African Americans. "Large cities," sociologist Seth Ovadia writes, "tend to have high levels of residential segregation and low levels of occupational segregation; smaller cities tend to have the opposite pattern." Seth Ovadia, "The Dimensions of Racial Inequality: Occupational and Residential Segregation across Metropolitan Areas in the United States," *C&C* 2 (December 2003): 313–333. The quotation is on p. 329.

34. Neil R. McMillen, *Dark Journey: Black Mississippians in the Age of Jim Crow* (Urbana: University of Illinois Press, 1989), 12; Leon F. Litwack, *Trouble in Mind: Black Southerners in the Age of Jim Crow* (New York: Knopf, 1998), 237; Spencer R. Crew, *Black Life in Secondary Cities: A Comparative Analysis of the Black Communities of Camden and Elizabeth, N. J., 1860–1920* (New York: Garland, 1993), xiv, 181, 184; Myra B. Young Armstead, *"Lord, Please Don't Take Me in August": African Americans in Newport and Saratoga Springs, 1870–1930* (Urbana: University of Illinois Press, 1999), 112.

CHAPTER FOUR

1. Introduction to *The Reason Why the Colored American Is Not in the World's Columbian Exposition,* in *The Life and Writings of Frederick Douglass,* ed. Philip S. Foner, 5 vols. (New York: International Publishers, 1950–75), 4: 477.

2. Quoted in Sundiata Keita Cha-Jua, *America's First Black Town: Brooklyn, Illinois, 1830–1915* (Urbana and Chicago: University of Illinois Press, 2000), 133.

3. H. C. Bradsby, "Cairo," in *History of Alexander, Union and Pulaski Counties, Illinois,* William Henry Perrin (Chicago: O. L. Baskin & Co., 1883), 55.

4. *Free American* (Columbus, OH), March 19, 1887.

5. Steven Hahn, *A Nation under Our Feet: Black Political Struggles in the Rural South from Slavery to the Great Migration* (Cambridge, MA: Belknap Press of Harvard University Press, 2003).

6. James N. Gregory, *The Southern Diaspora: How the Great Migrations of Black and White Southerners Transformed America* (Chapel Hill: University of North Carolina Press, 2005), 241–42.

7. This interpretation has its source in C. Vann Woodward, *The Origins of the New South, 1877–1913* (Baton Rouge: Louisiana State University Press, 1951); Woodward, *The Strange Career of Jim Crow* (New York: Oxford University Press, 1955); and Rayford W. Logan, *The Betrayal of the Negro: From Rutherford B. Hayes to Woodrow Wilson* (1954; reprint, New York: Macmillan, 1965).

8. David A. Gerber, *Black Ohio and the Color Line, 1860–1915* (Urbana: University of Illinois Press, 1976), chap. 9; Gerber, "A Politics of Limited Options: Northern Black Politics and the Problem of Change and Continuity in Race Relations Historiography,"

JSoH 14 (Winter 1980): 235–55. James W. Loewen attributes European Americans' decreasing tolerance for an African American presence in their communities to the worsening racial climate across the nation. James W. Loewen, *Sundown Towns: A Hidden Dimension of American Racism* (New York and London: New Press, 2005), chap. 2.

9. Gerber, *Black Ohio*, 248–49; Nina Silber, *The Romance of Reunion: Northerners and the South, 1865–1900* (Chapel Hill: University of North Carolina Press, 1993); Heather Cox Richardson, *The Death of Reconstruction: Race, Labor, and Politics in the Post-Civil War North, 1865–1901* (Cambridge: Harvard University Press, 2001).

10. A federal income tax was levied in the North during the Civil War and nationally afterward, but only a tiny minority were required to pay it, and it was discontinued in 1872. It was briefly resurrected in 1894 before being ruled unconstitutional by the Supreme Court. Robert H. Stanley, *Dimensions of Law in the Service of Order: Origins of the Federal Income Tax, 1861–1913* (New York: Oxford University Press, 1993).

11. For an inside look at this process from a wandering manufacturer's perspective, see Frank Clayton Ball, *Memoirs of Frank Clayton Ball* (Muncie, IN: Privately printed, 1937).

12. Paul Kleppner, *The Third Electoral System, 1853–1892: Parties, Voters, and Political Cultures* (Chapel Hill: University of North Carolina Press, 1979), 36.

13. Quoted in Gerber, *Black Ohio*, 231.

14. Ibid.

15. Lawrence Grossman, *The Democratic Party and the Negro: Northern and National Politics, 1868–92* (Urbana: University of Illinois Press, 1976).

16. *Evansville (IN) Daily Journal*, July 8, 1867, quoted in Darrel E. Bigham, *On Jordan's Banks: Emancipation and Its Aftermath in the Ohio River Valley* (Lexington: University Press of Kentucky, 2006), 374n13.

17. Ibid., 80–98; Gerber, *Black Ohio*, 235–36; Emma Lou Thornbrough, *The Negro in Indiana before 1900: A Study of a Minority* (1957; reprint, Bloomington: Indiana University Press, 1993), 260; Roger D. Bridges, "Equality Deferred: Civil Rights for Illinois Blacks, 1865–1885," *JISHS* 74 (Summer 1981): 104–107. Illinois Democrats also supported a strengthened civil rights law in 1891.

18. Gerber, *Black Ohio*, 236–43, 250–53, 332; Gerber, "Lynching and Law and Order: Origin and Passage of the Ohio Antilynching Law of 1896," *OH* 83 (Winter, 1974): 33–50.

19. Thornbrough, *Negro in Indiana*, 250, 260, 266, 280–83, 323–29.

20. Bridges, "Equality Deferred," 94–97; Robert L. McCaul, *The Black Struggle for Public Schooling in Nineteenth-Century Illinois* (Carbondale: Southern Illinois University Press, 1987), chaps. 8–9. The school law may be found in *Revised Statutes of the State of Illinois, 1874* (Springfield: Illinois Journal Co., 1874), 983. After these changes, according to historian Robert McCaul, Afro-Illinoisans believed they had gained all the statutory support possible for equal rights at the state level, and now turned their efforts to progress within their local communities. African American efforts at the state

level did not end, however, with the schools law of 1874, nor with the civil rights act of 1885.

21. Charles Branham, "Black Chicago: Accommodationist Politics before the Great Migration," in *The Ethnic Frontier: Essays in the History of Group Survival in Chicago and the Midwest,* ed. Melvin M. Holli (Grand Rapids, MI: Eerdman, 1977), 225–30; Grossman, *Democratic Party and the Negro,* 94.

22. For a survey of the means of communication that allowed African Americans to coordinate protest and political action, see Jack S. Blocker Jr., "Building Networks: Cooperation and Communication Among African Americans in the Urban Midwest, 1860–1910," *IMH* 99 (December 2003): 378–86.

23. Gerber, *Black Ohio,* chaps. 8, 12; Thornbrough, *Negro in Indiana,* chaps. 9–11; Bridges, "Equality Deferred"; McCaul, *Black Struggle,* 149–50; Sundiata Keita Cha-Jua, "'A Warlike Demonstration': Legalism, Violent Self-Help, and Electoral Politics in Decatur, Illinois, 1894–1898," *JUH* 26 (July 2000): 625n45, 627n68; David A. Gerber, "Peter Humphries Clark: The Dialogue of Hope and Despair," in *Black Leaders of the Nineteenth Century,* Leon Litwack and August Meier (Urbana: University of Illinois Press, 1988), 173–190; John Roy Squibb, "Roads to Plessy: Blacks and the Law in the Old Northwest, 1860–1896" (PhD diss., University of Wisconsin–Madison, 1992), 28, 201–202, 204–205; *Indianapolis Leader,* July 17, 31, August 7, 1880; *State Capital* (Springfield, IL), August 27, 1892; *Illinois Record* (Springfield, IlL), May 21, September 17, 1898.

24. Emma Lou Thornbrough, "The National Afro-American League, 1887–1908," *JSH* 27 (November 1961): 494–512; Thornbrough, *Negro in Indiana,* 389–90; Cha-Jua, "'A Warlike Demonstration,'" 627n68; Christopher Robert Reed, *Black Chicago's First Century: Volume 1, 1833–1900* (Columbia and London: University of Missouri Press, 2005), 311–13; *State Capital,* October 3, 1891; *Illinois Record,* November 27, 1897, October 1, 1898.

25. Gerber, *Black Ohio,* 337.

26. Ibid., 243–44.

27. Thornbrough, *Negro in Indiana,* 260–66; Gerber, *Black Ohio,* 257–63; Irving Dilliard, "Civil Liberties of Negroes in Illinois since 1865," *JISHS* 56 (Autumn 1963): 594–95.

28. John A. Garraty, ed., *The Barber and the Historian: The Correspondence of George A. Myers and James Ford Rhodes, 1910–1923* (Columbus: Ohio Historical Society, 1956), xix–xxi.

29. Gerber, *Black Ohio,* 263–66. A careful history of Cincinnati's separate school system may be found in Nikki M. Taylor, *Frontiers of Freedom: Cincinnati's Black Community, 1802–1868* (Athens: Ohio University Press, 2005), chap. 8.

30. McCaul, *Black Struggle,* chaps. 8–9. Quotation is from p. 142. The schools law may be found in Harvey B. Hurd, comp. and ed., *Revised Statutes of the State of Illinois, 1874* (Springfield: Illinois Journal Co., 1874), 983.

31. Thornbrough, *Negro in Indiana,* 329–39.

32. Squibb, "Roads to Plessy," 105–8.

33. Reed, *Black Chicago's First Century,* 224–26.

34. Gerber, *Black Ohio,* 354–55.

35. Gerber, "Politics of Limited Options"; Branham, "Black Chicago."

36. Gerber, *Black Ohio,* 338–39; Thornbrough, *Negro in Indiana,* 315. Lawrence Grossman dates Republicans' loss of interest in the northern African American vote even sooner, to the early 1890s, and explains it as a response to Democratic success in courting African American voters. Grossman, *Democratic Party and the Negro,* 156–72.

37. Squibb, "Roads to Plessy," 262–63.

38. For recent and forceful statements of this view in the context of African American history, see Robin D. G. Kelley, "'We Are Not What We Seem': Rethinking Black Working-Class Opposition in the Jim Crow South," *JAH* 80 (June 1993): 75–112, and Hahn, *A Nation under Our Feet,* 3. A theoretical basis for such an expanded definition, and a rubric, "infrapolitics," for the category are in James C. Scott, *Domination and the Arts of Resistance: Hidden Transcripts* (New Haven, CT: Yale University Press, 1990).

39. Thornbrough, *Negro in Indiana,* 271–72; Darrel E. Bigham, *We Ask Only a Fair Trial: A History of the Black Community of Evansville, Indiana* (Bloomington: Indiana University Press, 1987), 51.

40. *Illinois Record,* June 25, 1898; *Recorder* (Indianapolis), January 7, 1899.

41. Gerber, *Black Ohio,* 284–85; Bigham, *We Ask Only a Fair Trial,* 50–51, 133; Emma Lou Thornbrough, *Indiana Blacks in the Twentieth Century,* ed. and with a final chapter by Lana Ruegamer (Bloomington: Indiana University Press, 2000), 7; Reed, *Black Chicago's First Century,* 289–93.

42. Thornbrough, *Negro in Indiana,* 274–76.

43. Gerber, *Black Ohio,* 285; Thornbrough, *Negro in Indiana,* 272–74; Bigham, *We Ask Only a Fair Trial,* 50–51, 133.

44. Gerber, *Black Ohio,* 285–86.

45. I recorded all arrests during every third year beginning in 1875. In addition, I recorded all arrests in 1894 because it was the year of the lynch mob. Figure 4.1 reports the total number of jailings, not the number of individuals arrested. Some persons were arrested more than once in the same year, but the numbers generally fluctuate together. In any case, the same procedure was used for blacks and whites.

46. Richard R. Wright Jr., *The Negroes of Xenia, Ohio: A Social Study,* U.S. Department of Labor Bulletin No. 48 (September 1903), 1030.

47. Allie Hopkins Memoir, August 16, 1974, OHUIS; Beverly A. Bunch-Lyons, "And They Came: The Migration of African American Women from the South to Cincinnati, 1900–1950" (PhD diss., Miami University, OH, 1995), chap. 2.

48. Pauline Parker, interview, no date, BOHCO; Geraldine Daniels, interview, October 28, 1986, SJOHP.

49. The Arnett Law repealing the law conferring power to create separate schools is House Bill 71, passed February 22, 1887, in *General and Local Acts . . . Adopted by the 67th General Assembly . . . of Ohio* (Columbus: Columbian Printing, 1887). The repealed section may be found in *Ohio Revised Statutes, 1884* (Columbus: H. W. Derby & Co., 1884), 823.

50. J. Morgan Kousser, *Dead End: The Development of Nineteenth Century Litigation on Racial Discrimination in Schools* (New York: Oxford University Press, 1986), 14–15.

51. Gerber, *Black Ohio,* 263–67; Thornbrough, *Negro in Indiana,* chap. 12; Squibb, "Roads to Plessy," 99–100, 132–41, 179–81; Kenneth W. Goings, "Blacks in the Rural North: Paulding County, Ohio, 1860–1900" (PhD diss., Princeton University, 1977), 82; David W. Zang, *Fleet Walker's Divided Heart: The Life of Baseball's First Black Major Leaguer* (Lincoln: University of Nebraska Press, 1995), 114, 120.

52. Squibb, "Roads to Plessy," 188.

53. Hessie Williams, interview, November 29, 1972, and Rosetta Lacey Ellis, interview, no date, BOHCO; Hermann R. Muelder, *A Hero Home from the War: Among the Black Citizens of Galesburg, Illinois, 1860–1880* (Galesburg, IL: Knox College Library, 1987), 11–16.

54. Isabella Maud Rittenhouse Mayne, *Maud,* ed. Richard Lee Strout (New York: Macmillan, 1939), 175; Joanne Wheeler, "Together in Egypt: A Pattern of Race Relations in Cairo, Illinois, 1865–1915," in *Toward a New South? Studies in Post-Civil War Southern Communities,* ed. Orville Vernon Burton and Robert C. McMath Jr. (Westport, CT: Greenwood Press, 1982), 125–26; Christopher K. Hays, "The African American Struggle for Equality and Justice in Cairo, Illinois, 1865–1900," *IHJ* 90 (Winter 1997): 278–84; Luther Wheeler Memoir, October 17, 1983, OHUIS.

55. Kousser, *Dead End,* 5.

56. Ibid., table 1. Some of the cases are described in greater detail in Squibb, "Roads to Plessy."

57. Squibb, "Roads to Plessy," 184.

58. Hays, "African American Struggle," 281.

59. Squibb, "Roads to Plessy," 163–73.

60. Edwin Smith Todd, *A Sociological Study of Clark County, Ohio* (Springfield: Springfield Publishing, 1904), 66.

61. *Cleveland Gazette,* June 26, 1886. Other, similar incidents are described in Squibb, "Roads to Plessy," 190–92.

62. Charles F. Bunch Sr. Memoir, August 20, 1974, OHUIS.

63. In Ohio resegregation is known to have been carried out in only one community, but the exception is a significant one: Columbus, the state capital, where gerrymandering and a new black junior high school segregated many African American students in 1911. Gerber, *Black Ohio,* 266–67.

64. Shirley J. Portwood, "The Alton School Case and African American Community Consciousness, 1897–1908," *IHJ* 91 (Spring 1998): 2–20; Portwood, "'We Lift Our

Voices in Thunder Tones': African American Race Men and Race Women and Community Agency in Southern Illinois, 1895–1910," *JUH* 26 (September 2000): 740–58.

65. Edna Boysaw, interview, no date, *AS,* vol. 6: 23–24.

66. Herbert G. Gutman, "Reconstruction in Ohio: Negroes in the Hocking Valley Coal Mines in 1873 and 1874," *LH* 3 (Fall 1962): 243–64; Ronald L. Lewis, "Job Control and Race Relations in the Coal Fields, 1870–1920," *JES* 12 (1984): 35–64; Herbert G. Gutman, "The Negro and the United Mine Workers of America: The Career and Letters of Richard L. Davis and Something of Their Meaning: 1890–1900," in *The Negro and the American Labor Movement,* ed. Julius Jacobson (Garden City, NY: Doubleday, 1968), 49–127; Herbert Hill, "Myth-Making as Labor History: Herbert Gutman and The United Mine Workers of America," *PCS* 2 (Winter 1988): 132–200; John H. Keiser, "Black Strikebreakers and Racism in Illinois, 1865–1900," *JISHS* 65 (Autumn 1972): 313–26; Warren C. Whatley, "African American Strikebreaking from the Civil War to the New Deal," *SSH* 17 (Winter 1993): 525–58; Gerber, *Black Ohio,* 66.

67. Caroline Waldron, "'Lynch-Law Must Go!': Race, Citizenship, and the Other in an American Coal Mining Town," *JAEH* 20 (Fall 2000): 50–77; Felix L. Armfield, "Fire on the Prairies: The 1895 Spring Valley Race Riot," *JIlH* 3 (Autumn 2000): 185–200.

68. Victor Hicken, "The Virden and Pana Mine Wars of 1898," *JISHS* 52 (Summer 1959): 263–78; Keiser, "Black Strikebreakers and Racism."

69. Whatley, "African American Strikebreaking," table 1. European American workers also served as strikebreakers against African American strikers, although this topic has been less studied. Sidney H. Kessler, "The Organization of Negroes in the Knights of Labor," *JNH* 37 (July 1952): 251. Kessler also notes the use of African American strikebreakers in a strike of quarrymen in Joliet and Lemon, Illinois, apparently in 1886. Ibid., 252.

70. Loewen, *Sundown Towns,* 165–66.

71. Quoted in Kessler, "Organization of Negroes," 249.

72. Joe B. Kewley, Richmond, Indiana, to T. V. Powderly, May 14, 1883, in *The Black Worker in the Era of the Knights of Labor,* ed. Philip S. Foner and Ronald L. Lewis, vol. 3 of *The Black Worker: A Documentary History from Colonial Times to the Present,* 8 vols. (Philadelphia: Temple University Press, 1978–84), 244.

73. Kessler, "Organization of Negroes," 259; Jonathan Garlock, comp., *Guide to the Local Assemblies of the Knights of Labor* (Westport, CT: Greenwood Press, 1982); Reed, *Black Chicago's First Century,* 244–46.

74. Leon Fink, *Workingmen's Democracy: The Knights of Labor and American Politics* (Urbana: University of Illinois Press, 1983).

75. Gerber, *Black Ohio,* 212–13; Bigham, *We Ask Only a Fair Trial,* 92; Hays, "The African American Struggle for Equality," 275.

76. For examples, see *Indianapolis Leader*, July 17, 31, and August 7, 1880; *Illinois Record*, May 21 and September 17, 1898.

77. Gerber, *Black Ohio*, 212; Wheeler, "Together in Egypt," 126–27; Shirley J. Carlson, "Black Migration to Pulaski County, Illinois, 1860–1900," *IHJ* 80 (Spring 1987): 45; transcript of *Inter-Ocean*, December 6, 1881, "Negro in Illinois" collection, IWP; *Cleveland Gazette*, May 6, 1893.

78. Reed, *Black Chicago's First Century*, 198–200.

79. Gerber, "A Politics of Limited Options."

80. Kathryn Grover, *Make a Way Somehow: African American Life in a Northern Community, 1790–1965* (Syracuse: Syracuse University Press, 1994), 215–16.

81. William B. Hubbard Memoir, January 28, 1975, OHUIS.

82. Gerber, *Black Ohio*, 234–43.

83. *Indianapolis Leader*, January 17, 1880. For other examples of political independence on the local level, see *Weekly Review* (New Albany, IN), April 16, 1881; *Freeman* (Indianapolis), September 8, 15, 1888; *Illinois Record*, January 29, August 27, and September 10, 1898.

84. Hays, "African American Struggle," 276–77; Wheeler, "Together in Egypt," 127.

85. In 1888 the *Freeman*, normally a loyal Republican paper, reported on a series of assaults by black Republicans on black Democrats. *Freeman*, September 29, 1888. For an analysis of divisions within the African American community of Decatur, Illinois, during a hotly contested election with considerable salience to African Americans, see Cha-Jua, "'A Warlike Demonstration,'" 616–17.

86. Gerber, "Peter Humphries Clark," 186–87.

87. *Cleveland Gazette*, July 24 and November 13, 1886, and April 16, 1887; *Free American* (Columbus, OH), March 19, 1887; *Xenia Semi-Weekly Gazette*, June 24, 1887.Tuppins was not the first African American mayor of a biracial town, as John Evans had become mayor of the village of Brooklyn the year before. Ten years after Tuppins's election, Mason, Tennessee, elected an African American mayor, J. W. Bush. Cha-Jua, *America's First Black Town*, 243n11.

88. *Cleveland Gazette*, April 11, 1891, and May 6, 1893.

89. Gutman, "The Negro and the UMWA."

90. See any issue of the *Ohio State Register* during the period.

91. Willard B. Gatewood Jr., ed., *Slave and Freeman: The Autobiography of George L. Knox* (Lexington: University Press of Kentucky, 1979), 111–12.

92. Jack S. Blocker Jr., *"Give to the Winds Thy Fears": The Women's Temperance Crusade, 1873–1874* (Westport, CT: Greenwood Press, 1985), 130. For other examples of African American charges of Republican betrayal, see *Illinois Record*, January 29, March 12, April 9, August 20 and 27 (Springfield, IL), and September 10, 1898 (Cairo).

93. My model thus differs from that of James Loewen in *Sundown Towns*. Where Loewen views African Americans as victims of such forces beyond their control as

white desires for reconciliation of Civil War divisions, imperialism, anti-immigrant prejudice, and final destruction of Native American resistance, I see African American actions as threatening whites' exclusive control over local communities. Where Loewen portrays nationwide factors influencing behavior on the local level, I emphasize as well the effect of local conflicts in making white Midwesterners receptive to racist doctrines emanating from elsewhere. Racist actions in the Lower Midwest, including denial of equal rights, rejection of African American demands for change, reduction of black political influence, and antiblack collective violence, in turn encouraged white racists in other regions to push forward their offensives against African Americans' constitutional rights.

94. Barbara J. Fields, "Ideology and Race in American History," in *Region, Race and Reconstruction: Essays in Honor of C. Vann Woodward,* eds J. Morgan Kousser and James M. McPherson (New York: Oxford University Press, 1982), 143–78; Robert R. Dykstra, *Bright Radical Star: Black Freedom and White Supremacy on the Hawkeye Frontier* (Cambridge, MA: Harvard University Press, 1993).

CHAPTER FIVE

1. *Recorder* (Indianapolis), January 7, 1899.
2. "The Industrial and Social Conditions of the Negro," a Thanksgiving sermon at Bethel AME Church, Chicago, November 26, 1896, Box 15, Reverdy C. Ransom Papers, WUL.
3. *Illinois Record* (Springfield), December 17, 1898.
4. W. Fitzhugh Brundage, *Lynching in the New South: Georgia and Virginia, 1880–1930* (Urbana: University of Illinois Press, 1993), 17; Stewart E. Tolnay and E. M. Beck, *A Festival of Violence: An Analysis of Southern Lynchings, 1882–1930* (Urbana: University of Illinois Press, 1995), 260. A recent study by Christopher Waldrep shows the politically contested character of the term "lynching": "War of Words: The Controversy over the Definition of Lynching, 1899–1940," *JSH* 66 (February 2000): 75–100.
5. Tolnay and Beck, *Festival of Violence,* 29–31.
6. Richard Wright, *Black Boy: A Record of Childhood and Youth* (1937; reprint, New York: Signet, 1951), 190.
7. Luther Wheeler Memoir, October 17, 1983, OHUIS.
8. Sundiata Keita Cha-Jua, "'A Warlike Demonstration': Legalism, Violent Self-Help, and Electoral Politics in Decatur, Illinois, 1894–1898," *JUH* (July 2000): 591–629. See also Fitzhugh Brundage, "The Darien 'Insurrection' of 1899: Black Protest during the Nadir of Race Relations," *GHQ* 74 (July 1990): 252; and Larry J. Griffin, Paula Clark, and Joanne C. Sandberg, "Narrative and Event: Lynching and Historical Sociology," in *Under Sentence of Death: Lynching in the South,* ed. W. Fitzhugh Brundage (Chapel Hill: University of North Carolina Press, 1997), 21–47.

9. I counted lynchings and other incidents of antiblack collective violence during the period 1885–1910. These years were chosen because they enclose the period when African Americans in the Lower Midwest were making the crucial locational choices that would lead them away from the nonmetropolitan places where so many of them initially settled. An act of "antiblack" violence is indicated by an intended or actual African American victim or victims; "collective" means three or more attackers. European American initiative is presupposed, except where the evidence indicates otherwise. But while casting a wider net for antiblack violence makes better analytical sense—at least for my project—it virtually guarantees the incompleteness of the catch. Violent attacks by groups of European Americans upon African Americans no doubt went unrecorded or were noted only in fugitive sources. Indeed, careful students of lynching agree that even this more commonly reported form of violence is quite likely underrecorded. See Tolnay and Beck, *Festival of Violence,* 261; Brundage, *Lynching in the New South,* 295; George C. Wright, *Racial Violence in Kentucky, 1865–1940: Lynchings, Mob Rule, and "Legal Lynchings"* (Baton Rouge: Louisiana State University Press, 1990), 5; Waldrep, "War of Words," 99–100; Neil R. McMillen, *Dark Journey: Black Mississippians in the Age of Jim Crow* (Urbana: University of Illinois Press, 1989), 229. My tally, therefore, should be regarded as no more than a minimum estimate.

The list in table A.4 was constructed by beginning with the list of lynchings compiled by the NAACP and the annual tally of lynchings published on or shortly after the first of January in each year, beginning in 1882, by the *Chicago Tribune.* Each incident was then traced to at least one local newspaper and a full description recorded, or, in the case of fraudulent reports, the listing was discarded. Violent occurrences other than lynchings were recorded from a variety of primary and secondary sources, and, where possible, reports were filled out from local newspapers.

Three attempted lynchings in Ohio were reported by Marilyn Kaye Howard after my database and analysis were completed and were not added to the database. These took place in Hicksville, Defiance County, October 21, 1894; Lorain, Lorain County, July 28, 1903; and Lockbourne, Franklin County, March 15, 1904. Marilyn Kaye Howard, "Black Lynching in the Promised Land: Mob Violence in Ohio, 1876–1916" (PhD diss., The Ohio State University, 1999), 144–46, 197–201.

10. Brundage, *Lynching in the New South,* 18–19.

11. Ibid., chap. 1.

12. *New Castle (IN) Courier,* February 14, March 28, and May 16 and 23, 1890.

13. *Cyclone and Fayette County Republican* (Washington Court House, OH), April 3, 1889. The use of violence as a political weapon in a small town (Greenfield, IN) is abundantly illustrated in Willard B. Gatewood, ed., *Slave and Freeman: The Autobiography of George L. Knox* (Lexington: University Press of Kentucky, 1979), esp. 105.

14. Caroline Waldron, "'Lynch-law Must Go!': Race, Citizenship, and the Other in an American Coal Mining Town," *JAEH* 20 (Fall 2000): 50–77; Felix L. Armfield, "Fire on the Prairies: The 1895 Spring Valley Race Riot," *JIIH* 3 (Autumn 2000): 185–200.

15. Waldron, "'Lynch-Law Must Go!'" 62; Armfield, "Fire on the Prairies," 194–97.

16. Copies of articles from the *Chicago Tribune,* August 5, 7, 8, and 10, 1895, and *Daily Inter Ocean,* October 21 and November 2, 18, and 25, 1895, in Box 27, Negro in Illinois File, IWP.

17. Copy of article from *Daily Inter Ocean,* October 21, 1895, Box 27, Negro in Illinois File, IWP.

18. Waldron, "'Lynch-Law Must Go!'"; Armfield, "Fire on the Prairies." For a discussion of the roles played by the African American press, see Jack S. Blocker Jr., "Building Networks: Cooperation and Communication among African Americans in the Urban Midwest, 1860–1910," *IMH* 99 (December 2003): 381–86.

19. *West Union Scion,* January 4 and 18, 1894.

20. David A. Gerber, "Lynching and Law and Order: Origin and Passage of the Ohio Antilynching Law of 1896," *OH* 83 (Winter 1974): 33–50; Gerber, *Black Ohio and the Color Line, 1860–1915* (Urbana: University of Illinois Press, 1976), 250–52; Howard, "Black Lynching in the Promised Land," chap. 5.

21. *Xenia Semi-Weekly Gazette,* June 14 and 17, 1887; *Cleveland Gazette,* June 25, 1887; Howard, "Black Lynching in the Promised Land," 90–93.

22. E. M. Beck and Stewart E. Tolnay, "When Race Didn't Matter: Black and White Mob Violence against Their Own Color," in *Under Sentence of Death: Lynching in the South,* ed. W. Fitzhugh Brundage (Chapel Hill: University of North Carolina Press, 1997), 132. See also Brundage, *Lynching in the New South,* 23, 29–30, 45. Compare Wright, *Racial Violence in Kentucky,* 103.

23. *State Capital* (Springfield, IL), December 3, 1892.

24. *Broad Ax* (Chicago), September 30, 1899.

25. *Broad Ax,* July 25, 1903.

26. *Broad Ax,* September 30, 1899, July 25, 1903.

27. *Freeman* (Indianapolis), December 2, 1893.

28. National Association for the Advancement of Colored People, *Thirty Years of Lynching in the United States, 1889–1918* (1919), table 3.

29. *Rockport Journal,* December 21, 1900.

30. Ibid.

31. Only two sheriffs were removed from office in the Lower Midwest under the provisions of an antilynching law. The first was Sheriff John Dudley of Sullivan County, Indiana, who was removed from office under the state's recently strengthened antilynching law after failing to protect James Dillard from a lynch mob in November 1902. He was removed by Republican governor Winfield Durbin. The incident is described in *Sullivan Democrat,* November 20, 1902; *Sullivan Union,* November 19 and 26, December 3, 1902; and *Indianapolis News,* November 21, 1902. Dudley's removal is reported in Emma Lou Thornbrough, *The Negro in Indiana before 1900: A Study of a Minority* (1957; reprint, Bloomington: Indiana University Press, 1993), 283.

The second was Sheriff Frank E. Davis of Alexander County, Illinois, who was dismissed by Governor Charles S. Deneen after failing to protect William James, who was on a train in Davis's custody, and European American Henry Salzner, who was seized from the county jail and lynched on suspicion of a crime unrelated to James's. The lynchings are described in *Cairo Bulletin,* November 10–20, 1909, and Davis's dismissal is noted in *Illinois State Journal,* January 12, 1910. Davis's successor, Sheriff Fred D. Nellis, successfully defended John Pratt, a suspected purse snatcher, from a lynch mob three months after the James and Salzner lynchings by ordering his deputies, including several African Americans, to fire into the mob, killing one man and wounding four others. *Illinois State Journal,* February 18–22, 1910.

32. Thornbrough, *Negro in Indiana,* 281–82.

33. *Chattanooga Daily Times,* January 29, 1901. I am indebted to Darrel Bigham for this reference.

34. Fayette County Jail Register, 1894, Fayette County Jail, Washington Court House; *Ohio State Journal,* October 17, 1894.

35. My understanding of this event is based on the following sources: *Cyclone and Fayette Republican,* October 1894–March 1895; *Circleville Democrat and Watchman,* October 19, 26, November 23, 1894, March 8, 1895; *Xenia Democrat-News,* October 20, 1894; *Columbus Evening Dispatch,* October 17–18, 1894; *Ohio State Journal,* October 16–20, 1894; Adjutant General of Ohio, *Annual Report, 1894,* 292–301, and *Annual Report, 1895,* 16–23; Charles A. Peckham, "The Ohio National Guard and Its Police Duties, 1894," *OH* 83 (Winter 1974): 51–67.

36. *Cyclone and Fayette Republican,* November 8, 1894.

37. Adjutant General of Ohio, *Annual Report, 1894,* 292.

38. *Cyclone and Fayette County Republican,* October 11, 1894.

39. See two documents in the library of the Ohio Historical Society: *Argument of Judge Joseph Hidy Before the Judiciary Committee of the Ohio Senate On the proposed Bill to reimburse Col. Coit. . . . ;* and *Protest To the Seventy-second General Assembly of the State of Ohio. . .* (by a meeting of the Board of Trade and other citizens of Washington Court House and Fayette County).

40. *Cyclone and Fayette County Republican,* September 4, 1889, and April 23, 1890; Fayette County Jail Register, 1881, 1884, 1887, 1890, and 1894.

41. Harry M. Daugherty to Ray Baker Harris, June 7, 1938, Ray Baker Harris Collection, Warren G. Harding Papers, OHS.

42. *Cleveland Gazette,* November 3, 1894.

43. *Cleveland Gazette,* October 20 and November 10, 17, and 24, 1894.

44. Gerber, *Black Ohio and the Color Line,* 254. In 1900 there were only 525 African Americans in Akron, 1.2 percent of the population.

45. *Akron Beacon Journal,* August 23, 1900.

46. *Akron Beacon Journal,* August 21–29, and September 1, 4, and 5, 1900; *Akron Daily Democrat,* August 23 and 25, 1900; Howard, "Black Lynching in the Promised Land," 187–97.

47. Brian Butler, *An Undergrowth of Folly: Public Order, Race Anxiety, and the 1903 Evansville, Indiana Riot* (New York: Garland, 2000), 3, 187.

48. *Evansville Journal-News,* July 5–10, 15, 17, and 18, 1903; *Evansville Courier,* July 7, 1903; *Freeman* (Indianapolis), July 11, 1903; Butler, *Undergrowth of Folly,* 186–94, 211–25; Darrel E. Bigham, *We Ask Only a Fair Trial: A History of the Black Community of Evansville, Indiana* (Bloomington: Indiana University Press, 1987), 104–107; Thornbrough, *Negro in Indiana,* 284–87.

49. Bigham, *We Ask Only a Fair Trial,* 107.

50. See, e. g., Gerber, *Black Ohio,* 249; W. Fitzhugh Brundage, introduction to *Under Sentence of Death: Lynching in the South,* ed. W. Fitzhugh Brundage (Chapel Hill: University of North Carolina Press, 1997), 4. In contrast, however, James Loewen argues that the violence that played a part in creating "sundown towns" where blacks were unwelcome was more common outside the most southern parts of the South. James Loewen, *Sundown Towns: A Hidden Dimension of American Racism* (New York and London: New Press, 2005), chap. 3.

51. Tolnay and Beck, *Festival of Violence,* 32–34, 142–49.

52. Brundage, *Lynching in the New South,* 106.

53. Grace Elizabeth Hale, *Making Whiteness: The Culture of Segregation in the South, 1890–1940* (New York: Vintage, 1998), 132 and chap. 5.

54. Tolnay and Beck, *Festival of Violence,* 81 (quotation), 108–11. See also Leon F. Litwack, *Trouble in Mind: Black Southerners in the Age of Jim Crow* (New York: Knopf, 1998), 151, 309.

55. For a full description and analysis of the Springfield riots, see Jack S. Blocker Jr., "Race, Sex and Riot: The Springfield, Ohio Race Riots of 1904 and 1906 and the Sources of Antiblack Violence in the Lower Midwest," *OVH* 6 (Spring 2006): 27–44.

56. *Springfield Press-Republic,* March 16, 1904.

57. *Urbana Informer,* April, August 1903; Myra B. Young Armstead , *"Lord, Please Don't Take Me in August": African Americans in Newport and Saratoga Springs, 1870–1930* (Urbana: University of Illinois Press, 1999), 132–33; *Freeman,* August 29, 1908, quoting Booker T. Washington; Kevin C. Mumford, *Interzones: Black/White Sex Districts in Chicago and New York in the Early Twentieth Century* (New York: Columbia University Press, 1997), 32; Tera W. Hunter, *To 'Joy My Freedom: Southern Black Women's Lives and Labors after the Civil War* (Cambridge, MA: Harvard University Press, 1997), 161–64. The hatred was mutual. After the Rev. Reverdy C. Ransom, pastor of the Institutional Church in Chicago, denounced policy-shop gambling from the pulpit, a bomb blew up the end of the church in which he and his family lived. *Broad Ax* (Chicago), May 9, 1903.

58. Joe Trotter argues that Milwaukee was such a place. Joe William Trotter Jr., *Black Milwaukee: The Making of an Industrial Proletariat, 1915–45* (Urbana: University of Illinois Press, 1985), 229.

59. Loewen, *Sundown Towns.*

60. For a recent discussion of this point, see James H. Madison, *A Lynching in the Heartland: Race and Memory in America* (New York: Palgrave, 2001), 16, 156n6. On p. 72, Madison quotes a Georgia newspaper in 1930 claiming that the "only reason there are more lynchings in the South than in the balance of the country is because there are more negroes in the South."

61. Wright, *Racial Violence in Kentucky*, 5. My count is based on confirmations in local newspapers, but I began with the same sources used for other inventories: reports in the metropolitan press. I have not made an exhaustive search of local sources. Tolnay and Beck point out (*Festival of Violence*, 262) that inventories based on the metropolitan press overcount a significant number of lynchings (one-sixth of their initial list), but this point does not apply to Wright's locally based tally or my locally confirmed count.

62. George M. Fredrickson, *White Supremacy: A Comparative Study in American and South African History* (Oxford: Oxford University Press, 1981), 251. James C. Scott, *Domination and the Arts of Resistance: Hidden Transcripts* (New Haven, CT: Yale University Press, 1990). Fredrickson also cites the antebellum South as a society in which a system of domination was well entrenched. But slaves were lynched. For evidence see Christopher Morris, *Becoming Southern: The Evolution of a Way of Life, Warren County and Vicksburg, Mississippi, 1770–1860* (New York: Oxford University Press, 1995), 79, and Elizabeth Pleck, *Rape and the Politics of Race, 1865–1910*, Working Paper No. 213 (Wellesley, MA: Wellesley College Center for Research on Women, 1990), 5.

63. For examples, see *Freeman*, June 12, 1897; *Cleveland Gazette*, January 21 and April 21, 1894, August 31, 1895, July–August 1897, and September 1, 1900; *Illinois Record*, December 11, 1897, and September 17, 1898; *Broad Ax*, May 2, June 13, and August 15, 1903.

64. *Cleveland Gazette*, June 19, July 24 and 31, and August 14 and 21, 1897; *Illinois Record*, December 10, 1898; *Broad Ax*, June 13, 1903; *Indianapolis World*, July 29, 1899; copy of article in *Inter Ocean*, June 16, 1902, Negro in Illinois file, IWP; Emma Lou Thornbrough, *Indiana Blacks in the Twentieth Century*, ed. and with a final chapter by Lana Ruegamer (Bloomington: Indiana University Press, 2000), 21.

65. *Cleveland Gazette*, January 20 and April 21, 1894, August 31, 1894, and June 12, 1897.

66. *Freeman*, March 2, 1901.

67. *Freeman*, November 29, 1902.

68. *Freeman*, July 11, 1903.

69. *Recorder*, July 18, 1903.

70. *Indianapolis Leader*, August 30, 1879. See also the issue of May 8, 1880. For a pioneering brief survey of African American responses to violence, see William Lux, *A Survey of the Blacks' Response to Lynching* (N.p.: New Mexico Highlands University, 1973).

71. *Conservator* (Chicago), September 8, 1883; *Recorder,* April 22, 1899; *Broad Ax,* June 6, 1899, July 4, 1903, March 26, 1904, and August 22, 1908.

72. *Cleveland Gazette,* July 17, 1897.

73. *Freeman,* March 3, 1906. For Knox's urgings against violence, see the same issue and that of August 29, 1908.

74. Instances of armed self-defense to prevent lynchings in Kansas between 1870 and 1900 are noted in Randall B. Woods, "Integration, Exclusion, or Segregation? The 'Color Line' in Kansas, 1878–1900," *WHQ* 14 (April 1983): 195. For an overview, see Elliott M. Rudwick and August Meier, "Negro Retaliatory Violence in the Twentieth Century," *NP* 5 (Winter 1966): 41–51.

75. Leonard Harding, "The Cincinnati Riots of 1862," *CHSB* 25 (October 1967): 229–39.

76. For an example of reflexive and personal (and successful) armed self-defense, see Rosetta Lacey Ellis, interview, no date, BOHCO. For an incident in which the threat of violence stopped harassment, see Albert Harris Memoir, March 28, 1974, OHUIS.

77. *Cleveland Gazette,* January 27, 1906.

78. *Leader,* August 30, 1879.

79. *Leader,* May 8, 1880. However, James Loewen reports that Aurora remained a sundown town until at least 2002. Loewen, *Sundown Towns,* 240–41.

80. Sundiata Keita Cha-Jua, "'Join Hands and Hearts with Law and Order': The 1893 Lynching of Samuel J. Bush and the Response of Decatur's African American Community," *IHJ* 83 (Autumn 1990): 187–200; Cha-Jua, "'A Warlike Demonstration.'"

81. Roberta Senechal, *The Sociogenesis of a Race Riot: Springfield, Illinois, in 1908* (Urbana: University of Illinois Press, 1990).

82. "The So-Called Race Riot at Springfield, Illinois," *CC* 50 (September 19, 1908): 710.

83. Senechal, *Sociogenesis of a Race Riot,* 41.

84. Quoted in ibid., 42.

85. Ibid., 73–84.

86. Ibid., chap. 4; Margaret Ferguson Memoir, February 11, 1975, OHUIS; Marie Cunningham Memoir, December 7, 1971, OHUIS; Albert Harris Memoir, March 28, 1974, OHUIS.

87. The projects were directed by Professor Cullom Davis, and the transcripts of the interviews are held at the Oral History Office, University of Illinois–Springfield.

88. *Broad Ax,* August 22, 1908.

89. See chapter 4 above.

90. Charles Flint Kellogg, *NAACP: A History of the National Association for the Advancement of Colored People,* 2 vols. (Baltimore: Johns Hopkins University Press, 1967), 1: 9–12; Robert L. Zangrando, *The NAACP Crusade against Lynching, 1909–1950* (Philadelphia: Temple University Press, 1980), 22–24; Carolyn Wedin, *Inheritors of the*

Spirit: Mary White Ovington and the Founding of the NAACP (New York: John Wiley & Sons, 1998), 111–16.

91. Graham Taylor, "The Race Riot in Lincoln's City," *CC* 50 (August 29, 1908): 627–28; Senechal, *Sociogenesis of a Race Riot,* 177.

92. William English Walling, "The Race War in the North," *Independent* 65 (September 3, 1908): 634.

93. James L. Crouthamel, "The Springfield Race Riot of 1908," *JNH* 45 (July 1960): 178–79; Walling, "Race War in the North."

94. *Public* 11 (August 21, 1908): 493.

95. *New Outlook* 89 (August 22, 1908): 869.

96. *Freeman,* August 22, 1908.

97. Ibid.

98. Mattie Hale Memoir, April 30, 1974, OHUIS.

99. Edith Carpenter Memoir, January 1975, OHUIS. For another account of armed self-defense, see the William B. Hubbard Memoir, January 28, 1975, OHUIS.

100. Rev. Harry Mann Memoir, April 8, 1974, OHUIS.

101. John and Hazel Wilson Memoir, March 25, 1971, OHUIS. Allie Hopkins, who came to Springfield in 1923, was also told that "there was quite a few white people killed." Allie Hopkins Memoir, August 16, 1974, OHUIS.

102. LeRoy Brown Memoir, April 29, 1974, OHUIS.

103. Albert Harris Memoir.

104. Margaret Ferguson Memoir.

105. See, e. g., LeRoy Brown Memoir.

106. Springfield's share of the state's African American urban population dropped 1.8 percent, from 5.3 in 1890 to 3.5 in 1910. Cairo lost 4.5 percent and Quincy 3.4. See chapter 7.

107. Margaret Ferguson Memoir; LeRoy Brown Memoir.

CHAPTER SIX

1. Letter to editor, *Chicago Defender,* March 31, 1917, copy in IWP.

2. "Migration of Negroes from Georgia, 1916–17," in U.S. Department of Labor, Division of Negro Economics, *Negro Migration in 1916–17* (Washington, DC: Government Printing Office, 1919), 75.

3. "Negroes Move North I. Their Departure from the South," *Survey* 40 (May 4, 1918): 115.

4. To examine northern migration solely from a northern perspective is "methodologically wrong," writes Nelson Ouellet, because to do so "neglects how African Americans coped with similar situations before their arrival in cities of the North and how earlier experiences were tools to improve their condition, whether socially,

economically, or politically." Nelson Ouellet, "The Great Migration in Gary, Indiana (1906–1920): A Note," *IMH* 96 (March 2000): 81.

5. Robert Higgs, *Competition and Coercion: Blacks in the American Economy, 1865–1914* (Chicago: University of Chicago Press, 1977), 33–35. See also W. E. B. Du Bois, "The Negro North and South," in *Writings by W. E. B. Du Bois in Periodicals Edited by Others,* comp. and ed. Herbert Aptheker, 4 vols. (Millwood, NY: Kraus-Thomson Organization, 1982), 1: 253 (originally published in *Bibliotheca Sacra* [Oberlin, Ohio] 62 [July 1905]: 500–13); Neil Fligstein, *Going North: Migration of Blacks and Whites from the South, 1900–1950* (New York: Academic Press, 1981), 123–25; Robert Cook, *Sweet Land of Liberty? The African American Struggle for Civil Rights in the Twentieth Century* (London and New York: Longman, 1998), 30; Leon Litwack, *Trouble in Mind: Black Southerners in the Age of Jim Crow* (New York: Knopf, 1998), 483; and Kimberley Phillips, *AlabamaNorth: African American Migrants, Community, and Working-Class Activism in Cleveland, 1915–1945* (Urbana: University of Illinois Press, 1999), 17, 30.

6. Carole Marks has presented the most ample form of this argument, in *Farewell— We're Good and Gone: The Great Black Migration* (Bloomington and Indianapolis: Indiana University Press, 1989). Both the dynamism of southern urban black communities and the two-step nature of the migration process are emphasized in Zane L. Miller, "Urban Blacks in the South, 1865–1920: The Richmond, Savannah, New Orleans, Louisville and Birmingham Experience," in *The New Urban History: Quantitative Explorations by American Historians,* ed. Leo F. Schnore (Princeton, NJ: Princeton University Press, 1976), 184–204. See also Gavin Wright, *Old South, New South: Revolutions in the Southern Economy since the Civil War* (New York: Basic Books, 1986), 203–5; Neil McMillen, *Dark Journey: Black Mississippians in the Age of Jim Crow* (Urbana: University of Illinois Press, 1989), 267–70; and Peter Gottlieb, "Rethinking the Great Migration: A Perspective from Pittsburgh," in *The Great Migration in Historical Perspective: New Dimensions of Race, Class, & Gender,* ed. Joe William Trotter (Bloomington and Indianapolis: Indiana University Press, 1989), 75.

7. Lyonel C. Florant, "Negro Internal Migration," *ASR* 7 (December 1942): 785–86.

8. Urban places were one kind of transition zone to urban-industrial ways, but they were not the only such setting. As Joe William Trotter has pointed out, extractive industries such as mining and lumbering "operated at the interface between the black agricultural experience . . . and the black transition to an urban-industrial foundation." Joe William Trotter Jr., *Black Milwaukee: The Making of an Industrial Proletariat, 1915–45* (Urbana: University of Illinois Press, 1985), 232.

9. Don H. Doyle, *New Men, New Cities, New South: Atlanta, Charleston, Nashville, Mobile, 1860–1910* (Chapel Hill and London: University of North Carolina Press, 1990), 12–13. Doyle's remarks were meant to apply to all southern cities. See also David R. Goldfield, *Cotton Fields and Skyscrapers: Southern City and Region, 1607–1980*

(Baton Rouge and London: Louisiana State University Press, 1982), 105–18. After describing the slow pace of black urbanization and the limits to black achievement in cities, however, Goldfield adds that "this restricted urban life was still better than what the countryside offered them" (117). Other treatments include Zane Miller, "The Black Experience in the Modern American City," in *The Urban Experience,* ed. Raymond Mohl and James Richardson (Belmont, CA: Wadsworth, 1973), 50; and Howard N. Rabinowitz, *Race Relations in the Urban South, 1865–1890* (1978; reprint, Athens: University of Georgia Press, 1996).

10. Miller, "Urban Blacks in the South," 188–89; Rabinowitz, *Race Relations in the Urban South,* 19.

11. Cook, *Sweet Land of Liberty?,* 30; Goldfield, *Cotton Fields and Skyscrapers,* 105; William Cohen, *At Freedom's Edge: Black Mobility and the Southern White Quest for Racial Control, 1861–1915* (Baton Rouge: Louisiana State University Press, 1991).

12. James Weldon Johnson to Charles S. Johnson, January 17, 1918, National Urban League Papers, Series 6, Box 86, Folder "Migration Study: Correspondence," Manuscript Division, Library of Congress, Washington, DC. For another contemporary observation, see William M. Tuttle Jr., *Race Riot: Chicago in the Red Summer of 1919* (New York: Atheneum, 1970), 95. For a recent expression of the view that northern migrants were "unaccustomed to life in an urban setting," see Spencer R. Crew, *Black Life in Secondary Cities: A Comparative Analysis of the Black Communities of Camden and Elizabeth, N.J., 1860–1920* (New York: Garland, 1993), 70.

13. *12 Million Black Voices: A Folk History of the Negro in the United States* (1941; reprint, New York: Arno Press, 1969), 93.

14. J. W. Johnson to C. S. Johnson, January 17, 1918.

15. Quoted in George E. Haynes, *The Negro at Work in New York City* (New York: Columbia University, 1912), 14.

16. Everett S. Lee et al., *Methodological Considerations and Reference Tables,* vol. 1 of *Population Redistribution and Economic Growth, United States, 1870–1950,* ed. S. Kuznets and D. S. Thomas 3 vols. (Philadelphia: American Philosophical Society, 1957–64), 310, 311, 332.

17. Raymond Mohl, "The Settlement of Blacks in South Florida," in *South Florida: Winds of Change,* ed. Thomas D. Boswell (Miami: Prepared for the Annual Conference of the Association of American Geographers, 1991), 117–19.

18. My conclusions about population shifts across the urban hierarchies in the four east south central states are based on tables similar to tables A.1–A.3 constructed from published federal census data for the periods 1860–1890 and 1890–1910.

19. Michael P. Johnson, "Out of Egypt: The Migration of Former Slaves to the Midwest during the 1860s in Comparative Perspective," in *Crossing Boundaries: Comparative History of Black People in Diaspora,* ed. Darlene Clark Hine and Jacqueline McLeod (Bloomington: Indiana University Press, 1999), 227–28.

20. For an examination of African American life in Louisville, see George C.

Wright, *Life Behind a Veil: Blacks in Louisville, Kentucky, 1865–1930* (Baton Rouge: Louisiana State University Press, 1985).

21. George C. Wright, *Racial Violence in Kentucky, 1865–1940: Lynchings, Mob Rule, and "Legal Lynchings"* (Baton Rouge: Louisiana University Press, 1990).

22. Between 1860 and 1890, Kentucky's African American population grew by only 13.5 percent, while its European American population increased by 73 percent. Between 1890 and 1910, the African American population dropped 2.4 percent, and the European American population grew by 27.5 percent.

23. This movement will be closely analyzed in chapter 7.

24. Lester C. Lamon, *Blacks in Tennessee, 1791–1970* (Knoxville: University of Tennessee Press, 1981), 62, 80.

25. Ibid., 64.

26. C. Warren Thornthwaite, *Internal Migration in the United States* (Philadelphia: University of Pennsylvania Press, 1934), 12.

27. Louis M. Kyriakoudes, "Southern Black Rural-Urban Migration in the Era of the Great Migration: Nashville and Middle Tennessee, 1890–1930," *AH* 72 (Spring 1998): 341–51.

28. Nashville's African American population grew by 24 percent during 1890–1910, while Memphis's increased by 83 percent; the statewide urban growth rate was 32 percent. The African American experience in Memphis is discussed in Dernoral Davis, "Against the Odds: Postbellum Growth and Development in a Southern Black Urban Community, 1865–1900" (PhD diss., State University of New York at Binghamton, 1987), and Kenneth W. Goings and Gerald L. Smith, "'Unhidden' Transcripts: Memphis and African American Agency, 1862–1920," *JUH* 21 (March 1995): 372–94. Nashville is examined in Faye Wellborn Robbins, "A World-Within-a-World: Black Nashville, 1880–1915" (PhD diss., University of Arkansas, 1980).

29. Richard Wright, *Black Boy: A Record of Childhood and Youth* (1937; reprint, New York: New American Library, 1951).

30. For a discussion of Mississippi urbanization and outmigration, see McMillen, *Dark Journey*, chap. 8.

31. For a more detailed breakdown of migration destinations by decade for the east south central states, see William Edward Vickery, *The Economics of the Negro Migration* (New York: Arno, 1977), tables 49–52.

32. Goldfield, *Cotton Fields and Skyscrapers*, 131.

33. David R. Goldfield, "A Regional Framework for the Urban South," in *Region, Race, and Cities: Interpreting the Urban South,* ed. David R. Goldfield (Baton Rouge: Louisiana State University Press, 1997), 37–68. A survey of one hundred African American residents of Champaign-Urbana, Illinois, in 1932 found substantial groups of Tennesseans, Kentuckians, and Mississippians. Sixty percent of respondents had lived in southern Illinois before moving to Champaign-Urbana, and the average number of moves in Illinois was three. Janet Andrews Cromwell, "History and Organization

of the Negro Community of Champaign-Urbana, Illinois" (MA thesis, University of Illinois, 1934), 51–57.

Whether life in small and midsize towns and cities provided migrants with training in industrial skills as well as exposure to urban ways of life cannot be answered without examination of the specific places through which they moved. The local economies of some nonmetropolitan urban places were heavily based on industry, but others were primarily commercial centers.

34. Calculated from sources used for the tables tracing movement across the urban hierarchies of the east south central states and from Vickery, *Economics of the Negro Migration*, table 37. Some of the outmigrants, especially during the early years of the period, of course traveled to other east south central states.

35. Mrs. Jimmie D. Smith, interview, no date, BMP.

36. Jack E. Martin Memoir, October 25, 1974, OHUIS.

37. U.S. Bureau of the Census, *Negroes in the United States, 1920–32* (Washington, DC: Government Printing Office, 1935), table 8.

38. Barbara J. Fields has criticized historians who picture black Southerners as "perpetually poised on the edge of migration." She claims that "[f]reedmen and their descendants went to extraordinary lengths to gain an independent base on the land and persisted in the teeth of repeated defeats. . . . For them, . . . mass migration or emigration was the last resort when the rural economy could no longer accommodate them." Barbara J. Fields, "The Advent of Capitalist Agriculture: The New South in a Bourgeois World," in *Essays on the Postbellum Southern Economy*, ed. Thavolia Glymph and John J. Kushma (College Station: Texas A & M University Press, 1985), 94n37. Data from the published census on rural population changes in the four states of the east south central region furnish an opportunity to test this claim. Eight comparisons are possible: for each state during 1860–1890 and 1890–1910. If black farmers went to "extraordinary lengths" to remain on the land, then black rural populations should have increased faster or declined more slowly than white rural populations. In seven out of eight cases, however (Mississippi during 1860–1890 is the sole exception), this was not true. Black rural populations nearly always grew more slowly than white rural populations or shrank while white rural populations grew, suggesting higher rates of African American than European American outmigration from rural districts. This is a crude comparison since it may have been affected by differential fertility and mortality as well as migration. While completed families of black farm families were larger than those of white farm families, however, child mortality among rural black southern families was also higher than among rural white southern families. See Stewart E. Tolnay, *The Bottom Rung: African American Family Life on Southern Farms* (Urbana and Chicago: University of Illinois Press, 1999), 75–79; Samuel H. Preston and Michael R. Haines, *Fatal Years: Child Mortality in Late Nineteenth-Century America* (Princeton, NJ: Princeton University Press, 1991), table 3.2. The comparison here at least throws some empirical light on an obscure area. I do not view black Southerners as "perpetually

poised on the edge of migration," but rather as continually exploring the various options available to them.

39. U.S. Department of Labor, *Negro Migration in 1916–17*, 38.

CHAPTER SEVEN

1. W. T. Casey, "History of the Colored People in Sangamon County," in *Directory of Sangamon County's Colored Citizens* (1926).

2. Don Wallis, *All We Had Was Each Other: The Black Community of Madison, Indiana: An Oral History* (Bloomington: Indiana University Press, 1998), 45.

3. W. E. B. Du Bois, "The Negro North and South," in *Writings by W. E. B. Du Bois in Periodicals Edited by Others,* comp. and ed. Herbert Aptheker, 4 vols. (Millwood, NY: Kraus-Thomson Organization, 1982), 1: 256.

4. Leon F. Litwack, *Trouble in Mind: Black Southerners in the Age of Jim Crow* (New York: Knopf, 1998), 411.

5. A massive literature chronicles the turbulent events of the 1890s. My understanding of Populism is grounded on Lawrence Goodwyn, *Democratic Promise: The Populist Moment in America* (New York: Oxford University Press, 1976), and C. Vann Woodward, *Origins of the New South, 1877–1913* (Baton Rouge: Louisiana State University Press, 1951). The classic major work on the wave of segregation legislation is C. Vann Woodward, *The Strange Career of Jim Crow* (New York: Oxford University Press, 1955), and the most recent is Edward L. Ayers, *The Promise of the New South: Life after Reconstruction* (New York: Oxford University Press, 1992), chap. 6. The basic work on disfranchisement is J. Morgan Kousser, *The Shaping of Southern Politics: Suffrage Restriction and the Establishment of the One-Party South, 1880–1910* (New Haven, CT: Yale University Press, 1974). The most recent study of cultural reconciliation is Nina Silber, *The Romance of Reunion: Northerners and the South, 1865–1900* (Chapel Hill: University of North Carolina Press, 1993).

6. *Illinois Record,* September 17, 1898.

7. Everett S. Lee et al., *Methodological Considerations and Reference Tables,* vol. 1 of *Population Redistribution and Economic Growth, United States, 1870–1950,* ed. S. Kuznets and D. S. Thomas, 3 vols. (Philadelphia: American Philosophical Society, 1957–64), 310–11, 332.

8. Neil R. McMillen, *Dark Journey: Black Mississippians in the Age of Jim Crow* (Urbana: University of Illinois Press, 1989), 259, 261.

9. Glenda E. Gilmore, *Gender and Jim Crow: Women and the Politics of White Supremacy in North Carolina, 1896–1920* (Chapel Hill: University of North Carolina Press, 1996), 131.

10. Compare Lee et al., *Methodological Considerations,* 314, with George C. Wright,

Notes to Chapter 7

Racial Violence in Kentucky, 1865–1940: Lynchings, Mob Rule, and "Legal Lynchings" (Baton Rouge: Louisiana State University Press, 1990), 71.

11. For a discussion of circulation in the South of midwestern African American newspapers, see Jack S. Blocker Jr., "Building Networks: Cooperation and Communication among African Americans in the Urban Midwest, 1860–1910," *IMH* 99 (December 2003): 381–85; Robert A. Margo, *Race and Schooling in the South, 1880–1950: An Economic History* (Chicago: University of Chicago Press, 1990), 7.

12. Midwestern newspapers regularly reported violent incidents as well as discussing possible responses. See, for example, *Freeman* (Indianapolis), June 12, 1897; *Cleveland Gazette*, July 10, 1897; *Illinois Record*, September 17, 1898; Indianapolis *Recorder*, December 22, 1900, March 2, 1901, November 22–December 6, 1902, June 13, and July 11, 1903; *Broad Ax* (Chicago), August 1, 1903.

13. Jacqueline Jones, *Labor of Love, Labor of Sorrow: Black Women, Work, and the Family from Slavery to the Present* (New York: Basic Books, 1985), 159.

14. For a description of the population examined, see appendix C. For 1860–1930, *n* = 160; for the period 1890–1915, *n* = 30.

15. Undated interviews with Tolbert Bragg, Preston Tate, and Mary Emily Eaton Tate, *AS, Supplement, Series 1*, vol. 5: 20–21, 212–21. Other accounts illustrating forms of the "men first, women later" pattern are in: Julia Williams, interview June 19, 1937, *AS, Series Two*, vol. 16: 107; John Henry Gibson, interview, no date, *AS*, vol. 6: 97.

16. Clyde Vernon Kiser, *Sea Island to City: A Study of St. Helena Islanders in Harlem and Other Urban Centers* (1932; reprint, New York: AMS Press, 1967), 166–67. Joe Trotter points out that during the entire pre-Great Migration movement, African American women dominated the migration stream to the older northeastern coastal cities of Philadelphia, Boston, and New York, while men were more numerous among those traveling to the newer, dynamic industrial cities of the Midwest. This differential he attributes to the greater availability of domestic and personal service jobs for women in the older cities. Joe William Trotter Jr., "Blacks in the Urban North: The 'Underclass Question' in Historical Perspective," in *The 'Underclass' Debate: Views from History*, ed. Michael B. Katz (Princeton, NJ: Princeton University Press, 1993), 59. Further research is required, however, to determine whether a low sex ratio characterized the northeastern metropolitan migration consistently throughout the period 1860–1915 or if a shift took place at some point from a high to a low sex ratio.

17. Carol Stack, *All Our Kin: Strategies for Survival in a Black Community* (New York: Harper & Row, 1974); Judith Walzer Leavitt, *Brought to Bed: Childbearing in America, 1750 to 1950* (New York: Oxford University Press, 1986).

18. John Lucas, interview, no date, BMP. For other accounts of family migrations during 1890–1910, see Elva Williams, interview, July 16, 1980, BMP; Mrs. Mayhouse, interview, July 1 and 8, 1980, BMP; Carl Boone, interview, no date, *AS*, vol. 6: 16; Louis Watkins, Henry Bedford, Wade Glenn, and Tap and Susie Payne Hawkins, interviews,

all no date, *AS, Supplement, Series 1,* vol. 5: 231, 281, 348–51, 355–58; Celia Henderson, interview, no date, *AS, Series 2,* vol. 16: 42–43; Clarence Liggins Memoir, March 8, 1974, OHUIS; and Bruce K. Hayden Sr. Memoir, January 31, 1975, OHUIS.

19. Bertha Craig Memoir, September 1981, OHUIS.

20. Carter Woodson described northern migration during the years before the Great Migration as "mainly due to political changes." Carter Woodson, *A Century of Negro Migration* (New York: Association for the Study of Negro Life and History, 1918), 159.

21. William C. Mace, Glasgow, Kentucky, to Martha Lattimore, Noblesville, Indiana, January 9, 1880, Martha Lattimore Papers, IHS.

22. Bruce K. Hayden Sr. Memoir. For Fulton County's lynching record, see Wright, *Racial Violence in Kentucky, 72–73.*

23. Stewart E. Tolnay and E. M. Beck, *A Festival of Violence: An Analysis of Southern Lynchings, 1882–1930* (Urbana: University of Illinois Press, 1995), 231–32.

24. Ibid., 30.

25. Ibid.; Wright, *Racial Violence,* 71.

26. George Wright shows that the number of legal executions of African Americans in Kentucky remained fairly steady as lynching declined. Wright, *Racial Violence,* 227. An exception, however, is the decade 1900–1909, when the number of legal executions fell.

27. James A. Glass, "The Gas Boom in East Central Indiana," *IMH* 96 (December 2000): 313–35.

28. Robert Higgs, "Race and Economy in the South, 1890–1950," in *The Age of Segregation: Race Relations in the South, 1890–1945,* ed. Robert Haws (Jackson: University Press of Mississippi, 1978), 91.

29. Ayers, *Promise of the New South,* 208, 429–30; Neil Fligstein, *Going North: Migration of Blacks and Whites from the South, 1900–1950* (New York, Academic Press, 1981), 83, 95–96; Loren Schweninger, *Black Property Owners in the South, 1790–1915* (Urbana: University of Illinois Press, 1990), chap. 5. The African American proportion of farm owners in the Lower South, however, fell slightly between 1900 and 1910.

30. Lee et al., *Methodological Considerations,* 135–39, 190–91.

31. George W. Knepper, *Ohio and Its People* (Kent, OH: Kent State University Press, 1989), 302; Clifton J. Phillips, *Indiana in Transition: The Emergence of an Industrial Commonwealth, 1880–1920* (Indianapolis: Indiana Historical Bureau and Indiana Historical Society, 1968), 367–70; John H. Keiser, *Building for the Centuries: Illinois, 1865 to 1898* (Urbana: University of Illinois Press, 1977), 116–18.

32. As we shall see below, the biggest gainers of African American urban population share in Illinois were Chicago and East St. Louis. Other towns besides East St. Louis in the metro-east region may also have drawn African American migrants because of the pull of St. Louis across the Mississippi River. Madison and Venice may have gained African American share, although Belleville, Collinsville, and Edwardsville definitely lost share. The attraction of East St. Louis seems to allow an argument that

Illinois experienced a metropolitan shift toward its *two* regional centers, Chicago and St. Louis. Even when the attraction of the metro-east region is taken into account, however, the overall pattern of parallel black and white flows to places distributed across the urban hierarchy remains unchanged, since other urban places beyond the urban shadow of St. Louis also attracted significant numbers of African American migrants.

33. Compare the state totals in Lee et al., *Methodological Considerations,* 310–11, 332.

34. U.S. Census Office, *Twelfth Census, 1900, Vol. 1: Population, Part 1* (Washington, DC: Government Printing Office, 1901), 706–29.

35. Emma Lou Thornbrough, *The Negro in Indiana before 1900: A Study of a Minority* (1957; reprint, Bloomington: Indiana University Press, 1993), 228–30; David A. Gerber, *Black Ohio and the Color Line, 1860–1915* (Urbana: University of Illinois Press, 1976), 271–79.

36. In her posthumously published history of African Americans in twentieth-century Indiana, Thornbrough suggests that, in addition to the factors cited above, "white hostility was also sometimes a factor." Emma Lou Thornbrough, *Indiana Blacks in the Twentieth Century,* ed. and with a final chapter by Lana Ruegamer (Bloomington: Indiana University Press, 2000), 3.

37. James W. Loewen, *Sundown Towns: A Hidden Dimension of American Racism* (New York and London: New Press, 2005), chaps. 2–5. Andrew Wiese also describes "growing racial exclusivity in the suburbs," but dates its onset to the 1940s. Andrew Wiese, *Places of Their Own: African American Suburbanization in the Twentieth Century* (Chicago and London: University of Chicago Press, 2004), chap. 4. The quotation is from p. 95.

38. Willard B. Gatewood Jr., ed., *Slave and Freeman: The Autobiography of George L. Knox* (Lexington: University Press of Kentucky, 1979), 135.

39. Ibid., 16, 73–122.

40. Data on state-by-state origins of native-born African Americans are not given for any place below the state level in the federal censuses of 1890 and 1900, but they can be calculated for many large towns by subtracting the native-born whites of native parentage and native-born whites of foreign parentage from the total of native-born persons.

41. Gerber, *Black Ohio,* 273–74. David Macleod notes higher rates of child mortality among urban compared to rural black populations. David Macleod, *The Age of the Child: Children in America, 1890–1920* (New York: Twayne, 1998), 40.

42. There were only 216 out-of-state newcomers in Terre Haute and 173 in Fort Wayne.

43. For a careful and thorough portrait of the African American community in the late nineteenth century, see Darrel E. Bigham, *We Ask Only a Fair Trial: A History of the Black Community of Evansville, Indiana* (Bloomington: Indiana University Press, 1987), chaps. 2–6.

44. The dependent variable is absence from a subsequent census of individuals present in the community ten years before. Since data were not available to identify those who died, one should keep in mind that some of those who are recorded as missing did not leave the community through choice. This problem can be addressed, however, by including age among the variables to be examined.

45. Chi-square for cross-tabulation of persistence with "color" among both men and women is significant at the .05 level.

46. David Gerber, personal communication with the author, December 7, 1998. See also Jack S. Blocker Jr., "Race, Sex and Riot: The Springfield, Ohio Race Riots of 1904 and 1906 and the Sources of Antiblack Violence in the Lower Midwest," *OVH* 6 (Spring 2006): 27–44.

47. Chi-square for the cross-tabulation of persistence and "color" is significant at the .05 level for women, but not for men.

48. Everett S. Lee, "A Theory of Migration," *Demography* 3 (1966): 56–57.

49. *Slave and Freeman,* 16, 133–34.

50. The list is as follows, with year of violence in parentheses, followed by the percentage share loss in black population: Coshocton (1885, –.02), Washington Court House (1894, –.61), Urbana (1897, –.59), Akron (1900, –.09), Springfield (1904, 1906, –1.01).

51. Because of this the overall correlation between violence and change in black urban share, while negative, is not statistically significant.

52. Change in share of the state's African American urban population during 1890–1910 correlated positively and significantly with size of African American population in 1890 across one hundred urban communities; $r = +.42$, significant at the .05 level.

53. Cincinnati lost 6.5 percent in share of total urban population between 1890 and 1910 and lost 2.4 percent in share of adult manufacturing workers between 1899 and 1909, but gained 0.9 percent of black urban population share during 1890–1910. Manufacturing statistics are found in U.S. Census Office, *Twelfth Census, 1900, Vol. 8: Manufactures, Part 2: States and Territories* (Washington, DC: Government Printing Office, 1902): 1006–39; U.S. Bureau of the Census, *Fourteenth Census, 1920, Vol. 9: Manufactures, 1919* (Washington, DC: Government Printing Office, 1923): 1144.

54. In figures 7.5–7.6 and 7.13, circles are proportional to the increase or decrease in share of the African American urban population. Only towns and cities that experienced a change of more than one percent are shown.

55. Across one hundred urban places, change in African American urban share correlated positively and significantly with change in total urban share during 1890–1910; $r = +.29$, significant at the .05 level.

56. Across thirty-five urban places for which data on manufacturing employment are available, change in African American urban share during 1890–1910 is positively

and significantly correlated with change in share of the state's manufacturing work force during 1899–1909; r = +.47, significant at the .05 level. Among the same places, change in share of Ohio's manufacturing work force, 1899–1909, is correlated positively and significantly with change in share of total urban population, 1890–1910; r = +.74, significant at the .05 level.

57. Cleveland's tolerant racial atmosphere at the turn of the century is described in Kenneth L. Kusmer, *A Ghetto Takes Shape: Black Cleveland, 1870–1930* (Urbana: University of Illinois Press, 1976), 55–57.

58. Gerber, *Black Ohio*, 259–63.

59. Ibid., 296.

60. The regional dimension is emphasized in Thornbrough, *Indiana Blacks in the Twentieth Century*, 2.

61. Although changes in total urban share and African American urban share varied together, the swings in the latter were much wider than those in the former. Regression analysis shows that for every change of one percent in total urban share, African American urban share changed by 2.7 percent in the same direction.

62. Change in share of the state's African American urban population during 1890–1910 correlated positively and significantly with size of African American population in 1890 across 60 urban communities; r = +.45, significant at the .05 level.

63. For fifty-nine urban places, r = −.89, significant at the .05 level.

Stepwise regression analysis with Indianapolis included indicates the importance of the capital's large African American population. Change in total urban share by itself "explains" 66 percent of the variance in change in black urban share. With the effect of change in total urban share accounted for, size of black population adds another 14 percent to the equation's explanatory power. Size of black population was statistically unrelated to, and therefore acted independently of, change in total urban share. The equation is: Change in Black Urban Share = 0.19 + 2.6 [.35] (Change in Total Urban Share) + .0005 [.0001] (Size of Black Population). Standard errors for *b* are in brackets.

64. Bigham, *We Ask Only a Fair Trial*, chap. 5.

65. Emma Lou Thornbrough, "African Americans," in *Encyclopedia of Indianapolis*, ed. David J. Bodenhamer and Robert G. Barrows (Bloomington: Indiana University Press, 1994), 5–14; Ruth Hutchinson Crocker, *Social Work and Social Order: The Settlement Movement in Two Industrial Cities, 1889–1930* (Urbana: University of Illinois Press, 1992), 68–93. See also articles in the *Encyclopedia of Indianapolis* on "African American Businesses," "African American Churches," "African American Press," "African American Women's Organizations," "Flanner House," and "Senate Avenue YMCA." The work of Flanner House, then known as Flanner Guild, was sympathetically reported in a front-page story in the *Freeman*, June 21, 1902. At this time the *Freeman* circulated, in addition to many towns in Indiana and elsewhere in

the North, in Anniston and Birmingham, Alabama; Monroe, Louisiana; Hot Springs, Arkansas; Tampa, Florida; Columbus, Georgia; Meridian, Mississippi; and Clarksville and Nashville, Tennessee.

66. Chicago increased its share of the Illinois black urban population from 42 percent in 1890 to 52 percent in 1910.

67. James R. Grossman, *Land of Hope: Chicago, Black Southerners, and the Great Migration* (Chicago: University of Chicago Press, 1989), 74–79; Allan H. Spear, *Black Chicago: The Making of a Negro Ghetto, 1890–1920* (Chicago: University of Chicago Press, 1967), 114.

68. Christopher Robert Reed, *Black Chicago's First Century: Volume 1, 1833–1900* (Columbia and London: University of Missouri Press, 2005), 203–208, 315–32, 395–17; Spear, *Black Chicago*, 91–126.

69. Reed, *Black Chicago's First Century*, 406–407; Spear, *Black Chicago*, 95–96.

70. Mary Carbine, "'The Finest Outside the Loop': Motion Picture Exhibition in Chicago's Black Metropolis, 1905–1928," *CO* 23 (May 1990): 9–41.

71. Chicago's share of Illinois's total urban population dropped from 64.8 percent in 1890 to 62.9 percent in 1910. This explains why the correlation between change in share of black urban population and change in share of total urban population is inverse for the period 1890–1910. For 75 urban places, $r = -.32$, significant at the .05 level.

72. Chicago's increase in share of the state's manufacturing workers, 5.26 percent, dwarfed all other places. The manufacturing census of 1910, which contains the 1909 figures, however, was less thorough than that of 1900, containing the 1899 statistics. The 1900 census counted industrial workers in seventy towns, whereas the 1910 census reported figures for only thirty-one.

73. Because of the Windy City's much larger African American population, the number of violent incidents relative to population was actually smaller there than in Illinois's other violent communities. But because lynchings of individual African Americans was the most common form of violence elsewhere, while mob attacks on groups of strikebreakers was the usual form taken in Chicago's antiblack violence, the likelihood of any individual becoming a target of a white mob was probably higher in Chicago. My point in noting Chicago's violence, however, is simply that it occurred and thereby demonstrated to potential migrants that Chicago was not free from mob attacks on blacks.

74. Those that lost share are Belleville (–0.46 percent), Cairo (–4.54 percent), Pana (–0.05 percent), and Springfield (–1.85 percent). In addition, the census enumerator in Carterville, whose African American population was not recorded in 1890 since the town had less than 2,500 population, found no African Americans living there in 1910, although many had come in 1899 as strikebreakers. Furthermore, the 84 African Americans recorded in Spring Valley in 1910 are measured for this analysis as an increase over the one living there in 1890, but the 1910 figure represents a decline following the arrival of African American strikebreakers in 1894 and 1895. In 1900, 135

African Americans lived in Spring Valley. Those that gained share are Chicago (+9.43 percent), Danville (+0.99 percent), and Decatur (+0.21 percent). Virden's African American population was not recorded in 1890, but the nine African Americans enumerated there in 1910 undoubtedly represented a decrease from the number who came as strikebreakers in 1898.

75. Joanne Wheeler, "Together in Egypt: A Pattern of Race Relations in Cairo, Illinois, 1865–1915," in *Toward a New South? Studies in Post-Civil War Southern Communities,* ed. Orville Vernon Burton and Robert C. McMath (Westport, CT: Greenwood Press, 1982), 103–34; Christopher K. Hays, "The African American Struggle for Equality and Justice in Cairo, Illinois, 1865–1900," *IHJ* 90 (Winter 1997): 265–84.

76. With Chicago excluded, change in total urban population share and change in African American urban share during 1890–1910 were positively and significantly correlated across 74 urban places; $r = +.66$, significant at the .05 level.

77. As early as 1906, the pioneer African American sociologist Richard R. Wright Jr. wrote that "few women go to the rural districts, while there is great demand for men on the farms [of the North]." Richard R. Wright Jr., "Migration of Negroes to the North," *Annals of the American Academy* 27 (May 1906): 564.

78. Janice L. Reiff, Michael R. Dahlin, and Daniel Scott Smith, "Rural Push and Urban Pull: Work and Family Experience of Older Black Women in Southern Cities, 1880–1910," *JSoH* 16 (Summer 1983): 41.

79. During the 1890s, Mississippians provided about 1,700 of the 22,200 black interstate migrants to Illinois, and about 1,500 of the 17,200 during the first decade of the twentieth century. Approximately 1,500 Alabamians came to Illinois during the 1890s, followed by about 800 during 1900–1910. All figures are minimum net estimates derived from the birth-residence index. Lee et al., *Methodological Considerations,* 310. See also William Edward Vickery, *The Economics of the Negro Migration, 1900–1960* (New York: Arno, 1977), tables 34 and 52.

CHAPTER EIGHT

1. Kathleen Borboza, interview, no date, BOHCO.

2. George Johnson, interview, December 18, 1992, and April 1 and 12, 1993, in Timuel D. Black Jr., *Bridges of Memory: Chicago's First Wave of Black Migration: An Oral History* (Evanston and Chicago: Northwestern University Press and DuSable Museum of African American History, 2003), 344–45. Johnson is the founder of Johnson Products personal care company.

3. Scott, *Negro Migration during the War,* chap. 14.

4. Daniel M. Johnson and Rex R. Campbell, *Black Migration in America: A Social Demographic History* (Durham, NC: Duke University Press, 1981), 73.

5. The "watershed" label is applied in Carole Marks, *Farewell—We're Good and Gone: The Great Black Migration* (Bloomington and Indianapolis: Indiana University Press, 1989), 1. The First Great Migration is the subject of a voluminous literature. For a review of interpetations, see Joe William Trotter Jr., "Introduction. Black Migration in Historical Perspective: A Review of the Literature," in *The Great Migration in Historical Perspective: New Dimensions of Race, Class, and Gender*, ed. Joe William Trotter Jr. (Bloomington: Indiana University Press, 1991), 1–21. Other major works include James R. Grossman, *Land of Hope: Chicago, Black Southerners, and the Great Migration* (Chicago: University of Chicago Press, 1989), and Peter Gottlieb, *Making Their Own Way: Southern Blacks' Migration to Pittsburgh, 1916–30* (Urbana: University of Illinois Press, 1987). For an insightful comparison of the twentieth-century migrations of white and black southerners, see James N. Gregory, *The Southern Diaspora: How the Great Migrations of Black and White Southerners Transformed America* (Chapel Hill: University of North Carolina Press, 2005).

6. Continuities are emphasized in Johnson and Campbell, *Black Migration*, 71; Gottlieb, *Making Their Own Way*.

7. William Edward Vickery, *Economics of the Negro Migration, 1900–1960* (New York: Arno Press, 1977), 28–31. See also Grossman, *Land of Hope*, ch. 1. Seasonal migration prior to the movement north is emphasized in Gottlieb, *Making Their Own Way*, chap. 1.

8. Vickery, *Economics of the Negro Migration*, table 6.

9. Alonzo Parham, interview, October 4, 1996, in Black, *Bridges of Memory*, 117. For another example of step migration from Georgia—Albany to Macon to Atlanta to Chicago—see Wayman Hancock, interview, September 17, 1991, in ibid., 143. For another example of the men-first, women-later pattern of migration, in this case from New Orleans, see John Levy, interview, August 12, 1992, in ibid., 194. A concern for education similar to that shown by the Parham family is noted in Mildred Bowden and Hermene Hartman, interview, July 29, 1995, in ibid., 253.

10. Wanda A. Hendricks, *Gender, Race, and Politics in the Midwest: Black Club Women in Illinois* (Bloomington and Indianapolis: Indiana University Press, 1998), 105–11, 120.

11. Marc Fried, "Deprivation and Migration: Dilemmas of Causal Interpretation," in *On Understanding Poverty*, ed. Daniel P. Moynihan (New York, Basic Books, 1969), fig. 5–1; Johnson and Campbell, *Black Migration*, 75.

12. Everett S. Lee et al., *Methodological Considerations and Reference Tables*, vol. 1 of *Population Redistribution and Economic Growth, United States, 1870–1950*, ed. S. Kuznets and D. S. Thomas, 3 vols. (Philadelphia: American Philosophical Society, 1957–64), 134–39, 189–91.

13. Sallie Hopson, interview, January 30, 1987, SJOHP.

14. Edward L. Ayers, *The Promise of the New South: Life after Reconstruction* (New York: Oxford University Press, 1992), 9–13; *Travelers' Official Railway Guide for the*

United States and Canada (June 1893), timetables for the East Tennessee, Virginia, and Georgia; Queen & Crescent; Cincinnati, Hamilton & Dayton; Yazoo & Mississippi Valley; and Illinois Central railroads; *The Official Guide of the Railways . . . of the United States . . . , January 1930* (New York: National Railway Publication Co.), timetables for the Southern; Cleveland, Cincinnati, Chicago & St. Louis; Yazoo & Mississippi Valley; and Illinois Central railways.

15. David Ward, *Cities and Immigrants: A Geography of Change in Nineteenth-Century America* (New York: Oxford University Press, 1971), 4–5.

16. Geraldine K. Moreland, interview, April 18, 1978, OH-TPL.

17. For 128 urban places, the *r* values for correlations between change in share of the state's black urban population on one hand and change in share of the total urban population and size of African American population in 1910 on the other were +.23 and −.09 respectively. Only the first was significant at the .05 level. As in the previous periods, black migration during 1910–1930 was not deterred by the presence of proportionally large immigrant populations.

18. *The Official Guide of the Railways . . . of the United States . . . , January 1930.* See, for example, William H. Murdock, interview, September 19, 1986, SJOHP. In 1920 Murdock and his family traveled by train from Montgomery, Alabama, to Cleveland, changing trains in Cincinnati. So did Emma Thomas, traveling from Columbus, Georgia, two years earlier. Emma Thomas, interview, November 5, 1986, SJOHP.

19. For thirty-three urban places, the correlation between change in share of black urban population, 1910–1930, and change in share of manufacturing workers, 1909–1929, was positive and significant; *r* = +.50, significant at the .05 level. See also William W. Giffin, *African Americans and the Color Line in Ohio, 1915–1930* (Columbus: The Ohio State University Press, 2005), 14–15, 90.

20. During 1899–1909, Akron increased its share of the state's manufacturing workers from 2.7 to 3.5 percent, but its share of the African American urban population fell from 0.9 to 0.8 percent between 1890 and 1910. Springfield's share of manufacturing workers fell from 2.0 to 1.7 percent from 1899 to 1909, while its share of the African American urban population dropped from 7.0 percent to 6.0 percent during 1890–1910.

21. Between 1909 and 1929, Akron's share of the state's manufacturing workers shot from 3.5 to 8.1 percent, by far the greatest gain in Ohio. During 1910–1930, its share of the total urban population increased from 2.6 to 5.7 percent, while its share of the black urban population rose from 0.8 to 4.1 percent. Akron's boom is discussed in Jon C. Teaford, *Cities of the Heartland: The Rise and Fall of the Urban Midwest* (Bloomington: Indiana University Press, 1993), 107–108. City data on manufacturing employment are in U.S. Bureau of the Census, *Fourteenth Census, 1920: Vol. 9, Manufactures* (Washington, DC: Government Printing Office, 1923), 310, 315 (Illinois); 374, 378 (Indiana); and 1140, 1144 (Ohio); and U.S. Bureau of the Census, *Fifteenth Census: Manufactures: 1929, Vol. 3* (Washington, DC: Government Printing

Office, 1933), 139, 141 (Illinois); 161, 163 (Indiana); and 397, 399 (Ohio).

22. Harvey S. Firestone (in collaboration with Samuel Crowther), *Men and Rubber: The Story of Business* (Garden City, NY: Doubleday, Page & Company, 1926), 137.

23. Between 1909 and 1929, Springfield's share of the state's manufacturing workers declined slightly from 1.66 to 1.62 percent, while its share of the total urban population fell from 1.8 to 1.5 percent between 1910 and 1930 and its share of the black urban population dropped from 6.0 to 3.0 percent.

24. Kenneth L. Kusmer, *A Ghetto Takes Shape: Black Cleveland, 1870–1930* (Urbana: University of Illinois Press, 1976), chap. 9.

25. Ibid., 163–73 and chaps. 10–11. For a biography of the founder of the Phillis Wheatley Association, see Adrienne Lash Jones, *Jane Edna Hunter: A Case Study of Black Leadership, 1910–1950*, vol. 12 of *Black Women in United States History*, ed. Darlene Clark Hine (Brooklyn: Carlson Publishing, 1990); and Jane Edna Hunter, *A Nickel and a Prayer* (N.p.: Elli Kani Publishing, 1940). The widespread impact of these institutions is evident in the oral history interviews collected by Cleveland's St. James African Methodist Episcopal Church during the late 1980s. See, for example, the interviews with Carrie Turner, August 27, 1986, SJOHP, and Gwendolyn Lucille Stokes Williams, September 15, 1986, SJOHP.

26. Cleveland's African American population grew from 34,451 in 1920 to 71,899 in 1930. Constricting job opportunities are discussed in Kimberley L. Phillips, *AlabamaNorth: African American Migrants, Community and Working-Class Activism in Cleveland, 1915–1945* (Urbana: University of Illinois Press, 1999), 78, 96–97; and in Kusmer, *A Ghetto Takes Shape*, chap. 9, who emphasizes "stability" in occupational opportunity until about 1928, when ominous indicators of contraction began to appear.

The rapid growth of Cleveland's African American population, together with the lack of correlation across the state between African American population size in 1910 and change in African American urban population share between 1910 and 1930, argues against a simplistic assumption that the operation of chain migration will make a destination's attraction proportional to the size of its black community. Instead, we must take into account the content as well as the quantity of communication.

27. Clifton J. Phillips, *Indiana in Transition: The Emergence of an Industrial Commonwealth, 1880–1920* (Indianapolis: Indiana Historical Bureau and Indiana Historical Society, 1968), chaps. 4–7; James H. Madison, *Indiana through Tradition and Change: A History of the Hoosier State and Its People, 1920–1945* (Indianapolis: Indiana Historical Society, 1982), chaps. 6–8.

28. For an examination of chain migration from one distinctive African American rural community in Kentucky to Indianapolis, see William Lynwood Montell, *The Saga of Coe Ridge: A Study in Oral History* (Knoxville: University of Tennessee Press, 1970).

29. Emma Lou Thornbrough, *Indiana Blacks in the Twentieth Century*, ed. and with a final chapter by Lana Ruegamer (Bloomington: Indiana University Press, 2000), 35–36.

30. This estimate is based upon patterns of net migration. See Lee et al., *Methodological Considerations*, 311.

31. For Gary, see Nelson Ouellet, "The Great Migration in Gary, Indiana (1906–1920): A Note," *IMH* 96 (March 2000): 81; Elizabeth Balanoff, "A History of the Black Community of Gary, Indiana, 1906–1940" (PhD diss., University of Chicago, 1974).

32. For eighty-four urban places, the correlation between change in black urban population share and change in total urban share, 1910–1930, is positive and significant; $r = +.85$, significant at the .05 level. For twenty-four urban places, the correlations are positive and significant between change in share of the state's manufacturing workers, 1909–1929, and change in share of black urban population ($r = +.56$, significant at the .05 level) and change in share of total urban population ($r = +.66$, significant at the .05 level).

33. Madison, *Indiana through Tradition and Change*, chap. 1.

34. Indiana's last lynching occurred in Marion in 1930. For an analysis of race relations focusing on the Marion lynching, see James H. Madison, *A Lynching in the Heartland: Race and Memory in America* (New York: Palgrave, 2001). For an account by one of the intended victims, see James Cameron, *A Time of Terror: A Survivor's Story* (Baltimore: Black Classic Press, 1982). The Indiana Klan is described in Leonard J. Moore, *Citizen Klansmen: The Ku Klux Klan in Indiana, 1921–1928* (Chapel Hill: University of North Carolina Press, 1991).

35. For eighty-four urban places, the correlation between the incidence of antiblack collective violence, 1885–1910, and change in black urban share, 1910–1930, is negative and significant; $r = -.20$, significant at the .05 level.

36. Stepwise regression analysis supports the primacy of economic opportunity, as no other variable adds to the explanatory power of the equation once change in total urban population share has been entered. Change in share of manufacturing workers, 1909–1929, is too strongly correlated with change in total urban population share to exert an independent effect. The coefficient of determination is .71.

37. The changes in share of Indiana's manufacturing workers between 1909 and 1929 were: Anderson, +1.75 percent; Muncie, +1.35 percent; Fort Wayne, +1.26 percent; South Bend, +1.87 percent. The changes in share of the state's black urban population, 1910–1930, were: Anderson, +0.25 percent; Muncie, +0.49 percent; Fort Wayne, +1.11 percent; South Bend, +2.08 percent.

38. For the origins of Afro-Munsonians in 1920, see Jack S. Blocker Jr., "Black Migration to Muncie, 1860–1930," *IMH* 92 (December 1996): 308. No data are available for Anderson, but I surmise that the origins of its African American population were similar, since the two towns were located in the same part of the state and their patterns of growth in black population were parallel.

39. The African American populations of the four cities in 1910 were: Anderson, 532; Muncie, 1,005; Fort Wayne, 572; South Bend, 604. By 1930 these figures had increased to 1,387, 2,646, 2,360, and 3,431, respectively.

40. Evansville lost 0.28 percent in share of manufacturing workers and lost 0.40 percent in share of total urban population between 1910 and 1930. These two factors combined with the race riot and the fact that few industrial jobs were open to African Americans to produce a loss of 6.62 percent in share of African American urban population.

41. Correlation analysis is of marginal utility in Illinois. This is because Chicago, when analyzed as part of the state's urban system, is such an extreme outlier in every comparison. By itself, Chicago is capable of transforming a strong positive correlation into an equally strong negative and vice versa. To include Chicago, then, means obscuring the relationships between variables that obtain among the rest of the urban system. But to exclude Chicago distorts reality even more.

42. A discussion of the lynching's political aftermath is in Sundiata Keita Cha-Jua, "'A Warlike Demonstration': Legalism, Violent Self-Help, and Electoral Politics in Decatur, Illinois, 1894–1898," *JUH* 26 (July 2000): 591–629.

43. Chicago's share of total urban population fell from 62.9 percent in 1910 to 60.25 percent in 1930, and its share of total manufacturing workers dropped from 63.1 percent in 1909 to 58.6 percent in 1929.

44. Gareth Canaan, "'Part of the Loaf': Economic Conditions of Chicago's African American Working Class during the 1920's," *JSoH* 35 (Fall 2001): 147–74.

45. The definitive study is William M. Tuttle Jr., *Race Riot: Chicago in the Red Summer of 1919* (New York: Atheneum, 1970; reprint, Urbana: University of Illinois Press, 1996).

46. Representative Corneal Davis, interview, October 20, 1991, in Black, *Bridges of Memory*, 52–53.

47. The riot, its background, and aftermath are described in Elliott M. Rudwick, *Race Riot at East St. Louis, July 2, 1917* (1964; reprint, New York: Atheneum, 1972).

48. East St. Louis lost 0.36 percent of urban population share between 1910 and 1930 and its share of the state's manufacturing workers fell by 0.16 percent.

49. The populations of all-white towns ranged from 2,504 (Riverdale) to 14,863 (West Frankfort). Over the years since 1860, the number and percentage of towns reporting less than ten African Americans also steadily increased: In 1860, four towns (12.1 percent); in 1890, 12 (15.6 percent); in 1910, 39 (27.1 percent); and in 1930, 78 (40.6 percent). James Loewen argues that Illinois contained even more towns where few or no African Americans were permitted to live. James Loewen, *Sundown Towns: A Hidden Dimension of American Racism* (New York and London: New Press, 2005), 59–65.

50. Lodge Grant, interview, January 17, 1980, OHUIS, 48–49; John H. Keiser, "Black Strikebreakers and Racism in Illinois, 1865–1900," *JISHS* 65 (Autumn 1972): 314; John H. Keiser, personal communication with the author, October 1997.

51. Loewen, *Sundown Towns*, 59–65.

52. For Robbins, see Tyrone Haymore, *The Story of Robbins, Il.* (Robbins, IL:

Robbins Historical Society, 1989). For Evanston, see Andrew Wiese, "'Life on the Other Side of the Tracks': African Americans in a Domestic Service Suburb, Evanston, Illinois, 1916–1940," *Locus* 2 (Spring 1993): 163–83.

53. For the use of deed restrictions to control suburban development in Columbus, see Patricia Burgess Stach, "Deed Restrictions and Subdivision Development in Columbus, Ohio, 1900–1970," *JUH* 15 (November 1988): 42–68.

54. For women's part in building community in Chicago and across the state, see Anne Meis Knupfer, *Toward a Tenderer Humanity and a Nobler Womanhood: African American Women's Clubs in Turn-of-the-Century Chicago* (New York: New York University Press, 1996), and Hendricks, *Gender, Race, and Politics in the Midwest.*

55. For a recent study of the history of Chicago's West Side African American community, see Christopher Robert Reed, "Beyond Chicago's Black Metropolis: A History of the West Side's First Century, 1837–1940," *JISHS* 92 (Summer 1999): 119–49.

56. Chicago's African American world is explored in Grossman, *Land of Hope*, chs. 5–9, and Allan H. Spear, *Black Chicago: The Making of a Negro Ghetto, 1890–1920* (Chicago: University of Chicago Press, 1967). An extraordinarily valuable source is Timuel Black's *Bridges of Memory*. See also Mary Carbine, "'The Finest Outside the Loop': Motion Picture Exhibition in Chicago's Black Metropolis, 1905–1928," *CO* 23 (May 1990): 9–41.

57. Junius Gaten, interview, Grand Boulevard Oral History Project, 1995, CHS.

58. Grace Elizabeth Hale, *Making Whiteness: The Culture of Segregation in the South, 1890–1940* (New York: Vintage, 1998), 35.

59. In each of the three states in all three periods correlation analysis reveals no inverse relationship between change in African American urban population share and percentage foreign-born. This finding, as noted above, directly contradicts the argument of William J. Collins, "When the Tide Turned: Immigration and the Delay of the Great Black Migration," *JEH* 57 (September 1997): 607–32.

60. Johnson and Campbell, *Black Migration in America*, 68. Gavin Wright agrees, in *Old South, New South: Revolutions in the Southern Economy since the Civil War* (New York: Basic Books, 1986), 206.

61. Clyde Vernon Kiser, *Sea Island to City: A Study of St. Helena Islanders in Harlem and Other Urban Centers* (1932; reprint, New York: AMS Press, 1967), 112–13; Spencer R. Crew, *Black Life in Secondary Cities: A Comparative Analysis of the Black Communities of Camden and Elizabeth, N.J., 1860–1920* (New York: Garland, 1993), 68–69; Myra B. Young Armstead, *"Lord, Please Don't Take Me in August": African Americans in Newport and Saratoga Springs, 1870–1930* (Urbana: University of Illinois Press, 1999), 54; Joe William Trotter Jr., *River Jordan: African American Urban Life in the Ohio Valley* (Lexington: University Press of Kentucky, 1998), 98–99; Phillips, *AlabamaNorth*, 17; Morton Rubin, "Migration Patterns of Negroes from a Rural Northeastern Mississippi Community," *SF* 39 (October 1960): 64–65; Fredric Miller, "The Black Migration

to Philadelphia: A 1924 Profile," *PMHB* 108 (1984): 327–29; Wiese, "'Life on the Other Side of the Tracks,'" 169. See also Carole Marks, "Lines of Communication, Recruitment Mechanisms, and the Great Migration of 1916–1918," *SP* 31 (October 1983): 73–83.

62. U.S. Department of Labor, Division of Negro Economics, *Negro Migration in 1916–17* (Washington, DC: Government Printing Office, 1919), 28, 66, 86, 100.

63. Milton C. Sernett, *Bound for the Promised Land: African American Religion and the Great Migration* (Durham, NC: Duke University Press, 1997), 224.

64. Rudwick, *Race Riot at East St. Louis,* 159.

65. See, e.g., Blocker, "Black Migration to Muncie," 306–7.

66. Stewart E. Tolnay, "Educational Selection in the Migration of Southern Blacks, 1880–1990," *SF* 77 (December 1998): 499–502; Jason Carl Digman, "Which Way to the Promised Land? Changing Patterns of Southern Migration, 1865–1920" (PhD diss., University of Illinois at Chicago, 2001). Robert A. Margo, in *Race and Schooling in the South, 1880–1950: An Economic History* (Chicago: University of Chicago Press, 1990), chap. 7, shows that literate African Americans were more likely than illiterate African Americans to migrate.

67. Tuttle, *Race Riot,* 95; Crew, *Black Life in Secondary Cities,* 70; Sernett, *Bound for the Promised Land,* 90, 125.

68. The notion of migration as a structured process is central to modern migration scholarship. See, for example, Charles Tilly, "Transplanted Networks," in *Immigration Reconsidered: History, Sociology, and Politics,* ed. Virginia Yans-McLaughlin (New York: Oxford University Press, 1990), 88, and Ewa Morawska, "The Sociology and Historiography of Immigration," in ibid., 189–90.

69. For the procedure to use in calculating the number of African Americans born in each state, see note 40 in chapter 7, above.

70. *The Official Guide of the Railways . . . of the United States . . . , January 1930.*

71. The shift in origins of Toledo's African American settlers to the Deep South is noted in Lee Williams, "Newcomers to the City: A Study of Black Population Growth in Toledo, 1910–1930," *OH* 89 (Winter 1980): 7.

72. Jacqueline Jones, *American Work: Four Centuries of Black and White Labor* (New York: W. W. Norton, 1998), 306. A study of occupational mobility in Cincinnati between 1917 and 1920 shows that southern-born migrants suffered no disadvantage compared to northern-born Cincinnatians. Thomas N. Maloney, "Migration and Economic Opportunity in the 1910s: New Evidence on African American Occupational Mobility in the North," *EEH* 38 (2001): 147–65. Across the urban North, however, southern-born male migrants found less desirable jobs than northern-born African Americans. Stewart E. Tolnay, "African Americans and Immigrants in Northern Cities: The Effects of Relative Group Size on Occupational Standing in 1920," *SF* 80 (December 2001): 573–604.

73. Spear, *Black Chicago,* chap. 2; Kusmer, *A Ghetto Takes Shape,* chap. 4, 190–91;

Emma Lou Thornbrough, *The Negro in Indiana before 1900: A Study of a Minority* (1957; reprint, Bloomington: Indiana University Press, 1993), 350; J. S. Himes, "Forty Years of Negro Life in Columbus, Ohio," *JNH* 27 (April 1942): 143–43; Abraham Epstein, *The Negro Migrant in Pittsburgh* (1918; reprint, New York: Arno Press, 1969), 30–31; Nancy Bertaux, "Structural Economic Change and Occupational Decline among Black Workers in Nineteenth-Century Cincinnati," in *Race and the City: Work, Community, and Protest in Cincinnati, 1820–1970,* ed. Henry Louis Taylor Jr. (Urbana: University of Illinois Press, 1993), 146; Trotter, *River Jordan,* 100.

74. Grossman, *Land of Hope,* chap. 7. Before 1930, the African American unemployment rate in the North was generally lower than the European American. Edna Bonacich, "Advanced Capitalism and Black/White Relations in the United States: A Split Labor Market Interpretation," *ASR* 41 (February 1976): 35.

75. Spear, *Black Chicago,* 181–86; Kusmer, *A Ghetto Takes Shape,* 191–95; David A. Gerber, *Black Ohio and the Color Line, 1860–1915* (Urbana: University of Illinois Press, 1976), 309–19; Giffin, *African Americans and the Color Line in Ohio,* 23–28, 97–104; Himes, "Forty Years," 143–44; Wilma L. Gibbs, "African American Businesses," in *Encyclopedia of Indianapolis,* ed. David J. Bodenhamer and Robert G. Barrows (Bloomington: Indiana University Press, 1994), 233–35. George Johnson, the founder of Johnson Products Company and who is quoted at the beginning of this chapter, was one of the most successful of those entrepreneurs. He testifies how the compact size of segregated African American communities created efficiencies in marketing his hair care products, in Black, *Bridges of Memory,* 379.

76. Richard. R. Wright Jr., "The Migration of Negroes to the North," *Annals of the American Academy* 27 (May 1906): 563; U.S. Department of Labor, *Negro Migration in 1916–17,* 144; Gerber, *Black Ohio and the Color Line,* 273.

77. See note 60, chapter 2, above; Richard R. Wright Jr., *The Negroes of Xenia, Ohio: A Social Study,* U.S. Department of Labor Bulletin No. 48 (September 1903), 1019; Wright, "The Economic Condition of Negroes in the North," *SW* 41 (June 1912): 334–35. But tuberculosis, the most destructive killer of urban blacks, affected rural residents as well. Kenneth W. Goings, "Blacks in the Rural North: Paulding County, Ohio, 1860–1900" (PhD diss., Princeton University, 1977), 68.

78. U.S. Bureau of the Census, *Fourteenth Census, 1920: Vol. 2: Population* (Washington, DC: Government Printing Office, 1922), 1282. The census reported what proportion of homes were owned or rented, not what percentage of families owned their homes. Since more than one family could occupy a dwelling, the percentage of families owning their home would probably be lower than the percentage of homes owned by their occupants. Nevertheless, the contrasts drawn in the text should be sufficiently great to make the point that most migrants moved from a setting in which homeownership was more possible to one in which it was less so.

79. Jack S. Blocker Jr., "Wages of Migration: Jobs and Homeownership among Black and White Workers in Muncie, Indiana, 1920," in *The African Diaspora: African*

Origins and New World Identities, ed. Isidore Okpewho, Carole Boyce Davies, and Ali A. Mazrui (Bloomington: Indiana University Press, 1999), 122.

80. Committee on Negro Housing, *Negro Housing* (Washington, DC: President's Conference on Home Building and Home Ownership, 1932), 81. Toledo in 1923 appears to have had a surprisingly high rate of African American home ownership, 27.6 percent. Williams, "Newcomers to the City," 18. A sample of male and female "household heads" drawn from metropolitan areas outside the South in 1920 shows rates of homeownership ranging from 17 percent (southern-born) to 22 percent (non-southern-born). Gregory, *Southern Diaspora,* table A.15.

81. These processes are clearly described in such works as Spear, *Black Chicago,* and Kusmer, *A Ghetto Takes Shape.*

82. Scott, *Negro Migration during the War,* chap. 14.

83. Charles Tilly, "Race and Migration to the American City," in *The Metropolitan Enigma,* ed. James Q. Wilson (New York: Doubleday, 1970), 146.

84. Florette Henri, *Black Migration: Movement North, 1900–1920* (Garden City, NY: Doubleday, 1975), 142.

85. Darrel E. Bigham, *We Ask Only a Fair Trial: A History of the Black Community of Evansville, Indiana* (Bloomington: Indiana University Press, 1987), 154–63.

86. LeRoy Brown Memoir, April 29, 1974, OHUIS; Allie Hopkins Memoir, August 16, 1974, OHUIS; Margaret Ferguson Memoir, February 11, 1975, OHUIS.

87. Milton Sernett points to another advantage of large cities for African American women: "Discouraged or proscribed from holding the office of ordained minister in the mainline denominations, women exercised their spiritual gifts by establishing independent Holiness, Pentecostal, and Spiritualist churches, often of the storefront and house varieties. Women needed no male approval to set up as mediums, healers, and spiritual leaders of congregations of the dispossessed." Sernett, *Bound for the Promised Land,* 195.

88. These trends are noted in U.S. Department of Labor, *Negro Migration in 1916–17,* 145, 150; Lyonel C. Florant, "Negro Internal Migration," *ASR* 7 (December 1942): 787; Tuttle, *Race Riot,* 215; Phillips, *AlabamaNorth,* 42, 129.

89. In eleven cases, a falling sex ratio accompanied an increasing share of the state's black urban population: Chicago, Indianapolis, Cleveland, Columbus, and Toledo in 1890–1910 and Chicago, Cleveland, Akron, Gary, Dayton, and Youngstown during 1910–1930. In three cases, a falling sex ratio appeared while the city's urban share was falling, in Indianapolis, Cincinnati, and Columbus in 1910–1930. In these periods for these three cities, urban share was being captured by more rapidly growing industrial cities, in the Calumet and northeastern Ohio respectively. In four cases, a rising sex ratio accompanied increasing urban share: Cincinnati, Dayton, and Youngstown in 1890–1910 and Toledo in 1910–1930. In one case, Akron during 1890–1910, a falling sex ratio occurred while urban share was declining. This of course was the period of Akron's race riot.

90. As Florette Henri (*Black Migration*, 96) points out, census marshals probably substantially undercounted African American men in northern cities. For purposes of comparison, however, this is not a major problem, so long as we can assume that undercounting was fairly consistent from one midwestern city to another.

91. For oral history evidence on the gendered experience of women during the Second Great Migration after 1940, see Valerie Grim, "From the Yazoo Mississippi Delta to the Urban Communities of the Midwest: Conversations with Rural African American Women," *Frontiers* 22 (2001): 126–44.

92. U.S. Census Office, *Twelfth Census, 1900, Vol. 1: Population, Part 1* (Washington, DC: Government Printing Office, 1902): 702–29; U.S. Bureau of the Census, *Negroes in the United States, 1920–32* (Washington, DC: Government Printing Office, 1935), 24, 28–31, 34–36.

93. A minimum estimate of the number of Mississippi-born blacks living outside Chicago in 1910 can be obtained by comparing the number of Mississippi-born blacks living in Illinois (4,612) with the number of Mississippi-born persons living in Chicago (2,978), yielding 1,637. The maximum number of Mississippi-born blacks who could have been living outside Chicago is, of course, 4,612. U.S. Bureau of the Census, *Thirteenth Census, 1910, Vol. 1: Population* (Washington, DC: Government Printing Office, 1913), 743, 776. The number of Mississippi-born blacks living in Illinois in 1930 was 50,851, of whom 38,356 resided in Chicago, leaving 12,495 in the remainder of the state. U.S. Bureau of the Census, *Negroes in the United States, 1920–32*, 30, 35–36. Subtracting the maximum and minimum estimates for 1910 from the non-Chicago number for 1930 produces the range of estimates for the increase in Mississippi-born nonmetropolitan black population between 1910 and 1930. Mississippians contributed 23 percent of Illinois's African American migration during the 1910s and 27 percent during the 1920s.

94. [Emmett J. Scott], "Letters of Negro Migrants of 1916–1918," *JNH* 4 (July 1919): 303, 309, 331, 337, 340; *JNH* 4 (October 1919): 415, 429, 435–36, 440.

95. [Scott], "Letters of Negro Migrants," 436.

96. Phoebe Mitchell Day Memoir, March 25, 1974, OHUIS. A later migrant to Chicago from a small town recalled how hard it was for her to become accustomed to the "coolness"—the impersonality—of the metropolitan world. Edith Ellis, interview, June 14, 1995, in Black, *Bridges of Memory*, 30.

97. Jobs in coal-mining towns in western and southern Indiana were increasingly open to African Americans at the turn of the century. Thornbrough, *Negro in Indiana*, 350.

98. Elyria, Massillon, Middletown, and Warren all gained share of Ohio's total urban population between 1910 and 1930, and as well increased their share of the state's manufacturing workers between 1909 and 1929. Share changes in manufacturing workers cannot be calculated for Barberton, East Cleveland, and Niles because the census did not report their worker numbers in 1909, but in 1929 they all held a significant

share of industrial workers, in rough proportion to their growing share of total urban population.

99. The number of African American residents fell between 1910 and 1930 from ninety-nine to forty in Norwood, from seven to five in Cicero, from thirteen to nine in Blue Island, and from eighteen to five in Granite, while each city gained share of its state's total urban population.

100. Edna Christian, interview, December 5, 1972, BOHCO.

101. James E. DeVries, *Race and Kinship in a Midwestern Town: The Black Experience in Monroe, Michigan, 1900–1915* (Urbana: University of Illinois Press, 1984), 134–35.

102. Alexander and Bell Kelley, interview, no date, *AS, Supplement, Series 1,* vol. 5: 105, 106.

103. Scott Ray, "The Depressed Industrial Society: Occupational Movement, Out-Migration and Residential Mobility in the Industrial-Urbanization of Middletown, 1880–1925" (PhD diss., Ball State University, 1981), 125–33.

104. U.S. Bureau of the Census, *Negroes in the United States, 1920–1932,* 55. For a more detailed analysis, see Blocker, "Black Migration to Muncie."

105. James Davis, interview, June 6, 1980, BMP.

106. Blocker, "Wages of Migration," 119–22.

107. Blocker, "Black Migration to Muncie," 314–15.

108. See, for example, *Muncie Evening Press,* January 2, 1920.

109. Hurley Goodall and Elizabeth Campbell, "A City Apart," in *The Other Side of Middletown: Exploring Muncie's African American Community,* ed. Luke Eric Lassiter, Hurley Goodall, Elizabeth Campbell, and Michelle Natasya Johnson (Walnut Creek, CA: AltaMira Press, 2004), 54; Hurley Goodall and J. Paul Mitchell, *A History of Negroes in Muncie* (Muncie: Ball State University, 1976), 7.

110. Moore, *Citizen Klansmen,* 54, 96. Goodall and Mitchell record only one quasi-violent incident, when in 1898 a group of whites threatened to burn a tavern owner's shed to force him to fire his black porter. It is not known if the tavern owner complied. Goodall and Mitchell, *History of Negroes in Muncie,* 6.

111. Dorothy Armstrong, interview, no date, BMP; Thomas Wesley Hall, interview, no date, BMOHP; Mrs. Mayhouse, interview, July 1 and 8, 1980, BMP; Mrs. Geraldine Springer, interview, June 17, 1980, BMP; Elva Williams, interview, July 16, 1980, BMP.

112. Henry Sims, interview, June 10, 1980, BMP. Actually, the Klan paraded twice through Muncie, in 1920 and again in 1924. Goodall and Campbell, "A City Apart," 60. Henry Sims recalled "a kind of a race riot," "once at the fairgrounds," in an unknown year in response to a question about antiblack violence in Muncie. Emma Lou Thornbrough describes the advance of segregation in some Indiana cities during the 1920s, but argues that this development, while motivated by the same racist attitudes that bolstered the Klan, was not produced by Klan activity. Emma Lou Thornbrough, "Segregation in Indiana during the Klan Era of the 1920s," *MVHR* 47 (March 1961): 594–618.

113. Blocker, "Wages of Migration," 129.

114. Muncie city directories, 1903–1904, 1913–14.

115. Thornbrough, *Indiana Blacks in the Twentieth Century,* 14; *Muncie Evening Press,* January 7, 1920. See also Goodall and Campbell, "A City Apart," 52–61.

116. African Americans' mean age was about two and one-half years less than European Americans'; 86 percent of African Americans were southern-born while 64 percent of European Americans were northern-born; and only 26 percent of African Americans had lived in Muncie for at least ten years, compared to 34 percent of European Americans. Blocker, "Wages of Migration," 128. Some information is available on the wealth of homeowners in local tax assessment records. Among 28 adult members of home-owning families in 1917, the median value of African American real estate stood at $600, compared to $900 for European Americans. Among 73 adult members of home-owning families in 1923, the African American median was $728.50 compared to $1,680 for European Americans. Neither difference, however, was statistically significant. *Tax Duplicate and Delinquent List, 1917, Delaware County, Indiana,* vols. 1 (last names A–G) and 2 (H–O); *Tax Duplicate and Delinquent List, 1923, Delaware County, Indiana,* vols. 1 (M–R) and 4 (S–Z), Archives and Special Collections, Bracken Library, Ball State University, Muncie, Indiana.

117. This is an inference from the ages and states of birth of the Blackburn children.

118. U.S. federal manuscript census, Delaware County, Indiana, 1910, 1920. The Whitely community was founded by William Whitely, the reaper manufacturer whose bitter conflict with the Knights of Labor in Springfield, Ohio, had destroyed his operation there, but the factory he built in his eponymous model town near Muncie burned in 1894, shortly after opening, and William Whitely played no further role in Muncie. The racially integrated character of the Whitely neighborhood, annexed to Muncie in 1919, is noted in Goodall and Campbell, "A City Apart," 54–55.

119. There is a substantial literature on African American suburbanization, most of it focusing on the period since the 1960s. For a historical overview, see Leslie E. Wilson, "Dark Spaces: An Account of Afro-American Suburbanization, 1890–1950" (PhD diss., City University of New York, 1992). African American suburbanization's most prominent historian is Andrew Wiese. See his "The Other Suburbanites: African American Suburbanization in the North before 1950," *JAH* 85 (March 1999): 1495–1524; "Black Housing, White Finance: African American Housing and Home Ownership in Evanston, Illinois, before 1940," *JSoH* 33 (Winter 1999): 429–60; "Places of Our Own: Suburban Black Towns before 1960," *JUH* 19 (May 1993): 30–54; "'Life on the Other Side of the Tracks,'" 163–83; and *Places of Their Own: African American Suburbanization in the Twentieth Century* (Chicago and London: University of Chicago Press, 2004).

120. Wiese, "Black Housing, White Finance," 431.

121. T. J. Woofter Jr., *Negro Problems in Cities* (1928; reprint, New York: Negro Universities Press, 1969), 142–43.

122. Wiese, "The Other Suburbanites," 1500.

123. Wiese, "'Life on the Other Side of the Tracks,'" 169, and "Places of Our Own," 37, 45–46.

124. Wiese, "'Life on the Other Side of the Tracks,'" 179. These seem to have been located mainly in northeastern cities. YMCAs, YWCAs, and other community institutions probably developed somewhat later in the Midwest.

125. Wiese, "The Other Suburbanites," 1496.

126. Since in 1910 a majority of each state's African American population lived in nonmetropolitan places (57 percent in Ohio, 64 percent in Indiana, and 60 percent in Illinois), and because large cities typically showed higher death than birth rates for African Americans, a larger portion of the increase in nonmetropolitan compared to metropolitan communities would have been the result of natural increase rather than migration.

CONCLUSION

1. Welton E. Barnett, interview, Toledo, Ohio, July 7, 1976, OH-TPL.

2. Alain Locke, "The New Negro," in *The New Negro: An Interpretation*, ed. Alain Locke (New York: Albert and Charles Boni, 1925), 6.

3. Robert Higgs, *Competition and Coercion: Blacks in the American Economy, 1865–1914* (Chicago: University of Chicago Press, 1977), 32; Higgs, "Race and Economy in the South, 1890–1950," in *The Age of Segregation: Race Relations in the South, 1890–1945*, ed. Robert Haws (Jackson: University Press of Mississippi , 1978), 113; Daniel M. Johnson and Rex R. Campbell, *Black Migration: A Social Demographic History* (Durham, NC: Duke University Press, 1981), 146; Neil McMillen, *Dark Journey: Black Mississippians in the Age of Jim Crow* (Urbana: University of Illinois Press, 1989), 263; James N. Gregory, "The Southern Diaspora and the Urban Dispossessed: Demonstrating the Census Public Use Microdata Samples," *JAH* 82 (June 1995): 113; Gregory, *The Southern Diaspora: How the Great Migrations of Black and White Southerners Transformed America* (Chapel Hill: University of North Carolina Press, 2005), 327 and passim.

4. Florette Henri, *Black Migration: Movement North, 1900–1920* (Garden City, NY: Doubleday, 1975), chap. 10; Joe William Trotter Jr., *Black Milwaukee: The Making of an Industrial Proletariat, 1915–45* (Urbana: University of Illinois Press, 1985), 277; Peter Gottlieb, *Making Their Own Way: Southern Blacks' Migration to Pittsburgh, 1916–30* (Urbana: University of Illinois Press, 1987), 219–20; James R. Grossman, *Land of Hope: Chicago, Black Southerners, and the Great Migration* (Chicago: University of Chicago Press, 1989), 260–61. Carole Marks, however, disagrees. See her *Farewell—We're Good and Gone: The Great Black Migration* (Bloomington: Indiana University Press, 1989), chap. 7.

5. Glenn N. Sisk, "Negro Migration in the Alabama Black Belt, 1875–1917," *NHB* 17 (November 1953): 34; Higgs, *Competition and Coercion,* 75–76; McMillen, *Dark Journey,* 248–49, 305, 306, 308, 314–15; Nell Painter, "'Social Equality,' Miscegenation, Labor, and Power," in *The Evolution of Southern Culture,* ed. Numan V. Bartley (Athens: University of Georgia Press, 1988), 64; Darlene Clark Hine, "Black Migration to the Urban Midwest: The Gender Dimension, 1915–1945," in Joe William Trotter Jr., *The Great Migration in Historical Perspective: New Dimensions of Race, Class, and Gender* (Bloomington: Indiana University Press, 1991), 134; Gregory, *Southern Diaspora.*

6. Jan Lucassen and Leo Lucassen, "Migration, Migration History, History: Old Paradigms and New Perspectives," in *Migration, Migration History, History: Old Paradigms and New Perspectives,* ed. Jan Lucassen and Leo Lucassen (Berne: Peter Lang, 1997), 11–12. The discussion cited deals with the distinction between voluntary and forced migrations, but the argument applies with equal force, in my view, to the push-pull distinction.

7. Anna-Lisa Cox, *A Stronger Kinship: One Town's Extraordinary Story of Hope and Faith* (New York and Boston: Little, Brown and Company, 2006).

8. James E. DeVries, *Race and Kinship in a Midwestern Town: The Black Experience in Monroe, Michigan, 1900–1915* (Urbana: University of Illinois Press, 1984), 86, 91.

9. David W. Zang, *Fleet Walker's Divided Heart: The Life of Baseball's First Black Major Leaguer* (Lincoln: University of Nebraska Press, 1995), 14.

10. Frances V. Halsell Gilliam, *A Time to Speak: A Brief History of the Afro-Americans of Bloomington, Indiana, 1865–1965* (Bloomington: Pinus Strobus Press, 1985), 63–64.

11. Bruce K. Hayden Sr. Memoir, January 31, 1975, OHUIS.

12. Phoebe Mitchell Day Memoir, March 25, 1974, OHUIS. See also the Leota Harris Memoir, February 5, 1975, 2 vols., OHUIS.

13. Bruce K. Hayden Sr. Memoir.

14. Zang, *Fleet Walker's Divided Heart,* 45–46.

15. This is one theme, though by no means the only one, of the classic by Lewis Atherton, *Main Street on the Middle Border* (1954; reprint, Chicago: Quadrangle, 1966). The helplessness of small cities in the face of economic centralization is a major theme in Timothy R. Mahoney, "The Small City in American History," *IMH* 99 (December 2003): 311–30.

16. James W. Loewen, *Sundown Towns: A Hidden Dimension of American Racism* (New York and London: New Press, 2005), chap. 11.

17. Sinclair Lewis, *Babbitt* (Toronto: G. J. McLeod, 1922), and *Main Street* (New York: Collier, 1920); Sherwood Anderson, *Winesburg, Ohio: A Group of Tales of Ohio Small Town Life* (New York: Modern Library, 1919); Louis Raymond Reid, "The Small Town," in *Civilization in the United States: An Inquiry by Thirty Americans,* Harold E. Stearns (New York: Harcourt, Brace, 1922), 285–96.

18. I estimated these figures by applying to the 1890 and 1910 African American populations of the cities that reached 100,000 total population by 1930 the African American urban growth rate for their state during 1890–1910 and 1910–1930, respectively, then subtracting the result from the actual 1910 and 1930 African American populations. Cities whose African American populations fell below what would have been expected if the city had grown at the statewide urban rate were considered to have zero growth, rather than a negative figure.

19. These figures were estimated by comparison of tables A.6 and A.7 with tables A.15 and A.16 and by use of table A.17.

20. There is no contradiction between this conclusion and the finding that African Americans generally moved from economically lagging towns to prospering ones. As was noted above, the African American movement to the region's cities was distinctive. Although both European Americans and African Americans responded to changing conditions, because African Americans were among the most vulnerable, they were more sensitive to economic swings.

21. Loewen, *Sundown Towns.*

22. For a similar conclusion regarding African American migrants from St. Helena Island, Georgia, see Clyde Vernon Kiser, *Sea Island to City: A Study of St. Helena Islanders in Harlem and Other Urban Centers* (1932; reprint, New York: AMS Press, 1967), 217–18.

23. Joshua L. Rosenbloom, "Looking for Work, Searching for Workers: U.S. Labor Markets after the Civil War," *SSH* 18 (Fall 1994): 383.

24. A brief statement of this view was made by historian Harold Forsythe in a posting on H-Afro-Am, February 17, 1999. Cited by permission.

25. Henri, *Black Migration,* 336, articulates a common view. The case is most powerfully made in Grossman, *Land of Hope,* esp. 259–65. See also David Gordon Nielson, *Black Ethos: Northern Urban Negro Life and Thought, 1890–1920* (Westport, CT: Greenwood Press, 1977).

26. Jack S. Blocker Jr., "Building Networks: Cooperation and Communication among African Americans in the Urban Midwest, 1860–1910," *IMH* 99 (December 2003): 370–86.

27. Kimberley L. Phillips, *AlabamaNorth: African American Migrants, Community and Working-Class Activism in Cleveland, 1915–1945* (Urbana: University of Illinois Press, 1999), 186; James H. Madison, *Indiana through Tradition and Change: A History of the Hoosier State and Its People, 1920–1945* (Indianapolis: Indiana Historical Society, 1982), 12; Ruth Hutchinson Crocker, *Social Work and Social Order: The Settlement Movement in Two Industrial Cities, 1889–1930* (Urbana: University of Illinois Press, 1992), 197; Donald F. Tingley, *The Structuring of a State: The History of Illinois, 1899–1928* (Urbana: University of Illinois Press, 1980), 309; Marcus Garvey, "Why I Have Not Spoken in Chicago Since 1920," undated typescript, and "Interview with William A. Wallace," no date, both in Box 46, IWP.

APPENDIX C

1. For a recent summary and assessment of the historiography of migration see Ewa Morawska, "The Sociology and Historiography of Immigration," in *Immigration Reconsidered: History, Sociology, and Politics,* ed. Virginia Yans-McLaughlin (New York: Oxford University Press, 1990), 187–238.

2. Carole Marks and others have made this argument about the First Great Migration. Carole Marks, *Farewell—We're Good and Gone: The Great Black Migration* (Bloomington and Indianapolis: Indiana University Press, 1989).

3. I also conducted interviews, but these were with longtime residents of midwestern communities, not migrants.

4. George Rawick, ed., *The American Slave: A Composite Autobiography,* 41 vols. (Westport, CT: Greenwood Press, 1972–79). Two collections of oral histories from midwestern communities have been drawn upon for qualitative evidence on migration and community life, but their subjects have not been included in the database for quantitative analysis, either because the source contains little information on the migration experience (the Wallis volume) or because it was published after the database had been completed and analyzed (the Black volume). Don Wallis, *All We Had Was Each Other: The Black Community of Madison, Indiana: An Oral History* (Bloomington and Indianapolis: Indiana University Press, 1998), and Timuel D. Black Jr., *Bridges of Memory: Chicago's First Wave of Black Migration: An Oral History* (Evanston and Chicago: Northwestern University Press and DuSable Museum of African American History, 2003).

5. The archives in which migrant interviews were found are listed in appendix B. Interviews were also collected of lifelong residents of midwestern communities, but these will not be discussed here.

6. For a summary of criticisms of the FWP project as oral history, see David Henige, *Oral Historiography* (London: Longman, 1982), 116–18.

7. Most of the FWP interviews took place in 1937 or 1938. The median year of migration north for the forty-nine ex-slaves who gave this information was 1869; the range was 1859–1929.

8. The range of age at migration was four to eighty-four years; $n = 39$. Age at migration was calculated by subtracting the year of migration reported in the interview from year of birth.

9. The range of age at migration north was from less than one year to forty-eight years; $n = 83$.

10. For 214 respondents the median year of migration north was 1917; the range was 1865–1930.

INDEX

Aurora, Indiana, 128

Ballard, Clergy, 129
Baptisttown (neighborhood of
    Evansville, Indiana), 120
Barberton, Ohio, 208
Barnett family, 16
Beardstown, Illinois, 197
Beck, E. M., 8, 9, 289n61
Belleville, Illinois, 195, 196,
    298n32, 302n74
Betters, Peter, 109
Bibb, Scott, 96
Binga Bank, 177
Birmingham, Alabama, 139, 143
birth rates: in Fayette County,
    Ohio, 67
Black Laws, 28–30
Blackburn, James, 212
Blackburn, Lula, 212
Bloomington, Illinois, 195
Bloomington, Indiana, 128
Blountsville, Indiana, 106
Blue family, 16
Blue Island, Illinois, 208
Boonville, Indiana, 111
Boyd, Elmer, 114, 117
Boyd, Mary Parrett, 112, 114
Boysaw, Grace, 96–97
Bragg, Tolbert, 154
Brewer, Grace, 96
Broad Ax (Chicago), 127, 131–32
Brooklyn, Illinois, 109, 283n87
Brown, LeRoy, 133
Bruce, Henry Clay, 16
Brundage, Fitzhugh, 8, 9, 106
Bunch, Charles, 96
Burton, Scott, 130
Bush, J. W., 283n87
Bush, Samuel J., 128

Cairo, Illinois, 16, 35, 94, 99,
    101, 179, 195, 196, 265n96,
    291n106, 302n74
Calumet region, Indiana, 190, 191
Cambridge, Ohio, 187

Campbell, Rex, 200
Canton, Ohio, 93, 208, migration to,
    170
Carpenter, Edith, 132–33
Carterville, Illinois, 98, 302n74
Cementville, Indiana, 98
census data: disadvantages of, 247
Centralia, Illinois, 96
Cha-Jua, Sundiata, 272n62
Chagrin Falls Park, Ohio, 212, 213
Champaign-Urbana, Illinois, 294n28
Chattanooga, Tennessee, 147
Chester, Addie Anderson, 60
Chester, Eugene, 59–62, 117, 168
Chester, Frances, 59–60
Chester, Lewis, 59–61
Chester, Madora, 59–60
Chester, Mary Good, 59–61
Chicago, 25, 81, 99, 107, 108, 109;
    advantages of, 176–79, 198–99;
    economy of, 178–79, 195, 302n72;
    institutional network in, 177–78,
    198–99; migration to, 143, 179; mob
    violence in, 196, 302n73; popula-
    tion of, 26, 31, 35, 176, 195, 263n86,
    302n74; Knights of Labor in, 98;
    origins of migrants to, 164; sex ratio
    in, 205–6; strikebreaking in, 98, 106
Chicago Heights, Illinois, 197
Chicago Tribune, 285n9
Cicero, Illinois, 195, 208
Cincinnati, 26, 29, 31, 35, 81, 89, 106,
    127–28, 158, 188–89, 265n94,
    266n9, 300n50; migration to, 170,
    201–202; origins of migrants to,
    164; sex ratio in, 205–6
cities, northern: advantages of, 175; dis-
    advantages of, 203–4; migration to,
    141–42, 187
cities, southern: advantages of, 138;
    disadvantages of, 139; role in migra-
    tion, 138–39, 149
civil rights acts (state), 86
Civil War, impact of: on African
    American migration, 15–18; on race
    relations, 28–30

Urban Life and Urban Landscape
Zane L. Miller, Series Editor

The series examines the history of urban life and the development of the urban land-scape through works that place social, economic, and political issues in the intellectual and cultural context of their times.

Reading London: Urban Speculation and Imaginative Government in Eighteenth-Century Literature
Erik Bond

Lake Effects: A History of Urban Policy Making in Cleveland, 1825–1929
Ronald R. Weiner

High Stakes: Big Time Sports and Downtown Redevelopment
Timothy Jon Curry, Kent Schwirian, and Rachael A. Woldoff

Suburban Steel: The Magnificent Failure of the Lustron Corporation, 1945–1951
Douglas Knerr

New York City: An Outsider's Inside View
Mario Maffi

Merchant of Illusion: James Rouse, America's Salesman of the Businessman's Utopia
Nicholas Dagen Bloom

The Failure of Planning: Permitting Sprawl in San Diego Suburbs, 1970–1999
Richard Hogan

Faith and Action: A History of the Catholic Archdiocese of Cincinnati, 1821–1996
Roger Fortin

Regionalism and Reform: Art and Class Formation in Antebellum Cincinnati
Wendy Jean Katz

Making Sense of the City: Local Government, Civic Culture, and Community Life in Urban America
Edited by Robert B. Fairbanks and Patricia Mooney-Melvin

Suburban Alchemy: 1960s New Towns and the Transformation of the American Dream
Nicholas Dagen Bloom

Visions of Place: The City, Neighborhoods, Suburbs, and Cincinnati's Clifton, 1850–2000
Zane L. Miller

A Right to Representation: Proportional Election Systems for the Twenty-First Century
Kathleen L. Barber

Boss Cox's Cincinnati: Urban Politics in the Progressive Era
Zane L. Miller

Columbus, Ohio: A Personal Geography
Henry L. Hunker

Domesticating the Street: The Reform of Public Space in Hartford, 1850–1930
Peter C. Baldwin

The Rise of the City, 1878–1898
Arthur Meier Schlesinger

Lancaster, Ohio, 1800–2000: Frontier Town to Edge City
David R. Contosta

Cincinnati in 1840: The Social and Functional Organization of an Urban Community during the Pre-Civil War Period
Walter Stix Glazer

For the City as a Whole: Planning, Politics, and the Public Interest in Dallas, Texas, 1900–1965
Robert B. Fairbanks

www.ingramcontent.com/pod-product-compliance
Lightning Source LLC
Chambersburg PA
CBHW030637270326
41929CB00007B/113